Body Evidence

Body Evidence

Intimate Violence against South Asian Women in America

SHAMITA DAS DASGUPTA

RUTGERS UNIVERSITY PRESS

NEW BRUNSWICK, NEW JERSEY, AND LONDON

LIBRARY OF CONGRESS CATALOGING-IN-PUBLICATION DATA

Body evidence : intimate violence against South Asian women in America / [edited by]
Shamita Das Dasgupta.
  p. cm.
  Includes bibliographical references and index.
  ISBN-13: 978-0-8135-3981-2 (hardcover : alk. paper)
  ISBN-13: 978-0-8135-3982-9 (pbk. : alk. paper)
  1. Family violence—United States.   2. Victims of family violence—United States.
  3. South Asian American women—Violence against—United States.   4. South
  Asian American women — Services for — United States.   5. Women immigrants —
  Violence against — United States. 6. Women immigrants — Legal status, laws, etc. —
  United States. 7. South Asian Americans — Social conditions. I. Dasgupta,
  Shamita Das.
  HV6626.2.B63 2007
  362.82'92208991073—dc22

                                                      2006015441

A British Cataloging-in-Publication record for this book is available
from the British Library.

This collection copyright © 2007 by Rutgers, The State University
Individual chapters copyright © 2007 in the names of their authors

Manufactured in the United States of America

For Kiru, Kiya, Tumku, and Boris
You are my loving inspiration

CONTENTS

PART TWO
The Wounded Body: Emerging Issues
in Domestic Violence Work

PART THREE
The Body Evidence: Law and
South Asian Battered Women

ACKNOWLEDGMENTS

Much thanks to—

Adi Hovav for guiding me through the editing process

Margaret Abraham for her compassionate critique

Natalie Sokoloff for her review and encouragement

Sujan DasGupta for his constant support and love

Manavi for inspiring me

the contributing authors for their patience, imagination, and commitment to social

change work

and

the many battered women in my community and their courageous advocates—you are

always in my heart!

Body Evidence

Introduction

SHAMITA DAS DASGUPTA

Abuse of women in the South Asian communities in North America is no longer a matter of conjecture, even though it might still be a matter of relative silence. In the past two decades, South Asian women's activism against domestic violence has indelibly changed the landscape of the community and the larger nation. The skepticism that many of us early activists faced when bringing up the issue of domestic violence in community forums is slowly fading, as is the palpable hostility toward agents who dared to air dirty laundry in public. Along with this intra-community cynicism, the mainstream disbelief of problems of a model minority is also in the wane. Since the 1990s, nearly twenty-five South Asian community-based organizations (CBOs) devoted to anti–domestic violence work have been established;[1] several books, articles, and special issues of journals on domestic violence have been published; many conferences have included sessions on South Asian American domestic violence; and some service and research grants have seeped into the community. Although none of this is adequate to meet community needs comprehensively, collectively they certainly testify to a burgeoning South Asian anti–domestic violence movement.

Besides validating women's experiences of violence in their homes in America, the existence of the South Asian anti–domestic violence movement underscores the distinctiveness of South Asians as a community characterized by culture, ethnicity, and special needs, as well as the uniqueness of ideas, issues, and intervention strategies that are effective in the community. The South Asian CBOs have successfully challenged the notion of universality of battered women's experiences and highlighted that successful intervention has to be culturally, emotionally, legally, and linguistically appropriate (e.g., Abraham 2000b; Agnew 1998b).

In a society where race and citizenship are organizing principles, although South Asians have some commonalities with other immigrants and communities of color, they remain distinct. Thus, understanding domestic violence in the community requires specialized knowledge and a singular perspective, one that

Margaret Abraham terms "*ethno-gender* approach" (1995:452). Abraham defines this framework as "one that examines the multiple intersection of ethnicity, gender, class, and legal status as significant categories in the analysis of domestic violence with a special emphasis on the relationship between ethnicity and gender" (2000b:6). The approach certainly shifts from the traditional binaries of black and white, victim and perpetrator, citizen and alien. Working from this intersectionality, the South Asian anti–domestic violence movement has been able to foreground social structures and ethnic cultures as these play out in the lives of individuals.

Naming the Violence

In the last three decades, the South Asian community has become an economic and political force in North America (see Kantrowitz and Scelfo 2004). Immigrants from South Asia arrived on North American shores at the tail end of 1800s. However, this early group experienced such severe attrition that by the dawning of the twentieth century, it was difficult to identify a cohesive community. It is only after the relaxation of the Immigration and Nationality Act of 1965 that the second wave of migration from South Asia began (Chandrasekhar 1984). At the center of today's anti–domestic violence movement is this South Asian community, which has congregated in the United States primarily after 1970.

In the first decade or so, the South Asian immigrant community was engrossed in settling down in its newly adopted homeland. Its focus was to achieve economic stability and socialize the next generation to retain the teachings of the natal culture. To help maintain the cultural identity that the immigrants brought over the continents, the community established numerous cultural organizations and religious centers all across North America. During these heady years of success, the immigrant community spent immense efforts in maintaining an impeccable image to the outside world by vociferously denying the existence of social problems such as domestic violence, sexual assault, disease, homelessness, poverty, mental illness, unemployment, delinquency, racism, and intergenerational conflict (Abraham 2000b; Bhattacharjee 1992; Dasgupta 1998a; Dasgupta and Warrier 1996). Although it ignored many social problems, perhaps the community was most oblivious to women's plight within the home. Consequently, little systematic information exists on violence against women in the South Asian contexts in North America. To date, no large-scale studies of incidence rate has been conducted to assess the extent of violence against women in South Asian American homes.

According to Census 2000, nearly 2.2 million South Asians live in the United States—a figure that does not take into account the sizable undocumented population that lives in obscurity, nor individuals residing on temporary work visas (U.S. Census Bureau 2002b). Despite the community's substantial political and economic influence in society, investigators and practitioners ignored it as a viable ground for domestic violence research until the mid 1980s (e.g., Abraham 1995,

2000b; Ahmad et al. 2004; Dasgupta and Warrier 1996; *Journal of Social Distress and the Homeless* 2000; Krishnan et al. 1998; Nankani 2000; Natarajan 2002; Raj and Silverman 2002b, 2003; Raj et al. 2004; Rianon and Shelton 2003; *Violence against Women* 1999).

Despite the meagerness of researched information, one can gain some understanding of the magnitude of domestic violence in the South Asian community by examining the small-scale studies that are available. For example, Raj and Silverman's recent survey conducted in the Boston area shows an alarming pervasiveness of domestic violence in South Asian homes (2002b). Among 160 highly educated and middle-class women surveyed for the study, nearly 35 percent claimed that they had experienced partner violence. In addition, nearly 19 percent asserted that they had experienced sexual abuse by their male partners. In both cases, a significant majority of the respondents stated they were still involved in the abusive relationship.

An informal survey of newspaper reports on domestic violence related deaths and near deaths since 1990 further indicates the seriousness of the problem. Between March 1990 and February 2006, community newspapers reported 115 murders and murder/suicides, twenty attempted murders, five attempted suicides after murder, at least four suspicious disappearances of women, and two deaths of perpetrators in the hands of police, bringing the total of domestic violence related fatalities and near fatalities in the U.S.-based South Asian community to 146.[2] Notwithstanding such extreme violence, there is little reliable data on the incidence rate of intimate abuse among South Asians. The fact of this nonexistence speaks volumes of the invisibility that shrouds the topic of family violence in South Asian immigrant communities and the dominant community's failure to notice the group with any seriousness.

Although many of the tactics of abuse that South Asian women experience are common to other immigrant victims and battered women, their emotional, material, and physical impact render them unique. For example, although the threat of deportation is used frequently against immigrant battered women by their spouses, it adds on vicious dimensions for South Asian women due to certain factors: stigmatization of divorce, shame of failing to please one's husband, fear of losing custody of children, and bringing dishonor to the natal family. The theme of deep shame, failure, and disgrace is echoed repeatedly in the voices of battered South Asian women, who have dared to seek assistance from CBOs (Abraham 2000b; Dasgupta and Warrier 1996; Gill 2004; Shirwadkar 2004; Supriya 1995, 1996). In a comparative study of three communities of color, Yoshioka and her colleagues report that fewer South Asian battered women were advised to leave their violent spouses than women in other groups, even when they had disclosed the abuse to their natal male relatives (Yoshioka et al. 2003). Such recommendations are tantamount to inflexible decisions, as most women would not be able to survive emotionally and financially without the support of their families. Furthermore, a ruined reputation due to divorce or the batterer's vindictiveness might make a woman the target of an honor killing, an action they might not be able to escape on Western soil (Amnesty International 1999; Baker, Gregware, and Cassidy 1999; BBC News 2004; Joseph 2002; Indo-Asian News Service 2002). In short, the commitment to "my husband, good or bad" is forcefully reinforced in women through emotional and material pressures, as well as the threat of physical obliteration.[3]

Expanding the Net of Understanding

The battered women's movements in North America had hitherto placed emphasis on domestic abuse perpetrated by a spouse or romantic partner. Inclusion of South Asian women's contexts in this work has necessitated extending the understanding. Although a South Asian battered woman's male partner is more often than not complicit in any abuse perpetrated against her, the sources of violence are certainly not limited to him. Historically in South Asia, older women in the extended family were responsible for socializing new brides in the family's ethos and behaviors and doling out punishment to recalcitrant and transgressing women. While the powerful males set the codes of conduct, their day-to-day implementation was left up to the family's older women. The process traditionally made close allies of mothers and sons, creating bonds that became the primary source of power to the older women (Fernandez 1997). This pattern has not quite disappeared in the immigrant milieu. As extended families continue to reconfigure in North America, the proverbial "mother-in-law abuse" has started to raise its ugly head. In addition, many battered women have reported to CBOs that other members of the affinal family, such as mothers- and fathers-in-law, sisters- and brothers-in-law, also inflict violence on them. At times, the spouse is the passive observer of this abuse, leading the wife to believe that the removal of the in-laws would end all violence in her life.

Along with this widening network of familial sources of abuse, South Asian women's ground realities have instigated a blurring of geographical boundaries in anti–domestic violence work. South Asian CBOs are now facing violence against women that is transnational in nature—desertion of women by their immigrant husbands (Gurnani et al. 2005). Although abandonment of wives is not a new phenomenon, in recent years the collective number has reached such proportions in India that it has attracted political, activist, and media attention (Khan 2004; Nayar 2004; Singh 2003; Ward 2005). Media estimates that Punjab and Gujarat are homes to 15,000 and 12,000 women abandoned by their immigrant spouses, respectively (*Asian Pacific Post* 2004; NRIinternet.com 2004). Not all abandoned wives are married to runaway grooms who live in North America, but a sizable number are. Although comparable information from other South Asian countries is not available, one can only assume the situation is similar.

To mainstream anti–domestic violence movements in North America, desertion might not be considered actionable violence; yet, in the South Asian context its emotional, material, legal, and social consequences are devastating enough on women to warrant such considerations. Most anti–domestic violence activists in India are now calling for changes at the policy and legal levels to address the situation. However, the National Commission for Women in India has asserted in a report that "in the absence of any common or bilateral understanding with the countries concerned, these issues may not be sorted out" (Khan 2004). The South Asian American CBOs are also beginning to organize to undertake this issue. Undoubtedly, the problem is likely to appear soon on the radar screen of mainstream domestic violence service providers and practitioners also.

In addition to the problem of deserted women, other transnational issues such as international child kidnapping, contradictory family laws in the host country and the country of origin, exportation and marketing of misogynist sex-selective reproductive technologies, and trafficking are becoming salient to South Asian anti–domestic violence work. Many of the articles of this book centralize this transnational nature of South Asian women's realities.

Lighting Concealed Corners

In the past two decades, South Asian community activists have been organizing to keep women safe from violence in the family. They have been challenging not only the patriarchal entitlements integral to the community but also the racialized marginalization by the larger community that would wrench power from South Asian women. Certainly, the movement has made remarkable progress in changing the ideology, boundary, and practice of anti–domestic violence activism in the United States. Still, the spotlight needs to be turned on two special areas of this work: (1) violence against young women, and (2) accountability of perpetrators and the community.

Twenty years ago, as South Asian domestic violence activists began their work with immigrant women, they tacitly believed that the problems would, if not end with the first generation, at least dwindle with the second. They hoped that the second generation of women, growing up in North America without some of the barriers their mothers faced, such as language and unfamiliarity with social and legal systems, would be more empowered and thereby capable of escaping abuse. Yet, most indications are that this might not be the case. Steadily, information about young women who have been victims of incestuous violence, sexual assault, and domestic as well as dating abuse is coming to light (Jiwani 2005; Poore 2000a; Rianon and Shelton 2003). Partially, such abuse arises out of the community's insistence on policing young women to protect their purity and chastity in an environment perceived as licentious (Dasgupta 1998c; Handa 2003; Jiwani 2005; Mani 1993). In addition, the culture conflict that is inevitably generated in the attempt to balance the strictures of the ethnic community and assimilatory pull of the dominant society also renders young women vulnerable to violence in contexts of dating and marriage (Dasgupta 1998c; Jiwani 2005). The possibility of violence is especially enhanced when the choice of one's partner is against the family and community expectations.

In addition to girls' and young women's issues, anti–domestic violence CBOs are yet to resolve how to treat perpetrators of violence. As most CBOs work with limited resources, the lion's share of their endeavors and ideas have been dedicated to meeting victims' needs. Almost no batterers' intervention programs (BIP) exist in the community. Thus, South Asian batterers are either treated by default, along with men of other communities, or get off scot-free, without experiencing any negative consequences for their brutality. Similarly, although some efforts have been made to engage communities with issues of woman abuse, these are indeed insufficient and allow the majority to conveniently disregard such challenges.

Writing Activism, Changing Lives

The chronicle of South Asian women's experience of domestic abuse in North America is not one of despair only; it is also one of hope and inspiration. In their adopted countries, as women found no respite from violence within the intimate space of home, they came together to organize and claim their lives and the right to be violence free. Women's activism to change society in North America has not been restricted to domestic violence, but has spread into struggles for community harmony; immigrant, labor, and reproductive rights; and equality for lesbian, bisexual, transgendered, and queer-identified women. This activism encompasses action and ideas, organizing and documentation. This collection of eighteen essays, *Body Evidence*, is witness to this activism.

The first part of this book charts the faces and nuances of domestic violence in the South Asian community. Anitha Venkataramani opens it with an essay that provides an overall picture of the problem and its uniqueness for the initiated and uninitiated alike. Ruksana Ayyub and Bidya Ranjeet and Bandana Purkayastha explore women's position and situation in Muslim and Nepali communities, respectively. Discourses on women's conditions in the Muslim community have generally been confined to examinations of the ideal context, as delineated by the Quran. While the Quran provides significant rights for women, those rights are routinely ignored in reality. Ruksana scrutinizes both the ideal and contextual realities of Muslim women in America and points to the path of recapturing the former. Women's activism in the Muslim community is already leading to claims for the right to pray in *Masjids* and lead *Namaz*, a privilege bestowed only upon men (Joshi 2004; Venugopal 2005), as well as demand accountability of batterers (Holmes 2005). Bidya and Bandana's trail-blazing study of Nepali women and domestic violence in the United States is an enormous contribution to the existing literature on South Asian women. They not only discuss the diversity of the community and the resultant complexity in designing intervention strategies, but also offer a lesson of inclusiveness to South Asian CBOs that are predominantly led by women of Indian origin. It is a lesson that is timely, important, and must be heeded.

Sandeep Hunjan and Shelagh Towson dissect how shame is associated with the South Asian obsession with women's chastity and virginity. It is this heavy and pervasive mantle of humiliation that silences South Asian battered women and keeps them from seeking justice. Maunica Sthanki documents how South Asian, Arab, and Muslim battered women have been placed in double bind after the destruction of 9/11. For this group of women, the state-sponsored war on terror has strengthened the terror at home. Simultaneously, the post 9/11 milieu of hate has snatched away from them the option of seeking help.

The second part of *Body Evidence* consists of chapters that provide a glimpse at the emerging issues in anti–domestic violence work. Both Diya Kallivayalil and Julie Rajan discuss the penalties in mental health that domestic violence frequently extorts from women. Mental health is one of the most neglected aspects of South Asian life, and these exposés underscore the pressing need for intervention. Rajan complicates the issue further by scrutinizing violence of distorted body image and eating disorders among South Asian women. Sunita Puri examines the topic of health care, a corollary issue, and how racism and xenophobia of providers, even in the context of multiculturalism, deprive battered South Asian women of their right to high-quality medical intervention.

Grace Poore has tackled one of the most secret topics in South Asian communities—incestual child sexual abuse. She has highlighted the silences and cover-ups that maintain the pretension of cohesion in the family and community. These acts, of course, end up protecting the perpetrator at the cost their daughters. Prajna Paramita Choudhury has elaborated on the violence of silence with which the South Asian community surrounds lesbian, bisexual, transgendered, and queer-identified women. She correctly asserts that such silence kills more than the physical body and calls for reconciliation with this marginalized community.

Choosing to go beyond the "language barrier," Mandeep Grewal has argued that practitioners and service providers have to understand not only battered women's words but also the shades of meaning they attempt to convey. This part ends with Shashi Jain and my study of domestic violence in the context of Jainism. We contend that religious directives are inadequate to erect protective factors against domestic violence and that invasive patriarchal beliefs supersede the strictest of nonviolent principles in our community.

The next part of *Body Evidence* is an engagement with the U.S. legal systems that South Asian battered women routinely come into contact. One of the major motifs that surface here is the issue of contradictory cultures: South Asian, American, legal, and domestic violence. Both Sharmila Rudrappa's and my essays probe into the U.S. court culture and the bewilderment it poses for battered South Asian women. Much of the incongruity women face in courts arises from a system that was designed for the dominant group (read: white, middle class, male) but is being executed for the marginalized (read: immigrant, South Asian, battered women). Shivali Shah has focused on battered women on dependent visas, specifically H-4, and scrutinized a new intersection of domestic violence, class, and immigration.

The last part is on activism, nationally and transnationally. Rupaleem Bhuyan has examined a complicated angle of intervention: advocacy for H-4 visa holders.

She has approached advocacy for this vulnerable group from different angles: individual and systems change. Sujatha Jesudason has analyzed the intricacies of a transnational trafficking case and the difficulties of searching for justice when the power differential between the involved nations, systems, communities, and individuals is vast. Elora Chowdhury's essay carries on this insight to discuss transnational involvement in organizing Bangladeshi victims of acid-violence to be treated in the United States. Her story of transnational activism disputes the possibility of forging an international feminist sisterhood any time soon without a serious shift in power between countries, nations, organizations, and socioeconomic classes.

While these chapters document some of the current work and emerging issues in anti–domestic violence activism in the South Asian community, they also lay out crucial questions regarding power, class, sexuality, violence, service, and social change. None are easy to answer or resolve. However, the authors offer an opportunity to struggle with them the best we can. *Body Evidence* is not complete; it is only a stone in the road ahead. It does not represent all perspectives, nor all communities. Many omissions, gaps, and wishes are not to be. Nonetheless, it is a map of our activism—a body of evidence that I hope will help us move forward.

NOTES

1.   See http://www.manavi.org/links.htm for a complete list.
2.   I informally collected fatality reports from one South Asian community-based newspaper, *India Abroad*.
3.   I have borrowed the phrase from Bandyopadhyay (1995) as it succinctly captures the attitude of South Asian women and their families.

PART ONE

The Body Chart

Mapping Domestic Violence in
South Asian Communities

1

Understanding South Asian Immigrant Women's Experiences of Violence

ANITHA VENKATARAMANI-KOTHARI

Gurpreet was an educated girl from India whose parents instilled strong traditional values in her around religion and appropriate behavior. At the age of 19 Gurpreet was married to a scientist living abroad. Gurpreet faced severe abuse in her marriage on a daily basis. Helpless in this abusive marriage Gurpreet sought assistance from her parents and her parents-in-law. While her parents were sympathetic to her situation, they refused to take her in. Meanwhile her parents-in-law passively supported the abuse since they felt it kept her "in-line." Gurpreet could not leave the marriage and live alone since single motherhood would lower her financial security and her daughters' social respectability. Gurpreet had no choice but to resign herself to a life of daily abuse. (Dasgupta and Warrier 1996:238–239)

The story above brings together many facets of abuse in the South Asian community. Domestic violence, while it is not unique to South Asians, takes on new and complex dimensions within the South Asian context. Due to various cultural factors, abuse and its effects in the South Asian community become complicated, and the problem continues to fester.

Ayyub (2000) defines domestic violence as a situation in which one partner uses various forms of abuse to systematically persecute the other. The threat of domestic violence to a community is apparent when we consider the evidence that untreated domestic abuse in the family can affect the structure and well-being of the entire home, and can be transmitted to future generations. Among the children in abusive families, the much-needed sense of safety and security in the growing years is also hampered.

In the South Asian community, the existence of this smoldering problem receives little or no public acknowledgement. Under the shroud of traditional practices and values, domestic violence continues to grow and women in the community continue to suffer. This chapter is an attempt to look at various cultural factors that cause, promote, and propagate physical, verbal, and emotional abuse in South

Asian homes. While shedding light on issues that complicate the lives of abused South Asian women, I attempt to highlight the stories of a few women who dared to seek help and probe at the definite likelihood of many more who suffer silently.

The Situation in South Asian Communities

The paucity of empirical research or strongly documented evidence of the prevalence of domestic violence among South Asians sheds light on the controlling and confining structures of the culture, and the consequent contribution to high and persistent incidences of abuse and battering. The scarce amount of quantitative data around abuse stands in stark contrast to the many incidents of family violence that South Asian women's organizations encounter and document in their work. Ayyub (2000) presents information from informal surveys of the South Asian population in 1998, wherein one in every four South Asian women reported domestic violence in their homes. She proposes that the actual number of domestic violence victims among South Asian women is likely to be significantly higher.

The preponderance of information reflecting the seriousness of domestic violence in the South Asian community is in the form of anecdotal accounts available to women's organizations in the United States. The rigid and patriarchal structures of the South Asian community at large leaves little room for researchers within the field to access victims of domestic violence, and simultaneously makes it impossible, if not unthinkable, for battered women to participate in empirical studies. Furthermore, several cultural factors discussed in the following section deter women from seeking legal help and participating in studies, as they fear that their identities might be exposed. However, Ayyub (2000) points out that the number of women seeking help from women's organizations for abuse is not only high, it is on the rise.

Various Facets of Abuse in the South Asian Community

Domestic violence comes in many forms in the South Asian community. The accounts below reflect the various ways in which a South Asian woman may be manipulated and coerced into enduring and hiding the abuse she faces. The examples below have been selected from a wider range and have been chosen to reflect the various types of domestic violence present in the South Asian community and the different cultural factors at play.

The Case of the Western Beauty

One issue that South Asian immigrant women confront is that of the Western image of physical beauty, which their husbands may have grown accustomed to in the United States. Dasgupta (2000a) cites the example of Poonam, who came to Manavi half starved. Her scientist/academician husband had controlled her food intake from the moment she landed in the United States, insisting that she remain slim. He made her weigh herself every morning and kept a chart of her weight. He punished her for small increases in her weight with forced fasting, public humiliation, silence, and withholding of affection. He controlled when and how much she ate and made sure she had no money so that she could not buy any food without his knowledge.

The Case of the Unpaid Servant

The fact that often the man is the primary immigrant and the one bringing in the money is a power-card that is frequently played to the victim's disadvantage. This is reflected in the case of Shahida (Abraham 2000a), whose husband carried out an affair with a next-door neighbor while she, since the day of her arrival in the United States, was locked at home. To curtail her movements, he gave her no money and kept her indoors at all times. He forbade her from even walking across the block and forced her to sleep on the living room couch. He simply used her for his cooking and cleaning purposes as an unpaid servant. Isolation and financial dependency kept Shahida trapped in the marriage, and the abuse was reinforced by threats of deportation and defamation to her family in Pakistan.

The Case of the Working Woman

Abuse and forced financial dependency may not be exclusive to homemakers. Women who work and make their own money may also be subjected to torture at home. Abraham (2000a) cites the case of Malti, a working woman, who had lived in the United States alone before her marriage. Her physician husband soon brought her under his control by curtailing her outside activities and controlling her finances. Even though she had her own money from her previous job, he gave her twenty dollars a week for all her expenses. Her husband and in-laws threatened physical assault if she questioned their behavior. Malti's cultural disadvantage was that she was already a divorcée and felt compelled to maintain her marriage at all costs. Although Malti was a working woman, she was constrained by her marriage because leaving her second husband would cause her to lose her reputation, especially among her relatives. Abraham (2000a) explains that divorce is seen as a violation of South Asian culture and may lead to isolation from a woman's natal family. In Malti's case, the fear of defamation was doubled since she had already endured one divorce.

The Case of the Educated Woman

Another case described by Abraham (2000a) indicates the role of law enforcement in abusive situations. For immigrant women, the fear of reporting abuse can be exacerbated by their lack of knowledge of legal rights in the United States, combined with the increase of police insensitivity and ignorance toward immigrants. Geeta was severely abused physically and emotionally, and her husband often threatened her with acts of violence, such as burning her body with hot oil. She was a physician in India, and upon her arrival to the United States she found herself to be completely helpless in a new environment where she knew no one. On one occasion, neighbors who heard her screams called the police. However, her husband convinced her that the person at the door was a security guard and that she should not say anything to him. While the police insisted on talking to her, they failed to notice that her husband was instructing her in her mother tongue to keep quiet (Abraham 2000a). It is important to note that while the police arrived at the scene, they left without actually speaking with the victim. This is even more likely in cases where the victim speaks no English at all.

The legal system might itself be hypersensitive to cultural issues, at times causing more woe to the victims. Dasgupta (2000a) cites the example of a New Jersey family court judge who vacated a South Asian woman's temporary restraining order by commenting that her husband's abusive behavior may be cultural. Furthermore, language barriers, cultural differences, lack of knowledge about their rights, and immigration policies all keep abused South Asian women from seeking help from shelters or other social services.

External and Internal Cultural Factors

Several inherent characteristics of the South Asian community can complicate the problem for victims and heighten the trauma that they suffer. The following are a few of the cultural factors at play in South Asian populations in the United States.

Family before Self

The family unit plays a role of paramount importance in the life of South Asians. The family is generally given higher value than the individual and an individual's behavior is often seen as a reflection of the family's worth in society. Relationships are other-generated rather than centered on self, and regardless of how personal the issue at hand is, family-centered decisions take priority over individual preferences. In addition, influential issues such as karma and good behavior lead to notions of tolerance and passivity (Hines et al. 1992). Family boundaries are clearly defined and a strict distinction is drawn between insiders and outsiders. Each individual is made aware of the prohibition regarding exposing family information to the outside world (Dasgupta and Warrier 1996).

A Model Minority

The South Asian community as a whole maintains a model minority facade by community leaders strongly upholding an image of the community as being devoid of any social problems, including sexual assault, mental illness, homelessness, and domestic violence (Dasgupta 2000a). Therefore, victims are often encouraged to suppress evidence of violent acts within the home and community (Dasgupta 1998a). As Dasgupta (2000a) points out, the nonexistence of reliable statistical data on the incidence of abuse in the community itself speaks volumes about the invisibility that shrouds the topic. Under its dictates of cultural chauvinism, the community sets up harsh standards for women to suppress their need to speak out about the violence they experience (Abraham 2000a).

The Unmarried Girl

Given the patriarchal structure of South Asian communities, men tend to have the advantage in family issues. The behavior of women is continually judged and tested not only by men but also by women. The South Asian girl's conduct is strictly restricted as a daughter, sister, wife, mother, and beyond. While growing up, younger women are taught by their mothers and sisters to idealize the image and role of the mother-in-law, which would grant her some power in the family (Hines et al. 1992).

Ayyub provides insight into some ideas within the South Asian Muslim population, an important part of the South Asian community. The recommendation laid out for Muslim women is *"Chador and Char Diwar* (the veil and the four walls of the house)" (Ayyub 2000:241). This concept, while it is not exclusive to Muslim women, recommends that women remain covered and confined in the house. While the Hindu culture is laxer on women being physically covered, it does encourage and commend women who primarily stay within the home and focus on their role as homemakers. More often than not, the South Asian girl is socialized with the sole intention of finding her a suitable match in marriage. The primary motivation for educating her is, first, the status it provides for her parents and, second, the image and material well-being that it brings to her in-laws (Ayyub 2000). Beyond this, her education may improve her quality as a mother and make her an effective tutor and guide for her children at home.

Requirements of Marriage

Marriage brings with it another set of rules for the woman to follow. From early childhood, South Asian parents teach their girl-child that she would bring dire shame to them if her marriage were to fail and she were to prove a bad wife (Ayyub 2000). They learn from childhood the order of power in a household: the eldest male possessing highest power, followed by his sons in order, the mother-in-law, any older unmarried daughters of the home, and finally the daughter-in-law (Hines et al. 1992). Many women may have witnessed this structure in their own natal homes and participated in it as a daughter. Women are also taught and encouraged to be passive, tolerant, and never look elders in the eye (Hines et al. 1992). As a result, a woman in a greatly androcentric marriage might accept domination as her destiny instead of leaving the unhealthy situation. A woman whose husband indulges her is seen as lucky, whereas one whose husband mistreats her is advised to accept things as her fate and misfortune (Ayyub 2000). Hence, a woman may see nothing wrong with suppression and dependence within marriage.

The Joint-Family Setup

Another cultural factor that increases the acceptance of violence by South Asian women is the extended-family system. Many new South Asian brides live with their in-laws, including their husband's siblings, so that they become answerable to many people. The sources of abuse tend to increase in such situations. At times, the husband may be a participant or observer of his wife's abuse at the hands of his parents and siblings (Dasgupta 2000a). In other cases, the woman's mother-in-law may encourage and/or expect her son to keep his wife under control (Hines et al. 1992). In such situations, the woman tends to place the blame on the in-laws and believes that her husband deserves no blame for the violence (Dasgupta 2000a).

Financial Dependency

Even a working woman married to a dominating man may not really enjoy the independence, finances, and identity that she has earned. For example, men usually control the family income regardless of women's working status. Thus, a South Asian woman's financial security becomes entirely dependent upon her spouse (Dasgupta 2000a). Cultural limitations and gender-role conditioning combine to lead even highly educated and financially independent women to feel accountable to their spouses and families (Abraham 2000a). For a woman living with her in-laws, it is expected that her income will be distributed first among her in-laws, who have the primary right to any money she earns while living in their home (Hines et al. 1992).

The Divorce Stigma

The South Asian woman's identity is primarily derived from marriage and motherhood. Therefore, a woman without a husband is seen as a woman who is lacking a major component of herself. A divorced woman and/or single mother is seen as having failed in the role of wife and mother, regardless of the conduct of her partner. Single motherhood is seen as severely detrimental to the development of the children (Dasgupta and Warrier 1996). Divorced South Asian women are further viewed as damaged goods, while the divorce is seen as their own fault, stemming from some intrinsic problem or flaw (Ayyub 2000; Dasgupta 2000a). Divorced women are also stigmatized and their participation in holy events or celebrations (particularly weddings) is discouraged, for they might bring bad luck (Ayyub 2000). To complicate matters, those women who endure a bad marriage in order to keep their families together are glorified within the culture. This glorification of suffering gives South Asian women an added incentive to keep the family together at all costs (Waters 1999).

Second-Generation Issues

The pressure to keep up the model minority image breaks generational barriers and affects immigrant parents raising second-generation Asian American children. Having been raised under strict scrutiny in their homelands, immigrant parents become overwhelmed by the omnipresent influence of Western culture on their children, as manifested through the child or teenager's increased freedom of expression and open sexuality. Families view adolescent struggles for independence as disrespect, because respect is expressed through obedience (Hines et al. 1992). As a result, educated immigrant parents, who themselves may have disapproved of the iron-fist in their own youth, turn to the same rules in an attempt to re-create the traditional family system. The application of these rules can lead to a new round of abusive scenarios, which may involve coerced and even tricked marriages for second-generation youth, particularly girls (Ayyub 2000).

Invalidation of Experiences

Given the gender relations and androcentric power distribution that is inherent to traditional South Asian cultures, the experience and understanding of violence can be complicated by the cultural context, leaving the victims unsure of the validity of their experiences (Dasgupta 2000a). This issue is spotlighted, for instance, by the family court judge (mentioned earlier), who vacated a restraining order on the account that abusive behavior may be cultural. If a judge in the position of legal power can assert that abuse of various types may be culturally sanctioned among South Asians, it is obvious that sheltered, immigrant South Asian women may try to make sense of the injustice they face in cultural terms as well. Dasgupta (2000a) also cites some informal cases from her own work where she found that South Asian victims tend to recognize physical abuse quite readily and yet are reluctant to acknowledge sexual coercion or abuse. Perhaps victims of domestic violence view their husbands as having the right to be sexually forceful with them and, on occasion, to beat them if they have failed to perform their conjugal duties. Dasgupta (2000a) further emphasizes that most battered South Asian women feel that marriage denies them sexual control and their husbands are entitled to unlimited access to their bodies. Marital rape may be an alien concept to South Asian women (Mazumdar 1998).

The Allure of the Green Card

The issues of financial control and immigration status jointly compound issues of domestic violence. As they are frequently the secondary and dependent immigrants, women often feel the need to justify themselves in the eyes of their husbands and to live by their rules. Threats of deportation, consequent defamation, and helplessness can only make women more vulnerable to the control of their husbands.

For South Asian girls, marriage may simply move them from one set of rules (parental) to another (affinal). The lack of confidence in themselves and their own ability to survive independently, combined with the stigma associated with failed marriages, are reason enough to endure abuse silently. For many, living with an abusive man who holds the key to her permanent residency in the United States is a better alternative than being forced to return home to a life of scorn and stigma for herself and her natal family.

Lack of Support Systems

A South Asian immigrant woman may also lack family support in the United States. The family and cultural support systems of her home country are often nonexistent with the shift to a new country (Abraham 2000a). As Shahida's account pointed out earlier, some women are forcibly isolated from any family or friends they may have in the United States, which may further exacerbate their feelings of despair and helplessness. Living solely in the domain of her abusive husband, she may have only him for emotional sustenance.

Another problem may be that mainstream shelters and social institutions are not sensitive to South Asian women's cultures. Dasgupta (2000a) cites experiences of her client who was turned away from a domestic violence shelter because there was no one there who spoke the woman's language. Furthermore, once in shelters women may also face problems such as cultural insensitivity, racism, xenophobia, classism, and ignorance about immigration policies (Dasgupta 2000a).

Psychological Impact of Domestic Violence

Given the incredible social pressures that battered South Asian women face, there is very little hope of finding participants for in-depth studies on violence within the community. Consequently, there is little research reflecting the psychological trauma that results from domestic violence among South Asians. In fact, agencies such as Manavi report that mental health counseling is sought by very few of their battered female clients. They observe that when the abuse stops, most clients prioritize education, employment, and the well-being of their children over their own mental health (Preisser 1999). However, given the nature of the issues at hand, it is expected that victims may incur some emotional damage as a result of being exposed to such extreme violence.

Loss of Self-Esteem and Identity

The loss of financial control, as exhibited by the cases of Malti and Shahida (Abraham 2000a), are likely to leave women feeling helpless and insecure. Since she has to depend on her husband for every penny, a woman may feel indebted or obligated to him. Shahida found that she was being treated like an unpaid maid and did not speak up when asked to clean her abusive husband's soiled bed (Abraham 2000a). It is almost as though she accepted her role as his servant and stopped expecting any more concern for herself.

Similarly, Geeta's case is also an example of how a woman may develop a helpless and distorted view of the self (Abraham 2000a). Geeta was a physician, but she was convinced that the policeman at her door was really a security guard. This shows how given enough abuse and dependency, a woman may be led to question her own perceptions of reality. As she loses her self-confidence, she becomes increasingly tied to her husband and his judgment, which only places more power in his hands.

Such insecurity can also shift a woman's locus of evaluation outside herself, such as in the case of Poonam (Dasgupta 2000a), who was put through rigorous diets to stay slim. Poonam viewed herself as unappealing and unsatisfactory because her husband withheld affection when she gained a few pounds. Her own sense of physical beauty and the personal worth that she attaches to it becomes heavily influenced by her husband's viewpoint.

All of the women cited in these studies explained that they tried to entice their husbands and win their love, often apologizing for making them angry and violent. The justifications indicate that the victims tend to view themselves through the lens of their abusers. Such a perspective makes it all the more difficult for battered South Asian women to leave abusive relationships. Altogether, they become caught in a vicious cycle, where they become increasingly insecure, endowing more power to their spouses, which in turn makes them more vulnerable to abuse (Mehrotra 1999).

Depression, Anxiety, and Post-Traumatic Stress Disorder

These subtle setbacks in an individual's self-worth can compound with other social factors such as joblessness and isolation, leading to serious mental health problems. Research with African American women in abusive relationships has found significant evidence of depression and post-traumatic stress disorder (Kocot and Goodman 2003). While there is considerable research on the psychological consequences of domestic violence in Western cultures, it is difficult to draw a direct parallel with South Asians because there are considerable cultural differences between the two. However, since there are several points of similarity between South Asian and Chinese cultures, a comparison between research on battered Chinese and South Asian women may reveal similar patterns of mental health.

The Chinese American communities deal with similar social issues and pressures as South Asians. The patriarchal structure, men's license to abuse, pressure to keep up the model minority status, and the reluctance of women to leave abusive relationships are characteristics found in the Chinese American population as well (So-Kum Tang 1997). So-Kum Tang's study of Chinese women living in a shelter found that wife abuse (verbal and physical) was related to negative affects of both depression and anxiety (1997).

Another important similarity between the Chinese and South Asian cultures is that they tend to downplay psychological problems, considering them worthy of little attention (Yick and Agbayami-Siewert 1997). This suppression of emotional problems may actually compound to cause greater difficulties. Studies have shown that suppressed anger, which is a commonly experienced emotion among abused women, can lead to depression (Dutton 1992; Foa et al. 2000). Anger suppression has also been seen to compound with post-traumatic stress disorder among abused women (Foa et al. 2000). Given the highly family-centered structure of the South Asian population and the compounding cultural factors mentioned earlier, it is possible that South Asian victims of domestic violence may also reveal similar behavior or symptoms characteristic of depression and/or post-traumatic stress disorder.

Somatic Problems

Studies with abused women from white and African American groups have found that abused women are likely to have more health problems than nonbattered women (Sutherland, Sullivan, and Bybee 2001). These issues may include sleep problems, fatigue, insomnia, recurring nightmares, headaches, chest pain, back and limb problems, disturbing physical sensations, stomach and gastrointestinal problems, respiratory problems, hyperventilation, asthma, pelvic pain, and menstrual problems (Sutherland, Sullivan, and Bybee 2001). It is likely that in some cases, the psychological problems become somaticized and expressed as a physical illness, which is far easier to express and address than abuse and psychological trauma. Given that the expression of psychological trauma caused by domestic violence is difficult to address because of the aforementioned cultural factors, somatization of psychological problems may also occur in South Asian women. However, without actual data from systematically conducted studies, this claim cannot be made with certainty.

Substance Abuse

Studies with Anglo and African-American women have also found a correlation between degree of violence and extent of substance abuse (Clark and Foy 2000). Substance abuse may be the result of suppression of psychological problems and negative emotions of hurt or anger. While any of these problems in a South Asian woman cannot be automatically assumed to be the result of domestic abuse, a battered South Asian woman may abuse substances as a way of self-medicating to alleviate the physical and emotional pain.

Strategies for Resisting and Coping with Abuse

An abused woman, lacking appropriate ways to address the problem, may often try to explain her husband's actions. Counselors at Manavi reported that the most common justification a battered woman provided for abuse was that her husband might have a lot of frustration and stress in his life (Mehrotra 1999). This justification may be compounded if the woman feels the need to maintain a good image of the husband for the children. A battered woman may endure abuse and resist seeking help from agencies and shelters if she worries that her children will see their father being led away by the police (Preisser 1999).

However, abused women may employ other strategies to resist the violence, protect themselves from further harm, and preserve a sense of self-worth. These strategies may include passivity during the abusive episode, face-saving strategies such as joking about the abuse in public, and fantasies of murder and suicide (Lempert 1996). Mehrotra (1999) cites cases of South Asian battered women who employed several subversive techniques of resistance. Some asserted control by refusing to cook, others by duplicating house and car keys without their partners' knowledge. Women also kept their important documentation such as passports and immigration papers in a secure place. In some instances, the abused women would spit into their partner's food before serving it to him.

The Reality of Domestic Violence in South Asian Communities

Given the cultural norm of keeping family problems hidden, domestic violence researchers have not been very successful at penetrating South Asian populations. As a result, there is little information on the proportion of South Asian immigrant women who endure violence in their homes. One can only speculate based on informal surveys and anecdotal evidence obtained by women's organizations that the proportion of abused South Asian women is growing. There is no research that submits evidence of the frequency of abuse in South Asian communities. The understanding of domestic violence in the South Asian community cannot be complete unless research data is comprehensive and accurate.

Information from Chinese American populations and other immigrant groups can only partially illuminate the issues faced by South Asians. These data signal the possibility of depression, anxiety, and post-traumatic stress disorder remaining untreated among members of the South Asian community. However, it is also possible that other confounding factors, exclusive to South Asians, may lead to different patterns of mental health in abused South Asian women. Strong claims about the psychological repercussions of abuse among South Asians can only be made when strong evidence for abuse is available.

Another issue to consider is that the battered women cited in this article are not representative of every South Asian woman. Depending on their own mentality and the opportunities accorded to them, different women may address cultural norms in significantly different ways. Intimate abuse may also be an issue that is addressed and ameliorated differently by each individual. These ideas can only be clarified when strong evidence from systematic studies is provided.

On the other hand, the information that is available cannot be ignored or taken lightly. Even if anecdotal, such documentation is still representative of the issues that are present in the community. Ideally, the anecdotal evidence must be taken to represent the urgency for research on domestic violence in the South Asian community. Encouraging the presence and work of women's organizations, while it is essential and effective, only scratches the surface of the problem. For the issue of domestic violence to be accurately and efficiently addressed, large-scale studies must be conducted.

Implications for Intervention with the South Asian Population

Work with victims of abuse in the South Asian population must take into consideration the cultural issues involved for the client, and the perception of abuse and marital problems within her culture. Specifically, these factors must be addressed by all of the different people a victim of abuse is likely to encounter in her quest to gain control over her life.

If a battered woman seeks legal counsel to remove herself from the abusive situation, her advocate and counselor come to play an important role in her life. Therefore, it is of paramount importance that she shares good communication with them. Effective communication and understanding can only occur if her attorney and counselor have full understanding of the cultural perceptions and duties that she cannot separate from. When South Asian women approach main-stream service providers, they are faced with communication problems around language and an understanding of cultural context (Preisser 1999). It is important for agencies working with South Asian women to provide legal and psychological assistance that is sensitive to the woman's social position. She may not, for example, be able to report her abusive spouse to the police because he holds her immigration papers or he is a distant relative of a member of her family. Agencies should particularly consider cultural values on tolerance, childrearing, dating and marriage, insider and outsider relationships, and appropriate codes for public and private behavior (Dasgupta and Warrier 1995).

Often community leaders such as temple priests or church leaders confirm the belief that being silent about the abuse women experience is the best option (Ayyub 2000; Dasgupta 2000a). Intervening agencies must take into account all the reasons that encourage women to keep silent. They must also actively reach out to the community to spread awareness of the availability of resources and to edu-cate women on their rights. While undertaking such outreach, educators should use terminology that is accepted within the community, and refrain from using words that may shock the client and deter her from seeking help (Huisman 1996).

Concluding Remarks

Domestic violence affects people all over the country regardless of race, class, sex-uality, and gender. This chapter provides a glimpse at how this problem affects immigrants from South Asia and a few factors involved in it. It presents cases of abuse in the South Asian population, cultural factors that encourage abuse, the possible psychological impact, the primary methods of resistance and coping, and the implications for working with abused South Asians. Although based primarily on anecdotal evidence, this essay underscores the seriousness of the problem of domestic violence for those it affects and emphasizes the need for academic and clinical attention to this population. While it focuses on South Asian immigrant women, it is not an attempt to say that women are the only victims of abuse. Research might reveal woman-to-man abuse as well as intragender abuse between South Asian same-sex partners.

Over the years, South Asian women's advocacy groups such as Manavi, Sakhi, Narika, and Raksha have continued to reach more and more women and enlighten them on their rights to safety and happiness. This trend is encouraging for all who want to see the status of women in the South Asian community improve. If more women are seeking out such support services, then perhaps South Asian women are slowly but surely waking up to their rights. Perhaps such women's groups and researchers within the field can encourage more women to bring their stories to the forefront, allowing for appropriate action to take place within the community and to put an end to domestic violence.

Immigration is a difficult process for all involved. Domestic violence in immigrant families only makes this process more complicated. Research into domestic violence can encourage more awareness and promote more facilities and sources of support for those in need.

2

The Many Faces of Domestic Violence in the South Asian American Muslim Community

RUKSANA AYYUB

Since September 11, 2001, Muslims have been thrust into the limelight in America. There is a great deal of interest in trying to understand the Muslim psyche. Muslims themselves feel scrutinized and under siege. Fear and suspicions are easily raised on both sides. In such an atmosphere, while Muslim religious and community leaders continue to point out the message of peace in Islam, others try to cover up and hide internal problems. In order to distance us from terrorism and violence in the world, many have started denying the violence that exists in our homes. As our outside world became an unsafe place, the worst affected were the victims of domestic violence, for it became even more difficult for them to speak out and seek help.

The Muslim immigrants from South Asia bring with them very strong cultural and religious beliefs. Islam plays an important and positive role in the lives of South Asian Muslim immigrants. Numerous Islamic Centers have been established in America, which act as religious and community centers to meet the community's needs (Haddad 1986). However, one subgroup of the Muslim population whose needs have not yet been adequately met is the victim of domestic violence, a subgroup that is overwhelmingly women.

Most South Asians prefer to see themselves as a model minority devoid of any problems like domestic violence (Bhattacharjee 1992; Dasgupta 1998a). To them, domestic violence is a problem of the modern Western woman. Nevertheless, a survey I conducted in the immigrant South Asian population indicated that one in four women experienced domestic violence in their homes (Ayyub 1998). Despite strong denials within the South Asian community, if 25 percent of women reported violence in their homes, one might surmise that the actual number was even higher.

Generally, Muslim women faced with domestic violence turn to their religion and families for help and support. The religion, culture, and families expect them to fit certain prescribed roles of wife, daughter, and mother. For those women who fit the prescribed role, the system offers certain benefits like status and respect. Women as mothers are elevated in Islam and given even more importance than the father; heaven is said to lie under their feet. As daughters, women are cherished as temporary guests in their parents' home. In the role of the obedient wife, they are idealized as the honor of the family and promised heaven after death. However, for a woman faced with domestic violence and needing help to leave an abusive marriage, the system offers strong resistance.

This chapter highlights some of the obstacles south Asian Muslim women face from their religion, culture, and families in ameliorating domestic violence. I write this article as an insider, a psychotherapist, who is concerned not only with the aftermath of 9/11 but also with violence against women in the South Asian Muslim community. This essay is based on my work as a member of a committee for the prevention of domestic violence in the Muslim community and a native informant, drawing from my personal experiences of South Asian Muslim cultures.

I grew up in Pakistan, hearing stories of my grandmother's marriage at the age twelve to my grandfather, who was forty and taking on a third wife with the full support and acceptance of my grandma's family. I witnessed my aunt being blamed for the beatings she got at the hands of her husband. I saw friends being forced into marriages. In America, I continue to see female friends from South Asia living comfortable lives on the surface and experiencing violence in their homes. On a personal level, I wonder about the silent violence in my own life. I have become acutely aware of the controls hidden in the gentle reminders and the delicate nudges that were used to tame the independent spirit in me into something deemed more culturally appropriate.

The Role of Religion in Community Life

Fourteen hundred years ago, Islam was revealed to Prophet Muhammad in Mecca, Saudi Arabia (Siddique 1985). The first person with whom he shared about his revelation was his wife, Hazrat Khadija, thus indicating the high esteem in which he held her opinion. Khadija herself was the first woman to embrace Islam, indicating her own firm belief in the truth told by her husband. Khadija was also a successful businesswoman. She had been impressed by Prophet Mohammad's character while he worked for her. She was the one who had proposed marriage to him. Throughout her married life, the Prophet treated her with utmost respect and kindness. The life she lived is a role model for women even in modern times.

Islam offered women rights that were unprecedented, such as the right to choose a marriage partner, the right to inheritance, and the right to divorce (Mernissi 1987). The religion made it so that a woman seeking divorce does not have to prove any major reason other than a dislike for her husband. The example of Hazrat Zainab is worth noting here. Hazrat Zainab was not happy with her marriage because she thought her husband's status was below her. She approached Prophet Mohammad, who first advised her to try and accept the marriage. When she insisted, he allowed her to divorce her husband; then, later on, he married her himself to show the respect and honor he gave to a divorced woman.

Islam established guidelines for relations between the sexes that are fair and humane. The Prophet's life is a living example of these humane principles toward men and women. He treated all people, men and women, friends and enemies, alike, with dignity and respect. He encouraged both men and women to be educated. His message of increasing self-awareness and growth was directed toward both genders. Women took full benefit of the message of Islam to come out of ignorance and subjugation and to assume important roles in their communities. Islamic history is full of examples of strong women in leadership roles.

Over the years, through cultural distortions, the religion itself has been used to suppress and oppress women. Since the Muslim communities tend to view American culture as promiscuous, there is great fear that women and girls living in America will adopt this sexual freedom. Today, in Muslim religious centers across America, debates continue on the need to protect women and girls from the environment around them. In addition, the community is rife with discussions about the status of women as less than men, and the limited roles women are expected to embrace to keep the family their first priority.

However, the concept of feminism is not unknown in Islamic communities. Islamic feminism is defined as a form of feminism that is appropriate for Muslim women. Islamic feminism refers to demanding certain rights, such as the right to work, within the confines of the family and the community (Fernea 1998).

Even as the extended family system fails to meet the growing needs of women, lack of state-sponsored resources and services for Muslim women has forced many into accommodating the patriarchal system (Sabbagh 1996). Muslim women in America look for and find limited help in government-sponsored programs such as shelters for battered women, support groups, as well as legal and social services. In addition, they face strong opposition from their religious and cultural institutions in utilizing these services. Their reaching out is viewed as airing dirty laundry in public and bringing dishonor to Muslims. Many observant Muslim women themselves hesitate to utilize state-sponsored shelters due to potential conflicts with their religious community, Islamic prayer, and dietary requirements.

Intimate Partner Violence against Muslim American Women

Rashida [a pseudonym, as are names of all survivors] was severely beaten by her husband and had sought counsel by her local Imam [religious cleric] many times. The Imam talked to her and her husband imploring both to stay calm for the sake of the children. Her husband would make promises and Rashida would forgive him much to the delight of the Imam. Through the work of a committee on prevention of violence, Rashida went into a shelter. The committee members faced harassing calls from the husband and pleas of cooperation from the community leaders to help pacify the

situation and not let it get to the court. On the day of the court appoint-
ment, her husband showed up with the Imam and over ten other prominent
members of the community. These community members made promises
and personal guarantees to Rashida that she will not be beaten again. They
asked her to go back home and not bring shame to the Muslim community
by going to the court. Unable to take a stand in front of so many people,
Rashida walked home with her husband. The promises of the community
were not enough to protect her and about six months later, Rashida returned
to the shelter with some more bruises on her body. The blame for her escape
was placed on the Western ideas implanted in Rashida's head by the committee members. The husband continued to enjoy support and acceptance
within the community along with compassion for the difficulties he was
now facing due to the loss of his wife.

Muslim women face certain difficulties that are unique because of their particular system of marriage and divorce. An Islamic marriage takes place by the performance of the *Nikah* by the Imam.[1] *Nikah* is an agreement to enter into marriage
by the bride and groom with an agreed upon sum of money (*Haq Mehr*) to be given
by the groom to the bride. In addition to the religious ceremony, Muslims in America also enter into civil marriages by having their marriages registered. However,
many men go back to their home countries to marry and bring their wives back with
them. It is helpful to both if they go through the process of registration of their marriage in America, as it saves future difficulties in proving the legality of the marriage.

Like marriage, divorce also occurs at two different levels: religious divorce,
called *Talaq*, and civil divorce. Generally, the man gives *Talaq* to his wife in the presence of witnesses, which ends the marriage at the religious level. The civil divorce
has to happen in the country's courts. Divorce, even though permitted in Islam, is
frowned upon. Prophet Mohammad is believed to have said that of all the lawful
acts, the most detestable to God is divorce. The laws in some countries, like Iran
and Egypt, only accept divorce if given by the man to his wife according to Islamic
rules. In America, many Muslim men divorce their wives in civil courts and then
refuse to grant them religious divorce. Men find it easy to remarry following a civil
divorce, since the lack of having a religious divorce does not stop them from remarriage. Islam allows men up to four marriages, but only under strict conditions. In
contrast, women cannot remarry unless they have the religious divorce. Women
who get only a civil divorce face problems when they travel back to their countries
where they are still registered as the wives of the men who have left them.

To ameliorate this situation, some Muslim religious institutions now accept a
civil divorce as a final divorce, ending the marriage at both legal and religious levels. However, the majority of religious institutions still require religious divorce to
legitimize women's single status. This contradiction has caused many Muslim
women much distress and has led to the call for the implementation of a standard
law recognized by both religious and civil institutions.

Jewish women have faced similar inconsistencies in obtaining a *get*, or religious divorce, even after the civil courts have issued a legal divorce. Although the courts cannot order the sanction of a religious divorce, New York State has a provision in the family laws whereby a judge, before giving the final divorce decree, can order both parties to remove all barriers to remarriage for each other. Since one barrier to remarriage is not obtaining a religious divorce, this judicial order forces a couple to end the marriage at the religious level before a final civil divorce is granted. Jewish women have used this clause successfully to obtain religious *get* before civil divorce is granted.

Likewise, Muslim women in America are using the civil courts to obtain a divorce at both the religious and civil levels. Nonetheless, most U.S. courts still do not understand the need of Muslim women to acquire a religious divorce. Women themselves lack understanding of the laws, so many women still leave the courts without getting a religious divorce, only to return years later to try to complete the comprehensive divorce process.

> Aleema's husband left her for a young white woman. He had been generous enough to offer her a continued place in his house as a second wife. Aleema, who did not speak a word of English and had survived years of abuse, stood up against this final injustice and refused the offer. Because he was interested in getting married again, Aleema's husband divorced her in the Family Court. However, he refused to give Aleema a *Talaq*. It took her many more years of knocking on doors and asking for help before her husband was finally convinced to show up at the consulate office of her country in New York, where he uttered the religious divorce and Aleema was freed.

There is a provision in Islam that at the time of *Nikah*, a condition can be added to the *Nikah Nama* (*Nikah* contract), allowing the woman the right to divorce. This clause makes the marriage agreement equal for both partners. Nevertheless, even women who have this provision in the *Nikah* have approached us to help them get a religious divorce. These women report going from one Islamic Center to another in search of a supportive Imam who would grant a religious divorce initiated by women.

> Alia had to go back to Bangladesh to get her divorce because no Imam was willing to help her in New York. Even though she had a written marriage contract that clearly indicated she had the right to initiate divorce, a right given to her in Islam, getting it was still dependent on the generosity and mood of the local Imam. Most Imams saw this as an oddity and considered it unfavorably.

Another area in which lack of understanding has hurt Muslim women is *Haq Mehr*. *Mehr* is separate from and in addition to the wife's right to alimony, which according to Islamic law, she is entitled to in the event of her spouse's death or divorce. In some cases, the American courts have inaccurately treated *Mehr* as a prenuptial agreement leading to an unfair denial of her right to alimony. In other cases, the courts have treated *Mehr* as enforceable as long as the requirements of a valid contract are met, thus recognizing *Mehr* as a simple contract to be upheld and not a prenuptial agreement replacing alimony. At times, competent lawyers have been able to help women get their full alimony benefits in addition to the promised *Mehr* (Awad 2002), although many face difficulties regarding *Mehr* in the U.S. legal system.

Women in early Islam were encouraged to marry after divorce and were able to find partners to remarry. Muhammad himself married both divorced and widowed women to encourage other men to accept divorced and widowed women in marriage. Over the years, however, the mix of culture and religion has created biases against divorced women. Often, they are viewed as damaged goods, and the divorce is seen as their fault. Divorced women, even more than widows, are seen as carriers of bad luck and thus are to be avoided at auspicious occasions. Whereas widows can get some sympathy for their loss, divorced women are seen as bad women and therefore not entitled to any sympathy. In Pakistan and India it is a common practice not to allow a divorced woman near a bride while the wedding ceremony is taking place for fear of bringing bad luck. These cultural beliefs make it hard for a woman to marry again, even if she wishes.

Islam allows a Muslim man to marry four women. This right was given to men under very limited circumstances and with very strict guidelines. In times of war that led to many deaths and a large number of widows, Islam encouraged men to marry widows as a way of protecting them and their orphaned children. The guidelines clearly required the husband to equally treat all his wives. The Quran further elaborates on the difficulty and almost impossibility of implementing such equal behavior and thereby recommends one marriage only.

Many immigrant Muslim men in America have abused this right of multiple marriages by having a first wife, to whom they are married in civil courts and by Islamic law, and then marrying other women by performing only the Islamic *Nikah* without the benefit of a civil registered marriage. This situation creates problems like jealousy, rivalry, neglect, and financial distress for all the women while they are married. These problems are magnified in the event any of the marriages fail and the women try to seek fair legal settlement. In the United States, except for the first, all subsequent marriages are neither registered nor legal.

Sheikh Sahib was well versed in Quran and every one in the community was impressed by his religious knowledge. When he married a new Muslim convert in a *Nikah* ceremony, no one questioned his intentions. No one knew that he had been married before. A year later, his first wife and children arrived in America from his home country where they had been waiting for visa papers. Conflict started between the two wives right away. Not wanting to let go of the mother of his two children Sheikh Sahib asked his second wife to leave his home with a quick pronouncement of verbal *Talaq*. The second wife had no recourse. Her brief marriage did not count.

Most Islamic Centers do not keep any record of *Nikahs* performed or proof of any previous marriages. This situation creates problems when marriages are unsuccessful and women need proof of marriage.

> Arfa came to us with a simple request; can we help her get a copy of her *Nikah*? The Imam of an Islamic Center in Queens had performed the *Nikah* in front of two witnesses. Her marriage had lasted five years and she was seeking divorce due to emotional and verbal abuse. Her husband denied that he had ever married her. He had destroyed her *Nikah* papers and all other evidence of the marriage such as pictures. The witnesses were friends of her husband and joined in his story to deny that the marriage had ever taken place. The Imam who had performed the *Nikah* had left the Islamic Center by then and the new Imam refused to even look for any documentation of the marriage, stating that they kept no records.

Several Islamic Centers are attempting to correct this problem by refusing to perform the religious marriage unless proof of a civil marriage is first presented. The Islamic Center of Long Island in New York has been one of the first to take this stand even in the face of strong opposition from many community members, who claimed such a decision was un-Islamic. Such bold efforts need public support and praise. Many Muslim countries have traditions of implementing new laws that go beyond Islamic parameters. For example, slavery was allowed in Islam, but all Muslim countries have unanimously taken a stand against it and it has been legally banned. One wonders if a similar position could be taken for multiple marriages.

In addition to the abovementioned violence, segregation of women and the use of *Hijab* are also becoming popular in South Asian Islamic communities. *Chador aur char diwari* (the veil and the four walls of the house) is the recommendation made to women in Islam to ensure safety. *Hijab*, the traditional head covering of Muslim women, is also gaining popularity among younger Muslim women in America (Bullock 1998). Many women look for and find safety and security in the *Hijab*. Going out in *Hijab* frees them from the objections of family members who might otherwise limit their mobility.

> Ruby came from a modern family; both her parents were working professionals. She described a loving home environment with two older brothers. As she grew older, Ruby noticed her parents treated her differentially. Her parents started to express concern about her social interests and outings. Even staying late at the library to study became a matter of conflict at home. If she wanted to go to the movies with her friends, she was expected to take her brother along. Ruby joined the Muslim Student Association in her college. Through them, she was exposed to *Hijab*; something women in her family had never worn before, even in India. Ruby started wearing the *Hijab* in the U.S. Since her interest in Islam grew, she said her parents started trusting her more and she faced less questions and harassment by them. She claimed she had more freedom after she began to wear the *Hijab*.

However, religion also places obstacles in a woman's career path. Islam allows limited work opportunities for women outside the home, provided work does not pose any conflict for the spouse. A woman's first responsibility is toward her husband and her household. The common belief is a woman who dies while her husband is pleased with her will enter heaven.

Violence in the Family

Islam takes a very strong stand on violence against women and categorically condemns it. However, a verse in Quran has been repeatedly translated to justify beating of wives. The verse is usually translated as follows: "As to those women on whose part you fear willfulness, admonish them first, then abandon them in beds and last hit them with a single strike: and if they obey you, seek not against them means (of annoyance or harm) for God is most high and Great above you all" (4:34).

Some interpret the verse as allowing a symbolic beating of a wife if she disobeys and others cling to a more literal meaning. While still others go to great details on what, where, and how severe a beating is allowed in Islam. This selective preference of one verse from the Quran over many others that speak about kindness and justice toward women has created an atmosphere that tolerates violence against women (Siddique 1985). As more and more women are studying the Quran, it is fascinating to see the same verse being interpreted without the patriarchal influence but in the true Islamic spirit of equity and fairness. The work of Sisters in Islam in Malaysia explaining the verse is worth noting. They point out a long list of meanings that can be ascribed to the word *idribuhunna*, which is traditionally translated as "beat them with a single strike": travel, set up, take away, ignore, condemn, explain, etc. (Badlishah and Kaprawi 2004). It has also been translated to mean "to part" or "go separate ways." Al-Hibri (2003) goes to great lengths to explain the word *nushuz* (willfulness), which traditionally meant any defiance of the will of the husband but had been shifted to mean obedience to Allah by both men and women. She encourages Muslim societies to view wife beating as a crime and to rise to a higher state of consciousness described in the Quran of marital ideal: "The parties should hold together on equitable terms or part in kindness" (2:229).

A recent survey showed that out of a 158 Islamic Centers in the state of New York, only a handful provided specific services to women (Ayyub 1998). The religious community, along with family and friends, tend to advise women who experience violence in their lives to be patient and give in to the will of the husband. In contrast, no clear stand is taken against a man who is violent. Violence in marriage is generally condemned, but when it does happen, the religious community offers no clear consequences for the abuse. Furthermore, the Islamic religious community tends to condemn any woman who seeks legal protection from an abusive spouse. Her actions are considered disloyal to the husband and the family. In addition, the Islamic Centers fail to impart any information on domestic violence protection and prevention programs that are available in the community, considering them radical. Yet, the services provided by the Islamic Centers often fail to include social problems such as domestic violence. The overall message given to women is to endure and accept. A religion meant to bring about peace in the lives of all mankind has become a way of justifying violence against women.

The Role of South Asian Cultures in Muslim American Communities

South Asia comprises many different cultural and ethnic groups, each with its own unique background, history, languages, customs, and traditions. Variations exist within the same group across different social class lines. Times are changing, and with the advent of satellite television, Internet, and other technology, the traditional cultural systems are feeling the vibrations of change. Still, much endures.

Traditional South Asian cultures resist the development of a strong sense of individual identity. Individuals are socialized to define themselves as part of a larger familial group. A person's identity is described in terms of the family he/she belongs to and the relationships the person has in the family. Thus, the South Asian Muslim woman's identity is more specifically based upon her role as mother, daughter, niece, sister, and so on. Identities outside of these relationships may seem inconceivable to her (Jayakar 1985). The system respects and supports women who can fit into these prescribed roles and both are harshly withdrawn from those who transgress—for example, lesbian, single, battered, and divorced women. Alan Roland (1988), in his analysis of the Indian self, describes three critical components: (1) a large familial self that derives its identity from the family, (2) a spiritual self, and (3) a very small individual self that tries to have its needs met within the context of the family. This obliteration of the individual self is even more exaggerated in women. Although focused on Indians, Roland's analysis speaks to South Asians in general.

Even though the extended family structure tries to meet the needs of its members within its rigid and strict rules, few allowances are made for individual differences. For the family, maintenance of the order of hierarchy is important. Thus, women at the bottom of this hierarchy face the most rigid controls, while the burden of maintaining it falls on them. The family system sustains itself by keeping its members within its borders by magnifying the concepts of honor and shame. While they apply to both men and women, they are central to a woman's role. Women bring honor to the family if they comply and maintain their prescribed roles; but any deviation not only brings dishonor to them but also brings shame to the entire family system. Any transgression by women rarely goes unpunished (Dasgupta 2000a).

When Muslim women maintain the traditional role of wife and mother, they are supposed to be protected by their husbands, brothers, or their fathers. A single woman is viewed as at risk of being abused by outsiders. Such beliefs fail to take into account the statistics that indicate most women face violence not from strangers, but at the hands of men they love, who are supposed to be their protectors (Walker 1984).

This focus on marriage and belittling of most other roles for women has tremendous impact on the socialization process of Muslim women. Many young women are pressured by their parents to marry. Parents themselves feel the stress of messages ingrained in them that requires them to marry off their daughters as soon as possible. Although many attempt to delay marriage in pursuit of higher education, they drop out in the middle of their studies due to pressure from parents. Those who persevere face continued escalation in pressures to marry. There is very little tolerance in society of a grown woman who is working, independent, and single. Islam encourages marriage for all adults both male and female. However, this recommendation is amplified for women to the point that a single woman is perceived as leading to *fitna*, or social disorder (Mernissi 1987).

Once married, the message implanted in women by parents, friends, and clergy is that the marriage must be maintained. They are encouraged to be in passive, dependent roles. No price a woman can pay is greater than the shame she would bring on the family if she were to choose to end her marriage. Therefore, many women, even in the face of extreme domestic violence, continue to stay in the marriage, because leaving would bring utter shame to their family.

Such beliefs are so strongly entrenched in South Asian cultures and individual psyches that abuse becomes almost invisible. A parent pressuring a woman to stay in a violent marriage is not perceived as abusing her; rather, such persuasion is viewed as an attempt to stop her from making an impulsive decision based solely on her personal interests. The interests of the family group have to be met above everything. If anyone has to be sacrificed for the maintenance of the family system, it must be the woman. She is expected to sacrifice herself willingly and without complaint. She is reminded of the rewards that will follow her after death for being a patient and tolerant wife. Oppression of women occurs on a continuum, ranging from extreme physical abuse to more subtle negation and putdowns.

In addition to violence by intimate partners, South Asian Muslim women face repression in their natal families. I have witnessed South Asian parents take independent or strong-willed teenage daughters on trips to their home countries, where they force them into arranged marriages. Oppression also continues in the more subtle forms of encouraging women to be passive, give in, and contain and control themselves. A traditional view of a decent and virtuous girl is one who walks slowly, never runs, never laughs out loud, and never ever takes care of her needs before that of the family.

Saima and her two friends went on a family vacation to Pakistan. During their stay, all three girls had *Nikah* done to suitable boys whom their families recommended. The marriages were to be consummated once the boys immigrate and reach New York. After their return to New York, the girls went back to school while immigration papers were filed for their husbands. Saima was allowed to write letters to her husband. Very soon, she came to realize the vast differences between her and her husband's ideas and mentality. She decided to seek divorce. The week in which Saima asked for a divorce, her father had a car accident. The accident became a tool to hold back Saima. Every time she talked about divorce, her parents reminded her of the father's car accident due to the stress she had caused him. Now Saima says she does not want her father hurt and will go through with the marriage. She says both her friends also do not want to continue their marriages, but probably will.

Although no statistics are available, my general observation has been that even in families where both parents are working professionals, they are choosing to marry off their daughters at a young age.

Re-creating the Familiar

For South Asian Muslim immigrants, life in America, which looked very attractive from their home countries, created stress. The freedom in the American culture that had first attracted the men, now scared them. Accustomed to patriarchal family systems, the men now found it difficult to share power with their wives. As their children grew, concerns about the impact of the American culture on them intensified. Habituated to submitting and complying with their parents' wishes while growing up, these immigrants were unprepared for their children questioning their actions and decisions. Freedom of expression, open sexuality, and 50 percent divorce rate in America became their biggest fears.

In working with South Asian Muslim families on domestic violence issues, I have found that only about 20 percent of the cases involve a second marriage or a second woman. An even smaller percentage of problems revolve around alcoholism or substance abuse. A majority of the cases have issues of power sharing and control. The men tend to demand total power and control over their families. They expect their wives to submit not only to their control but also to the control of their mothers and other family members. Even in situations where the wife works outside the home, the husband holds on to the power of deciding how and where she should spend her money.

> Fatima married Ahmad, twenty years older to her, in an arranged marriage. Ahmed was an engineer and made good money. Fatima stayed home and raised her two boys. As her youngest child left home to go to college, Fatima found a job and started working. Her husband ordered her to have her paycheck directly deposited in their joint account. Fatima says she was never allowed to operate the bank account or use any of the money; Ahmad was a good provider and paid for everything. Even though now she has been working for over fifteen years, Fatima is still not allowed to touch any of "their" money.

In the face of stress, another common reaction in Muslim immigrants is to return to religion as a solace. More and more religious centers are being established in response to this growing need for safety and security. Most of my colleagues and friends whose daughters are now wearing *Hijab* had never worn it in their own countries. It is also gaining popular support in the community.

Recently, a young Muslim woman was denied the right to wear *Hijab* at work. An employee of an Office Depot store, the girl was placed on administrative leave for showing up at work in a headscarf. Numerous Muslim organizations rallied to this young woman's support and helped her to win the legal battle and be reinstated in her job (Council on American Islamic Relations 1998). One wonders if these organizations would similarly rally on behalf of a woman who is battered or abused by her spouse.

The Role of Family of Origin in Muslim Women's Lives

South Asian Muslim women who have experienced violence in their marriages tend to idealize their families of origin in general and their fathers in particular. Whether it is the exaggerated way in which the father is described as a generous and loving parent, or how the mother is described as indulged and respected by the father, the overlying theme is always how wonderful things were in the parental home before the marriage. Thus, it is perplexing to observe women coming from supportive and nurturing environments with good educational opportunities who find it very difficult to protect themselves when facing domestic violence.

Yet, most South Asian Muslim women are aware of the harshness and cruelty toward women in their cultures. They recognize that in South Asian society, women's place is a few steps behind their men. They had grown up hearing stories of other women being abused by husbands, in-laws, and relatives, and about women who did not have the option to escape. They describe themselves as lucky that they did not have to face such oppression of women and invariably feel indebted to their families' generosity for it. They felt protected from the unfairness of society, not by their own strengths, but by that of their parents and family. Therefore, the self that emerges is dependent upon authority figures for its rights and grants.

Even the right to education becomes a privilege for women. Often, women are allowed to pursue education and a career because it makes their parents look good. Educating the daughter has the added benefit of enabling parents to find a better match for her. An educational degree could offset mediocre looks and a not-so-hefty dowry. Dowry is a totally un-Islamic practice that has become common among Muslims in South Asia. Frequently, the objective of a daughter's education is to attract an eligible marriage partner.

The history of education of women in South Asian countries records centuries of exclusion from the field of knowledge. The only knowledge traditionally considered right for them was religious education. The message of Quran that encouraged both men and women to gain knowledge and study was overlooked where women were concerned. Sir Sayyed Ahmad Khan, a prominent Indian Muslim philosopher, was totally opposed to women's education outside the home (Jalal 1991). The trend toward educating women is recent and a response to the "growing desire of educated

Muslims to find educated wives" (Jalal 1991). Perhaps motivated by reasons other than gender equality, the changes nevertheless are occurring.

In the midst of so much change in Islamic cultures, the relationship system that is resisting modification is that of husband and wife. Upon marriage, a young woman is considered fortunate if her husband indulges her, the default being a life of mistreatment. For those young women facing conflict or violence in the marriage, parents expect them to tolerate and submit totally to the authority of the spouse and his family. They are encouraged to accept it as their kismet. After having invested money and family resources in raising and marrying their daughters, the parents are often resistant to letting even bad marriages come to an end. Even when they leave an abusive marriage, the young women report strong feelings of obligations toward the family and suffer from guilt for letting down their parents.

Concluding Remarks

Awareness of the presence of domestic violence in the South Asian Muslim community is slowly increasing. Different cultural groups that may never have dealt with domestic violence in their home countries are springing up and trying to help their own constituencies. Battered women are finding the strength to break the cycle of violence and oppression and are questioning the wisdom of saving a marriage at all costs. The 50 percent divorce rate in America does not appeal to Muslim women, but neither does a 25 percent rate of marriages with ongoing violence (Ayyub 1998).

Domestic violence hurts the whole family. It hurts the victim at the physical, emotional, and psychological levels. It causes pain and suffering to the victim and also hurts the perpetrator by creating distance between him and his family. Furthermore, domestic violence hurts the children by taking away a sense of safety and security that they need to grow up. Being a witness to violence in the home teaches our children to solve problems with violence. Studies show boys growing up in violent homes are more likely to resort to violence as they grow up (Berry 1995).

Women have always depended on their families and religion for support. When facing abuse, women turn to these for answers. For a woman trying to end domestic violence in her life, it is very comforting to know that her religion supports her. When religious leaders, family, and friends discourage a battered woman to escape violence, it increases the oppression she is already experiencing. The first step toward resolution of any problem is to recognize that the problem exists. Community leaders, religious leaders, advocates, legal experts, mental health professionals, all need to collaborate to address this issue. Mental health professionals need to educate the community about the damage caused by domestic violence—not just to the woman, but to the whole family and, through the family, to the community.

Some minimum standards of knowledge and education for Imams should be established, which must include information on domestic violence. Only when the Imams are educated can they guide the community to overcome this social evil. Information on resources, culturally and linguistically appropriate supportive services, and shelters need to be made easily accessible to women.

The Islamic Centers need to allocate some funds to establish programs for supporting women and children affected by domestic violence. *Zakat* funds can be a good source of funding such programs. Some fundamental changes in Islamic structures would also empower Muslim women and lead them toward true equality. Religious rules and regulations surrounding marriage, divorce, *Haq Mehr*, separation, and custody need to be further clarified and standardized. The question of multiple marriages should be addressed and a uniform decision made to abolish it. The Imams who perform religious *Nikah* should be given strict guidelines on maintaining accurate records.

Religious and community leaders must come forward to express a strong and clear stand against violence against women. The community must be mobilized to make women safe and hold batterers accountable. Anyone who is violent toward their family members must be socially condemned and encouraged to make reparations to the victims and the community. The community must delineate clear consequences for abusive behaviors. Men who are abusive must not be allowed to hold prominent positions in the community as leaders. It is only through such clear messages that we can convey that woman abuse is unacceptable.

One recent trend that offers a hopeful sign is the work of scholars such as Fatima Mernissi, Kaukab Siddique, Aziza al-Hibri, and Nik Noriani Nik Badlishah. These pioneer scholars are trying to remove the cultural distortions from the religion and help women reestablish equality, dignity, and respect within the Islamic context.

Our parenting styles must be modified to enable the next generation to face the new millennium with a strong sense of self and an awareness of who they are, what they desire, and what their goals are. Our children need to learn to survive on their own and to become aware of their own strengths. Children must be allowed to make choices, to learn from their mistakes, and grow from their life experiences. Such child-rearing behavior is difficult for most South Asian parents, who feel the need to be overprotective. Furthermore, girls and boys cannot be brought up differently, with extra pressures placed on daughters to behave in socially prescribed ways. Such beliefs must be changed if parents want their children to develop into strong independent human beings and experience life free of violence.

NOTES

An earlier version of this article was published in 2000 as "Domestic Violence in the South Asian Muslim Immigrant Population in the United States," in *Journal of Social Distress and the Homeless* 9 (3): 237–248. It is reprinted here with kind permission of Springer Science and Business Media.

I.   See S. D. Dasgupta's *Battered South Asian Women in U.S. Courts* for explanations of *Mehr, Nikah, Nikah Nama*, and *Talaq*.

3

Minority within a Minority

Reflecting on Marital Violence in the Nepali American Community

BIDYA RANJEET AND BANDANA PURKAYASTHA

Compared to many other groups of Asian origin, Nepali Americans have remained below the radar in regards to both scholarly and activist interests about their lives in the United States. The lack of systematic governmental data on this community as well as the tendency of outsiders to consider Nepali Americans as no different from Indians contributes to their veritable invisibility. There are very few and scattered descriptions of the history, socioeconomic profile, numbers, and concentration of Nepali immigrants in the United States. Accounts of domestic violence in the Nepali American community, a subject that is often shrouded by cultures of silence, are even more difficult to track.

We have attempted to partially address these gaps of information in this chapter.[1] First, we describe the legal and sociocultural position of Nepali and Nepali American women. Second, based on our dialogues with several Nepali American women who are part of a Nepali women's network, we discuss dimensions of domestic violence, focusing particularly on underreporting of such violence and the culture of silence surrounding it. Third, we discuss the reasons for the relative (in)ability of Nepali American women to seek help from South Asian women's domestic violence organizations. Given the problems of gathering systematic data, we cannot describe exactly how often violence occurs or how prevalent it is across social strata. However, we discovered that almost all Nepali women we approached in different parts of the country were aware of some cases of domestic violence in the community. This persistent pattern of awareness within our small sample is indicative of the existence of wider patterns of violence throughout the Nepali American community writ large.

This chapter draws on both secondary and primary data to present several dimensions of domestic violence among Nepali Americans. We obtained much of the information by asking women on a Nepali American e-list about problems women face. The questions we asked the e-list participants were:

1. What domestic problems do you feel that Nepali women face in the United States?
2. What types of immigration problems and challenges do you feel Nepali women encounter in the United States?
3. Are there any South Asian women's groups or clubs in your area that you would recommend South Asian (or Nepali?) women to join and/or use their services? Please elaborate why or why not.

The cases we describe later are compiled from the information reported by the e-list respondents. To this, we have added our own experiences of working with South Asian women in domestic violence situations.

Immigration Pattern and Nepali Women's Status

Over the last decade, scholars have begun to describe a series of social conditions that increase the vulnerability of female immigrants (Abraham 2000b; Dasgupta and DasGupta 1997; Purkayastha, Raman, and Bhide 1997). Both their structural position, which is constructed through their labor market experiences and legal status as immigrants, as well as their sociocultural conditioning, shape the relative susceptibility of women to domestic violence. These scholars have collectively argued that the likelihood of an abused woman to stay with her abuser in order to save family honor or to fulfill her wifely obligation is increased if she has no legal right to work, which would give her the economic independence to move away from the abuser. These intersecting factors affect Nepali American women, like other immigrant women from South Asia.

Immigration Pattern and Its Consequences

Since the official policies of both Nepal and the United States discouraged migration until the 1970s, only a few people from Nepal came to the United States before the 1990s. Upadhyay (1991) reports that 1,229 Nepali citizens were admitted to the United States between 1970 and 1989, and the U.S. Citizenship and Immigration Service (USCIS) Yearbook shows a gradual increase in the number of Nepali admitted per year from 212 in 1992 to 1,138 in 2002 (Office of Immigration Statistics, Office of Management, and Department of Homeland Security 2002:Table 3). This growth is directly related to a change in the United States' immigration policy. While earlier policies encouraged the migration of highly educated people from Asia (a requirement that attracted a significant number of Chinese, Indians, and Filipino migrants), the emphasis since the 1990s has been on balancing the mix of immigrants (Espiritu 1997). Consequently, people in formerly underrepresented countries such as Nepal have been able to apply through a visa lottery, called the

40 BIDYA RANJEET AND BANDANA PURKAYASTHA

Diversity Visa program, which provides fifty thousand permanent resident visas annually to persons from countries with low rates of immigration to the United States. In order to achieve the balanced mix of immigrants, diversity visas are not given to citizens of countries that have sent more than fifty thousand immigrants to the United States within the past five years. Furthermore, no one country may receive more than 7 percent of the available Diversity Visas in any one year (Immigration and Naturalization Service Center n.d.). Applicants who meet the visa requirements, which seem to favor males over females in developing nations, are chosen through a computer-generated random lottery drawing.

The number of Nepali people in the United States has increased due to three factors: first, through the Diversity Visa Program; second, some Nepali students who came to the United States for higher education were able to change their status to work-related or permanent residency visas; and third, as the population of Nepali immigrants increased in the United States, they have been able to sponsor their nuclear families. In 2002, 442 Nepali entered the States on employer-based preference, while 328 were relatives of U.S. citizens, and another 331 arrived on diversity programs (Office of Immigration Statistics, Office of Management, and Department of Homeland Security 2002:Table 8). Although we do not have any census data documenting the socioeconomic status of Nepali Americans, we infer that given these various migration routes that Nepali Americans are from mixed educational and class backgrounds. The South Asian Journalists Association (SAJA) Web site estimates that there are 25,000 Nepali Americans in the United States (2005) who work in both white- and blue-collar occupations in large urban areas.

These seemingly neutral migration conditions have intensified gender inequalities in the Nepali immigrant community. Part of the inequality stems from larger social conditions. For instance, more male than female students are likely to seek higher education in the United States. Since 61.6 percent males and 26.4 percent females are literate in Nepal (United Nations Development Programme 2003), the proportion of females with high school or college degrees who are eligible for the diversity or student visas is correspondingly low. Thus, more males than females apply for diversity visas. When a male migrant arrives in this country, he establishes himself economically and politically (i.e., meets the criteria set by USCIS to sponsor his family) and sends for his spouse or marries someone and brings her to the United States. The trailing spouse, who often arrives several years later, is politically and economically dependent on the primary migrant. This dependency, in turn, creates new and reinforces existing power imbalances between the spouses. In her book on domestic violence among South Asian Americans, Margaret Abraham (2000b) illustrates how the structure of immigration laws often increases the vulnerability of immigrant women. She argues that as long as these laws require foreign-born wives to be sponsored for migration by their husbands, women are placed within a modern form of the law of coverture, where female spouses are nonpersons legally and husbands have sole legal authority over them.

Immigration laws that enhance women's political dependency also contribute indirectly to their economic disadvantage. As later entrants into the U.S. labor market, Nepali American women, like other South Asian women, are likely to suffer from cumulative disadvantages (Purkayastha 2005). They experience greater pressure to stay within the geographical area where their spouse is employed, and this geographical rooted-ness curtails their job choices. Even if Nepali American women are able to find paid employment, as immigrant women of color they typically hold lower-paid jobs than their male counterparts. Their job choices are further restricted because they are relatively less likely than Nepali men to possess skills that are valued in the labor market, such as fluency in English, professional training, or job experience in the United States. These factors, along with their near-total responsibility for all household tasks (to support the male family provider), means that they are mostly stuck in jobs that do not pay sufficiently.

When domestic violence occurs, women must weigh their economic and legal dependence against their need to break away from their spouses and be safe. Our discussions with Nepali American women indicate that because of their lack of knowledge about their rights as immigrants and their marginal position in the job market, they often consider staying in abusive marital relationships as a lesser evil. Thus, in the absence of real options, women stay in these marriages and tend to rationalize their decisions with references to the social beliefs that encourage them to fulfill their obligations in a marriage, irrespective of the spouse's deeds and behaviors.

Sociocultural Status of Nepali Women in Nepal and America

Nepali communities are not homogeneous. Even though outsiders perceive Nepali Americans as a monolithic group, in actuality they come from a country where thirty-five languages are spoken by at least fifty-nine different ethnic groups. Nepali is the official language and Hinduism is the official religion of the country, but members of this community practice a variety of syncretic traditions that create significant cultural diversity within the population.

As a Hindu kingdom (90 percent of the people are Hindus), Nepal promotes the symbolic worship of women. For instance, the country recognizes the pre-eminent position of Kumari, the living goddess in all secular and spiritual affairs. The Kumari is a young girl, who is chosen from a Buddhist household in Nepal by certain auspicious behaviors and characteristics she displays. After the choice is made by a group of priests, she is taken away from her natal family and installed with great pomp and ceremony in a palace in Kathmandu, the capital of Nepal. Popularly worshipped as a living emblem of the eternal spirit (*atman*) venerated by Hindus, the Kumari commands the reverence of all Nepali, including the royalty. Once the Kumari reaches menarche, a new Kumari replaces her. Grown up Kumaris revert to "normal" life; certainly, as ex-Kumaris they carry high social status the rest of their lives. However, few marry, since most men dare not affiliate with these goddesses, fearing their stronger astrological charts.

Apart from venerating the Kumari, Nepal emphasizes a variety of celebrations of Shakti, the cosmic female force. The powerful female goddesses Durga and Kali are widely celebrated in major festivals. This recognition of female power is evident in many household rituals as well. For instance, a Nepali American second-generation female narrated how her uncles came and touched her feet in the morning as a token of worship of Kumari when she visited Nepal.

Despite all this, even a cursory examination of women's legal and socio-economic position in Nepal tells a very different story. There are enormous disparities in literacy, earnings, and ownership of property among males and females in Nepal (Singh 1995). According to United Nations' data, the estimated yearly income for females was the equivalent of $891 in 2002, while the corresponding figure for males was $1,776; thus, females earned 50 percent of the amount that males earned (UN Development Programme 2003). While Nepal's Constitution states that everyone can own property, the actual laws maintain certain caveats that are complex and contradictory. Women can only own their dowries and have property rights if no male siblings or other male relatives exist. Additionally, they have to abrogate property rights upon (re)marriage.

Subedi (1997) argues that even in much of the recent "women-friendly" legislation, many female rights have been curtailed through addendums. For instance, the eleventh amendment of the civil code, which guarantees women equal property rights, was passed in 1999, but it still contains a clause that maintains when women get married they must return their property to their parents or brothers (Manzione 2001). Therefore, except for any dowry or *pewa* that is given to her by her parents, or property settled formally by her husband and/or his family with the written consent of all males over sixteen years of age in the household, a woman is entitled only to her own earnings. Since the use of her dowry is not wholly in a woman's control, it is not a guaranteed property right in actual practice. Similarly, women are not citizens in their own right. Nepali men can sponsor their foreign-born wives for Nepali citizenships, but Nepali women cannot sponsor their foreign-born husbands. Furthermore, a mother's citizenship does not guarantee citizenship for her children, if the father denies his paternity. Although this is not an everyday issue for Nepali women, it is a subject that permeates into everyday aspects of women's lives.

Until 2002, women were imprisoned, for up to twenty years, for having abortions, even in cases of rape (Singh 1995). As a direct result of women's groups' activism, abortion is now legally allowed during the first trimester, and later for the safety of natal health. However, awareness of this issue has not changed dramatically.

The position of young wives in the marital household in Nepal is especially precarious. A gender/age hierarchy places them in subordinate positions. While the level of power and privileges of males over females is unquestionable, the additional power of older women within the household shapes the subordinate status of new wives. Marriage is considered to be a relationship shaped and dictated by women, where the youngest and newest member has to conform to all the expectations and behavioral norms enforced by older women. As one of our interviewees explained, "a girl who never had to bow down to her own family members now has to touch the feet of her husband, mother-in-law, as well as other elder relatives everyday before she can break her fast in the morning." A series of such daily customs and behaviors are made obligatory to emphasize the new bride's subordinate status in many Nepali families.

As women's groups have grown stronger and more vocal in Nepal, they have begun to equate a series of behaviors within households with violence against women. Subedi (1997) lists child marriage, polygamy, sexual abuse, dowry-related pressures, wife battering, abandonment, alcohol-related negative conduct, violation of reproductive rights, trafficking, unequal pay for work, and caste-related violence as examples of violence against women. Pertinent to this discussion is the widespread practice of wife beating. Even among the educated middle class, corporal punishment of women and children is simply accepted as a normal method of chastisement. One highly educated Nepali American female activist residing in the northeastern United States said that while her father was like a Buddha in all other respects, she had seen him beat her mother regularly. This story is telling because this woman's mother had, by all accounts, been a remarkably high-achieving woman, even by Western standards.

Even when there is no overt physical violence, wives are expected to meet an extraordinarily high degree of unequal obligations toward their husbands and their affinal families. Such extreme expectations within marriage increases a woman's susceptibility to violence, as she is socialized to believe it is her religious and cultural duty to fulfill her obligations to her husband irrespective of his behavior toward her. Mythology about women who maintain their obligations amidst overwhelming adversities, such as the stories of Sati, Sita, and Savitri, act as ideal types and exert sociocultural pressure on women to live up to these exceptional models. Indeed, the perpetuation of patriarchal system is dependent on the promotion of selective stories of subordinated females as ideal role models for all women in society. While all Nepali or Nepali American women do not live by these codes of subordination, these myths continue to persist in all situations of domestic violence. Thus, when domestic violence occurs, both the perpetrators and the victims justify the abuse on the basis of their duties as a wife. Even though Hinduism, as a religion, provides a whole range of models of womanhood, including powerful goddesses and mythological warriors, the ability of some sections of Nepali society to perpetuate patriarchal control by referring to selective religious texts contributes to women's victimization.[2]

The Nepali experience suggests that a wide network of family members are likely to be complicit in and/or condone domestic violence to maintain the culture of subordinating females in the marital household. Thus, even when a woman is willing to lodge formal complaints to the police, it becomes extremely difficult to prove to legal authorities that domestic violence occurred, as many relatives are willing to swear that life was normal within the household. This pattern of denial and/or unwillingness to discuss woman abuse makes it difficult to address domestic violence in Nepal.

According to a Nepali American activist, such acceptance of physical and other forms of coercion and violence as a normal way of life is transported to the United States, where women are placed under extreme social pressure to conform to Nepali traditions and maintain Nepali culture. Consequently, the Nepali American community is reluctant to talk about domestic violence publicly and many simply do not recognize wife battering or extreme emotional control as a problem in the community. Similar to violence in the dominant community, where rape and violence against white women are normalized by "she provoked him" or "she should not have been there at that time" and are thus reframed as problems of errant or deviant individuals, the violence in Nepali American communities shows a comparable trajectory, even when the tools for constructing the normal public image are different. While several women's groups in Nepal are resisting and challenging the myths that help normalize domestic violence, in the United States, with its scattered and small Nepali population, there are few parallel attempts to take up such reforms. Overall, this culture of subordination and silence along with women's and men's unequal political and economic status makes Nepali American women vulnerable to domestic violence.

Violence against Women: Dimensions of the Problem

Violence among Nepali Americans in the United States, like violence experienced by other groups, ranges from physical beatings to extreme mental control. Nepali men are often unable to recapture the masculine privileges that they enjoyed in the natal country. In this new environment, some gain employment as less skilled laborers or, in the case of some highly educated Nepali men, as underemployed white-collar workers. Some men resort to violence out of habit and others may do it to reaffirm their masculinity. That is, some Nepali American men feel they need to establish and maintain their patriarchal power in the household by violently subjugating their spouses.

As one Nepali American woman pointed out, "It is hard for Nepali men to adjust to being the other equal half in a marriage since they have often been waited on hand-and-foot by their mothers and other female relatives as they were growing up." However, she acknowledged that the next generation of men would have to learn to live with empowered women. When other family members live close by, they are likely to participate in or condone the violence. At the same time, when there are no natal family members close by, women feel too isolated to seek trustworthy community support to intervene in the abuse. Unfamiliarity with their political rights and status, as well as their economic dependency, further contributes to women's marginal status. Thus, structural positions and cultural expectations intersect in ways that make women vulnerable to violence.

Given their socialization, Nepali American women are generally unwilling to talk about their experiences of domestic violence. In many instances, they do not recognize such abuse as a problem, especially if the abuse takes on the form of coercion or extreme control (i.e., nonphysical forms of abuse). A Nepali American woman may put up with abuse because of her psychosocial conditioning about a wife's obligations to her husband under any circumstances. Violence is thus rationalized to be a normal part of marital life.

> After coming to the United States, Sunita [a pseudonym, as are names of all survivors, perpetrators, and activists] quickly realized that her husband had a drinking problem. He found ways to fight with her and beat her when he was drunk. Sunita had to go to the hospital several times because of her injuries but she always made up excuses to hide the truth. Despite the efforts of a few South Asian friends, who encouraged Sunita to contact South Asian women's organizations in the United States, she did not seek any help. Her main aim seemed to be to "save face" and meet her "wifely obligations." She continued to maintain the public image of a "normal marriage."

Such loyalty is not entirely irrational. Nepali American women are frequently aware that many friends and family members are apt to condone the violence or ignore this one flaw in the man. Thus, women cannot rely on the support of community members to help them walk out of abusive situations.

A second case illustrates the effects of socialization where women stay in marriages even when they are aware of their spouse's problems.

> Rita arrived in the United States years after her husband, when her visa quota finally opened up. She soon found out that the husband was addicted to gambling. Even though she barely knew how to make long-distance calls when she got here, she found paid employment and began to support the family and pay off his debts. But her husband expected her to be there for him to ensure his life ran smoothly, so she constantly had to find work that would not "interfere" with her domestic responsibilities. Rita found out that the husband had filed for bankruptcy only when she was applying for citizenship. Over the years, she struggled to meet their basic needs through her meager earnings while he depleted their family resources through his increasingly uncontrolled gambling. She contemplated leaving her husband but felt that she had to stay in the marriage and look after him. She was also influenced by the fact that she had three children who did not want her to leave their dad. Additionally, she thought of most community members and her own relatives back home talking negatively about her if she left him and not meeting "her obligations" to take care of him much like the legendary Sati-Savitri.

In both of these cases, we find that abused Nepali women are unable to ignore more widely prevalent social opinions that overlapped with their own views on the endless obligations and duties that wives supposedly owe their errant husbands. Even when some friends and natal relatives encouraged these women to leave, victims saw the views of the majority as the normative expectation. This belief, then, ensures that women stay in abusive marriages and suffer in silence. The Nepali American women who responded to our questions indicated that they knew several women in similar circumstances who believed that it was the wife's duty to sustain the family irrespective of the violence they personally experienced.

In our study, the women we interviewed and who responded to our questions were reporting about others. They revealed stories about how they tried to encourage battered women to leave their abusive partners. But the community viewed most of the respondents, who were highly educated and mostly white-collar workers, as exceptions. They were also seen as unusual women. They were role models to the community and often community members sought their advice and support. Only when women are more confident about support of family and general community are they likely to resist their victimization.

> Bina had an arranged marriage with a man who had been living in the United States for several years. Within a year of coming to the United States, she found out that her husband was having an affair with another woman. Bina's husband's parents and siblings lived nearby and they had been aware of this affair for several years. When she questioned him, he beat her so badly that she ended up in the hospital. His family colluded to cover up his crime by changing her blood-stained clothes before the police and emergency personnel arrived. However, because of the extent of her injuries, he was ultimately arrested. A couple of Nepali American women urged Bina to leave him, pointing out to her that she could die from such beatings. Her family in Nepal also urged her to get a divorce. Initially, Bina felt she could not walk out of a marriage but later when he beat her again she made the decision to leave him. Some Nepali Americans provided her with the moral support and guidance to go through the steps for legal separation.

All three stories indicate that even though a few individual women tried to help the victims, most families and the community as a whole did not intervene. Two factors discussed below partially explain this pattern of nonintervention. First, the dense network of obligations and ties that bind various members of the community together can act as a deterrent to intervention. Pavitra, a Nepali American activist who had worked on women's empowerment issues, shared a story to explain why people do not act to support victims.

> On a visit to Nepal, Pavitra's sister disclosed that her husband used to beat her when she was newly wed. Pavitra said she had a hard time reconciling the public persona of her brother-in-law, who was unfailingly kind and nice to everyone, with his private role as a wife beater. Pavitra said that after hearing this story, every time she saw him in Nepal, she had the urge to

confront him about his acts. Yet, she could not bring herself to do this and continued to follow the customary rule of being nice and gracious to her brother-in-law. She felt trapped because such a confrontation would involve exposing too many people, including her sister, to public scrutiny. Pavitra said every time her children returned from holidays in Nepal and remarked "Uncle Shyam is so nice," she would want to let her teenage children "know his dark side." Yet, Pavitra said, "All I do is sigh and smile."

Second, the social organization of the community contributes to the exacerbation of the problem. The very small number of Nepali Americans in the United States and their geographically dispersed nature affect women negatively. Often, Nepali American women who are victims of violence are unlikely to find others they are comfortable with or trust sufficiently to disclose their own experiences of violence. However, even when there are Nepali Americans around, due to the smallness of the community and fear of losing confidentiality, women frequently choose to suffer in silence rather than seek assistance from their circle of acquaintances. As one Nepali American woman pointed out, in Nepal the extended family and friends network operates in ways that allows relatives to step in and ask questions about a range of marital issues. The family and community in Nepal are marked by close interdependence. But in the United States, it is difficult to re-create these invisible bonds because the community is spread out over vast geographical distances, as well as the pervasive culture of independence. On the one hand, women are reluctant to let the whole community know about the violence, and on the other, when community members get to know about the violence they are reluctant to step in and intervene. Pavitra asserted that

> here people don't want to step in and say this is wrong. Nepali people also feel uncomfortable to stand[ing] up for the women who may be in abusive relationship as they know the whole family and thus, would be alienating themselves from rest of the family members. It has also become part of living in this culture; it's your thing, [it's] your independence, [it's] none of our business.

The key issue in all of these cases is the culture of silence, who is willing to participate in it, and why. In addition to keeping one's place in the Nepali American community by maintaining silence, it can be stigmatizing and humiliating for a woman to confess that she is being beaten by her partner. Both the authors have encountered situations where groups of women in the community distanced themselves from abuse victims, simultaneously reframing the issue as the victims' fault. For instance, a Nepali faculty member reported that she has heard women discussing a case of domestic violence and commenting that the victim must have somehow provoked her husband. In all of the cases described above, only a few women offered help and advice to the victims. Those who did were often involved in community activism.

Namita, a Nepali American faculty member, remarked that while she was studying Nepali women's health issues, she had included a question related to domestic violence in her survey. She stated that most people left the question blank, again indicating the cultural grip (or pervasiveness of silence) even in total anonymity. In another case, Namita related how she was surprised to hear a comment by another Nepali colleague, Suchitra, when they had gone to an international conference. At the conference, there were a few women from Nepal who were presenting the problem of Nepali women forced into prostitution in the brothels in Mumbai (formerly Bombay), India. Suchitra argued that the topic was too degrading to discuss in an international forum. Whatever her exact motivation, Suchitra's reactions, along with the majority of Nepali peoples', appears to keep the topic of violence against women out of the public realm while continuing to uphold the symbolic importance of women.

The unwillingness to get involved in others' private affairs is also a response to living in the United States, where a great deal of emphasis is placed on privacy and independence. It overpowers the moral obligation of mutual support that is latent in community ties. Domestic violence, which is often conflated with women's affairs, is stringently separated from issues that involve men and women, even though as victims, women are most negatively affected by it. The larger roles of the family and community, as well as the impact of laws and policies, are made invisible in this redefinition of domestic violence as a woman's issue. For instance, a Nepali American woman described how she had heard of another woman in the community dying unexpectedly. People in the community had learned that her husband had beaten this woman to death. However, other Nepali people, who lived in that area, did not know whether her death was part of an earlier pattern of violence or if she had tried to seek help. Her home in the United States had become totally separated from the community and larger society.

Why Don't Nepali American Women Seek Help? South Asian Organizations and the Question of Inclusiveness

The cases mentioned above reveal two patterns. First, several individual women tried to help victims; second, none of the victims sought help from South Asian women's organizations in the United States. Yet, the cases occurred in locations where there were prominent South Asian women's organizations. Abraham (2000b) and Dasgupta and DasGupta (1997) have asserted that throughout the 1970s, 1980s, and 1990s, the American mainstream women's domestic violence organizations were neither willing to centrally consider the effects of institutionalized racism on immigrant women, such as the deleterious effects of immigration laws and labor market disadvantages, nor were they able to provide culturally competent support for victims of domestic violence in immigrant communities. In response, a range of South Asian organizations had sprung up to meet the unaddressed needs of South Asian women. Thus, a crucial question for our discussion on domestic violence among Nepali Americans is "Why are these Nepali women unwilling or unable to seek the help and support of the existing South Asian organizations?"

The answer is twofold. All the activists we spoke with explained that at an individual level Nepali American women are unwilling to discuss domestic violence until they are 100 percent sure that they are going to leave their husbands. Our own experiences reinforce their observations. In most cases, women keep trying to find a solution to the violence while attempting to keep their marriages intact. Activists in the community state that they are generally unsuccessful in convincing victims to take measures to change their situations.

The other facet of this answer is related to the structural position of Nepali Americans within the South Asian community. Experiences of one prominent Nepali American activist, Krishna, illustrate the problems of inclusion in many of the South Asian community based organizations. We would like to caution that the specific conditions Krishna describes might not represent all South Asian domestic violence organizations. However, her experiences replicate one of the author's, Bandana's, perceptions during her tenure at a local domestic violence agency.

First, Krishna pointed out that battered Nepali American women are afraid of others in the community finding out about their situation if they call the domestic violence hotlines. Moreover, individual women do not always understand how calling a toll-free number and talking to advocates is likely to help them. They are rarely aware of other Nepali American women who have successfully gone through the process. Second, even when individual women are aware of South Asian domestic violence organizations (SADVOs), they hardly ever see anyone from the Nepali American community in these organizations evoke trust in the agencies. Krishna pointed out that most SADVOs are numerically and structurally dominated by Indians and there is very little social interaction between Indian and Nepali American women at a community level to create a sense of community between the two groups. Third, the dearth of Nepali American women in these organizations means that there is little systematic outreach to this community. The lack of outreach also means that there are few sustained attempts to raise consciousness about domestic violence as a problem of the collective community. Thus, a lack of familiarity with the work of such organizations and the inability of the organizations to create a sense of trust and ownership in Nepali American women complicate the relationship of Nepali American victims with existing SADVOs.

Fourth is the related issue of cultural competency at an organizational level. Krishna argues that there are serious questions about how culturally appropriate the South Asian support and interventions are for Nepali American women. Since Nepali women are reluctant to seek help in the first place, a lack of understanding of their cultural ethos and social positions simply exacerbates the idea that these organizations are not suitable for the minority Nepali American community. Krishna articulates "When you are already socialized not to call, why would you call a group that has no one from your culture and area? To what extent are these organizations able to help in a culturally appropriate way?" While she did not generalize, Krishna pointed out that her own experience in one organization showed that since many Nepalis are Hindus, there is an extraordinary degree of complacency among many Indian activists that their practice of Hinduism gives them complete insight into the Nepali American culture. With little knowledge of the diversity of cultures within Nepal, the migration and economic status of Nepali Americans, the degree of isolation of the community, or even the increasingly complicated political situation in some parts of Nepal that increase the feeling of insecurity among Nepali Americans, too often activists from the other South Asian communities erroneously assume that their knowledge of Indian Hinduism makes them culturally competent in Nepali matters. Krishna felt that the SADVO model was drifting toward a charity model for minorities among the dominant South Asians. That is, Nepali Americans and other South Asian minority groups were treated with a "they-are-all-in-a-mess, we-have-all-the-answers" attitude.

Krishna described her own experience with SADVOs as "a minority within a minority," which indicates structural problems of building truly inclusive South Asian organizations. She said that Indians have been in the United States for many years and are very well established. The Nepalis, who arrived much later, are still in the process of establishing themselves economically; yet, they do not want to be swept under the Indian cultural hegemonic field. The SADVOs reflect some of these intracommunity majority-minority dynamics. For instance, most SADVO programming and fund-raising events highlight programs and speakers from India to primarily target their numerically largest base. As a result, the South Asian minorities do not participate in large numbers. Krishna also explained that during her tenure with SADVOs she at times felt that most of the Indian women were threatened by her involvement in the organization, and at others she felt like a second-class citizen. She said, "When they [Indian women at SADVOs] spoke with me they were very condescending. The behavior of that group as a whole was shocking, as I did not expect such educated people with a mission statement of unity to be so discriminating." Krishna asserted "they wanted a Nepali representative but were not willing to learn about Nepali women and were afraid of changes that I may bring to the organization. Thus, instead of meeting the main objective of helping all South Asian women, the SADVO created a chasm and the place where isolated women needed to feel confident enough to call trustworthy, respectful people was being lost in the process." She felt compelled to leave the SADVO she had joined within one year because of her negative experiences.

Krishna argued that if SADVOs are unable to be respectful of various cultures, their ability to help women of other cultures remains a hope rather than a reality. She added that it was not simply a case of Indians degrading Nepali people; the larger problem is that no South Asian groups were making sufficient efforts to increase interaction and build trust and respect for each other.

Concluding Remarks

Our brief account of Nepali American women's experiences of domestic violence highlights some themes that are important for developing effective activist strategies. The information on Nepali Americans and domestic violence raise some critical issues. First, we think cultural competency in individual ethnic groups is a crucial issue that requires constant attention. There is a critical need to learn about various cultures and not fall back on the essentialist position, which assumes that because we share some commonalities we are culturally all the same. Understanding the culture of silence and the specific reasons that lead to the existence of this culture among minorities is crucial in understanding domestic violence in the Nepali American community. Both minority communities in the United States and minority groups within pan-minorities, such as South Asians, reflect a complex combination of structural and cultural factors that lead to such cultures of silence. Since most activists (and we include ourselves in this category) do not arrive with sufficient cultural competency in a variety of related cultures, repeated training may be necessary to successfully bridge the knowledge gap. However, being familiar about cultures is not sufficient. We must educate ourselves about the ways in which structural conditions and cultures intersect. We contend that successful activism is based on one's openness to learning and willingness to understand the intersecting dimensions of domestic violence in order to address the complex underlying factors.

Second, understanding particular cultures of victims and helping them in ways that make them feel empowered and respected is key to all successful activism. The Nepali American experience, as far as we have been able to glean from our readings and conversations, points to the need for South Asian groups to centrally work on creating culturally inclusive spaces. Simultaneously, SADVOs need to conduct culturally appropriate outreach programs for minority South Asian communities, both to raise awareness about domestic violence as a community problem and to recruit more minority activists to address the needs of victims. Programming, including fund-raising events, must be more inclusive, either by organizing several separate fund-raising events or by making annual events more attractive to minority groups such as Nepali, Pakistani, Sri Lankan, and Bangladeshi. We are aware that in most SADVOs a few overworked individuals shoulder the burden of organizing and implementing all events and programs. Thus, our suggestion of more culturally inclusive events or customized outreach may not seem feasible. Yet, the status quo is clearly problematic for minority groups such as the Nepali Americans. We hope that awareness of the problem might encourage some groups to initiate change. Effective intervention has to centralize plans for creating an inclusive South Asian identity by overcoming the organizational and structural barriers.

While individual victims are most negatively affected by domestic violence, in the end, it diminishes all of us as women and men. Ultimately, understanding minority social locations constitute a crucial step toward a more effective challenge to the problem.

NOTES

1. We would like to caution that the findings of this study are not generalizable to all Nepali American women. The objective of this chapter is not to present empirical data but to document the stories we have heard and situate these within larger structural conditions, so that the dimensions of the problem are evident for later analysis. Mindful of the size of the community and the possibility that outing people might affect their lives and work detrimentally, we have maintained confidentiality of all those we spoke with, including the activists. We believe that domestic violence is not about individual deviance or Nepali culture alone, but about the coalescence of a series of structural, cultural, and individual factors.

    We wish to make our position as researchers transparent by asserting that Bidya is of Nepali origin and Bandana is of Indian origin, and both of us are highly educated women who work in academia. We have been formally and informally involved with domestic violence activism for over a decade.

2. We wish to emphasize this point about *selective* use of texts to justify domestic violence and caution about overgeneralizing the influence of myths in women's lives. Hindu mythology provides numerous stories of strong women, such as Amba, Draupadi, or Chitrangada, who challenged patriarchal systems. However, the subordination of women is based on downplaying these stories and using the other models as ideals. The supposedly religion-sanctioned myths from South Asia justify violence against victims and need to be scrutinized as controlling symbols. Legitimating myths, religious or secular, serves as means of ideological control and helps maintain patriarchal power in all societies.

4

"Virginity Is Everything"

Sexuality in the Context of Intimate Partner Violence in the South Asian Community

SANDEEP HUNJAN AND SHELAGH TOWSON

Although violence against women by their intimate partners and family members is a global phenomenon (Levinson 1989), there is a great deal of cultural variation in the patterns and manifestations of domestic violence (e.g., Ellsberg et al. 1999; Heise et al. 1994; Sorenson 1996; Walker 1999). Triggers for, responses to, and consequences of intimate partner violence may differ across cultural groups. As Vandello and Cohen (2003) put it, some of the reasons for domestic abuse may reside within the abusive male, but culture also plays a causal role by providing the scripts for the ways in which males and females are to behave.

South Asian culture is characterized by various norms that serve not only to maintain violence against women but also to silence those who experience it (e.g., Abraham 1999; Almeida and Dolan-Delvecchio 1999; Dasgupta and Warrier 1996). From the time they are born, if they survive the abortion, infanticide, malnutrition, and femicide that result in a low ratio of girls to boys in most parts of South Asia, girls learn that they are valued less than boys but are duty bound to provide service, sacrifice, and devotion (Kumar 1991; Sen and Seth 1995). This emphasis on duty and service (Sethi and Allen 1984) is central to the South Asian family system, "an elaborate network of male-centered relationships" (Almeida and Dolan-Delvecchio 1999, 662). When they marry, women are expected to leave their natal, "temporary" family (Kumar 1991) and move in with their "real" family, their husband's family, where power is determined by age and gender hierarchies and new brides enter near the bottom (Almeida and Dolan-Delvecchio 1999; Kumar 1991; Moghadam 1992). This transfer of a woman as property from father to husband, combined with beliefs regarding a woman's destiny and duty to her husband, may normalize the occurrence of rape and other violence in marriage and make it more difficult for women to reveal their abuse (Abraham 1999; Coomaraswamy 1995).

The lack of information on South Asian women's experience of domestic violence in North America is especially apparent in the area of sexual abuse of women

by intimate partners. Control of female sexuality is an important value in traditional South Asian cultures, maintained by social, economic, political, and legal
institutions (Abraham 1999). Daughters are expected to be chaste and asexual
before marriage. In fact, the social stigma against any kind of premarital sexuality
is so strong that women are held responsible for any assumed promiscuity, including
rape (Dasgupta 2003; Prasad 1999). A woman's nonparticipation in sexual relations
after marriage implies shyness due to lack of sexual experience, which is expected
because of gender role socialization, and which must be overcome, even with force,
by her husband (Abraham 1999). Within this context, it is not surprising that little
research exists on South Asian women's perceptions of their sexuality or their
experience of intimate sexual violence.

For the research reported here, the first author interviewed thirteen South
Asian women living in Canada who had experienced intimate partner violence.
The analysis of the narratives of the women presented first identifies the centrality
of two cultural gender norms in experiences of their sexuality: the acceptance of
female inferiority as a given and the importance of virginity in conferring value on
women. The discussion, then, moves to an exploration of the meaning of intimate
sexual abuse, its normalization as an accepted part of the husband's role, and the
central importance of silence as a cultural norm. Finally, possible sources of and
prospects for individual and cultural change are discussed.

Method

The emphasis in the analysis on women's narratives reflects a feminist perspective (Acker, Barry, and Esseveld 1991; Greaves et al. 1995; Lykes and Stewart 1986);
women who have experienced abuse can best describe the beliefs, values, and
actions that contribute to violence (Abraham 1999; Heise 1993).

The thirteen participants who tell their stories here were recruited through
word of mouth, posters, a South Asian radio show interview, and referrals from South
Asian community-based organizations. All the women were heterosexual, of South
Asian descent, and living in southern Ontario, Canada, and all had experienced
violence by spouses or partners. The women participated in semistructured face-
to-face taped interviews conducted between 2000 and 2001, which ranged from
one and a half to three hours, and they received twenty dollars in compensation
for their time. At the end of the interviews, participants were given a feedback
sheet including the researcher's contact information and a list of community
resources provided in an inconspicuous lipstick case to ensure individual safety.

The participants ranged from twenty to fifty-three years. As indicated in table 4.1,
the women were from diverse backgrounds, with diverse experiences. The violence
these women experienced also differed in intensity, ranging from emotional neglect,
threats, and financial control to beating, sexual assault, and attempted murder.

Qualitative and inductive analytic techniques guided data collection and analysis, including the QSR NUDIST Vivo program (QSR NVivo 1999), with which patterns

TABLE 4.I

Participant Demographics

Participant	Age	Age of Immigration	Age of Marriage	Children	Education Status	Marital Status	Place of Birth	Occupation	Religion
Amar	20	15	18	0	High school	Separated	India	Unemployed	Sikh
Asha	30	3.5	NA	0	BA	Single	England	Health Professional	Sikh
Belinda	53	23	16	3	High school	Divorced	Kenya	Nanny	Sikh
Bubbly	41	6	21	3	Diploma	Married	England	Medical Technician	Sikh
Enza	47	41	39	0	BA	Divorced	India	Secretary	Hindu
Fari	28	27	24	1	BMed	Separated	Pakistan	Unemployed	Muslim
Meena	29	29	19	0	BA	Divorced	India	Unemployed	Hindu
Muskaan	26	20	17	1	High school	Separated	India	Counselor	Sikh
Palvsha	25	23	18	0	—	Separated	Pakistan	Unemployed	Muslim
Shameem	40	38	20	4	High school	Divorced	Pakistan	Unemployed	Muslim
Simran	32	NA	21	2	—	Married	Canada	Student	Sikh
Sonia	32	29	17	2	Home schooled	Separated	Afghanistan	Unemployed	Sikh
Zharguna	35	34	NA	0	MA	Single	Pakistan	Unemployed	Muslim

Note: All unemployed women were receiving social assistance from the government. Dashes indicate that information was missing during the interview.

in the women's narratives were categorized as meaningful themes (Abraham 1995; Cresswell 1994; Strauss and Corbin 1990). Themes related to ethnicity and gender were central; the focus was on emerging themes related specifically to sexuality. Quotes from the interviews are presented here as transcribed, with filler phrases such as "um" and "like" removed to facilitate clarity.

Gender Norms

No Respect for Women

Violence against women is rooted globally in beliefs in male dominance over women (Abraham 1995). Like other patriarchal systems, the South Asian cultural context is characterized by inequalities in male-female roles, legitimized and institutionalized by social norms that place men in dominant positions in the lives of women (Fernandez 1997). Males are valued more than females, and in her lifetime a woman is expected to be dependent on her father, husband, and eldest son (Segal 1991). These attitudes regarding women's subordinate status to men constituted a predominant theme in the narratives. All thirteen women described pervasive gender-related messages that reinforced their dependence on men and their domestic, subservient, and passive role in the family (Walker 1981).

These women's socialization into gender inequality started early. Nine of the respondents recalled that boys were given more freedom inside and outside the home, while girls were responsible for household chores, and their activities outside of the home were restricted. Zharguna (a pseudonym, as are names of all interviewees) is a thirty-five-year-old Muslim woman from a tribal area in Pakistan with five sisters and one brother. Engaged at eighteen to a supposedly single man, Zharguna discovered a week before her wedding that he was already married with children. For thirteen years, Zharguna and her family fought to break the engagement. During this time her fiancé attacked her brother and, after the engagement was successfully broken, threatened Zharguna's new fiancé, who as a result, canceled the wedding. Zharguna detailed the characteristics of a "good girl":

> In the beginning they will tell us talk slow, softly, wear your *dupatta* [head scarf] all the time, be a good girl, don't talk, ask too many things this is for a good girl. I'm not allowed to go at late hours. I don't make noise when men are around; if they men, boys are doing [making noise]—okay, for them it's acceptable.

Amar, a twenty-year-old Sikh woman who immigrated to Canada five years ago with her natal family, endured a physically, emotionally, and sexually abusive marriage with a man from India, whom Amar had sponsored for immigration. When she left him after eleven months, her parents refused to take her in and she was forced to seek refuge in a women's shelter. Amar recalls how her brother was allowed more freedom, while she was confined to home. "He allowed to do, he can go out with anyone, but not me. I have to finish my school and come back home and I have to do housework and everything."

Some research suggests that these traditional patriarchal power imbalances may be even more strongly maintained or emphasized in the immigrant community in the hope of ensuring cultural continuity (e.g., Abraham 1999; Almeida and Dolan-Delvecchio 1999; Dasgupta and Warrier 1996; Singh and Unnithan 1999). Bubbly, a forty-one-year-old Sikh woman born in England who immigrated to Canada at the age of six, has three children and remains married to her abusive, alcoholic husband. Bubbly reflects this reality, "We were just really brought up as Canadian kids, but we were taught to stay home, the women are supposed to stay home. The boys always have that extra priority, where they can do what they want."

Meena, a twenty-nine-year-old Hindu woman, born, raised, and married in India, was beaten and abused by both her husband and in-laws, who had attempted to murder her by throwing her off a balcony. Eight years after this crime, her husband was finally sentenced to five years in jail, but his threat that he would kill her on his release led her to seek asylum in Canada. Meena summarizes the patriarchal view: "In India there is a man-dominated society. They don't have a respect for women."

Gender inequality was a defining theme in the respondents' lives; men are more valued than women and virtually the only way that women can attain value is through their relationships with men, primarily as wives and mothers. The message is that since men are more powerful, they will be responsible for taking care of women. A woman is raised with strict rules regarding behavioral norms and is expected to be dependent on the men in her life (Abraham 2000a; Almeida and Dolan-Delvecchio 1999; Kumar 1991; Moghadam 1992). Zharguna knew that the number of male members measured the strength of one's family. Thus, having only one younger brother and five sisters reduced her family's power: "In our tribal society, men is, the number of men is considered as, power. If there are too many men in a family, they are a strong family, so I had, in my case I had only one younger brother with me."

This message of male superiority is translated into married life such that women look up to their husbands as the person who defines them. Muskaan, a twenty-six-year-old Sikh woman was born in India and was married at seventeen to a man from Canada, who turned out to be a criminal gang leader. He became emotionally and physically abusive toward her immediately after their wedding and attempted to murder her numerous times. However, Muskaan kept returning to her husband because "your husband is your God, without him you're nothing." Meena takes this one step further when she describes what she thought was expected of her after her marriage: "I should wear the *bindi* [dot worn on forehead], I should wear the *tikka* [jewelry worn in the hair to indicate that a woman is married], and I have an *izzat* [honor] with the *ghar* [home]; my husband is my God. I should pray my husband what he's saying I never refused him. This is in my mind, that marriage is the word, to always keep your mouth shut and follow the rules. I thought only this marriage is a compromise, you, women should do the compromise, men is saying this, you should do the compromise."

The expectation of women's dependence and sacrifice was a common theme. Four women described their understanding of the underlying message that if they fulfilled their duties and sacrificed their needs for others, they would be rewarded later. Simran, a twenty-six-year old Sikh woman born in Canada, married a man from India who was emotionally and physically abusive toward her. She sponsored both her husband and father-in-law for immigration and for some time was the sole financial support for the family, including two children. Simran related that "I was always told how Indian woman always sacrifices and then you reap the benefits later." This model of the ideal Indian woman as a combination of service, sacrifice, and devotion is embodied in the form of the Hindu heroine Sita from the Sanskrit epic the *Ramayana* (Kumar 1991; Sen and Seth 1995). Sita's acts of loyalty and sacrifice set the ideal for wifely love and devotion and play a central role in defining what is expected of a South Asian woman.

Belinda, a fifty-two-year-old Sikh woman born in Kenya, grew up with an alcoholic and abusive father and married a physically and emotionally abusive man at sixteen. The abuse continued through the birth of their three children and immigration first to England and then to Canada. Although she tried to leave her husband many times, her natal family intervened on his behalf. As Belinda puts it, "I was brought up, man is everything; you please the man, and you do everything for a man and a man loves you."

This theme of self-sacrifice, putting the needs of their husbands before their own, regardless of the situation, means that unreasonable male behavior is often indulged or justified in the family. At her wedding, Simran's father-in-law warned her of her husband's psychological problems. Despite her husband's neglectful and abusive behavior, Simran continues to live with him. Here, she recounts her mother's dismissal of her husband's temper tantrums: "He would have these temper tantrums; my mom told me, 'Oh Indian men they're like that. You have to, you have to give them, their way, so that their ego is satisfied, this is just the way it is, just don't talk back to him, because they're not used to that, so try to, try to please him.' So I, I was a very submissive woman in the beginning."

Thus, South Asian women are socialized from birth into patriarchal norms that reinforce a female identity that privileges men. Women are given to men through marriage. They gain respect and power through their sons and later through their position as mothers-in-law (Moghadam 1992). Furthermore, a culture that legitimizes male dominance and female subordination silences women by teaching them that they are less important than men and therefore need a man's protection.

The same patriarchy that socializes women to powerlessness contains a paradox, the patriarchal belief that women do have power, that this power is located within their sexuality, and that this power must be controlled. This belief leads to various methods of control in economic, social, and sexual realms (e.g., Mernissi 1987, 1989, 1996) and to the emphasis in the sexual realm of female virginity and purity. In fact, as discussed next, the second central cultural norm is maintenance of a woman's premarital virginity at all costs.

Virginity Is Everything

In the South Asian view, femininity is equated with submissiveness, while female sexuality is associated with power (Abraham 2000a; Bannerji 1993; Kumar 1991; Mazumdar 1998). "The concept of 'Shakti,' femininity in control of her own sexuality, and its real-life translation, 'Virangana' (warrior woman)," contradicts the idea of the ever-subservient woman (Dasgupta and Warrier 1996, 255). However, the patriarchal need to control female sexuality is reflected in the contrasting images of woman as goddess, the chaste and life-giving mother who supports the dominant social order, and as whore, who has the power to destroy men with her commanding sexuality (DasGupta and Dasgupta 1998).

The South Asian family controls female sexuality by making explicit the link between family honor and women's sexual purity. A woman must protect her virginity before marriage and her virtue afterward; not to do so brings dishonor not only to herself but also to her entire family, and her primary duty is to protect her family from rumor and scandal (Hasnat 1998; Vandello and Cohen 2003). Thus, the only legitimate space for women's sexuality is marriage and the creation of a family (DasGupta and Dasgupta 1998).

As with socialization into an acceptance of female inferiority, lessons regarding the importance of repressing sexuality begin early. As Meena expressed it, "In my childhood, first thing that we can't talk with a boy, we can't love with a boy, we should do the work in a kitchen, and, this is too much difference." Ensuring a daughter's chastity benefits the entire family (Abraham 1999; Coomaraswamy 1995), so family members influence their daughters to be dutiful and act in accordance with community expectations (Hennink, Diamond, and Cooper 1999). These messages regarding appropriate gender-related behaviors are so pervasive that they need not be explicit. Social norms that communicate the shame and social ostracism that will accompany loss of virginity before marriage help to ensure that girls will think twice before engaging in premarital relationships (Abraham 1999; Hennink et al. 1999). In Muskaan's words, "We always went to school with our cousins, we came back with them. We went to the same school; we weren't even allowed to talk to any guys even in the class, even to ask for a book or anything. So, that was, no, no, no you'll be killed if we see you anywhere near a guy."

Palvsha, a twenty-five-year-old Muslim woman, was married by telephone to a man in Canada, whom she saw for the first time five years after the wedding, after his family finally initiated the immigration process. She realized upon her arrival in Canada that he was mentally "disabled" and physically abusive. She did not allow a sexual relationship with her husband until her mother-in-law threatened to lie to her parents and tell them Palvsha was seeing another man. Palvsha describes the meaning of her virginity and its loss: "A woman's virginity is everything for her and mine was snatched from me by him."

A woman's premarital virginity ensures her family's honor in alliances between families secured through marriage, the legitimacy of heirs, and the maintenance of caste purity. Consequently, general modesty is encouraged, sexuality is controlled, and interactions with the opposite sex are discouraged in girls and women (Abraham 1999; Almeida and Dolan-Delvecchio 1999; Hennink et al. 1999). Simran describes her experience: "I guess I was very innocent, I had never dated before, I'd never had a relationship with a man before. I only had girlfriends, that's the way I was brought up, because I knew, I knew dating was a no-no and I just tried to be the good girl that didn't do anything like that."

This control of female sexuality in order to ensure male honor may differentiate patriarchy in Asian cultures from that in Western cultures (Almeida and Dolan-Delvecchio 1999; Moghadam 1992). For South Asian immigrants invested in maintaining cultural continuity in the West, such cultural prescriptions may be magnified by a stronger adherence to cultural values. "By linking the burden of sexual chastity and cultural traditions, and placing both on the Indian-American daughter's shoulders, the Indian immigrant community protects itself from mainstream threats of assimilation" (DasGupta and Dasgupta 1998, 125).

A young woman's understanding of her sexuality is based largely on media stereotypes and experiences of coercion by a family friend or relative (Abraham 1999). The media glorify motherhood and subservient wifehood and make it difficult for girls to think and act outside prescribed gender roles. Media images (e.g., South Asian films) reinforce the cultural attitude that female sexuality is dangerous both outside and within marriage and must be repressed for the good of society (Derné 1995). Derné (1999) noted that Indian films often eroticize and legitimize violence against women and portray women as sexually exploitable, with rape scenes a common part of the script. South Asian films also often depict punitive personal and societal outcomes for women who experiment with their sexuality, especially outside marriage (Abraham 1999).

Thus, protecting her virtue (and family honor) before and after marriage becomes the South Asian woman's primary responsibility (Hasnat 1998; Vandello and Cohen 2003). South Asian cultures view marriage as an ideal, a duty, a social responsibility, and a sacrament where religion, caste, and regional affiliations guide mate selection. Getting one's daughter married is considered the parents' prime responsibility. Amar sponsored her husband's immigration after marriage; when he arrived in Canada, he started to beat her daily and told her that he had only married her so that she could sponsor him. Amar commented, "They [parents] think husband is everything for a girl." There is considerable cultural stigma associated with remaining unmarried, which puts considerable pressure on women to marry (Abraham 2000a).

Marriages in South Asian cultures are traditionally arranged by parents and are a contract between families rather than individuals. Arranged marriage practices are reinforced by strong beliefs in destiny, including the idea that one's mate and fate are preordained by supreme forces within the universe (Gupta 1976). Since youth, beauty, and desirability are conflated, the earlier a woman is married the better. Parents also fear that girls allowed to remain single until an age when autonomy is possible may choose their own partners. Muskaan's marriage to the man who ultimately attempted to kill her was arranged when Muskaan was seventeen, prompted partly by "fear of either that they might end up dating somebody else or deciding for themselves."

A South Asian woman's primary identity is that of a daughter until she is wed, after which she is a wife. Thus, marriage serves as the border between childhood and adulthood, and between asexuality and sexuality. Essentially, women are given to men through marriage. The denial of a woman's personhood through her transfer from father to husband formalizes her status as property and entitles the groom and his family to every right over her (Mazumdar 1998). Zharguna describes women's position as chattel: "It's happened with tribal families. If a person died, the woman has no right to go back or to marry again with another person. It's like a property if her husband died, the second, the brother of her husband will marry her, if he is younger than her or if he is older. I can give you an example, there are many, sixty years old men married with women fourteen, twenty years old women, because her husband died and she, she is property. She has no choice."

In preparation for her duty to her husband, the woman may be given cursory instructions prior to her wedding night regarding her wifely responsibility to satisfy her husband's sexual needs (Abraham 1999). Reluctance is interpreted as appropriate shyness due to lack of sexual knowledge or experience, and the possibility that her husband may have to use force to initiate sexual relations is commonly accepted. All twelve of the married participants in this study had gone through an arranged marriage process whereby they had very little or no time to get to know their husbands. After a lifetime of being told to stay away from boys, these women were expected to be intimate with their husbands soon after the wedding. Not surprising, then, were the reactions described by women who, with little or no knowledge of sexuality, faced physical intimacy with virtual strangers. Simran describes her fear and uncertainty regarding what she should do on her wedding night: "I thought, okay we'd get married; we would fall in love later. However, I was still very, I was very scared of, your first night and everything. I don't even know this person; now, what am I supposed to say? Can I say no, that's what I was really scared of, because I had never had a relationship, and, when you don't know somebody and you're expected to share yourself physically, with someone you don't even know."

South Asian cultures are collectivist cultures, and in collectivist cultures, love, intimacy, and the bond between marriage partners are not considered to be as important as the responsibility of the married couple to the man's family (Dion and Dion 1993). Central to the maintenance of the family is the concept of honor, or *izzat*, defined as virtuous behavior, good moral character, integrity, and respect. This code of family honor dictates precedence and toughness for males and modesty, shame, and avoidance of immoral behaviors for females (Vandello and Cohen 2003). Women bring honor to their family if they comply with their prescribed roles, and dishonor and shame if they deviate from them (Ayyub 2000). Thus, while South Asian women are subordinate to men and strictly controlled, they are also central to the family's status. In fact, speaking of South Asian cultures, Vandello and Cohen point out that "it is often said that in such cultures, the honor of the family goes through the female" (2003, 998). This means that women must maintain purity and chastity while performing their duties, which ultimately include getting married and producing male heirs.

Closely associated with the idea of family honor is the importance given to the transmission of cultural values. It is here that South Asian women, while being dutiful and devoted, are also powerful agents of cultural transmission, playing a central role in carrying the teachings of their culture to their children. Of course, women socialized to accept cultural norms of female inferiority and chastity, as the primary source of whatever female value exists, may contribute in their roles as mothers and mothers-in-law to the perpetuation of these norms. Both Meena and Palvsha describe significant abuse at the hands of their mothers-in-law.

However, six of the women indicated that since experiencing intimate violence, they have decided to parent their children differently. Asha, a thirty-year-old Sikh woman who immigrated to Canada from England when she was three, described a long-term relationship with an abusive boyfriend and indicated that if she had a daughter in the future, she wanted to teach her the values of strength and independence, "so that she understands that no one should be able to take advantage of her." Bubbly described how she is raising her children with more egalitarian roles and responsibilities than she was raised with: "What my mom was doing was wrong 'cause it's not right, it's not fair, everybody should be helping out, we're, all of us make the mess so we should all clean it up so that's what I'm telling my kids now, that it's your responsibility, you guys all help out. If you made the mess there shouldn't have to be a border, where the boys do one thing and the girls do another. So I'm trying to make them equal." Sonia's new message to her children reinforces the importance of living a life that pleases them, rather than keeping up appearances. She said, "I have had an arranged marriage for my family's sake and I have done this, but I won't force my daughters to do this. Some people stay for appearances, in our society, because we can't leave our husbands, what will people say, these people are stupid."

This duality of duty and power is also reflected in popular images of South Asian women as passive, docile, chaste, and self-sacrificing, on the one hand, and as the powerful, creative, life-giving force whose mystical powers are often feared, on the other (Bannerji 1993; Kumar 1991). These dual associations allow South Asian women to be simultaneously active and passive (Sethi and Allen 1984), resulting in the potential for powerful forces of change, whereas cultural norms serve to control women and protect against such change.

Sexuality and Intimate Violence

The Meaning of Sexual Abuse

The limited sexual experience South Asian women have prior to marriage may make them more vulnerable in their relationships, as sex often becomes a means through which men can appropriate power. Ten of the thirteen women inter-viewed reported experiencing physical abuse, ranging from battering to attempted murder. Eight women reported experiencing different forms of sexual abuse, includ-ing rape, attempts at reproductive control, and using the threat of another woman to demean and humiliate them. However, regardless of what they experienced, women were most reticent about talking about their sexual abuse.

Even when women did talk about their sexual abuse, they often would not label it as rape. Meena was an exception: "Slowly my husband talk with me, of course he want the sex with me, so he talk with me and, but he, he come only at the night time with me, he want the sex only, then in the morning he is the strange person to me. I'm like a stranger in their house, just your room is in the kitchen like the servant, the working in the home and then they beat me daily. Then when I was feeling hurt, I have a pain, and then he want with me sex, but I, I never say no. I never refused. He, he raped me always."

Other women described their partners' attempts to control their reproductive rights. In Muskaan's case, the month following her wedding at age seventeen was the only sexual contact she had with her husband before he returned to Canada. After his departure, Muskaan discovered she was pregnant; her husband did not believe the child was his and wanted her to get an abortion, which ultimately she decided not to have.

In Simran's case, her husband refused to use adequate birth control and then encouraged her to have an abortion: "He, was irresponsible not using his condom and stuff. Even when I asked him to, and then at the end what does he do? He tells me to get an abortion after, and I said, no, I'll try to make the best of this now."

Meena's husband used physical abuse as a form of birth control. She stated, "My husband beat me every day in my stomach, he kicked me that he don't want me to become pregnant. Every day he, he did the sex with me, and every next day he'd kick me."

Four of the women interviewed (Enza, Asha, Belinda, Shameem) described how their husbands used the idea of being with another woman to control, humiliate, or neglect them, a form of abuse labeled as use of the sexual other (Abraham 2000b). Enza, a forty-seven-year-old Hindu woman born and raised in India who immigrated to Canada to join her husband after her wedding at the age of thirty-nine, describes how her abusive husband tried to force her to invite his mistress into their social network, "He wanted me to be friends with her. I said, look, you want to be friends with her, you want to be with her, I will not say anything, I'll just be at home, let me be here you go you do whatever you do, don't come and tell me. And, I don't want to make her a part of our social life."

Asha described how her abusive boyfriend continually denied that he was having an affair, despite her strong suspicions after observing her partner and the other woman together. Shameem, a forty-year-old Muslim woman born and raised in Pakistan, detailed how her husband of ten years left for Canada soon after the birth of the youngest of their four children. He did not return or make contact for ten years, at which point he sent for the family. Soon after their arrival, Shameem became aware that he was involved in a sexual relationship with his sister-in-law. He became physically and emotionally abusive, finally forcing Shameem to leave their home so that he could continue the relationship.

Thus, the risk of sexual violence for South Asian women is increased by the interaction of three factors (Abraham 1999): (1) culturally prescribed premarital sexual purity for women; (2) the notion that sex is part of the obligation for exchange of goods; and (3) the definition of sex as being for men's pleasure and gratification within marriage. Furthermore, the denial of a woman's personhood through her transfer as property from father to husband at marriage, combined with beliefs regarding a woman's destiny and duty to her husband, normalizes marital rape (Abraham 1999; Coomaraswamy 1995; Mazumdar 1998). This normalization and the shame associated with sexual violence maintain its invisibility, as women do not speak out and prosecute the perpetrators (Abraham 2000a; Mazumdar 1998).

All the Husbands Beat Their Wives

Spousal abuse is a common method by which men assert dominance, with both husband and society viewing abuse as a legitimate manifestation of power and control (Abraham 2000a). Traditionally, there was the belief that beating those of lower status was acceptable (e.g., teachers beating students, parents beating children, husbands beating wives) (Dasgupta 2000a). Muskaan describes this norm, "I didn't wanted to hurt [my family by disclosing the violence]. I thought it might change. Probably it won't get to a point where I have to tell them. *Qnukay* (because) there's norm like all the husbands beat their wives, not in my family, but . . . ."

Some South Asian societies ignore the murder of female relatives or treat it very leniently, in the name of family honor (Dasgupta 2000a; Khouri 2003). Amnesty International's 1999 report provides evidence of the acceptance of the family honor defense in Pakistan as a mitigating circumstance at all levels of government, including the police, judiciary, and legislature. "In our society, honor killing, a man can kill his wife and there's laws to protect men."

Meena, whose sexual abuse began on the first day of her marriage, thought this was a normal part of marriage: "First day, almost he raped me. I'm crying, illiterate, crying and, just he finished his work and I'm, I'm so, I felt so bad, but I think, this is supposed to happen."

Dasi Na (Don't Tell)

On a global level, the private nature of abuse, the lack of definitional consensus regarding types of violence, the methodological limitations in research, and the reluctance of women to report these crimes keeps the enormity of violence hidden (Kazarian and Kazarian 1998; Koss, Heise, and Russo 1994). This reluctance is exacerbated by social norms against discussing sexual and private matters, distrust of authorities or fellow citizens, and the desire to maintain privacy in small communities (Koss et al. 1994). Regardless of culture or crime, when people are identified as victims some degree of devaluation occurs (Koss 1990).

Until recently, gender role conditioning in South Asian families and ideas regarding the home as a private institution have allowed domestic violence to remain hidden and unaddressed (Abraham 2000a). Shame as a societal control mechanism has a powerful impact on the acknowledgment and reporting of violence (especially sexual assault) and on proposed intervention strategies. The stigma of public humiliation prevents families and communities from discussing personal problems (Kanuha 1987). Not surprisingly then, there is not a lot of community, family, or financial support for South Asian women who want to leave their abusive husbands (Agnew 1998a).

In a caste-based, collectivist society like India, in which family honor overrides personal freedom and the group takes precedence over the individual, prohibitions against exposing private information are strong and it is common for women to remain silent to save their families' honor (Prasad 1999; Winter and Young 1998). The stigma of revealing problems within the family and fear of losing face in front of one's community, as well as the sense of failing her marital commitments may keep a woman silent about her victimization (Dasgupta 2000a). Bubbly remained in the relationship for fear that her husband would kill her and/or her three children if she attempted to leave. As she stated in her interview: "It's really hard to let other people know [*last few words said softly*] what's going on in your life. And you don't want them to know, you want to cover up."

This statement reflects the desire of many women, regardless of cultural background, to keep negative information within the family. The silencing of women is even more complex when women are socialized to expect violence in their relationships. Muskaan's situation illustrates the interaction of a few of these variables in keeping women silent: "I said but he drinks, but my in-laws had told them [my family] that he doesn't drink or does anything. So, they were in a shock too. I said he drinks, he smokes, he takes drugs so, but then they said, oh don't tell anyone then it will be embarrassment for us. That was first shock like at the wedding day and he first started hitting me on the third day after the marriage, but, I didn't tell my parents that, because you feel embarrassed. You have grown up with that thinking that, that's what husband is supposed to do." In addition to the fear of shaming one's family, many women are afraid to talk about their situations for a variety of other reasons. For several women, fear for their families and for themselves kept them silent. Given that most women never live alone and are seldom allowed to make their own decisions, telling someone or leaving the marriage would render a woman quite vulnerable (Dasgupta 2000a).

In the North American context, this message is reinforced by the notion of maintaining an image of the South Asian model minority, whereby family problems are kept hidden and seeking outside help is shunned. Women may also remain silent about their victimization to maintain their family's support in other areas of life (e.g., racial, ethnic, and class discrimination in a new country). In fact, the struggle between the gender discrimination in their own community and the racism of the dominant culture can further act to silence women and maintain abusive situations (Abraham 1999; Agnew 1998a).

Concluding Remarks

Consistent with a feminist analysis, which reframes the problem of intimate violence against women as "one of misuse of power by men who have been socialized into believing they have the right to control the women in their lives, even through violent means" (Walker 1989, 695), this investigation shows that the secondary status of women within South Asian patriarchal family hierarchies engenders many of the issues that the women identified as meaningful in terms of spousal violence. A woman's subordinate position, regardless of culture, sets up a situation where others are given the right to, and responsibilities over, her life. The community's responsibility appears to be focused on raising the girl and getting her to her wedding day, at which time the responsibility for her life is handed over by her parents to a husband and in-laws who, in most cases, are virtual strangers to her.

The focus on ethnicity advocated by the ethno-gender approach (Abraham 1995), takes this analysis one step further and reveals certain factors specific to the South Asian cultural context. One such factor is that marriage is perhaps the only route through which women obtain value. Within this cultural group, the existence of rigid gender role norms and prohibitions regarding sexuality gives women the message that their day-to-day behavior must be dictated by and for the needs of others. Through this behavior, especially in terms of marriage, they will have the opportunity for a happy life. Even in the personal sphere, sexual identity is inhibited and women are expected to be the gatekeepers of family and community honor. Even though women are given the responsibility of representing the South Asian community, they are allowed little if any decision-making power over their own lives.

This situation obviously leaves lower status women, usually the daughters-in-law in a family, vulnerable. However, as South Asian women are encouraged to maintain their relationships at all costs, and are taught that suffering and sacrifice are the virtues for which they will be rewarded, their struggles may remain silent. Cultural norms that stigmatize women who are not married or who leave their marriages provide additional pressure to keep their sufferings secret. Furthermore, the lack of training in decision making and self-sufficiency, within a system that makes women's rights unimportant, leaves many women with few options but to endure their oppressive situations. Therefore, it appears that these South Asian women are being sold a bill of goods from birth that states that women are less important than men but identifies women as so integral to maintaining the family's honor that they must be protected, even from themselves, at all costs. Women who do not adhere to cultural standards are blamed, stigmatized, and as Belinda, who divorced her husband after years of abuse, put it, "made to feel like outcasts."

Within the immigrant context, the pressure of being a successful "model minority" and the added stresses of racism, financial instability, and lack of extended family support mean that people who could potentially help women may avoid looking critically at their own communities. Portraying the community in a positive way may become so important for members of immigrant groups that they may oppress some segments, including women, by denying the violence perpetrated against them. The social control of intimate violence also marks an intrusion into the private realm of the family, an arena controlled by "domestic patriarchy," another factor that maintains the invisibility of intimate violence (Abraham 2000a, 14).

However, the paradox regarding women's power, and the fact that women are the primary transmitters of cultural norms, means that women may prove to be powerful agents in changing these oppressive forces. Many of the women interviewed noted that they were already parenting or would parent their children differently than they had been parented. For some, this meant more egalitarian gender role socialization for their sons and daughters, while for others it was teaching their daughters independence and self-sufficiency. The dynamic nature of culture is reflected in these changing attitudes toward culturally prescribed gender-related norms, a change that bodes well for reducing the generational transmission of attitudes that may facilitate violence against women.

Ultimately, the problems related to violence against women cannot be understood and solved by focusing exclusively on the individual, but must involve changing the cultural and social institutions that provide a framework for these problems. The problem calls for social scientists and policy makers to work together and create change in the attitudes and institutions that perpetuate men's violent acts against women.

5

The Aftermath of September 11

An Anti–Domestic Violence Perspective

MAUNICA STHANKI

The attacks of September 11, 2001, temporarily paralyzed the United States, as Americans attempted to make sense of the tragedy and deal with personal issues of hate, fear, and sadness. In many ways, the entire nation seemed to form a support group and individuals shouldered the burdens of their neighbors, friends, and families. However, this collective support group was not always welcoming to members of the South Asian, Arab, and Muslim communities. These communities were victimized by the attacks of September 11, and many returned to their daily lives only to be revictimized by their neighbors and friends (Iyer 2003; also, see South Asian Leaders of Tomorrow 2001). Victims of domestic violence within these communities were, then, re-revictimized as they encountered violence inside as well as outside their homes.

Domestic violence did not cease to exist in the aftermath of September 11; instead, many social service agencies reported that domestic violence in the Muslim communities increased after the day of the attack. An article in *Newsweek* attributed the increase to "the weak economy, an insulated culture and intense scrutiny from law enforcement and locals" (Childress 2003, 37). The Arab-American Family Support Center explained that the increase in domestic violence in the Arab community was due to the high level of fear and stress after September 11. The *Newsweek* article related the story of a Muslim-American batterer whose temper turned violent after the attacks of September 11. His victim, Lila (pseudonym), explained that September 11 "changed him from an angel to a monster" (37).

While the actual rate of domestic violence may have increased after September 11, several organizations reported an initial drop in calls from women in the South Asian and Muslim communities (Katz 2003). The New York Asian Women's Center (NYAWC) noticed that there was a reduction in calls from the South Asian community, despite initial reports of increase in domestic violence from a comparable group, East Asian women. NYAWC maintained that reports of domestic violence from East Asian women increased significantly in the immediate aftermath of September 11 and complaints by Chinese women rose 50 percent. NYWAC attributed the increase in domestic violence to tensions in Chinatown after the attacks, yet acknowledged that calls from Muslim women dropped significantly (Katz 2003).

NYAWC's executive director, Tuhina De O'Connor, a woman of South Asian descent herself, explained that the fear of persecution was the reason why many Muslim women stopped reporting their abuse (Katz 2003). Consequently, NYAWC staff increased their outreach in the South Asian community; nonetheless, many Muslim women remained afraid to report domestic violence.[1] Purvi Shah, executive director of Sakhi for South Asian women (Sakhi) in New York, explained that Sakhi also experienced an initial drop in calls between September 2001 and December 2001, yet remarked that calls nearly doubled in 2002 and have been on a steady rise since then.

The effects of September 11 crossed borders, as many Muslim women in the United Kingdom also felt reluctant to seek assistance from domestic violence service providers (Ebrahim 2001). Najma Ebrahim, coordinator of the Muslim Women's Helpline in the United Kingdom, reported that calls dropped significantly during the month of September 2001. She attributed this drop in calls to women's greater concern for Islamaphobia and racism (2001). While statistical numbers concerning reporting is useful, it is not an absolute way of measuring the rate of domestic violence in the South Asian, Arab, and Muslim communities due to gross underreporting by women. Because of cultural, societal, familial, and religious issues, many women in these communities are reluctant to report abuse.

Clarifying Terminology

Even though I recognize that ethnically Muslims can be South Asian or Arab, I have categorized "South Asian," "Arab," and "Muslim" distinctly. This is because South Asian and Arab Muslims, and those who look like them, were the particular recipients of post-9/11 backlash in the United States. While Arab and South Asian Muslims were the chief targets, many non-Muslims in these communities were also victimized during this period. For example, the first victim of 9/11 backlash murder in the country was a South Asian Sikh man (Real Sikhism n.d.). At the same time, although many whites and African Americans belong to the Muslim community, the primary focus of this article is on the Arab and South Asian communities because they bore the brunt of discrimination after 9/11.

I also recognize that South Asian and Arab Muslim communities vary drastically in many cultural, religious, and ethnic aspects; yet, I use the three labels nearly interchangeably. The purpose of grouping these communities together is not to deny their individuality, but rather to acknowledge that after September 11 these communities were similarly subjected to backlash and abuse due to their perceived connection to the September 11 attacks. Thus, throughout this chapter, I list these groups separately, while continuing to draw parallels among them.

The "Culture of Fear" after 9/11

A study conducted in 2003 by the Center for the Prevention of Hate Violence (CPHV) at the University of Southern Maine found that immigrant and refugee communities in the United States are more frightened than ever (Solomon 2004; Wessler 2002). The study found that certain federal policies have immigrants terrified that they will be held, questioned, and sent away even if they have the correct documents, or that their friends or family will suffer these consequences. The center's study also found that immigrants are hesitant to report crimes, afraid to tell their landlords about poor housing conditions, and the women are afraid to report domestic violence assaults (Wessler 2002).

While the immigrant community as a whole remains on alert, the South Asian, Arab, and Muslim communities are particularly afraid because of the immense backlash directed at them after September 11 (Gerson 2003; Iyer 2003). The CPHV study found that Muslims worry about whether their homes and phones are bugged by the government; question whether to attend religious services at mosques for fear of government infiltration; and fear immigrant detention and deportation (Wessler 2002). Furthermore, Muslims continue to face abuse in the form of bias, prejudice, and harassment. Much of this abuse arises from the decisions by members of these communities to wear traditional clothes, adding to the perception of them and their appearances as foreign (Wessler 2002).

Mohamad, a twenty-one-year-old Pakistani resident of New York City, was stabbed in the stomach in the foyer of his apartment building by three assailants as he returned home from work (Solomon 2003). He received forty stitches for a three-inch-deep wound and currently has an eight-inch-long scar on his torso from the attack. When the ambulance and paramedics came to the scene, Mohamad told them that he had stabbed himself. He said, "I don't have no papers, no documents. I didn't want to make a police report" (Solomon 2003, 26). Nihad Awad, the former executive director of the Council on American-Islamic Relations (CAIR), explains, "We get reports by people who are assaulted, and they are afraid to report it to authorities because of their status. We don't force them to go forward. . . . People feel they are vulnerable to bias attacks and also to those who should protect them" (Lee 2001, 44).

Recently, the FBI has reported a markedly significant increase in hate crimes against the Muslim, Arab, and South Asian communities (Abedelkarim and Riad 2003). In 2000, the FBI reported 28 instances of hate-crime abuse in these communities, whereas in 2001 the figure rose to 481. Some organizations believe this number to be a low estimate, as many South Asian, Arab, and Muslims did not report instances of abuse for fear of further persecution by law enforcement officials. CAIR estimates that between September 2001 and February 2002, the number of hate crimes in Muslim communities could be as high as 1,700.

Most reported hate crimes involve physical attacks; however, many South Asians, Arabs, and Muslims face less violent forms of racism every day of their lives.

A December 2004 Cornell University study indicated that approximately 44 percent of Americans believe that the civil rights of Muslims should be curtailed and approximately 27 percent of Americans believe that Muslims should be required to register with the U.S. government, regardless of their citizenship or immigration status (Cornell News 2004). While people holding the belief that Muslims should have fewer rights than non-Muslim Americans cite the need to protect the security of the United States, the very sentiment dramatically increases the degree of fear experienced by Muslims and those who appear to be Muslim.

Many individuals in the South Asian, Arab, and Muslim communities fear local and federal law enforcement intrusion into their lives while also worrying whether their neighbors will report them to law enforcement officials, and whether strangers they encounter will hold biased or prejudiced views (Wessler 2002). The Department of Justice's (DOJ) attempted creation of Operation TIPS (Terrorism Information Prevention System) was based on encouraging ordinary Americans to spy on suspicious individuals and unusual situations (Pickett 2002). Operation TIPS encouraged deliverymen, neighbors, and telephone installers to report suspicious activity to a DOJ hotline. Operation TIPS was not implemented but made community members wary of strangers.

South Asian, Arab, and Muslim communities are, therefore, increasingly isolated, not trusting of outsiders, and scared about the possibility of a continuing backlash against them. Ahmad Razvi, codirector of the Council of Pakistan Organization (a New York City community center founded in the wake of 9/11), explained, "People are really afraid . . . FBI, INS, police—they've gone to businesses and homes in this neighborhood conducting raids. Why would our people trust them?" (Solomon 2003, 26).

The United States' decision to initiate a war with Iraq only exacerbated this situation, as many within these minority communities felt as if America was at war with their ethnicities and/or religions (Breznikar 2003; Solomon 2003). The home of Upindar Kaur, a Sikh American woman, was vandalized by assailants using racial slurs a week after the Iraq war started (Evans 2003). Kaur reported the incident to the local police but did not receive a response, nor did the police have a report on file. Also, in the months after the Iraq war, CAIR reported an increase in hate crimes and created a bomb threat checklist for South Asian, Muslim, and Arab organizations to keep handy (Solomon 2003).

Numbers of criminal acts are not always the best indicators of fear, as community members may experience violence in the form of hate speech, xenophobia, and general racist comments. Because these forms of hatred are not characterized by physical violence or law enforcement cooperation, many members of the community choose not to report such incidents to officials (Wessler 2002). For example, Barbara Ghaddar, a Muslim resident of Laramie, Wyoming, was forced to leave a Wal-Mart with her two daughters because someone approached them and yelled, "Oh my God—the terrorists are here!" (Egan 2001, 1). Saha Waheed, also a Muslim resident of Laramie, was wearing a *hijab* while walking down her street when two men rushed up behind her and said that anyone who wore a scarf on her head should die (Egan 2001).

Muslim women are often easily identifiable because many of them wear a *hijab*, a traditional Islamic head covering worn by women (Wessler 2002). Because of this visible indication of their faith, they are often accosted, yelled at, and sometimes physically assaulted. One young woman reported, "I was so afraid [on 9/11] because one guy he was like, um . . . late adulthood and he tried to hit us and said "take this shit off" and I was so afraid I took my *hijab* off because I was afraid I was going to get killed" (Hallak and Quina 2004, 331). Ebrahim notes that their organization in the United Kingdom received numerous e-mails in the fall of 2001 from women in the United States worrying about violence because of their decision to wear a *hijab* (2001). The CPHV study found many Muslim women who wear a *hijab* "reacted to the risk of being victims of hateful and degrading conduct by staying in their homes" (Wessler 2002, 6).

Backlash from wearing ethnic clothing was not limited to Muslim women, as many non-Muslim South Asian women also became afraid to wear traditional clothing such as *sari* and *salwar kameez*. For example, Sakhi reported that all of the survivors at a support group meeting in October 2001 chose to dress in Western clothes. Many of these survivors would often wear South Asian clothes but chose not to wear them in the wake of September 11. Shah explained that the women were attempting to look American out of fear of the post-9/11 backlash.

For South Asian, Arab, and Muslim victims of domestic violence, the world outside their homes became a violent place after September 11, just as their homes continued to be violent. Many women have hesitated to report domestic violence in the years since the terror attacks out of fear that they would be greeted with responses similar to those they had encountered on the streets (Childress 2003). In a *Newsweek* article, Nora Alarifi Pharoan, a psychologist with the Arab American Family Support Center in Brooklyn explained that even before September 11, many Muslim and Arab women were unwilling to report their abuse because of cultural issues, the acceptance of patriarchy, and the notion that help-seeking and counseling are Western ways not appropriate for their communities. However, Pharoan claimed that after September 11, many women who might have considered reporting their abuse were afraid of law enforcement and federal officials threatening arrest and deportation (Childress 2003).

Obstacles Faced by South Asian, Arab, and Muslim Victims of Domestic Violence

Many immigrant victims of domestic violence do not report their abuse out of fear that they will be deported or become entangled in the immigration legal system (Cowen 1998; Thompson 1999). This fear was heightened after September 11 as immigration officials began increased enforcement and deportation of individuals in certain immigrant communities (Wessler 2002).[2]

In post-9/11 America, many South Asian, Arab, and Muslim victims of domestic violence faced prejudice as they sought relief from their abusive relationships (Nagpaul 2005). Some women faced instances of subtle bias and the inability of people outside their communities to adequately understand South Asian, Arab, and Muslim cultures. Others were confronted with the popular assumption that their men were inherently violent while they were inherently meek and submissive; or that they themselves were complicit in some sort of suspicious activities because of their ethnicity (Nagpaul 2005).

For instance, a Pakistani woman in a shelter in New York City faced verbal abuse by her housemates soon after the September 11 attacks. The shelter residents had gathered for their support group and used the opportunity to personally attack the Pakistani resident by demanding to know "how her country could support terrorism" and "how she could condone the loss of so many innocent lives." What was most troubling about this episode was that the shelter employees did not intervene in this discussion and allowed the verbal attack to continue. It is important to note that while such cultural, racial, and social barriers were not created by September 11, they gained greater visibility due to the nation's intensified awareness of South Asian, Arab, and Muslim communities.

The language barrier many South Asian, Arab, and Muslim women routinely struggle with was also exacerbated by September 11, as Arabic and other South Asian languages became viewed as indicators of criminal acts; thus, prompting some community members not to speak in their native tongues in public.[3] For example, many Arabs have been reported to law enforcement because a deliveryman or postal service worker overheard them conversing in Arabic (American Civil Liberties Union 2004; Cable News Network 2002; Iyer 2003). In the mass hysteria since September 11, speaking in Arabic or languages that may be mistaken as Arabic has been enough in many cases to justify the investigation, detention, and deportation of individuals (Iyer 2003).[4]

As language was criminalized, women, who conversed primarily in Arabic or South Asian languages, were silenced by a nation who viewed their speech as inherently suspicious. Many South Asian, Arab, and Muslim victims of domestic violence, therefore, became even less likely to report any abuse to police or seek language translators out of fear that simply speaking in Arabic to a law enforcement official would make them suspects of terrorism. In addition, women who spoke in Arabic or South Asian languages feared seeking outside help or support because of the fear that the outside world was at war with them.[5]

However, attorney Nooria Faizi explains that the language issue is not the only inhibitor for Muslim victims of domestic violence. "Many Muslims do not believe that the Western system is suited to solve their problems. . . . [E]ven when there are no language barriers, many Muslim women will not be open with non-Muslims about their domestic problems" (Faizi 2001, 218). Faizi explains that Muslim women sometimes worry about non-Muslims, who might not be able to understand their culture and worry about the ability to relate to other non-Muslim shelter residents.

The problem is common in South Asian victims of domestic violence from other communities (Abraham 2000b).

Critical Race Analysis: Understanding
Battered Women's Revictimization

Critical Race theorists explain how women of color are victimized because they are both the oppressed race and the oppressed gender. Consequently, women of color often feel their loyalties are split and they must choose to identify with and protect either their race or gender (Crenshaw 1997).[6] For example, an immigrant South Asian woman might not want to report an abusive husband out of fear that he will be detained and deported. Similarly, an African American woman might not want to report her abusive husband out of fear that he will be imprisoned and mistreated by law enforcement (Crenshaw 1997). Women of color worry about their loyalties to their cultures and the impression that a domestic violence offense may have on a prejudiced society. As a result, they might not report their abuse or seek divorces from their abusers. In a study that examined South Asian, African American, and Hispanic battered women, researchers found that many of the South Asian women worried not only about the shame and negative social implications that a divorce would bring on their family, but also how a divorce would make the South Asian community look in relation to other ethnic and racial groups in the United States (Yoshioka et al. 2003).

Adrien Katherine Wing, law professor at the University of Iowa, explains that women of color often internalize their dual oppression because they are devalued by the outside society of the racial oppressor, the internal society of their culture, and the intimate context of their families (1997). The result of this internalization is the decision for some women of color not to report abuse, as they pick their loyalties. Women of color abuse victims, "would not even think of going to outsiders, i.e., the police or other officials, to seek relief from repressive practices or to report their own men for abuse. This would make women collaborators or traitors. Thus, they suffer in silence, perhaps unaware of the 'patriarchal bargain' they have made in their own subordination" (Wing 1997, 952).

Similarly, South Asian, Arab, and Muslim women are torn between the allegiances to their race, ethnic community, family, and gender. After September 11, patriotic nationalism in the United States projected the message that you are either with "us" or you are with "them" (Perlez 2001). South Asian, Arab, and Muslim women, who felt as though American people perceived them as decidedly not one of "us," have been hesitant to report instances of abuse out of a fear that the nation was at war with their ethnic group. As a result, victims of domestic violence were trapped between wanting to live an abuse-free life within their homes and not wanting to betray their people by reporting another "wife-beater."

Wing also explains how many men of color (or men of any oppressed group) are emasculated within the majority society and therefore some assert their dominance on women of color as a means of retaining their manhood. "The only sphere where 'emasculated' men can take out their frustration is the private one affecting women and children" (Wing 1997, 951). Consequently, some men engage in violent attacks on women within their homes, again resulting in the dual victimization of women of color. For instance, there was a speculated rise in domestic violence within Muslim communities after 9/11. A potential reason for the abuse could be that Muslim men felt emasculated and oppressed by American society and therefore took their anger out on Muslim women as a way of reasserting their gender dominance (Childress 2003).

The idea of dominating women to gain legitimacy and power is not a new notion. Some black nationalists in the 1970s viewed domination over women as the only way to reach equality with the white race. For example, Eldridge Cleaver, one of the founding members of the Black Panther Party, was arrested and jailed for raping several black and white women. Cleaver explained that he wanted to rape white women as a way of asserting his dominance over the white race and practiced on black women in preparation (Cleaver 1968). Huey P. Newton, another founding member of the Black Panther Party, explained that many black males "want to hit the woman or shut her up because we are afraid that she might castrate us, or take the nuts that we might not have to start with" (Newton 1972, 152). While Newton did not advocate abusing women, he acknowledged that some black men felt threatened by women, which deterred them from treating women as political and revolutionary equals. Although made a number of years ago, Newton's statement is an example of the tensions between gender and racial power struggles and is reflective of this imbalance in society.

Similarly, Wing uncovered some undertones of threatened masculinity in her comparative analysis of black South African and Palestinian men (Wing 1997). She found that although apartheid had officially ended, a significant number of black South African men were unable to find jobs, and when they did find jobs they were often working for non-black employers. Simultaneously, there was a significant number of rape and domestically violent acts perpetrated against black South African women by black South African men. Wing argues that black South African men felt emasculated by the invasion of their land by whites and took their frustration out on women. Consequently, South African women were abused on multiple levels, both internally in their families and externally by a society that still exhibited significant racism (Wing 1997).

Palestinian men living under occupation experienced a similar type of emasculation (Albina 2003; Wing 1997). Wing found high rates of domestic violence in Palestine but admits that it was hard to obtain legitimate numbers because so much was still unreported (Alexander 2000; Wing 1997).[7] One domestic violence provider in the Gaza Strip reported, "Men have a lot of aggression and very few channels for ventilating it. . . . Men . . . use women to ventilate" (Wing 1997, 964). There have been reports that in attempts to mimic their oppressors, Palestinian men have used Israeli torture techniques on their wives. In one case, a Palestinian man, who had been recently released from prison, "covered his wife's head with a sack and beat her with pipes and cable" (Wing 1997, 964).

Several parallels can be drawn between the situations of South Africans and Palestinians and that of South Asian, Arab, and Muslim men in America after September 11. In both South Africa and Palestine, men of color are criminalized to such an extent that officials assume men of color are inherently involved in illegal activities (Bernstein 2004; Foderaro 2004). After September 11, South Asian, Arab, and Muslim men in America were immediately looked upon in suspicion and distrust. This presumption of guilt instantaneously made these men criminals regardless of their actions or characters (Ahmad 2004).

For instance, immediately after September 11, thousands of South Asian, Arab, and Muslim men were rounded up and detained for an indefinite period of time. Although only one detainee was ever formally charged with a crime and those charges were eventually dropped, many were detained on minor immigration violations, while others were held on suspicions of criminal activity (American Civil Liberties Union 2004). A 2002 report by the Office of the Inspector General found that many of the detainees experienced severe physical and sexual abuse while in prison (Office of the Inspector General 2005). It is possible that the aggression and emasculation these detained men experienced contributed to the increase of violence against women in their households.

It is worth noting that much of the aggression by white males that manifested in the form of hate crimes against South Asians, Arabs, and Muslims following September 11 was also an expression of masculinity. Ahmad (2004) claimed that the post–September 11 culture emphasized honor, loyalty, and betrayal, which ultimately became imprinted on the nation's psyche and was internalized by individuals seeking to protect the sanctity and safety of America. He argued that "post–September 11 violence constituted an attempt to protect male honor, which in turn helps to explain how violence against South Asians, Arabs, and Muslims has been normalized" (1270). As white males exerted their dominance and masculinity on South Asians, Arabs, and Muslims, some men from these communities, in turn, exerted their dominance and masculinity on women within their homes (Childress 2003).

Similar to the black South African and Palestinian communities, many South Asians, Arabs, and Muslims faced extreme economic hardship due to the mass deportation of male members of these communities. A new federal immigration policy called "Special Registration" resulted in over 82,000 South Asian, Arab, and Muslim men registering with the U.S. government (American Civil Liberties Union 2004). Of these individuals, 13,000 were deported, many for minor immigration violations and the inability to comprehend the complex provisions of the registration policy (American Civil Liberties Union 2004; Swarns 2003; Swarns and Drew 2003). The result of these mass deportations has wreaked economic devastation on women, as the male members in these communities, often the primary breadwinners, were no longer able to provide for their families. Neighborhoods with a majority population of South Asians, Arabs, and Muslims were empty as thousands of men, who were shopkeepers and restaurant owners, were suddenly deported (Swarns 2003; Swarns and Drew 2003).

The tremendous loss of the male figure within these communities scared many women and made them grateful to have any male companion at all, despite instances of abuse. Studies show that economic sustenance is a primary reason why women stay in abusive relationships (Buel 1999). After September 11, South Asian, Arab, and Muslim women feared not only economic hardship but also prosecution for immigration violations, indefinite detention, and abuse by law enforcement officials.

Concluding Remarks

After the attacks of September 11, the United States' attention was focused on terrorism, al Qaeda, and Osama bin Laden. The safety of the nation was a primary concern; yet, the safety of the South Asian, Arab, and Muslim communities was not considered, nor was the safety of women, who faced violence both inside and outside their homes. While there are some who may argue that the United States had greater concerns to deal with, the reality is that Americans prioritized whose safety they chose to protect and whose safety was dispensable. South Asian, Arab, and Muslim communities were low on the totem pole of American safety concerns, and domestic violence victims within these communities were even a step lower.

However, individuals can make a difference by acknowledging these complex issues, educating themselves about these cultures, and examining the motives behind exclusionary actions. It is crucial to engage in outreach with the South Asian, Arab, and Muslim communities and acknowledge that they, too, are in need of protection and deserve to live violence-free lives. Only after demonstrating solidarity with the South Asian, Arab, and Muslim communities will trust and equal understanding be gained to engage in outreach to domestic violence victims who experience terrorism in their daily lives.

DEDICATION

For Ba and Nanima

NOTES

1.   This is not a definitive statement, as some Muslim women did report their abuse. Hadayai Majeed, network coordinator of the Baitul Salaam shelter for Muslim women in Atlanta, Georgia, stated that while many Muslim women were afraid to report their abuse, others sought the opportunity to finally seek help and escape their abusers. Majeed claimed that these women were often the victims of the most serious and severe forms of physical abuse.

2.   The federal government's crackdown on undocumented immigrants, entitled Operation Compliance, focused intense investigatory tactics on foreign nationals from countries with suspected ties to al Qaeda. See http://region.princeton.edu/issue_35.html.

3.   Author's personal experience.

4.   See Janofsky and Chen (2001) for an example of the scrutiny of written Arabic in mail.

5.   Majeed points out that some Muslim victims of domestic violence sought help after 9/11 because they realized that while the United States had an anti-Muslim sentiment, it was largely directed at Muslim men and not women. Majeed explains that many victims of severe abuse, therefore, took this opportunity to seek help, when they had not done so before.

6.   Kimberle Crenshaw explains how male members of a community often define racism, much in the same manner as white women define sexism. "Because women of color experience racism in ways not always the same as those experienced by men of color and sexism in ways not always parallel to experiences of white women, antiracism and feminism are limited, even on their own terms" (Crenshaw 1997, 1252).

7.   "Violence against women in Gaza basically means domestic violence," says research consultant Aitemad Muhanna. "Women are beaten by their husbands, beaten by their fathers, and even beaten by their brothers. Women are beaten for not fulfilling traditional roles such as cooking, cleaning, and tending to their appearance to a husband's satisfaction. Other abuses include harsh insults, sexual abuse in family, and marital rape" (Alexander 2000).

PART TWO

The Wounded Body

Emerging Issues in
Domestic Violence Work

6

Mental and Emotional Wounds of Domestic Violence in South Asian Women

DIYA KALLIVAYALIL

Despite the growing literature on domestic violence in the South Asian immigrant community, research has not yet focused on the psychological outcomes of family violence on women of South Asian origin in the United States. Mainstream literature indicates that the psychological corollaries of being a survivor of domestic violence are extremely severe and long lasting, and cites depression, anxiety, posttraumatic stress disorder, and suicide as the most significant of these outcomes (e.g., Jones, Hughes and Unterstaller 2001). Given the lack of research in this area, however, it remains a theoretical and empirical question whether such diagnoses and attempts at traditional forms of assessment will prove to be meaningful to the South Asian immigrant population. This, in turn, has implications for the provision of a range of support services to this group.

Using in depth interviews with two South Asian survivors of domestic violence, this chapter addresses the challenges that may be involved in gaining information on personal psychological outcomes with this population. The interviews indicate that South Asian women are more likely to mobilize more familiar forms of discourses such as cultural and pragmatic, rather than that of mental and emotional health and suffering to discuss their abuse experiences. The essay also presents information from South Asian mental health practitioners to suggest that the power of such cultural and pragmatic mobilizations reflect their acceptability and use in the larger South Asian community as opposed to the aura of silence, stigma, and lack of prioritization that exists around both domestic violence and mental health issues. These popular discourses make the processes of gaining information and treatment more challenging. I conclude by arguing that greater efforts must be made by practitioners and members of the community to prioritize mental health issues among survivors of domestic violence.

Mental Health Issues in the South Asian American Community

Despite the growing literature on intimate abuse in the South Asian community, little work has been done to examine the psychological outcomes of domestic violence on women of South Asian origin in the United States. This may be due to a "double silence" in the community on issues of both domestic violence and mental health; certainly any attempt to develop a discourse on the relationship between the two might engender additional obstacles. Since the silence on domestic violence in the community has been well documented by other researchers (see, e.g., George and Rahangdale 1999; Nankani 2000; Preisser 1999), I will instead address what the literature indicates about attitudes in the community toward mental health.

The literature on South Asian Americans and mental health is meager (Das and Kemp 1997; Durvasula and Mylvaganam 1994). There are two separate but closely linked issues in this regard, on which little empirical data exist: community attitudes toward mental illness and community attitudes toward mental health services. A few recently published works have attempted to develop theoretical frameworks on these topics, presumably to assist in developing culturally competent therapeutic practices, and reflects themes of silence and shame in the community discourse on mental health issues. For example, Durvasula and Mylvaganam (1994) show that recent studies document the shame and stigma attached to mental illness in India, and since most Indians have immigrated to the United States in the last thirty years, they are likely to "have retained some traditional Indian beliefs about mental illness" (101).

Further, the research that does exist suggests that South Asians in the United States have negative impressions of psychological counseling and in general under-utilize mental health services (Durvasula and Mylvaganam 1994; Johnson and Nadirshaw 1993). Das and Kemp (1997) identify three major veins of explanations for this phenomenon: first, the so-called model minority myth. Many members of the South Asian community have achieved financial success in the United States, and scholars argue that members of the community are preoccupied with maintaining cultural integrity and cohesion, as well as a positive image to the outside world (Bhattacharjee 1992; Dasgupta 2000b; Prashad 2000). This effort ensures a certain amount of denial of "unpleasant" issues such as mental illness. Second, research also documents a "cultural proscription" that inhibits South Asians from discussing intimate problems and emotional difficulties with anyone outside the family, because the family is viewed as the major and most appropriate support structure for individuals (Das and Kemp 1997; Tewari, Inman, and Sandhu 2003). Lack of awareness and education about the complex dimensions of mental health problems may have led to a stigmatization of psychopathology in the community and the view that seeking counseling is a sign that a person is insane. As a result, the acknowledgment of such issues may stigmatize the person seeking counseling and his or her family (Das and Kemp 1997).

This is a particularly salient issue for survivors of domestic violence, because being labeled or diagnosed, even with good intentions, may undermine a woman's credibility in the community at large and the legal system when fighting for custody of children. There is the very real risk of turning protest to pathology by mental health professionals' focusing on the internal emotional problems of women, rather than the larger patriarchal structures that maintain and condone violence

(Davar 1999). However, minimizing the psychological problems that result from domestic violence may also be oppressive and prevent women and children from seeking needed help.

Finally, the literature indicates that the western model of individual psychotherapy can be unfamiliar and threatening to members of the South Asian community (Durvasula and Mylvaganam 1994; Preisser 1999), suggesting that goals such as individual self-actualization and self-disclosure could be foreign to people of South Asian origin, as the culture minimizes the importance of any particular individual in the family. There appears to be a relationship between degrees of acculturation and seeking professional help. In her study of help-seeking behaviors, Sheikh (2001) found in a sample of Indians and Pakistanis in the United States that acculturation tends to have a positive impact on seeking mental health help. However, many South Asians continue to utilize nonpsychological options such as family members, primary care physicians, and community religious leaders rather than mental health professionals for treatment and relief of emotional or mental health problems (Das and Kemp 1997; Lloyd 1992).

These research conclusions were also supported by the anecdotal experiences of South Asian mental health practitioners who work in the field of domestic violence and acknowledge the pressing need for attention to mental health issues with this population. For example, a South Asian social worker who works at a community mental health agency in a metropolitan area with a large proportion of South Asian clients shared with me her strategy to combat the stigma attached to domestic violence and mental illness and engage South Asian clients:

> One of the things we have been doing is outreach, going out to shops to put up flyers about our agency and the work we're doing and the main thing is to create awareness about domestic violence and substance abuse but as we've realized, we're not bringing up that topic so openly, we're saying we're helping children, other things. So it's not a very easy topic to talk about. Because if you talk to [members of the community] about it, they will say, "No, *esa tho kuch nahi hai* (there's nothing like that)."

Another South Asian social worker, who works with South Asian substance abusers at a mental health agency in a large metropolitan area, addressed the stigma prevalent in the community:

> Mental health, people do not want to acknowledge it. It's an issue that should be kept in the closet; you don't speak about it. With South Asians in particular, it adds to it because of the culture that everything should stay in the family. No one should know about it. Very much like victims of domestic violence. The husband may have hit the wife and she will tell all sorts of lies about that. What happened? I fell; I banged my head against the cabinet. Definitely, there's denial. With South Asian families, one of the major issues is shame.

Purpose of Study

The in-depth narrative interviews referred to in this chapter were conducted with battered South Asian women as part of an ongoing project on the mental health consequences of domestic violence among women of South Asian origin in the United States. South Asian practitioners who work in the field of domestic violence were also interviewed about their experiences of working in mental health within the community. Using two case examples of women and the perspectives of practitioners, I will discuss the challenges and implications for intervention and reflect on the values of the South Asian community with respect to mental health.

Methodology

Given the findings that mental health is not an openly addressed issue in the South Asian community, I developed a number of strategies within the interview context to approach the topic in an indirect way, staying open to the complex subjectivities such an encounter was bound to draw. This approach guided all aspects of the process, beginning with the consent forms I asked the participants to sign before the interviews commenced. However, the forms did not use the term "mental health" or any other uncolloquial or professionalizing term.

Similarly, the interview protocol moved very gradually toward the topic of emotional difficulties, giving the participants time to first discuss their backgrounds and experiences in their marriages before delving into more specific issues of emotional distress and coping. The questions on suffering and help seeking were very much blended into the larger frame of the interview. The structure of the protocol was not rigid; when important issues arose, they were explored. All the questions were open ended.

The participants were recruited through a mental health agency in a large metropolitan area that serves the South Asian immigrant community. The women agreed to participate in the study voluntarily. The methodology for this project involved a qualitative interview (described above) along with a more structured psychological assessment to examine the relationship between gender, suffering, and psychological outcomes with women who have survived domestic violence. The in-depth interview was conducted with each participant to learn about her family and immigration history, class and educational background, marriage experiences, the severity and kinds of abuse she had faced (e.g., physical, sexual, emotional, financial), and how she explained the abuse. The interview also examined the idioms of suffering that women used, as well as their descriptions of the mental and physical problems they experienced. This information was critical in assessing the extent to which local metaphors and symptoms of suffering map onto traditional categories of mental health. The next part of the interview involved a more formal psychological assessment using a clinician-administered tool, the Structured Clinical Interview (SCID) of the Diagnostic and Statistical Manual of Mental Disorders IV (DSM-IV), to obtain a clinical picture of both past and present symptoms and diagnoses. I personally conducted all the interviews with the women. I also interviewed mental health workers who serve South Asians to assess their experiences with mental health and domestic violence issues in the community.

Results

An Overview of Mental Health Outcomes of Domestic Violence

Given the lack of mental health research on South Asian immigrant survivors of family violence, what could we expect in terms of outcomes of surviving violence? The mainstream literature may serve as an initial guide. Research that has primarily focused on white American women identifies (in addition to extremely severe medical injuries), depression, post-traumatic stress disorder (PTSD), anxiety, panic attacks, and suicide as the significant mental health outcomes of domestic violence (e.g., Jones et al. 2001). It also indicates cognitive distortions (including memory distortion and loss), the disruption of relationships, and feelings of worthlessness and self-blame as common outcomes of experiencing intimate trauma (Gleason 1993; Walker 1984).

Scrutiny of the research on typical human responses to personal assault (whether or not the attack is initiated by an intimate partner) indicates that often victims initially experience shock, denial, and confusion, and may be unable to react to the trauma (Chapman 1962; Herman 1992). When the abuse is chronic, as is the case with domestic violence, victims may consider their options for coping and safety. This process may reduce externally visible activity, sometimes giving the impression that the victim is apathetic (Withey 1962). Research reviewed by Koss and her colleagues (Koss et al. 1994) indicates that abused women's psychological responses to violence parallel that of survivors from a cross section of other traumatic events. For example, their initial reactions appear to be focused on self-protection and survival and often include shock, denial, psychological numbing, and fear (Browne 1987; Kerouac and Lescop 1986). Walker's (1979) in-depth study of more than 120 abused women reveal that most report low self-esteem, depression, severe stress reactions, helplessness, and physical complaints.

There is also evidence that such symptoms manifest differently after a while. Over time and chronic abuse, women may experience sleeping and eating disturbances, nightmares, physical complaints, and difficulty in planning, and/or making decisions (Herman 1992). Women who were the most severely battered suffer very high levels of distress, including a sense of danger, flashbacks and memories, and suicidal thoughts (Browne 1987). Compounding these reactions are often feelings of betrayal, loss, and vulnerability when women realize that someone they love and were supposed to rely on and trust is attacking them (Browne 1991; Walker 1979).

Some recent work has focused on international contexts (see summary by Fischbach and Herbert 1997) and indicates the severity of the psychological impact of domestic violence in diverse populations. A study conducted with ninety abused women in south India found constant tension/anxiety, feelings of shame, guilt and alienation, insomnia, and severe emotional trauma to be the health consequences of abuse (Panchanadeswaran and Koverola 2005). Over half the women in this study also reported suicidal thoughts and/or attempts.

However, the major researchers and practitioners in the area of South Asian domestic violence acknowledge the lack of research on mental health outcomes with South Asian immigrant women in the United States (e.g., M. Abraham, personal communication, October 25, 2002; S. D. Dasgupta, personal communication, April 30, 2003). A South Asian psychiatrist working in a community mental health agency in the United States indicated the high rates of depression and PTSD among abused South Asian immigrant women, based on anecdotal evidence (R. Boppana, personal communication, November 6, 2002). In addition, Sakhi for South Asian women, a New York—based domestic violence agency, conducted an informal survey in their health clinic and found that many women reported symptoms of depression. Unquestionably, gaining a better understanding of the mental health effects of abuse for South Asian women is an essential step in providing these women with appropriate intervention.

Western Tools and Techniques: A Cultural Psychology Approach

An added layer of complexity in the process of psychological assessment is the potential ethnocentric bias that comes with evaluating and treating mental disorders initially identified in the West with culturally different populations. According to Kleinman (1980), explanatory models or beliefs about illness and treatment are community specific. For example, researchers have examined the psychiatric relevance of descriptions of "sinking heart," an experience of heart distress in Punjabi communities (Krause 1989), and "thinking too much in the heart," as a description of feelings given by South Asian women (Fenton and Sadiq-Sangster 1996). As Gone (2001) has persuasively argued, examining locally situated conceptions of "disorder" is incomplete without acknowledging that they follow from locally defined ideas of "order." The study of local conceptualizations of mental disorders is important in privileging local knowledge and leaves open the exploration of whether these conceptions connect to traditional notions of symptomology in a meaningful way. This approach had significance for my project, as I sought to evaluate emotional states while paying attention to the linguistic, social, and community dimensions of affective experience.

Marsella, Friedman, Gerrity, and Scurfield (1996) suggest that there is ethnocultural variation in the expression and phenomenology of PTSD and, presumably, all clinical disorders. They argue that the biological, psychological, and social aspects of clinical disorders are culturally defined because they are influenced by local conceptions of health, disease, definitions and attitudes toward trauma, and concepts of abnormality. Also, symptoms of distress exist in the context of the ongoing stress of acculturation as well. Finally, although physical and psychological distress may be experienced individually, it often arises from and is resolved in a social context. The presence of such symptoms and being labeled may serve in isolating women from their community. Therefore, traumatic events may result in immediate and long-term negative consequences for individuals, families, and communities.

Examining the importance of local/religious metaphors and understandings of suffering is also an attempt to capture the vast diversity in the South Asian community. However, despite this variability, people of varied South Asian descent appear to be perceived similarly by the outside world as well as helping agencies. The reality of living in an immigrant community provides many similar material experiences for women, such as racism and legal dependency. I contend that it is this perceived similarity, beyond actual individual and group differences, that is a powerful influence on South Asian women's experiences.

Uncovering Mental and Emotional Histories

My experiences of interviewing women indicated a challenging path to uncovering issues of mental health and emotional coping. In the narratives of the interviews, it seemed that women displayed a certain level of familiarity (which is not to say comfort) with recounting their background and abuse histories. This may be because by the time they spoke with me, they had all negotiated varying aspects and levels of the system, including the legal, medical, welfare, and at times, the mental health system. So, women were used to being asked about their age, the current status of their marriage, their abuse history, the number (if any) of order of protections they had obtained, and other demographic and legal information, and were able to address these questions directly and in some cases, without even being asked. For example, one woman, Gayatri (a pseudonym, as are names of all survivors), began the interview by talking about her divorce and child custody battles before these questions were directly asked. Despite what I told them what the interview was generally about (i.e., emotional difficulties), the participants often seemed puzzled by the nature of (and perhaps motivation behind) my questions regarding physical and emotional problems or concerns. A psychiatrist working with this population confirmed this observation. She indicated that her clients were not used to being asked questions about their feelings and did not always understand some of the routine assessment questions placed to them.

It was not that the women simply did not answer specific questions, or that information on mental health was impossible to gain. At times, women volunteered some aspects of this information. In most cases, when I began to ask them the more structured and specific questions of the SCID, women answered the questions more succinctly and directly (it is worth mentioning that the SCID is an alarmingly thick and somewhat intimidating document). In general, however, the experience of interviewing indicated that women mobilized at least two distinct but closely related discourses about their experiences: one was contextual and reflected the material or concrete realities of the difficulties they faced, and the other reflected a cultural discourse, or what I have come to see as a master narrative of domestic violence in this community. In other words, women seemed more comfortable describing and instrumentally using notions of traditionalism and cultural norms, or focusing on their day-to-day pragmatic difficulties to explain their experiences, regardless of the nature of the interview questions. An example of the latter strategy is what one woman articulated when I asked her if she had been sad in the past few months, saying she had "no time to worry about feeling sad with five kids."

The use of a cultural discourse within which to think about domestic violence and the role and inevitability of marriage was even more common. This was clear not just from the interviews with women, but also from practitioners and other professionals with whom these women interacted. A psychiatrist who worked with the South Asian immigrant community in a community mental health agency said, "I would say there definitely are some cultural characteristics associated with South Asian culture, it tends to be paternalistic. Women very often are encouraged to keep quiet, whatever problems they may have, for the sake of face or the way [that] the family looks, they have to deal with things on their own." The mobilization of such a discourse in research and professional contexts and also in the larger community may thus work to frame what is important to talk about and consider, which is, in turn, reflected in women's own representations of their experiences. This may sometimes overshadow narratives of emotional distress. My interview with Aditi is in some ways representative of the use of an iconic vocabulary of culture, especially as it relates to family and marriage.

Aditi is a woman in her early thirties from India. She moved to the United States with her parents when she was about fifteen. Her father ran a store and she remembers her transition into the U.S. school system as difficult because she spoke no English. Despite this, she eventually made friends and became proficient in English. She went on to college, but dropped out when her parents arranged a marriage for her to a man from India. Aditi sponsored him to come to the United States. She has two daughters and has never worked outside the home. Aditi reported that her husband had never physically assaulted her, but that once his parents moved in with them from India, he did not offer her any support or protection when they emotionally tortured her. She did not label his behavior as emotional abuse, although at times during the interview she expressed how scared she was to live in their home. She also said that she felt devastated because the situation had degenerated to the point of her husband wanting a divorce.

Throughout the interview, Aditi referred to and articulated ideas about culture and its impact on marriage and family, choices (or lack thereof), and subsequent difficulties, in a manner that, perhaps unwittingly, diverted attention from her subjective emotional experiences and decisions. For example, when I asked her to describe the experience of how she got married, she said, "In our culture when the girls get certain age, they get married, you know? So, my father and my mother they were looking for somebody. It was time, you know? I didn't know I was going to get married, sometimes you don't know, you know?"

Here, Aditi used the culture argument as an explanation for how her marriage was decided/arranged and her lack of involvement in the process. By "culture," it is unclear if she meant her own state, community, or India in general. She implied that I (being a South Asian myself) understood the background to what she was saying. She also implied that there is a time for getting married that people are aware of and which applies more to girls. That is, there is a natural stage of life progression at which girls "get" married. Aditi seemed to have endorsed and internalized this notion. When I asked her about physical or emotional problems or reactions, she addressed my questions briefly, but did not focus on them (although she cried, sometimes breaking down completely, for most of the interview), preferring instead to discuss concrete family issues of the past and future.

Q: And since you started having problems, have you had any problems like sleeping, headaches?

A: Yeah, I'm sleeping less. I cry a lot.

Q: And in your mind, what worries you or makes you sad?

A: I don't know what's going to happen to my future, you know . . . because he told me three times about the divorce thing [*sobs*] and now, in my mind it's always, I don't know, this is his parents' work; oh, we are not going to leave, we are going to become here citizens [*sobs*]. They have two sons and one more daughter, actually they have two daughters but she ran away; so there's a lot in my mind. My husband once time told me when the test [for citizenship] comes, I will give you divorce, and maybe they [his parents] will become citizen so when they become citizen and when my husband finishes his residency, so maybe that time . . . [*breaks down and sobs for several seconds*].

Here, when I asked her questions about being sad, Aditi spoke briefly about her worries but swiftly moved into specifics. She talked about family composition and history including the fact that her in-laws' other child had run away from home and perhaps such a transgression implied that she is no longer considered part of the family, reflecting community discourse on the ideal family and the behavior of its members. She elaborated his parents' strong involvement and imposition in their marriage, whom she blamed for the situation and for the particular form of verbal abuse she suffered. She also seemed to express fear of this residency deadline he placed on her and was approaching it with a sense of doom.

When probing her emotional reactions to the situation, Aditi recounted specific incidents of difficulty or abuse and her immediate reaction with a great amount of detail. However, her descriptions tended to be very context specific and she was less sure of how to think of her emotional reactions to the abuse in more general and decontextualized terms. Indeed, her idea to get some help was spurred on by her husband's initial suggestion that they try marriage counseling. It seemed that her goal was to improve and save her marriage, not necessarily to ameliorate her own distress. Since she did not know what services were available, she approached her primary care physician and told her that she wanted an Indian counselor because she would feel more comfortable with someone who understood her culture and, by extension, her marital situation. Aditi had had limited interactions with white Americans in her life, and it appeared that neither she nor her husband were opposed to marriage counseling per se, but declined going to an American. Aditi's reluctance is, of course, reflected in many South Asian women highlighting the need for community specific services.

Aditi mobilized a keen understanding of such gender issues that she saw as inherent to the community, even when she spoke about her thoughts of death, obliquely referring to suicide. She did not consider death as a reasonable solution to her problems, as she had realized early on the primacy given to male children in her new family, and understood that her daughters' lives would be in graver straits if she were not around to protect them. Thus, she focused on her role as a mother. Concerns for her daughters put her own distress in shadow.

A: Like there is nothing in my life. I have my baby [*sobbing*] what in case if I die? He might go get another woman. My daughters they are going to have problem. So, I don't know what to do.

Q: Do you think about death a lot?

A: Yes, sometimes I do. But right now I'm pregnant you know so [sobs] so I cannot do anything right now because if I die, then two people die and this is a like a little baby and it'll be like sin.

By the time I interviewed her, Aditi had been in therapy for many months. Coming to therapy was the only help-seeking behavior she had executed at the time. Her approach to therapy was very much based on a cultural familiarity she felt with her Indian therapist. It seemed she was glad to have an Indian woman to talk to and seemed less focused on and aware of specific therapeutic issues such as emotional symptoms, psychological reframing, or explanations of her problems. She appeared to see therapy as primarily practical; that is, she has a problem with her marriage and goes for support. The idea of a larger mental health issue within a system of therapy seemed distant to her. Although in the context of the current study, she had received a diagnosis of major depression and generalized anxiety disorder (GAD), words like "therapy" and "diagnosis" did not appear to have much resonance for her. Given her context, meeting with an Indian therapist gave her familiarity, comfort, and strength.

The process of subverting questions about emotional distress to focus on material and immediate problems is well illustrated by my interview with Sonea, a woman from India in her thirties. Sonea moved to the United States with her parents when she was less than ten years old. Her family, which is lower-middle class, arranged her marriage after high school to a much older man. Sonea was not working at the time I met her. Her husband was an alcoholic and abused her physically. She offered that information without prompting but was not forthcoming about the abuse. I asked her about the abuse a number of times in different ways (e.g., did he give you a hard time, did he hit you or harm you?). She responded affirmatively, but would not offer any details or elaboration. I finally asked:

Q: Do you feel you have suffered a lot?

SONEA: Yes, but why think about that? What can I do? This is life. I have to manage with it and my responsibilities.

Sonea was financially stressed and was struggling with public assistance and public housing. While I was asking questions about her sleep and health, she interrupted many times asking for advice and information on services she can access, including how long Section 8 housing takes to come through. She did not report any physical difficulties, but said that she worried about her children's financial future. I asked her specifically about sleep, pain, appetite, and health problems, but she denied them all. I also asked the screening and depression questions from the SCID, prefacing them by saying that sometimes people feel sad. She did not endorse any of these statements and stated that she had never been in therapy. Her action against the abuse was to get an order of protection against her husband barring him from the home.

Why was it difficult to elicit this information from Sonea? I believe that if I were her social worker, or had developed a more lasting and trusting relationship with her, she may have eventually confided some difficulties to me. In one sense, Sonea was confiding difficulties to me, just not the kind that I was expecting to hear. She implied that the financial and survival issues trumped the physical and emotional ones, and reflected the professional discourse that I frequently encountered in this regard: therapists taking on a holistic role and helping their clients negotiate a range of material and legal issues. The therapists pointed out to me that it was often unproductive to expect clients to be able to engage wholeheartedly in the therapeutic process as long as there were more pressing and pragmatic concerns. Other South Asian professionals, who worked in the field of domestic violence but were not mental health workers, sometimes expressed a more pointed lack of prioritization of mental health issues, suggesting that the abuse was the problem and if women were assisted with their pragmatic difficulties, mental health needs would not arise. This perspective implied a certain threshold of emotional problems that was only crossed by some battered women, who would then need mental health assistance. This community view is prevalent and may influence women like Sonea to deemphasize their emotional needs. Although certainly not all women develop acute psychiatric disorders as a result of domestic violence since coping varies from case to case, domestic violence has been seen to lead to severe emotional consequences in the mainstream literature and needs to be more closely considered with South Asian women.

Nevertheless, it is unclear whether Sonea's unwillingness to discuss physical and emotional problems was a matter of not acknowledging them as primary or *actually not experiencing them* in some crucial way. In either case, as Veena Das (1995) articulates, "The idea of a reality independent of its description is very difficult to sustain" (31). Was Sonea practiced at not acknowledging her subjective suffering for her children's sake? It also seemed that the words, and perhaps even the concept of suffering and emotional functioning, were not critical issues to her. Perhaps she wondered what my investment in her suffering was. My questions, despite my best efforts to ask them contextually and to elicit her definitions of what she had been through, were still framed within a model of subjective difficulties that were relatively independent of daily events and tolerance. It is worth noting that despite her denials of suffering, Sonea appeared dysphoric and had a very flat affect at the time of the interview. Nonetheless, she was unlikely to receive counseling unless others in the community encouraged her to do so.

Concluding Remarks

In some sense, we could conceive of the path to uncovering the psychological scars of domestic violence as constrained by a productive silence on issues that may play a role in further stigmatizing South Asian women in the community. However, at least part of this path is strewn with mobilizations of other issues that are seen as more significant, both by survivors of violence and by the closely tied practitioner community.

What we could conceive of as emotional difficulties, or, if we dared to label them so, symptoms of a diagnosable condition, were so entwined with women's experiences of abuse and their suffering that they were able to recount specific evocative incidents of difficulty. But when asked about their emotions relatively decontextually, such as "Did you ever have trouble sleeping?" or "Were you worried all the time?" those questions did not always resonate with the women. Further, as evidenced by both Aditi's and Sonea's interviews, women were much more familiar with a larger cultural narrative of the institution of marriage and its inevitability, motherhood, and gender roles, which professionals also articulated. As one South Asian therapist who works with battered women said:

> Actually South Asian culture is a male dominated culture. And if you look at the families and see most of the men are well educated, working, bread earner. And the women are, most of them are housewives and culturally, we [are] taught from the early childhood that we are girls, that we have to be very respectful toward the men because they have such powers. In [the] South Asian culture when girls get married with someone, she got some idea from the parents, this is your husband now, he will be [the] one who will take care of you for all these things, so you have to be very respectful. And once they get married, they have this kind of education that like they have to stick with this man for the life long.

This cultural narrative has deep power and implication for articulations of marital suffering and in many ways indicates a giant leap forward in conceptualizing domestic violence as part of a complex terrain where gender, power, and community interact. However, part of what makes mental and emotional information relatively inaccessible is the very explanatory appeal of this narrative, which gains credence when espoused by the larger professional and community discourse. This also holds true for the emphasis on resolving concrete, pragmatic difficulties. However, if our task is holistic empowerment and recovery, expressions of subjective suffering must be given the space to be articulated.

Recommendations

A crucial step toward prioritization of mental health issues in the South Asian population, both by professionals, including researchers and activists, and by the larger South Asian community, is going beyond the explanatory appeal of gender and marriage discourse that surrounds these issues. Activists and others who do direct work with survivors of violence should consider and not deemphasize the potential need for therapeutic assistance and make appropriate referrals, as many women simply do not know where to go for help. This consideration will work against the stigma and silence that surrounds these issues. Therapists also need to be more vigilant in obtaining mental health information, as the process is often challenged by other narratives and needs. It is also worth mentioning that there is a stereotype prevalent in the community that if women go to therapy they have a severe mental health problem. However, many survivors of domestic violence derive support and understanding from the process of therapy that have been denied to them in other contexts.

Finally, given the literature on mental health, domestic violence, and the anecdotal experiences of practitioners, it is important that we in the community do not take part in a secondary victimization of battered women and their children by downplaying their emotional needs and sufferings. Not only is this approach unfounded in the literature, but in the worst-case scenario it could potentially be dangerous for women and their children. Pragmatic needs must be addressed, but denial of emotional needs is part of the stigma attached to mental health issues in the South Asian community. It may imply that women who need help are weak and thus may affect their help-seeking behavior. This chapter indicates how expressions of coping are influenced by community discourse, and a change in the larger community language could lead to healthier and more holistic outcomes for battered women and, by extension, the community.

ACKNOWLEDGMENTS

The research for this chapter was supported by University of Illinois Research Board, the Marianne Ferber Dissertation Award from the Women's Studies Program at the University of Illinois at Urbana-Champaign, and the Bardwell Memorial Research Fellowship from Mount Holyoke College. I thank my adviser, Sumie Okazaki; my dissertation committee members, Nancy Abelman, Nicole Allen, Manisha Desai, and Louise Fitzgerald; and the women who shared their lives with me.

7

Fragmented Self

Violence and Body Image among South Asian American Women

V. G. JULIE RAJAN

Eating disorders are one of the least visible and thereby least examined forms of violence experienced by women in the South Asian American community. However, the invisibility of eating disorders does not indicate its absence among South Asians. As more women of the South Asian diaspora are willing to discuss openly their challenges with body images and food, they are helping to raise the community's consciousness about eating disorders and the ways in which these disorders reflect the exacerbation of existing and initiation of new forms of gender violence in the community. Through a cultural and theoretical framework, this chapter assesses the identity politics circumscribing South Asian women's relations to food and body image in America.

Roots of South Asian Femininity

Whether they are members of the first- or second-generation immigrant groups, South Asians, male and female alike, are influenced by the traditions of their society.[1] Primarily, the culture's impact is rooted in the principles of shame and honor, which demand the subjection of individual desires in favor of those of the family and the larger community. This framework affects myriad social constrictions in order to stabilize patriarchal moral norms, which consistently privilege the agency and value of men over women in all processes such as social, political, economic, and religion. For example, in cultural parameters of shame and honor, any attention to the self is likely to incur a stigma of shame and weakness, whereas those who sacrifice for the larger community are viewed as strong and proper, and therefore worthy of respect. Furthermore, shame visited upon an individual is inevitably reflected onto all members of the person's family. Consequently, individuals in South Asian societies are expected to resolve their personal problems without displaying any need for assistance from outside (Waters 1999). Additionally, psychiatric treatments, or "talking through one's issues," are considered oddities that are often symbolically associated with immorality, weakness, and disease. Stemming from this logic, South Asian norms assume that there are no problems that cannot be handled privately. Consequently, the notion of individuals displaying problems that they cannot solve is considered abnormal.

As this chapter will underscore, these norms more heavily circumscribe the female gender in the South Asian community. Lata Mani (1993) notes, "Questions of tradition and modernity have, since the nineteenth century, been debated on the literal and figurative bodies of [South Asian] women. . . . It thus comes as no surprise that the burden of negotiating the new world is borne disproportionately by women, whose behavior and desires, real or imagined, become the litmus test for the South Asian community's anxieties or sense of well being" (34). In all patriarchal frameworks, especially in those emphasizing the community's desires over those of the individual, women's agencies are subjugated to those of men. In conservative communities, South Asian females of all ages are expected to defer to male relatives; first, in their natal families, and, second, in their marital families.

From the moment of birth, a South Asian woman's social, political, economic, and spiritual disenfranchisement is rooted in patriarchal mechanisms that require the control of female sexuality. Sonalde Desai (1994) notes how South Asian power structures purporting "seclusion, subservience, and self-denial" have a profound impact on women's subjectivities (16). Although complicated and impacted by layers of economic class and caste, certain basic processes of patriarchal sexual control permeate all class and caste divisions within the broader South Asian community (Pande 2003).

The theoretical beliefs of patriarchy are manifested physically in the community through the medium of the female body. The regulated masculine control of women's bodies (and therefore women's sexuality) allows for the production of consistent moral norms that support the code of shame and honor underscoring South Asian traditions (Desai 1994). Because these beliefs have been associated with South Asian traditions over the centuries, they have gained a symbolic moral significance and credibility that renders them proper and customary. Hence, the subjugation of women, though truly a social process, has attained the representation as being correct and normal in the traditional framework of South Asian society.

Since the well-being of the community is dependent on the proper sexual behavior of South Asian women, a restrictive nexus of shame and honor tempers their sexual expressions. As a means of guarding family honor, for example, certain South Asian families may equate women's observation of physical and social seclusion as a form of proper moral behavior (Desai 1994). The sacrifice of female sexual expression parallels a sacrifice in female agency in society, and, consequently, the social control of women's bodies functions as a core means by which to map social constancy—the moral index of society. The phenomenon of son preference, for example, underscores the links between women's behavior and patriarchal stability. Today, South Asian women across economic classes cater to their society's desire for the production of sons, either by undergoing consecutive abortions until they conceive a male fetus or by committing female infanticide, depending on their class status (Hegde 1999; Rajan 1996; Sen 1990). A 1990 study estimates that 300,000 more girls die every year in India than boys (Desai 1994), and a 1995 United Nations report cites that approximately fifty million females are missing from the Indian population (Rajan 1996). India's latest census survey indicates that the number of girls per 1,000 boys has dropped from 945 in 1991 to 927 in 2001 (Dugger 2001).

Women's willingness to undergo and participate in a process that is detrimental to them individually and collectively attests to not only their low agency in the family unit, immediate and broader communities, and the Indian nation, but also the degree to which women themselves have accepted symbolic slippages between their negative body image and social stability. In her interviews with fifty-four urban, middle-class women in Mumbai and New Delhi, Jyoti Puri (1999) discovered that "what is clear from the narratives on menarche, menstruation, and post-pubertal physical changes, is that the impositions and restrictions enforce a negative perception of womanhood. . . . The social/sexual restrictions shape women's ideas of what it means to be 'respectable woman' " (69).

By buying into social productions underscoring negative representations of their bodies, women are less likely to seek health care measures for themselves, believing it unnecessary (Rao, Levy, and Bhattacharya 2002). Desai (1994) notes, "Women tend to seek help only if an illness is advanced, thereby reducing their chances of surviving it" (55). Women's and society's joint devaluation of women's bodies reinforces a wide range of other patriarchal oppressions that ensure the subjugation of female agency.

Imperialism and Femininity: Color as Aberration

In addition to the community's androcentric parameters, images of femininity among South Asian American women are informed by the racialization of gender norms in postcolonial South Asian and modern-day Western societies. Both cultures are underscored by historical representations of the colonized native woman in Western society.

From the sixteenth century onward, as Western explorers encountered new populaces in foreign lands, their fears centered on the lack of abilities to comprehend and, therefore, accommodate the racial and cultural differences they perceived between themselves and the natives. Eventually, imperialism and a constructed hierarchy of human excellence that facilitated the dominance of non-Western peoples controlled these anxieties concerning new customs and territories.

The human value of all peoples globally was processed through this imperial lens that privileged Western peoples, the colonial center, as the superior model of humanity. Imperial success depended on the ability to define and secure the unquestionable status of that hierarchy. The answer lay in focusing on physical differences, primarily racial, through nineteenth-century studies of scientific racism.

Physical difference offered a permanent means of discerning and establishing otherwise undetectable discrepancies between the humanity of the colonizers and colonized. Racial difference, thus, produced a clear hierarchy of human merit, the increments of which correlated to moral and economic value to the empire. The top of the hierarchy was dominated by the most empowered in the empire, the British male. The value of non-Western lands, peoples, and goods was gauged on the basis of skin color and comprised the middle and bottom of the hierarchy; the races with the darkest skin were linked most closely with the animal kingdom (Loomba 1998). Imperial anxieties were further assuaged by the quantification of new spaces and peoples through maps and census counts, allowing colonialists to unquestionably appropriate, fix, and limit any previously unknown objects and environments into the Western symbolic order (Ashcroft 2001). Ultimately, race allowed for the translation of imperial visions of difference into pathology. Thus, the panoptic gaze rendered simultaneous the darker skins of native peoples and representations of disease and immorality—hence, aberrations of humanity (Gilman 1985).

Whereas this vision exerted over the racial colonial Other allowed for the regulation of the borders of the empire, the same control over Western women allowed for the regulation within the center of the empire, ensuring stability from the inside out. Victorian principles of nineteenth-century England demanded the repression of female sexuality for functional purposes (Foucault 1978). Women's social value became dependent on her ability to produce pure progeny for the empire, to ensure its continuance (Matlock 1995). However, as the British Empire grew, so too did consistent interracial contact between Western women and native men in the colonies, and the increased frequency of such contacts increased likelihood that Western women could produce racially mixed progeny. As a result, additional colonial fears concerning racial difference engendered essentialist views of and a tighter surveillance of Western women's sexual purity.

Western women's sexual agency was further limited by the imperial sexual representations of the native, colonized woman. Nineteenth-century studies in scientific racism unequivocally established black women as the ultimate marker of improper sexuality. Cultural representations of the empire, including artwork and literature bolstered the symbolic link between immorality and sexual depravity of black women and the morality and sexual propriety of white women (Gilman 1985). Hence, the native, colonized woman became the foil for Western, white beauty norms.

The assumptions of morality of white, Western women and the lack of native, colonized women were interpolated through the body of lower-class Western women. The (sexual) surveillance of Western women was class-based, for it was mainly women of the middle and upper classes who were automatically regarded as morally proper and therefore worthy of producing valuable progeny for the state. Women of the lower classes, such as prostitutes, were deemed receptacles of disease. Nineteenth-century studies in scientific racism assessed, quantified, and

compared in detail similarities between the physical aspects of the Western pros-
titute and the native, colonized black women as evidence of improper formula-
tions of the female gender in humanity and as the site of social pollution. Those
disturbing connections between white, Western prostitutes residing in the center
of the empire and native, colonized women on its borders pervaded every space in
the empire, and have been inherited by and integrated into the consciousness of
the postcolonial era, in both the global north and south (Gilman 1985).

Food and Femininity

As Western assumptions of food affect the subjectivity of South Asian American
women, an evaluation of the Western dynamic between food and femininity is
crucial to understanding the impetus behind eating disorders among South Asian
American women. Historically, the symbolism of types of food is rendered synonymous with its culture. Uma Narayan (1997) observes that food is synchronous with
a culture's prestige and social power. From ancient Greek culture to medieval
Christian spiritual practices, the regulation of food consumption was aligned with
Western beliefs concerning a range of acceptable and unacceptable philosophical
and spiritual identities (Bordo 1993). The control of bodily appetites through diet
was synonymous with achieving spiritual excellence (Bordo 1993). Food consumption allowed for the construction of a hierarchical dynamic of social, religious, and
economic merit, which accorded members of the aristocracy or spiritual sects
with human excellence.

Symbolic slippage between human value and food consumption underscore
patriarchal processes reinforcing women's bodies as the site of social anxiety and
negativity. Bordo (1993) writes, "The cost of such projections to women is obvious.
For if . . . *the body* is the negative term, and if woman *is* the body, then women are
that negativity, whatever it may be: distraction from knowledge, seduction away
from god, capitulation of sexual desire, violence or aggression, failure of will, even
death" (5). Thus, monitoring and regulating the body size of women satisfies patriarchal demands for their passivity—the less space women assume, the less visible
their present and potential agencies, the more stable the society. The feminine
beauty ideal of being slim is ultimately guided by patriarchal desires for a passive,
silent woman.

Gwyn Kirk and Margo Okazawa-Rey (2004) assert, "These notions of ideal
beauty are very effective ways for men as well as women to compare and judge
women and to keep them on the treadmill of 'body management'" (113). In particular, the patriarchal institution of capitalism has exaggerated the objectification
of women by suggesting certain feminine beauty ideals, casting women in constant competition with other women about the perfection of their bodies. In order
to access what they perceive as agency in the patriarchal framework, women feel
they must satisfy their culture's physical requirements of beauty. Managing their
bodies, therefore, requires women to accept negative images of femininity.

The hegemony of Western capitalism globally has fostered the legitimacy of those beauty ideals not only in the U.S. culture but also in non-Western, post-colonial societies. Consequently, the dominant image of beauty in major magazines, television shows, and advertisements throughout the West remains the thin, white woman; even more beautiful is the blond-haired, blue-eyed white woman. Beauty ideals throughout the non-Western world also resonate with this fair-skinned, light-haired, non-dark-eyed, thin woman. Alternatively, images of non-white women in mainstream America are symbolically linked to highly sexual images and therefore remain the foil of Western beauty norms (Bordo 1993). For example, black women are represented as "amoral Jezebels who can never truly be raped, because *rape* implies the invasion of a personal space of modesty and reserve that the black woman has not been imagined as having" (Bordo 1993, 9). Negative images of nonwhite women, no doubt, complicate their sexual agency by inviting correlations between their bodies and sexual violence. Thus, constructions of South Asian American feminine subjectivity are complicated by the racialized and gendered dynamic of Western consciousness.

Eating Disorders Worldwide

By internalizing Western racial and gender representations, South Asian women may feel at a disadvantage socially, politically, and economically in the United States. Frustrated by the inability to achieve Western beauty ideals, they may feel a sense of displacement and disenfranchisement. Psychically affected further by the gender demands of their own culture, South Asian women may resort to eating disorders as a way of coping with their personal frustrations.

Anorexia nervosa, bulimia nervosa, and *binge-eating disorder* (BED) (AllPsych Online 2004; At Health 2000; International Eating Disorder Referral and Information Center n.d.) are the most common categories of eating disorders diagnosed in current medical and psychological literature. Statistics cite that anorexia and bulimia together affect over eight million Americans, 95 percent of whom are adolescent girls and young women; further, individuals younger than ten years and as old as seventy years may suffer from eating disorders (National Eating Disorders Association 2002). Unlike the more visible effects of those diagnosed with anorexia nervosa, bulimia nervosa has proven to be a stealthier disease. Affecting 1–2 percent of adolescent women from a variety of ethnicities and economic classes, those diagnosed with bulimia nervosa are usually of average or above-average weight (International Eating Disorder Referral Organization n.d.).

The prevalence of eating disorders globally and primarily among females is directly linked to patriarchal processes of social control over women's agency, namely their sexuality and voice. The emergence of eating disorders in non-Western civilizations alludes to the hegemonic influence of Western culture worldwide and highlights the erasure/mutation of other forms of beauty standards. For example, Western influences have recently increased levels of eating disorders in Japan

(Shuriquie 1999). By 2000, Japanese women were affected with the highest percentage of eating disorders globally, after only the United States (nationmaster.com 2004). Proper female body images espoused by Western capitalism have also negatively influenced Zulu women in South Africa. Indeed, Zulu women display such an alarming number of eating disorders (BBC News, November 4, 2002b), that South Africa now presents the tenth highest proportion of cases involving eating disorders internationally (nationmaster.com 2004). In Fiji, studies suggest links between television viewing and body image (BBC News, May 31, 2002a). Even as there is solid evidence for the prevalence of eating disorders worldwide in non-Western countries, there is a marked lack of studies in South Asia (Kishwar 1995).

The absence of research is precisely why India is missing from the global list of countries most affected by eating disorders. Although Patel and his colleagues claim that eating disorders in India are rare because these conditions are Western-based, ironically, the study itself admits to its own limited statistical information (Patel, Phillips, and Pratt 1998). The invisibility of eating disorders among women in South Asia can therefore be attributed to a lack of research and cultural materials regarding the region's embrace of Westernization and capitalism and its concomitant acceptance of Western ideals of feminine beauty.

The rise of consumerism has had profound implications for representations of South Asian femininity in the subcontinent. Mankekar (1999) writes, "Indian advertisements created spectatorial subject positions that were crucially mediated by culturally specific discourses of gender, modernity, and tradition. As in the United States, many Indian advertisements segmented the female body into hair, face, legs, breasts, and so on" (90–91). Consequently, traditional South Asian women's beauty norms have been reshaped by Western perceptions of beauty. Kishwar (1995) discusses the resultant objectification of women popularized via beauty pageants has "more to do with marketing a self-view to women whereby they all try to look and behave like standardized products rather than normal human beings. This makes women self-hating by wanting to conform to a pre-set glamour doll image" (15). Further, imported Western beauty norms have complicated existing norms concerning women's bodies in various South Asian traditions. Sacred Hindu texts such as the foundational *Manu Smriti* suggest numerous ways to temper a woman's agency by controlling her body (Muller 1993). For example, "At her pleasure let her emaciate her body by (living on) pure flowers, roots, and fruit; but she must never even mention the name of another man after her husband has died" (5:157). The text also advises women that silence and the control of body and mind are appropriate behaviors of a virtuous wife (5:165). Through the figure of Sita, the *Ramayana* forges powerful junctures between women's proper sexual behavior, their silence, and representation of ideal beauty.

Additional layers of colonial impact of race and gender have engendered specific attention to the lightness of women's skin color. According to Kauser Ahmed (1999), "Despite the overt rejection of Western values in South Asia, there remains a strain of internalized racism particularly centered around color, with lighter skin clearly favored" (46). The preference for light skin internalized through multiple tiers of biases from religious-based Indian literature (Kishwar 1995), class norms, and beauty ideals of the British Raj has certainly been exacerbated by today's capitalist society. Thus, Indian women with lighter skin continue to be symbolically associated with higher-class status, higher sexual agency, and greater social, political, economic, and religious power. Analyzing the Miss India Beauty Contest, Susan Runkle (2004) reports the disturbing effects of light skin preference in the pageant contestants: "In the name of confidence, then, the contestants undergo chemical peels and daily medication, some of which have rather unpleasant side effects. Harsimrat, for example, often complained to the doctor that she felt nauseous and weak as a result of the medication prescribed to lighten her South Indian skin" (17). The preference for lighter skin in the general populace is evident in the popularity of skin bleaching treatments in beauty salons throughout South Asia.

The nexus of native, colonial, and present-day gender and racial ascriptions on modern-day South Asian female beauty norms is evident on the bodies of today's Bollywood film stars. A far cry from the more voluptuous, dark-hair, and sloe-eyed beauties in cinemas of the past, current South Asian actresses are exceedingly thin and often have light-colored hair and eyes. Take for example, the top Bollywood actress Aishwarya Rai, an ideal of South Asian beauty. In a recent photograph in *indiatimes*, Rai bears a striking resemblance to white, French-born model Leitita Casta, with whom she is posing (*indiatimes* n.d.). The dissemination of such images throughout South Asia has a startling negative effect on women in general. In an interview with the author, Kishwar (2004) remarked, "The Aishwarya Rais of India have so mesmerized people for the time being dieting and weight loss centers are proliferating at the speed of AIDS virus even though they involve making women both mentally and physically sick."

Reading South Asian American Female Subjectivity

The dominance of Western beauty ideals in the United States automatically marginalizes non-Western beauty norms within the same space and therefore renders body images of nonwhite women highly problematic. To an extent, the dominance of Western images of beauty may encourage nonwhite women to devalue their own natural bodies. In a 1995 interview, Black model Veronica Chambers noted, "We [black women] are still acculturated to hate our dark skin, our kinky hair, our full figures" (Kirk and Okazawa-Rey 2004, 115). As a result, for non-White women residing in the United States, the challenges of and social pressures to emulate Western beauty ideals may not only be extremely harmful and but also cause them to resort to eating disorders to assuage disenfranchisement and the subsequent alienation from their own bodies.

The limited history of South Asians in the United States has not allowed for a comprehensive study of the effects of Western beauty norms on their health. Such effects may be gauged by analyzing the influence of white beauty norms on Asian

American and British South Asian women, whose values and communal identities are similar to those of South Asian American women.

Ellen A. Kim (2003) observed the effects of racial internalization of beauty standards on Asian American girls who lighten their hair and tape their eyelids to affect Western-looking eyes. The rejection of their natural bodies results in eating disorders in the broader Asian American community. "The increasing number of new cases of anorexia nervosa and bulimia nervosa among Asian immigrants to Western countries and the consistent findings of abnormal eating attitudes and eating disorders among Asian and Arab teenagers indicate that these Eastern women have been exposed to Western values" (Shuriquie 1999). The stress of Western beauty images on the Asian community becomes apparent in a 1996 survey of 900 girls in northern California (National Asian American Pacific Islander Mental Health Association 2004). The study notes that the Asian American girls were more dissatisfied with their body images than were their white counterparts.

Asian American women experience additional pressures from the Asian community to conform to its traditional images of thinness. Korean American comedian Margaret Cho related how she felt pressured both by the American media and the Korean American community to govern her body weight while filming her 1994–95 ABC sitcom *All-American Girl*. These pressures led Cho to lose weight by dangerous methods such as constant exercise and the employment of laxatives and Fen-Phen, which caused her to drop thirty pounds in two weeks (Seattle Post-Intelligencer Reporter 2003). "I have never been a heavy person, but for some reason, my physique drives some Korean people insane. They feel that I am too large for them to be comfortable, too large to be one of them" (Cho, as quoted in Seattle Post-Intelligencer Reporter 2003).

One can also extrapolate from statistics concerning South Asian women's health in the United Kingdom. A 1991 British study notes that Asian [South Asian] girls who wore traditional dress and spoke Asian languages had a high propensity for eating disorders (Mumford, Whitehouse, and Platts 1991). A subsequent study notes that although British Asians comprised one-fourth of the total numbers of eating disorder cases, the statistics may have been skewed by South Asian cultural principles that prevent higher levels of disclosure (Ratan, Gandhi, and Palmer 1998).

It is interesting to examine how the framework of shame and honor impacts perceptions of women's body images in South Asian communities by posing a barrier to collecting information on women's health. However, sources addressing the subject of eating disorders among South Asian American women are scarce. For example, the recently published *A Brown Paper* by the South Asian Public Health Association in the United States (Rao et al. 2002) confirms the existence of eating disorders among South Asian American women but lacks actual studies on the phenomenon. Yet, even a random questioning of South Asian American women confirms its prevalence.

When I asked if she knew anyone of South Asian origin with an eating disorder, Kiran (a pseudonym, as are all names of affected women), a young woman in her early thirties replied, "Yes—the little sister of a friend. . . . I have to admit—had I been 'successful' at purging—I might have had one [an eating disorder] as well."[2] Another interviewee, Lata, who was in her early thirties offered, "Ever since I was eleven, I have been made to be so conscious about my weight, everyday. It has in many ways *consumed* my life—even leading me to an eating disorder in college." The number of women ready to speak casually about their negative experiences with eating, or who were contacted for this study, underscores the strong presence of eating disorders among South Asian American women.

Complicating South Asian American Femininity

The propensity for eating disorders in the South Asian community in the United States is informed by overlapping psychological and physical pressures ensuing from unyielding multicultural demands. These demands arise from the complicated dynamics between the South Asian immigrant and Western majority populaces in America. Uma Narayan (1997) reads those dynamics through Western appropriations of South Asian food in the United States. The American homogenization of the wide array of cuisines unique to each state in India is comparable to the West's homogenization of the range of unique cultural aspects of Indian culture. Narayan (1997) asserts, "Indian food, as it is represented by 'Indian restaurants' in Western contexts has, like most immigrants, undergone a series of adaptations and assimilations into the dominant context. . . . In much the same way as specific dishes get singled out as 'Indian cuisine,' certain practices and norms get singled out as emblematic of 'our culture and way of life,' both in Indian communities in India, and in Indian disaporic communities" (174–175).

In conjunction with Western secular appropriations of Hindu religious iconography, Western appropriations of food, for example, have increased the South Asian American community's fear of losing its identity. In response to American appropriations of South Asian traditions, South Asians themselves have singled out certain aspects of their heritage they feel are central to their communal identity, and at the root of those traditions lies the sexual control of its women (Narayan 1997).

The psychical paranoia exercised against South Asian immigrants by the dominant American society and vice-versa are displaced onto the bodies of South Asian women. Such restrictions have resulted in the exacerbation of both visible and invisible forms of violence against women of all ages and backgrounds within the family, and particularly against young women. For example, traditional associations between the sexual purity of South Asian women and cultural purity require even tighter regulations on young women's agency in America. "It thus comes as no surprise that the burden of negotiating the new world is borne disproportionately by women, whose behavior and desires, real or imagined, become the litmus test for the South Asian community's anxieties or sense of wellbeing. For instance, the fear of dating that consumes many South Asian families is primarily a fear of women dating" (Mani 1993, 34).

The negative psychological impact of such constrictions on South Asian women is powerful. Ahmed (1999) asserts that the inability of young South Asian women to reconcile their conservative values with the more liberal demands of the American society results in a psychological split. By attempting to satisfy the disparate cultural demands from the West outside of their homes and the traditions within their South Asian homes, young South Asian women experience "constant guilt and a sense of fracture in their lives" (45).

The conflation of South Asian and Western beauty ideals for women disseminated by both the Bollywood and Hollywood movie industries produces new, less visible forms of violence on South Asian female subjectivity in America. Existing Bollywood messages of women with light skin, light hair, and a thin body as beautiful are even more strongly pronounced in a Western context. For example, the entrance of Bollywood actress Aishwarya Rai into the American movie market demonstrates ways in which Indian femininity has been modified for Western consumption.

In a recent L'Oreal commercial on television, Rai's Indian accent was erased by American marketers and replaced with an American accent. Although L'Oreal's intention was to please the American public, the American public includes South Asian women, whose femininity may be complicated and problematized by such drastic modifications of physical images paralleling their own. Ahmed writes, "For South Asian American girls, pressures to meet unattainable standards of physical beauty can come not only from the dominant culture but from expectations internalized within their own community" (Ahmed 1999, 46). The combined pressures of the immediate community and broader American culture enact a dual oppression in which existing difficulties of attaining beauty standards espoused by Bollywood is exasperated by the physical impossibility of satisfying beauty standards of the prevailing American culture.

Additional forms of violence against South Asian perceptions of femininity arise from continued Western appropriations of South Asian femininity as exotic and therefore sexual. Amita Handa (2003) addresses the subtle ways in which Western representations of South Asian femininity may negatively affect South Asian feminine consciousness. In the Fall 2001 cover of the magazine owned by Mary Kate and Ashley Olsen, the twins don saris and bindis and are accessorized by Hindu-centric lunchboxes, bringing "the cool into school." "But I will wonder whether Mary-Kate and Ashley's cool is the same as ours," posits Handa. "It is doubtful that South Asians would be able to set a market trend on a cover of a magazine in the same way as the Olsen twins. Brown girls in saris are immigrant and ethnic, not mainstream and fashionable" (161).

Handa's observations highlight the ways in which dominant Western images reinforce negative stereotypes of and restrictive social controls over South Asian women. Western appropriations of Hindu sacred items reflect the continued objectification and exotization of the East as a sexual object of the West. Such aesthetic objectifications are inextricably linked to colonial beauty ideals noted earlier and, for that reason, resurrect and perpetuate them. Furthermore, the ability of the West to continue to objectify South Asia and, in particular, symbols specific to the female gender, such as dress, perpetuates Western and South Asian beliefs of the native, colonized woman as a passive and silent object that can be appropriated. Ultimately, the public sexualization of South Asian women may unconsciously raise South Asian communal fears over the loss of its identity, thereby resulting in the enactment of tighter sexual controls over South Asian American women.

The periodicity and intensity of these forms of violence are dependent on the patriarchal interface between the immigrant and dominant communities. The inability to reconcile neatly the imposition of Western cultural expectations onto the South Asian framework of shame and honor, may cause South Asian women to view their bodies as a burden, as a hindrance to recognizing their full agency and potential as individuals. Surrounded by American society's obsessive focus on weight, South Asian women are more likely to turn to eating disorders as a way of dissipating their own psychological anxieties concerning their own bodies and as a quick and immediate means of establishing agency.

In her article "Happiness in Quotation Marks" (forthcoming), Sunita Puri describes ways in which eating disorders may be employed by South Asian American women to mask and cope with a range of gender violence specific to their experiences in America. Unable to deal with the shame she feels about being raped by an older cousin, the author turned to anorexia as a mechanism of catharsis. She writes, "After my cousin left our home, I began to hate my body for the five years' worth of memories it lodged, for the loss of control those memories represented, for the guilt and shame over the choice I didn't have. And when you hate something that much, all you can do is destroy it. And after all, my body was a very easy target." Because images of weight control for women threaded her immediate American environment, eating disorders seemed the quickest, least taboo means of coping with additional forms of patriarchal violence engendered by her South Asian heritage, such as the incest. Soon, anorexia became a way of coping with academic pressures placed on her by her parents as well. "To me, anorexia is the ultimate representation of psychosomatic illness, of how social experiences translate into bodily breakdown. Those who gape, aghast, at anorexic women believe their behavior to be voluntary; I call it an involuntary survival strategy."

The psychological symptoms displayed by South Asian American women reflect a phenomenon that is specific to their multicultural struggles in the United States. The psychical angst of coping with visible and invisible violence resulting from an inability to integrate the South Asian expectations into those of the dominant American culture renders their exertions unique. Consequently, emphasizing only the symptoms of an eating disorder as a disease over the multicultural issues underlying the disorder enacts an erasure of the complicated identity struggles associated with South Asian American femininity. Thus, treatments for eating disorders for a South Asian woman require sensitivity to her cultural background. Writing about Kamelesh, an incest survivor who later developed an eating disorder,

Grace Poore notes how the lack of cultural sensitivity in American healthcare providers exaggerated her existing anxieties, thereby adding on to the layers of violence against her: "Some South Asian survivors growing up in Canada found nurturing friendships and roles models for positive nonabusive relationships among non–South Asians. But these relationships also came packaged with lack of cultural awareness and stereotypes, which fueled the survivor's own antifamily, anticultural resentments; resentments that intensified their sense of cultural alienation and struggles of being young South Asian immigrants in an Anglo-dominated country" (this volume).

Perhaps as South Asian women begin to express themselves in a variety of ways apart from mainstream American femininity, they may discover new ways to empower themselves. Sonia Shah (2003) writes, "Our shakti hasn't yet expressed itself on a nation stage accessible to our sisters. But we are entering a moment in our organizing when we will soon be able to create a distinctly Asian American feminism, one that will be able to cross the class and cultural lines that currently divide us" (540). Perhaps by raising awareness of and taking seriously the distinct oppressions that cause eating disorders in South Asian women, we can construct and pursue new feminine subjectivities.

ACKNOWLEDGMENTS

I would like to thank Anne M. Slocum McEneaney, Ph.D., and Dr. Santhi Periasamy for their contributions to this research. I am deeply grateful to the many South Asian women who have shared with me in private or for this study their personal struggles with eating disorders.

NOTES

1.   South Asian identity politics comprises varied economic, religious, ethnic, and linguistic differences that differentially affect speculations of South Asian femininity. This study employs the generalized term of "South Asian" feminine norms in the least complicated manner.

2.   The author personally conducted all interviews July 19–23, 2004.

8

Silences That Prevail When the Perpetrators Are Our Own

GRACE POORE

Although the term *incest* is frequently preferred by criminal, legal, mental health, and media professionals, in my work, I opt for the terms *incestuous sexual abuse* (ISA) and *incestuous child sexual abuse* (ICSA). Both labels grew out of the movement to prevent child sexual abuse in the United States. In the early 1970s rape survivors and their allies drew powerful parallels between child sexual abuse and rape and made it a public issue. They pointed out that rape, like child sexual abuse, is not a "singular act of sexuality but rather an expression of power and violence" (Berrick and Gilbert 1991, 10). These early articulations formed the core premise of the anti–sexual violence movement, including the movement to prevent child sexual abuse, which was primarily galvanized by women who were subjected to stranger rape or incest rape in childhood (Berrick and Gilbert 1991).

The terms ISA and ICSA more aptly communicate the violation of a person's human rights, integrity, and wholeness, rather than merely a violation of laws or social mores. Both do not condemn certain customs, such as cousin marriage or uncle-niece marriage, that are practiced in different cultures and communities around the world but do not involve abuse. Instead, by attaching *abuse* to *incest* the focus shifts from problematizing the blood relationship to problematizing the dynamics of abuse facilitated by the trusting relationship with the victim and victim's family.

Those who commit ICSA choose to gratify their sexual needs at the expense of someone with very little or no power to give or withdraw consent. They take advantage of family connections where members are related not only by blood but also by marriage and/or historical ties. For instance, in South Asian households, the notions of family include current and past family friends, frequent visitors to the house, distant cousins, and houseguests who may or may not be biologically related or even closely connected to the family. In addition, South Asian children in most parts of the world are in regular contact with people hired by the family, such as priests, doctors, domestic workers, childcare providers, tutors, tailors, dance instructors, and chauffeurs. Consequently, children experience ICSA in these settings because perpetrators' access to them is made possible by their access to familiar and familial spheres.

U.S.-born Preeti (a pseudonym, as are names of all survivors) recounts how an uncle took advantage of the home-care arrangements and spatial considerations in their home: "He was immigrating to the United States. My father sponsored him to come. Until he could get on his feet and find a job and establish himself, he needed a place to stay. I don't know how long he was with us when the abuse started. He had the responsibility for sometimes taking my sister and me to school, making sure that we took our naps, giving us baths. [My sister and I] actually had to sleep in the same room with him sometimes. He had access to everything in our family. Our house was his house."[1]

Neesha was born in India and came to North America with her parents when she was six. In her case, childcare arrangements involved a religious institution that her newly immigrated parents were relieved to turn to as a source of cultural and familial support.

> I was six years old when my family moved from India where we had few South Asian friends. My parents moved next door to a Sikh temple. This immediately gave my parents a sense of security. These were other people who were also Sikh, thereby trustworthy, immediately trustworthy. My parents worked a lot, we were a working class family. So, they left me and my brother at the temple. My brother was three and I was six. My mother would drop us off in the morning and pick us up at the end of the day. There were other young children there also for the same purpose. Their parents were working and they thought this was a good place, a safe place to leave their children. The priests in the temple would teach us how to read and write Punjabi, teach us how to play the tabla. Because my parents so unconditionally trusted these men at the temple, my brother and I had a sense of security. We did not at any point feel that we had to be careful or not trusting.

It is in this atmosphere of trust and familiarity that perpetrators often escape suspicion and therefore detection; they manage to disarm and confuse internal alarms that victims experience before or during the abuse and are able to violate with a high level of confidence and get away with it. Abusive intentions and actions are embedded within the normality of physically and emotionally affectionate relationships with the victim's family, as well as the cultural mandates that predetermine rights and privileges of those who are older, irrespective of blood ties. The same rights and privileges are not recognized for those who are underaged, particularly children. Under these circumstances, ICSA offenders often do not need tactics that involve overt force or terrorization because the balance of power already favors them. Their forms of abuse need not involve physical injury or pain—at least in the beginning, as Preeti's experience underscores:

> The abuse started as a game. We were playing one afternoon, and it was time for us to take a nap and I was a very playful child. I liked to run around and chase people and I was trying to tickle my uncle. He asked me to lie down and he said, "Okay I'm going to tickle you now." And he began to touch me and he called it tickling. That's the way it started. The tickling escalated. At first, it was just caressing and touching me. And it generally happened when nobody else was around. It would also happen at night after my parents went to sleep. And when it escalated, he started having intercourse with me. It then became "tickling me inside" when he was penetrating me and it didn't feel like tickling anymore. It was painful. I didn't understand what he was doing, what was happening. It started when I was six and lasted for about three years or so.

While children of both genders are frequently insulated from the knowledge that sexual abuse could happen within the family, South Asian girls, like girls in most cultures, also have to contend with the additional pressure of gendered upbringing. For many South Asian daughters, including those born and raised in a North American culture, there is an expectation by parents and relatives that they must behave in ways that are considered appropriately female or, more important, reflective of South Asian values from the home country.

For Nupoor, this upbringing left her vulnerable to a family member who took advantage of her niceness. "Part of being a child is openness and this is what was taken away. I was always the good girl, the nice girl. I was not taught to fight or how to ensure my safety. I was really naive. It was my mother's sister's husband who abused me. I remember being eight or nine, could be younger. He would take me to the amusement park or Niagara Falls and that way got me to be alone with him. When it first started, I felt it was normal but I knew something was wrong because of the secrecy."

With Neesha's parents, who wanted to present the image of good immigrants, it was imperative that their children cause little or no trouble to those who were older and, more important, in positions of religious authority. Neesha recounted:

> My mother made it very clear that she and my father were working very hard and that we needed to be self-sufficient, my brother and I, that I needed to take care of my brother, that if anything happened to me or my brother, it was my responsibility. My brother and I were in the temple every day for a year and a half. The second incident of abuse I remember; he was one of the older priests in the temple. He was very respected, a higher priest in the temple. I was sitting behind a counter on a stool and there were three or four other kids on the other side of the counter, kicking a ball or playing

and my brother was on the other side with them. He [perpetrator-priest] was sitting next to me. I wasn't looking at him but he started to put his hand into my pants. And I froze. I stared straight ahead. And he started to touch me and fondle me. I just felt my brain was scattering. I remember I clenched my hands really tight and I kept staring.

Language of Sexual Violence

In many South Asian languages, sexual molestation is minimized, even joked about as indiscreet touching, rather than being named for what it is: abuse, violation, rape. In this context, it is extremely difficult for South Asian women to name fondling or sexual touching as something serious, even if they felt "disgusted and dirty," "knew it was wrong," or wanted it to stop. Worse, if their bodies felt physically stimulated during the abuse, they frequently struggle with self-blame, shame, and self-deprecation. Many women are not sure if they even have the right to call such an experience abuse. In this case, disclosing becomes even more complicated because many South Asian women already know the stigma associated with inappropriate sexuality, sexual desire, and sexual pleasure. To talk about sexual abuse without conjuring images of pain and injury opens the door for all kinds of insidious accusations, including, "You liked it, that's why you didn't try to stop it" or "Don't pretend you didn't enjoy it," which revictimizes victims. In many cases, years after the abuse has stopped survivors are finally able to articulate why they felt forced into the situation, although the force did not feel overtly menacing.

Aparna's abuser was a close family friend, which placed her in the untenable position of having to keep the abuse a secret in order to preserve historically tight family relationships. Since there was no overt force, she had no framework to describe the abuse while it was happening.

> I wanted to tell someone so badly because I did not like the way I felt, I felt dirty. Maybe telling someone would have stopped the abuse. I think I really wanted to tell my parents but I never felt safe doing it. I was afraid of the repercussions because our families were so close. Lot of it included touching mainly in the breast area and genital area. It also involved forcing me to touch him, what I now define as force. Then it didn't feel like force to me. It was him guiding my hand to touch his genital area. Now I define it differently because I really didn't feel like I had the choice to say yes or no. Yes really has no meaning if you don't have the option to say no.

Like Aparna, Maya's reluctance to disclose was directly related to who the perpetrator was and the implications of revealing his identity. In addition, there was the fear of unveiling a form of abuse that she, like most people, believed happened only outside the home and not within. "In India, sex is only supposed to occur between husband and wife, only in marital relationships. It's treated as sacred. How could I tell what my brother was doing to me? What would I say? I did not have the words for it. It's true that if my brother had slapped me I would have told my mother. But sex, that's not something we could talk about. After I had grown up, we would discuss men pressing against women on buses. We talk about this kind of thing openly. But no one ever spoke of anything sexual in the family. So, in a way, it wasn't only about what was happening to me but also who was doing it."

Toronto-based psychotherapist, Smita Vir Tyagi explains why language is necessary when dealing with psychic violations: "There is a word for rape in Hindi but I haven't come across a word for incest. When people talk about sexual molestation by family, they don't talk about *zabardasti*, which is 'force'—a person forced you to do this or that. Sometimes they use a kind of minimizing language like *chher-chhaar*, which means 'a little bit here and there,' 'pushing and shoving,' playful kinds of things [it actually means teasing]. This language doesn't allow you to get the sense of how serious and how intrusive and what a deep violation this is." Vir Tyagi adds, "When you don't have adequate language with which to describe what is happening, it's very hard to construct it mentally, when it's very hard to construct something mentally, it's very hard to confront it. And when it's hard to confront something, it's hard to grapple with it, much less deal with it."

When my video *The Children We Sacrifice* was being translated into Tamil, Hindi, and Bengali, the linguists hired to handle the scripts declined to translate certain portions of the dialogue or on-screen text that described the nature of the abuse. They insisted on retaining the English because they felt there was no culturally appropriate way to describe explicit acts of sexual abuse without resorting to street lingo that would offend the audience, or clinical jargon that no one would understand. The conflict between me, the producer, and these senior movie industry scriptwriters came down to willingness versus unwillingness to talk publicly about something that was perceived as private and shameful. They would not give themselves permission to communicate the profane, while my goal was to destigmatize sexual violence for survivors so that shame could be detached from victimization and disclosure. Eventually, Indian feminist scholars resolved the stalemate by finding the right language to convey specific violations without disguising or turning away from what was being described (e.g., "penis put into the mouth," "pinching buttocks and breasts," and "asked to touch abuser's genitals").

Clearly, limited vocabulary for parts of the body or specific acts of sexual violence is only one part of the problem. The greater struggle is the inability to access the emotional language to talk about sexual abuse, for a variety of reasons involving culture, class, religion, family upbringing, age, and, perhaps, caste. Take, for instance, the Tamil culture's concept of *Naat Kunam* (Four Qualities): *maddam* (innocence), *naanam* (shyness or timidity), *payippu* (respect), and *accham* (fear).

According to Sudha Coomarasamy, a Sri Lankan women's advocate in Canada, *Naat Kunam* was originally devised as general principles for all humanity, the ethical precepts by which to live in society. *Payippu*, for example, was respect for others; *accham* was fear of doing anything unjust or evil; *maddam* was respecting the sacredness of one's mind, body, and spirit; *naanam* was timidity about committing an act that was bad for humanity. Over time, *Naat Kunam* came to be associated with feminine values. Coomarasamy notes, "These values have been quoted in Tamil poetry, literature, and used by the Tamil media and movie industries as a yardstick for women's virtue. Girls learn the principles of *Naat Kunam* at a young age. Often mothers, grandmothers, or other female matriarchs are the teachers. Consequently, it is the women in the family who are held responsible and told, 'You did not bring up your daughter properly' if a girl or woman falls short of the values instilled in her."

Chastity Equals Virtue

In a situation of sexual abuse within or outside the family, a Tamil girl or woman has to transcend the *Naat Kunam* value system that has come to symbolize her femininity, a daunting prospect when (1) *maddam* has come to mean sexual innocence, no knowledge of sex, or what sexual abuse is, so that when sexual violence does occur the shame is the woman's shame; (2) *payippu* now denotes a woman's self respect, which means it is her responsibility to thwart any unwanted sexual attention that is not from her husband; (3) *naanam* applauds a woman's shyness and timidity as desired characteristics; and (4) *accham* advocates a woman's fear of authority or anyone accorded power over her. By representing the nexus of chastity and virtue, virtue and femininity, *Naat Kunam* principles serve as a convenient mechanism to hold women and girls responsible for sexual abuse; consequently, letting sex offenders off the hook and preempting victim disclosure and perpetrator accountability. Coomarasamy explains:

> Say I am a twelve-year-old and I'm listening to my aunt, my mother, and my grandmother talking about these things. When something happens to me, even though [I] didn't have any part in it, I have now known the act that I am not supposed to know, the knowledge I [was] to wait for [my] husband to reveal to me. *Naat Kunam* is a prison for women [because] what a woman is being taught is that she has to hold it in, it's endurance that's a mark of womanhood; the earth is like a woman, it bears everything, it endures all. So the woman [who is a victim or survivor of incest] thinks that is what she has to be; [she] must be patient and give up on reparation. This is one reason why women don't talk about sexual abuse even if they have the opportunity and support to go through the legal system to get help, [because] what *Naat Kunam* does is that it tells women that they're doing the right thing; meaning you are a better woman if you do not speak. I have had women say, "I admire this woman a lot because she had this abuse for so long and she didn't tell a soul." And that's held up as a virtue.

Protecting Dumbness

While researching for *The Children We Sacrifice*, I asked Tamil and Sinhala women in Sri Lanka if they had an English transliteration that would capture the inability to speak out about being sexually abused. One phrase that emerged was "protecting dumbness." It encapsulates a complexity of feelings, initially a psychic paralysis from the treachery involved in the abuse and, later, anger and resentment at having to keep the secret, while also a sense of valiance from being able to protect self and others with silence. Within this context, protecting dumbness is more than the inability to speak because of fear, but also a way to deploy silence for personal sanity, where living inside silence becomes a kind of crucible experience in which to develop resilience and self-reliance. In North America, South Asian women who had to engage in protecting dumbness were faced with an added expectation that was related to them being not only South Asian daughters but also the children of a racially oppressed community.

Kamelesh's family migrated to North America long before the post-9/11 racial profiling and backlash against South Asians. But her fears about the United States' response to South Asian men were not much different twenty years ago.

> On an emotional level, I don't give a shit about [my father and uncle]. Yet, loyalty also plays a role in not wanting to expose my father to the police, the white police in a white justice system. Because I don't want them to think that all the things they say about South Asians are true. Also, if I exposed him, his business would be ruined and it would mean financial ruin for my mother as well. My parents are in their sixties and my mother constantly talks about how she needs to continue maintaining a good relationship with the extended family. She's still friends with my uncle although I told her what he did to me. And I have to accept that because I can't take care of my mother so I cannot expect her to give everything up just for me.

Kamelesh was severely abused sexually and physically by her father and later by her father's brother. Although her mother became aware of the abuse by her brother-in-law, Kamelesh never told her about the sexual abuse by her father. She had several complex reasons for protecting dumbness, including the need to protect her mother from the possibility of destitution and her perpetrator-father from racism in their new country. Similarly, Neesha, also the daughter of first-generation immigrants, felt the need to protect her parents from a greater injustice and did not report her abuse for a long time: "At the time, my parents were trying desperately to stay in the country, trying to survive, working very hard, feeling very lonely not knowing the language. I witnessed it every single day when we went grocery shopping, when my mother did laundry at the Laundromat— looks from people, the way people responded to me, adults. I am talking about white people. So there was a real sense at the time of wanting to protect my parents from the racism, a real sense that I wanted to do something, and I think my way of doing something was not telling anybody about what was going on, about the abuse."

In some instances, protecting dumbness prevails into adulthood, even after women are married and have their own children, as with Maya, whose long involvement with an organization that assists South Asian battered women in the United States did not detract her from an overwhelming need to maintain her silence in order to keep family harmony. She says that although the sexual abuse by her brother made her a defensive parent around men, especially with her daughter, she chose not to tell her husband or children about being an incest survivor, even after her children started college.

> When I got married, my sexual relations with my husband were very difficult and I know he's also suffered a lot because of that. Even until now I am not able to have normal sexual relations. My husband doesn't know I was abused and I don't think I'll be able to tell my husband that I have been. I think now if I told him, he would just be so angry that he suffered for so many years because of this. I don't think he would even understand what happened and now, I just think that it's too late. If I tell my husband, if I tell my parents, if I tell my in-laws, all it's going to do is cause unhappiness. Now looking back, I think if it had been an uncle, or a male cousin, or a servant, I would have told. But fathers and brothers—that's a sacred relationship. I think one reason for my living in the States is to be far away from all that. Whenever I go back to India and visit the family, he is there and I would look at him and wonder, how could you have done this to me? Didn't you know it was wrong? Didn't you realize I am your sister?

Shamita Das Dasgupta, founding member of Manavi for South Asian women in New Jersey, contextualizes Maya's anxiety about revealing her experience. "Even in our work with domestic abuse victims, we tend to avoid bringing up the topic of sexuality because of our uncomfortability with language, class-based sensibility, or lack of necessary information. . . . Women are more willing to speak on domestic violence. The same, however, is not true with issues of sexual violence" (Mazumdar 1998, 140).

Dasgupta's observation applies to a majority of the survivors I talked to, across age and circumstances of immigration, levels of awareness about sexual abuse, and levels of political activism. For those who did speak, it was a battle to be heard and understood. They were constantly evaluating which silences to break and which to preserve, how much to tell and when. Often keeping silent felt no different from speaking about the abuse; both brought long periods of inconsolable sadness and rage along with safety, relief, and sanity. For instance, silence preserved family alliances and important relationships, which prevented loss of emotional and physical safety, and loss of financial support. However, exposing the sexual abuse and the perpetrator brought a different kind of emotional and physical safety, for the survivors themselves, and for other potential targets.

Incest Survivor Warrior

Just as there were women for whom silence worked, other women chose to rebel, confront, and catalyze their rage. They refused to keep up appearances as dutifully silent South Asian daughters, often at great personal cost. Instead, they responded to a different call to duty. One such example was Nupoor:

> Everyone in my family is in denial and I am the reminder. That's why people don't support you. Breaking silence has a price. But not breaking silence almost killed me. I nearly killed myself. I am the one who has been mobilizing my cousins to talk and do something about [the abuse]. It was a major breakthrough in my dealing with the abuse: that I am not alone, that there are others, females in my family who were also abused and believe me, and are willing to support me and take action. My cousin says there are at least twenty others, all females, abused by my uncle. Right now, two cousins and I are talking about finding a way to get him. I feel overwhelmed sometimes and frustrated because the process of healing is so long and it impacts so many areas of life, like finding work, being unemployed, getting access to resources. Asking for help is hard and breaking silences is hard. When people say they can't help, it's hard. When there's really no place in the world where you can say, "I'm falling apart, I'm feeling emotional, I can't go on," that's hard. When vulnerability is seen as a sign of weakness, all this is hard.

Like Nupoor, Preeti did not stop being outspoken despite being disappointed from speaking up. She rescripted family relationships and vigilantly policed boundaries with family members:

> I decided to take a self-defense class. Through the class, I was motivated to write a letter to my father sharing with him that my uncle had abused me. I just didn't want to keep the secret anymore. I wanted [my father] to know and I wanted him to do something. I wanted him to, not necessarily kill my uncle, but reprimand him or confront him; [but] my dad kept saying, "How could he do it? I don't know what to do, what to say to him." That wasn't the way I wanted him to respond because I felt that I was put in the position to sort of explain why my uncle had done what he did. I wanted my father to sort of tell me that it was okay and that he was going to take care of it. He would often at the time say, "It's over now. It's okay. It doesn't matter anymore. It's finished." And that felt like a slap in the face because it clearly was not over for me. He wanted to give me money, to have me live at home, to assess my finances. But he still let the uncle, his brother, come to the house. When I was getting ready to return [home] for one month, I knew my uncle would be there. This is why I decided to confront him. I wrote him a letter, a short letter. It said, "I know what you did to me." I put boundaries— "Don't talk to me, don't touch me, don't come to the house." I told him not to respond to my letter and I said, "I don't care what you have to say. You

can't give me any information I need for my healing." Now there are several adults in my family who know—my father, sister, uncle, stepmother. They pretend no one knows.

To Deny Is to Collude

In March 2004, police in Clinton, Massachusetts, received a telephone call from a South Asian woman who reported that she saw her husband raping their two-year-old daughter. When the police arrived, they found the woman had slit her daughter's wrists and her own in a failed homicide-suicide attempt (Nugent 2004; Rosinski and Richardson 2004; Associated Press 2004). A key member of a local South Asian women's organization remarked about the incident, "I would definitely put this as the worst thing that could possibly happen. This is unheard of in the South Asian community. Incest is something that is almost unheard of, so I can see where this woman could have almost completely fallen apart, and that's what she did" (Walsh 2004). The president of the same organization said, "It was bone-chilling. . . . When I heard it for the first time I just sat down. I can't believe something like this can happen in the community" (Walsh 2004). It is unclear if these comments relate to the child sexual abuse or the homicide-suicide. Given previous media publicity around South Asian mother-child homicide-suicide attempts, I am inclined to believe that the remarks were about the ICSA—because of the age of the child, who the perpetrator was, and the mother's subsequent actions.

The case raises several troubling questions: Did the mother fear retaliation after calling the police? Did she believe that there was no protection for her and her daughter anywhere? Was there domestic violence going on besides ICSA? Did she feel that death offered them a way out that subjugation to her husband and family would not? Since the mother had family in the area, was she unable to turn to them because they responded in ways that made her feel trapped? Had she already suspected her husband might be a child sex offender and had no one to talk to about this? Could she have felt isolated because South Asian women's groups in the Boston area have been openly reluctant to acknowledge and address ICSA in the South Asian community?[2] Was there no place to go outside her own community because non–South Asian groups working to end sexual assault in the area had not built bridges with the South Asian community?

When community organizations take positions such as those quoted above, it drives sexual violence in the family underground and sends a dangerous message: South Asian families (mothers in particular) that need help protecting their children from sexual abuse should keep quiet. The message discourages girls and women from seeking timely redress or relief. I would even suggest that the positions taken actually facilitate the perpetration of child sexual abuse in South Asian communities in North America.

Several years earlier, there was a similar lapse in community response including those from South Asian women's organizations. In July 1998, National Public

Radio aired a story about a seventeen-year-old South Asian who had been sexually abusing his twelve-year-old sister and got her pregnant (Lohr 1998). The Michigan case drew national attention because a local judge had prohibited the victim's parents from getting her a third-trimester abortion. When prosecutors discovered that the parents planned to take their daughter to a doctor in Kansas who specialized in late-term abortions, they petitioned the court to prohibit the girl from leaving the state, arguing that the abortion was not in the girl's best interest, although she herself wanted the abortion (American Civil Liberties Union 1998; Merx 1999).[3]

Most South Asians will react with incredulity when the problem of ICSA is associated with the community, particularly the educated, middle, or upper middle classes. But a 1997 survey of 350 schoolgirls in New Delhi by Sakshi Violence Intervention Centre found that 65 percent had been sexually abused by a family member and 25 percent had either been raped, forced to masturbate the perpetrator, or perform oral sex (Poore 2000b). For one-third of the girls, the perpetrator was a father, grandfather, or male friend of the family. Another survey of 1,000 English-speaking, middle- and upper-class college-educated women living in Delhi, Kolkata, Mumbai, Goa, and Chennai found that 76 percent had been sexually abused in childhood and 40 percent of these by a family member. For 50 percent of the survivors, the abuse took place when they were under twelve and for 35 percent between twelve and sixteen years. While 48 percent had been abused by a single abuser, 52 percent had multiple perpetrators. Furthermore, 11 percent of the survivors said that the sexual abuse occurred once in their lives, while 42 percent was subjected to the abuse repeatedly, at different times, either by the same abuser or different abusers (RAHI 1999). There is no reason to believe that these statistics for South Asia do not also apply to South Asian children living in North America or who may travel between both continents, as might their perpetrators.

Home as Refuge and Site of Violation

In part, the rejection of ICSA as a phenomenon within South Asian communities is linked to myths about sexual abusers as strangers, maniacal perverts, the mentally ill, poorly educated, and those who troll parks and malls looking to snatch children. The South Asian immigration story makes no room for images of South Asians as perpetrators of domestic violence or child sexual abuse. Instead, members of the community strive for and project model minority status, which for survivors like Kamelesh, conflicted daily with lived reality.

> My father is the eldest son. He used to be a lawyer, the pride of our community. My father is the kind of husband who washes the dishes and does the laundry. He gives people money when they are in trouble. He's everybody's big guardian. I mean the community doesn't even know how physically violent he can be. And if the community does not believe that he's physically violent then how would they believe the incest? With my uncle,

the abuse started when I was fifteen. He was playful, the Casanova, cuddly. He was not violent and aggressive like my father. At fifteen, I wanted that attention and kindness from my uncle. I did not think that my uncle feeling me up was abuse. It was only later that he began being aggressive with me, after I started to deny him access to me.

When South Asian survivors of ICSA find no room to maneuver within their own family for support and understanding, many turn to non–South Asian friends, counselors, schoolteachers, and psychotherapists. Some South Asian survivors growing up in Canada found nurturing friendships and role models for positive nonabusive relationships among non–South Asians. But these relationships also came packaged with lack of cultural awareness and stereotypes, which fueled the survivors' own antifamily, anticultural resentments—resentments that intensified their sense of cultural alienation and struggles of being young South Asian immigrants in an Anglo-dominated country. The South Asian culture, which for them represented everything familiar, had turned into a place where there was trauma, pain, and secrets, while non–South Asian communities threatened cultural pride and loyalty to heritage.[4] In due course, identity conflicts overlapped with the painful realization that as South Asian incest survivors they were caught between two worlds and ended up being terribly isolated. Kamelesh recounts, "I have not told my therapist even to this day about the incest because my therapists have all been white and I went to them for an eating disorder. Can you imagine what they would think of me if I told them I wanted to marry my uncle? They have no idea about our culture, no context, and they don't even bother to hide their attitudes about South Asians. To them, I would be really bizarre. So, when I went to see the therapist about the food disorder, I never told her about the incest. And when I went to see another therapist about the anxiety attacks and agoraphobia, I didn't tell her about the incest either."

Often, survivors like Kamelesh and others I spoke to in North America had the option of moving away from their parents' home, away from the atmosphere of silence and enforced respect for family elders, to another city or another part of the country. While mobility brought economic vulnerability, it also provided relief and freedom from the family dynamics that contributed to the incest atmosphere. Cleaving from their biological families led to the creation of alternative kinship connections with close friends, colleagues, activist comrades, as well as intimate partners and their families. Again, the down side was the absence of visible or available South Asian networks. But even if these networks existed, for many survivors these were not always safe because of the inevitable questions—where is your family, why did you leave, do you keep in touch with them? By default, for women like Kamelesh, recovering from childhood sexual violation has meant having to exchange the comfort of being part of the culturally familiar for the 24/7 experience of being the cultural "other."

South Asians in North America are a diverse people. Despite the community's shared cultural references and political histories, there are differences in ethnicity, religion, language, regional traditions, immigration backgrounds, and diaspora origins. Frequently, nonfamily South Asians serve as each other's home away from home. However, when domestic violence or child sexual abuse are happening, families will most likely treat South Asian nonfamily members as outsiders to prevent their involvement in what are considered to be private matters. Yet, as insider-outsiders these individuals have a unique opportunity to provide cultural kinship to victims/survivors who need to leave home while also preserving their anonymity, privacy, and confidentiality. They could serve as foster homes for children who are being abused. Outsider-insiders are an untapped, potentially valuable resource who can be galvanized to make profound differences in improving support systems for and interventions with victims/survivors.

Justice and Healing

Like survivors from other cultures, South Asians are often pressured to put the abuse behind them and get beyond it. In many ways, it is unreasonable to place this onus on victims when little is done to restore the compromised home and prevent the abuse from happening again. Allocating responsibility for getting over it to victims takes the spotlight off those who perpetrated abuse and those who failed to protect. What frustrates most survivors is the attitude behind mandates like "don't dwell on it" and "get over it." Such advice communicates lack of caring and compassion, and denial of support that many survivors deeply yearn for in the immediate and long-term aftermath of abuse.

As Lata's story shows, survivors feel isolated in their healing process when family support is not forthcoming. It reminds them of the isolation they experienced while the abuse was going on and afterward, when disclosure was not possible, or even after disclosure occurred. "I want to be closer to my family but they are not trying. They only want to go on with their lives. They don't want to know or hear that I am in therapy. By the mere fact that I was abused, makes them so guilty [and] brings up the refrain, 'I blame myself, I have to blame myself.' What I want from my mother is for her to listen to me, to acknowledge the steps I am taking to heal and change, to hear my pain. Instead, all she wants to hear is that I am fine."

Moving on does not happen in a vacuum. Each party involved in the abusive situation has to go through a process. For victims, justice comes when someone besides them believes in the wrongfulness of the abuse; when others make an attempt to hold the perpetrator accountable and bring about reparation for the abuse; and when guardians are willing to accept responsibility for delayed or ineffective intervention without invoking guilt. For perpetrators, there must be genuine remorse and acknowledgment of the abuse; a consistent willingness to deal with the abuse and harm caused; a refusal to use culture as an excuse for avoiding responsibility; a serious commitment to stop abusing; and understanding how the abuse was a culmination, not the beginning, of a pattern of abusive thinking and behavior. For the family as a whole, the possibility of restoration is more achievable with open communication and an end to secrecy on which ICSA thrives. There must be sincere attempts made to address the profound betrayals experienced by victims and to be available to them during their healing process; a willingness to learn and prevent how boundaries are violated; while making sure that the perpetrator's interactions with all children are scrupulously transparent and supervised. Maya's experience speaks volumes: "All I can remember of that incident is standing at a darkened doorway with my parents at the far end, looking through the doorway at me. My brother was with me. And my parent's faces were angry. After that incident, we left the city and moved to another place. But my brother did not accompany us. He was sent to a boarding school. The redeeming feature was after he went to boarding school, he was only home once or twice a year. But my parents never thought of protecting me when he came home, because he continued abusing me for many years. Even up to the time I was twelve or thirteen, he would just indicate with his head that I should go up to the roof terrace and I would just go because I didn't know how to say no."

Intervention Is Messy

At a workshop I was presenting on ICSA, a South Asian woman sitting in the front row appeared upset. During the discussion, I invited her to share her thoughts and she revealed that several years ago she had walked in on her cousin molesting her little daughter. She immediately confronted the cousin and took whatever actions she had to. Although her daughter is fine now, the woman never got over the shock and grief of witnessing her daughter being abused and her cousin perpetrating the abuse. She said she could not accept that her daughter had to go through the molestation at all. It was obvious from this woman's demeanor that she was very shaken and still in mourning over what had happened. I believe that she was grieving not only over what happened to her daughter, but also for herself. Her own sense of safety in her own home was violated. This mother had to reckon with her favorite cousin's violation of her trust. He had compromised the comfortable space of their relationship and threatened the notion of family.

Intervening in an incest situation is complicated and scary. There may not be neat and easy formulas between reaction and intervention. For instance, a sexually abused niece can hate and love her uncle at the same time. An interventionist may find her- or himself caught in the middle of these conflicting emotions. A loving uncle, who is his sister's greatest ally, may be sexually abusing his sister's daughter. Part of being an interventionist is to recognize and acknowledge the gray areas that emerge when incest is exposed. But gray areas should not muddy the truth that there is a victim and there is a perpetrator, and perpetrators bear full responsibility for their choice to become abusers.

Often, people put off intervening for fear of errors in judgment. To keep damage from such errors to a minimum, psychotherapist Smita Vir Tyagi recommends that we find out ahead of time what is involved in intervention, who plays what role, which intervention is best within a particular time frame, what are the goals of each intervention, who benefits from these goals?

However, for many, intervention becomes hypothetical. Even if one was abused as a child, he or she does not expect it to happen to his or her own children. For instance, as an incest survivor, I never imagined that my sister could also be abused. I never imagined there could be classmates who were being abused. I believed for a very long time that I was the only one. When people believe they are the only one, there is no reason for them to think about protecting others, because they do not realize that there *can* be others. Detection, intervention, and protection only become necessary when we anticipate danger. Even more, they do not imagine that their children could engage in inappropriate sexual behavior or perpetrate abuse, which means that even if sexual abuse prevention is talked about, it will not include conversations that give permission to children to "come and tell" if they have done or wanted to do "a bad touch" on someone else.

Confronting Perpetrators

It is extremely difficult to get those who commit child sexual abuse, particularly on known victims, to acknowledge the wrongfulness of their actions. The majority of ICSA offenders will adamantly deny the abuse. Denial keeps them from acknowledging the damage they have caused and the deliberateness of their actions. Without denial, they cannot hide behind "No harm was done, it was just for pleasure."

If there is any admission of guilt, it tends to be an opportunity to confess an indiscretion or a momentary weakness caused by external forces such as "I didn't have sex for a long time"; "I have needs and my family won't tolerate my going to prostitutes"; "My religion doesn't allow masturbation"; "My family won't approve of dating the opposite sex"; "I was drunk and did not know what I was doing"; "I was under a lot of stress"; "The victim came on to me"; or "I don't know what made me do it." Such confessions minimize the harm done and deny the personal choices involved in committing child sexual abuse. They usually end with ardent promises never to do it again.

ICSA perpetrators also look for ways to take the blame off themselves by accusing their victims, even children, for causing them to commit the abuse. They discredit victims' allies and protectors by accusing them of misunderstanding what really happened, overreacting, or having a personal agenda to create family divisions. These tactics, whether conscious or unconscious, pit family members against each other and against the victim. They are a powerful way to elicit compliance and silence, to divert attention from holding perpetrators accountable. Neesha's story clarifies some of the abusive power dynamics operating within families where ICSA is occurring.

Around the age of twelve or thirteen, my grandfather started to sexually abuse me. He would come into my room at night, caress my legs, and try to get into my pajamas. Nobody inside the family had ever abused me. All of a sudden at twelve or thirteen, my grandfather's coming into the room. That was when I told my mom about my grandfather. She was outraged. She was angry. And when I told her she said, "That bastard. He did it to me and I hoped he would not do it to my daughter and how could he do it to my daughter?" She spoke with her brother about it and they both sat down and talked with my grandfather. And my grandfather said that I had provoked it. I went and sat on his lap. That it was my fault. I was wearing provocative clothing. What was he expected to do? And my uncle, my uncle basically said, "Yeah, you really need to keep a check on your daughter, look at how she's running around and what she is doing." When I came back later on that day, there was an eerie sort of icy silence in the house. And that was the last that anyone ever mentioned about that.

When Neesha's mother decided to intervene on behalf of her daughter, she chose to seek her brother's support and not her husband's. Most likely, she was trying to prevent the possibility of violent confrontations between her husband and her father. She also may not have told her husband about the sexual abuse by her father. She may have been afraid that her husband would blame her for failing to protect Neesha from a known perpetrator. When the alliance with her brother failed and she was blamed for raising a wayward daughter, it may have reinscribed the shame that she might have been carrying because of what her father did to her. Whatever the confrontation evoked for Neesha's mother, the result was that Neesha was revictimized by her uncle and her mother, while the perpetrator-grandfather escaped censure. Neesha stated, "After that [my mother] turned on me, around the clothing I wore, makeup, wanting independence. All of that was to her a pointer to the fact that I was bringing on sexual advances from men. She was the only support I had in my life, the only one, who backed me up in certain things I wanted to do. So, I think that made the betrayal much worse from my mother."

Since those who commit ICSA are part of our families, our communities, and our culture, they know how power dynamics within families operate, and use it to their advantage. Furthermore, cultural silences around sex and sexuality create an atmosphere where children can become easy targets for abuse. Their vulnerability is exacerbated by a climate within the home that provides physical refuge while being unreliable with regard to safety. Such was the case when my father's brother, one of my perpetrators, was able to easily convince me that if I told anyone about what was happening, my father, well known for his rages, would beat him up. At eight, I had no reason to doubt him and was able to fill in the blanks: my father would probably kill him, get in trouble, which would get me in trouble, the family would be dragged into the spotlight, and we would all be shamed. To have imagined anything else was outside my experience as a child growing up in that household.

ICSA perpetrators also use cultural and religious notions about virginity, female honor, chastity, and virtue to rationalize the sexually abusive acts they commit.

For instance, as noted by Radhika Chandiramani, who coordinates the Delhi-based organization, Tarshi, which deals with sexuality and reproductive health: "One man [who called the hotline] argued that it was because he was concerned about the child's virginity/virtue that he chose to masturbate by rubbing himself on his victim [and did not penetrate]. Another man said that because he had used his fingers [as opposed to a penis], he had not deflowered the girl" (Poore 2000b, 12).

The real significance here is that perpetrators understand very well and benefit from the high premium placed on family reputation, honor, and harmony to convince victims to be silent. They rely on being able to persuade the family to extend its protectionism in the event the abuse is discovered, where protectionism includes hiding or minimizing shame-creating incidents. This same protectionism becomes a double-edged weapon. It can be turned against victim-survivors who speak about the abuse and are seen to defy family loyalty and solidarity.

Under these circumstances, one would think that ICSA perpetrators have nothing to fear and are impervious to the threat of reprisals. Contrarily, most are afraid of being discovered because they, too, do not want to be ostracized and lose family ties. Moreover, knowing that society views child sex offenders as deviant sick people, ICSA perpetrators are even more secretive (Poore 2000a). For instance, in South Asian communities, where mental illness and seeking mental health services are still very much a stigma (Sheikh 2000), perpetrators will want even more to avoid the humiliation of being perceived as mentally defective or insane.

Sex offender treatment cannot ensure that perpetrators will not repeat their violations. However, there can be lower recidivism rates if (1) treatment is grounded in feminist analyses of patriarchy and violence against women; (2) practitioners are committed to cognitive and behavioral changes; (3) perpetrator-participants are willing to change not only their behaviors but also their power-over attitudes; and (4) perpetrators are able to transform shame and guilt into genuine remorse for their actions and commit to protocols for nonabusive behaviors. Without this reeducation, all perpetrators, even those who sincerely want to stop abusing and believe they can stop, will re-abuse—if not against the same victim, then another.[5]

Collective versus Individual Actions

What will it take for the South Asian community not to be passive bystanders? Many South Asians learned to become bystanders a long time ago—when we saw girls being touched on buses and women being brushed up against in public places and no one did anything. We saw that those who spoke out on those buses received no support and in some cases were scolded for making a scene. According to psychiatrist Judith Herman, "Without a supportive social environment, the bystander usually succumbs to the temptation to look the other way" (1992, 8).

In 2003, during workshops on the overlaps between domestic violence and ICSA in South Asian communities, I asked several participants to recommend community-based collective actions that would improve intervention and prevention. Their top three suggestions were (1) have members of the South Asian community sign a social contract with incest perpetrators to hold them accountable for their actions and keep them from minimizing their potential for repeat abuse; (2) train groups of incest survivors to meet with incest perpetrators who are not their own and use these face-to-face meetings to inform perpetrators of the harmful effects of child sexual abuse; and (3) make ICSA perpetrators aware of the consequences of their actions on the child and family, and remove perpetrators from the home or give them the option to leave.

Other recommendations spoke to family needs: train family members to provide peer support for those who are intervening on behalf of a child victim or adult survivor; provide support services for South Asian women who are trying to keep their children from being sexually abused by known perpetrators; develop appropriate terminology and language for talking about sexual abuse in the home; educate South Asian battered women about what signs to look for to help them detect if incest might also be happening; encourage mothers who are not supportive of the incest victim or unable to protect the child to consider letting someone else, such as a trusted family friend or extended family member, care for the child; help mothers of incest victims who were sexually abused as children to explore their own experience of incest and examine what helped or could have helped them at the time; and find reliable, safe, and trustworthy South Asian community members across different ethnic and religious groups to be part of an informal safe-homes network for child and youth victims of incest and/or their mothers, so that victims are not culturally displaced as they grapple with the trauma of abuse and consequences of disclosure (Poore 2004).

Clearly most of the recommendations target mothers, not fathers or other nonabusing male relatives. This speaks to the unfortunate realities that (1) mothers are most often the receivers of disclosure when it comes to child sexual abuse; (2) most fathers are less emotionally and/or physically available to their children; and (3) the majority of South Asian daughters have no language with which to talk to their fathers about sexual violence.

Campaign against Fear

I believe that we also need a South Asian intergenerational campaign against fear to address the worries that feed the community's collective indifference, denial, and apathy. By suggesting this campaign, I do not deny the many valid reasons behind peoples' fears, but a campaign could help individuals scrutinize their fears and reasons. Unmasking these fears could help families unravel the intricate, interwoven layers of silence and denial they use to distance themselves from the realities of family-based child sexual abuse. Perhaps this could translate into perpetrator prevention and child protection, where more family members and people who are in the lives of victims and perpetrators would be willing to step outside their comfort zones and discard the codes of silence. Part of the campaign against fear should also involve consciousness-raising groups to develop culturally relevant ways to assist South Asian guardians (who may or may not be the parents) of children needing protection from in-family perpetrators.

Given the prevalence of ICSA universally and within the South Asian community, there is a good chance that someone (maybe more than one person) we love and care about was sexually abused as a child by person(s) they knew and trusted. The effects of this abuse and the compounding effects of silence and isolation touch not only the victim, but also everyone who is closely connected to that victim; which means that, whether we are aware of it or not, someone else's experience of child sexual abuse is having an impact on us.

Instead of arguing whether ICSA happens in the South Asian community, or whether it can happen in "our" families or "our" homes, it would be more productive to acknowledge that it does happen and it happens a lot more than we care to admit. Then, do something about it. Otherwise, as Shamita Das Dasgupta has pointed out, "A house of cards is held together by spit not glue. So when it dries what happens? In a crisis, who keeps the house of cards going and at whose expense? Who does the house of cards benefit?"

NOTES

1. The anecdotal information presented in this article is based on interviews that were conducted for *The Children We Sacrifice* (TCWS) project, which involved the development of a resource book and video documentary, written, produced, and directed by the author and released by SHaKTI Productions (Poore 2000a).

2. The South Asian women's organization quoted here had previously taken the position that "this type of abuse does not happen in our community, to our children."

3. The perpetrator-brother was eighteen when he was sentenced to serve six months in jail, six months on a tether, and a three-year probation. He was subsequently deported and the parents, with their daughter and him, returned to India.

4. Personal communication with South Asian women in Canada and the United States, May 27–July 1, 1997; August 12–14, 1998.

5. Based on author's research and interviews for *Enemy on the Inside*, a video documentary on ICSA perpetrators (in preparation).

9

The Violence That Dares Not Speak Its Name

Invisibility in the Lives of Lesbian and Bisexual South Asian American Women

PRAJNA PARAMITA CHOUDHURY

In embarking upon writing this essay, I feel a great responsibility knowing that mine is the only representation of lesbian and bisexual women's experiences in an anthology on South Asian American women. Initially, I tried to assuage this pressure of representing my community accurately by soliciting the input and feedback of two other queer South Asian women working in the antiviolence movement.[1] The impossibility of incorporating the views and experiences of all queer South Asian women into one chapter soon became apparent, and my collaborators encouraged me to stay with one perspective. As with any sole representation of a minority group in a forum, I do not claim to represent all queer South Asian women, who are as diverse as our subcontinent and the diaspora. I share my own views and experiences, informed by many working to end violence within lesbian, gay, bisexual, and transgender (LGBT), immigrant, and people of color communities. I share this in the hope that we can begin recognizing, acknowledging, and responding as a South Asian community to the violence experienced by this segment of our community.

Unfortunately, while there is a growing body of literature by and about queer South Asians, there is a scarcity of research specific to this population. Thus, I pull from personal experiences, anecdotes, case studies, and the body of research on violence experienced by the *general* LGBT population in the United States. While some of the findings may be extrapolated to the South Asian LGBT community, there may also be specificities within this community that cannot be assumed by this body of work.

The Violence of Invisibility

When I think about the violence experienced by South Asian American lesbian and bisexual women, the most common and pervasive violence, the one underlying all the other forms of violence, is also the least easily named and identified. It is the violence that leads to only one article being submitted to this anthology on the experiences of this subgroup of South Asian American women, despite the large numbers of lesbian and bisexual South Asian activists and leaders in the antiviolence movement and despite the efforts to seek out such submissions. It is the violence that made me seriously question whether I should write this article at all, and then whether I should attach my name to it. Although I have worked for LGBT rights and wellness for nearly a decade, I have always attached my "nickname" to articles I have written for South Asian publications. This enigmatic violence against queer South Asian women that I speak of is the silencing and erasing of our existence, so effective that it makes us inflict further violence upon ourselves by silencing and erasing ourselves from our communities of origin.

The self-erasing women I speak of are not only the quiet, apolitical, and ashamed, we are also the vibrant, passionate, committed, often "out and proud" women working for equality, peace, and justice on the multiple fronts of race, gender, class, sexual orientation, environment, economics, healthcare, etc. We are also those women unashamed of who we are, living honestly and actively in the world. Yet, I hesitate to sign my proper name in an anthology that will be read in the mainstream South Asian American community.

I grew up in a tight-knit Bengali community, proud of my culture and not at all understanding those of my peers who seemed to want so much to "act white" or "just be American." After relocating to another part of the country to further my education soon after coming out, I very much wanted to connect to the local Bengali community—to once again be part of a community in which I could be myself, speak my language, and celebrate my culture. But in order to be comfortable expressing one part of myself, culturally and ethnically, it became clear that I would have to hide another part of myself—my sexual orientation—in order to become an accepted member of the community. I found myself not returning calls and unconsciously trying not to grow too close to (presumably) straight Bengalis that I met.

I gradually stopped attending Bengali cultural events, as one of the first questions I was always asked is whether I was married. I do not even know how to answer that question. Technically, the answer is "no," since my legal status, according to the state, is single. Nonetheless, that answer leaves me uneasy, making me feel I am lying.

I share my life with a partner, and we do everything that I grew up learning that married people do—taking care of our home and each other, maintaining social and familial relationships in addition to our careers. But answering this question truthfully holds many dangers—will the person think I have inappropriately shared too much information (although he or she is the one who asked)? Will the person walk away and not want to interact with me any further? Do I want to subject myself to such immediate judgment when I am just trying to be a part of my community?

My culture, thus, has become something I only practice privately at home—listening to music, cooking food, watching films, speaking my native tongue with family members—not something that I participate in *with* my community. And, I realize that I do this to myself: I erase myself from my community for fear of and preempting being erased by them. I do not fear rejection from non-Bengali communities because as an immigrant and a person of color in the United States, I am prepared for that. While certainly difficult and painful, exclusion from the mainstream community in the United States is not as anguishing as the fear of being excluded from my own people in a land that is not mine.

As LGBT people, we have to decide on a daily basis whether to come out. Mainstream Bengali circles are the only communities within which I have chosen repeatedly *not* to come out. As a result, I have become less and less involved with my community over the years. It takes too much energy to erase myself continually. How can I be part of a community that cannot acknowledge my relationship with my partner, the family that I have formed?

It is not just my sexuality that I speak of. Being queer is not just about whom we sleep with. It is about the structure of our families and our lives, including who we share our lives with, come home to, cook with, eat with, and do laundry with. It concerns who we socialize with; where our children come from; what type of art or activism we participate in; what films we like; what actors or actresses we follow; what causes we support; what events we go to; what fashions we subscribe to; what books we read; what politicians we vote for; what kind of work we engage in; and the nature of our relationships with our families of origin.

The question "Why do you have to flaunt it?" is shockingly common. In a community in which it is assumed that any woman over thirty is either married or defective and where people feel free to ask personal questions about one's life (e.g., one's marital status, profession, income, parents' professions and income, etc.), one has to try very hard—even lie—in order to *not* "flaunt it." What I experience as many straight people's perceptions of flaunting it is any discussion in which a queer person's sexual orientation does not remain completely hidden. The judgments and exclusions that my family members and I would face with honest responses to those questions are often devastating. It is frequently the family members that impose the invisibility in the first place, due to their own fears of marginalization.

I do not consider myself closeted, since I am out in every other space I inhabit. But there are so many in our community who are closeted, who see no other option but to keep a huge part of themselves hidden. I cannot believe closeting as a survival strategy is a passive choice, as being lesbian or bisexual informs every ordinary aspect of our lives. The closet is multidimensional, and many of us feel compelled to hide ourselves within the context of our families, workplaces, ethnic or religious communities, friends, public lives, and sometimes even from ourselves; that is, having romantic and/or sexual relationships with other women without acknowledging one's own desires.

There are, of course, valid reasons for staying in the closet. The emotional, financial, and/or physical violence that lesbian and bisexual women and possibly those we care about face is very real. What emerges (or sometimes what we only fear may emerge) when we are seen and heard is total rejection, disconnection, and often uncontrolled violence and rage. The closet provides at least some protection from the homophobia and misogyny we must face in a world that oppresses women for loving contrary to what is mandated and for daring to manifest our true selves.

Hate Violence

Despite some social tolerance, it is still impossible for many of us to think about sexual minorities without concurrent thoughts of the violence and persecution they face. Violence against lesbian and bisexual women is the concomitance of human rights abuses against sexual minorities and violence against women:

> Women who do not conform to dominant heterosexual norms, whether they identify themselves by terms such as lesbian, bisexual, single by choice, transgendered, or by any number of other words in any number of languages, are raped, assaulted, battered, coerced into heterosexual marriage, forced into psychiatric treatment, separated from their children, and denied education and employment in countries around the world. The context and often the form of these abuses . . . are determined not only by a woman's sexual orientation but by race, class, religion, age, ability, and other factors. The role that homophobia plays in violence against women . . . is rarely documented or acknowledged. (Minter and Rosenbloom 1996, 26)

LGBT individuals experience the highest rates of hate crime per capita than any other group in the United States. In 2003, 2,051 anti-LGBT incidents were reported to eleven community-based organizations tracking anti-LGBT violence in different regions of the country (Patton 2004). In the same year, the FBI reported 1,239 sexual orientation based incidents of hate crimes (FBI 2004). This number is also not a true reflection of the full extent of anti-LGBT hate crime across the United States, as reporting these statistics to the FBI is voluntary for local law enforcement agencies. In recent years, we have witnessed an explosion in the number of hate-motivated murders against the LGBT community, particularly of transgender individuals. Such crimes, as well as acts of hate violence that may not be crimes by legal definition (e.g., hate speech), may be perpetrated by strangers but are as often perpetrated by coworkers, neighbors, acquaintances, or friends/community members who come to know about or suspect the target's sexual orientation. Only in the last twenty years has violence against LGBT individuals come to be seen as *wrong* in the United States.[2] However, many perpetrators still view gay bashing as their civic duty or a rite of passage to heterosexual adulthood.

For LGBT people of color, such attacks are often combined with racial or ethnic hatred. For example, the National Coalition of Anti-Violence Programs (NCAVP), a network of twenty-seven antiviolence organizations that monitor and respond to incidents of violence affecting the LGBT community, reported substantial increases in victims who identified as Middle Eastern (e.g., +155 percent in 2001 over 2000, +26 percent in 2002 over 2001) and those outside the list of racial and ethnic categories provided by NCAVP's intake form (+244 percent in 2002 over 2001), due to increased numbers of people of Arab, Middle Eastern, and South Asian descent reporting both racist and anti-LGBT incidents they suffered after the 9/11 attacks (Patton 2002, 2003). The current hyperpatriotic and militaristic environment foments hate violence against anyone considered outside the bounds of mainstream culture and thus a threat to the American way. Members of the LGBT community are quite certainly assigned to this outsider category.

An example of violence targeting members of any number of groups considered cultural outsiders is an incident in which two buildings in San Francisco's Mission District were targeted for vandalism. The culprits spray-painted on the Women's Building: "Kill Arabs," "Kill Dykes," "Why Are Dykes So Ugly," and "Why Are Cunts Nasty?" The Women's Building houses many social justice organizations supporting women. Similar epithets were spray-painted on the building that houses Community United against Violence (an LGBT antiviolence organization) and other LGBT and progressive organizations. A flyer and poster advertising a peace event was defaced with graffiti that included "Die Sand Niggers" and "Dead Arabs = Peace" (Patton 2003).[3]

Interpersonal homophobia and violence—whether in the form of discrimination in housing, employment, or public accommodations; slurs and taunts; or physical violence leading to murder—is fueled by state-sanctioned homophobia and violence, both in our countries of origin as well as in the United States. Such sanctions include the law or custom of stoning or murdering lesbians in countries such as Iran and Saudi Arabia (SodomyLaws.org 2005), as well as outdated laws criminalizing sexual activity between consenting adults of the same sex. Section 377 of the Indian, Bangladeshi, and Pakistani penal codes punishes "carnal intercourse against the order of nature," with lifetime imprisonment. Originally a British law, it was later repealed from the country of its origin but not its former colonies (International Gay and Lesbian Human Rights Commission 1995, 2003; SodomyLaws.org 2005).

In the United States, state sodomy laws were not declared unconstitutional until 2003. Current state policies fueling anti-LGBT sentiment in the United States include recently imposed laws and a potential constitutional amendment to prevent the possibility of legalizing same-sex unions. Such legislation proactively prevents gays and lesbians from seeking basic rights all other citizens take for granted, such as being able to visit their partners in the hospital when critically ill; securing custody of a child they helped raised or a home they helped build if their partner should die; receiving health insurance benefits through their partner; and being able to immigrate in order to be with their life partner. In several countries, including the United States, lesbianism has been used as grounds for removing children's custody from mothers and granting it to even abusive fathers. According to U.S. federal law, it is perfectly legal to discriminate against someone in employment, housing, or public accommodation due to one's sexual orientation or gender presentation.[4] In addition to these forms of institutionalized homophobia and heterosexism, the frequent homophobic statements made by political and religious leaders also promote and give legitimacy to violence and discrimination at the interpersonal level. For example, the late Pope John Paul II's assertion, "It is legitimate and necessary to ask oneself if [same-sex marriage] is not perhaps part of a new ideology of evil" (Curtis 2005).

Victims of hate crime (e.g., robbery or extortion perpetrated on the basis of sexual orientation) are often specifically targeted because the perpetrator recognizes that the crime will not be reported. Victims often do not report such crimes because it would entail coming out and potentially facing revictimization by law enforcement authorities and the legal system. It may also carry the threat of losing livelihoods and social relationships for the victims if the nature of the crime is leaked. Underreporting of hate crimes is even more severe for LGBT people of color, immigrant, and other disenfranchised communities, as safety is routinely viewed as something they do not deserve or expect. Most often, lesbian and bisexual women of color expect to be revictimized rather than assisted by authorities due to the compounding jeopardy of race, sexual orientation, and gender, as well as potential class, immigration status, and language barriers.

Personal experiences of hate violence or hearing of hate violence perpetrated against someone in the community can drive people further into the closet. One may take greater precautions to hide anything that would identify them as LGBT to a potential perpetrator; or would prevent them from walking down the street or getting a cup of tea without being harassed; or hinder their efforts to obtain a job or an apartment. Many, of course, do not have the luxury of invisibility, particularly those who are differently gendered. Others struggle against the deep oppression involved in self-erasure but know that to exist in the world as who they are might unleash myriad forms of violence against them.

In addition to the fear of losing family and community support, the threats of violence keep a large number of LGBT individuals closeted. Ironically, secrecy is also a setup for violence, as it contributes to making a person more vulnerable to being controlled by the people who know or suspect one's dark secret. Furthermore, these attempts to not disclose one's sexual orientation makes a person afraid of authorities and community members to whom one could otherwise report violence and receive support.

Violence in the Family

Lesbian and bisexual women throughout the world face a high rate of psychological and physical abuse from their families (Minter and Rosenbloom 1996). This may be an escalation of a preexisting pattern of family violence against the woman or a new response to a woman's sexual orientation. In many of our countries of origin, lesbian and bisexual women may be tortured or held captive by their families while the legal system and authorities support the right of the families to do so. A lesbian couple's testimonial in India's *Savvy* provides a chilling example:

> Sheela's [violently abusive] father saw us. He chased us, and reached the FIRM office [Foundation for Integrated Research in Mental Health, where the couple was helping with an AIDS prevention project] with the police. On his request, the police bundled us into the jeep and took us to the Women's Cell. At the station, the police pushed us around, closed Sheela's mouth, didn't allow her to speak and used abusive language. They told us that Sheela would have to go with her father. When she objected, the police told us that they would book us under IPC 377 for being involved in unnatural sex. (Nandu and Nandu 2004, 20)

The potential for such abuse and torture is particularly acute for youth, who already have few legal rights or socioeconomic resources (Minter and Rosenbloom 1996). The violence may take many forms, such as throwing a young or dependent woman out of the home, attempting to control her by forcing her to go to reparative therapy, compelling her to submit to an arranged marriage through physical violence or threats of violence, and withdrawing financial or emotional support.

The violence and control exerted by families on their lesbian daughters, often stemming from the fear of their own or the daughter's marginalization, in combination with living in a society in which women have little autonomy over their own lives, have driven many South Asian lesbians to suicide:

> A recent example . . . is the series of lesbian suicides in Kerala. When two women decide to take their own lives purely on the grounds that society will not tolerate their love, one needs to expand the traditional focus of civil rights activism beyond the state as violator and seriously examine how institutions such as the family and the community deny a basic autonomy to lesbian women leading to the taking of one's life. . . . *Humjinsi*, a resource book on queer rights, documents over 30 cases of lesbian couples committing suicide in a period of five years. According to Deepa V., a lesbian rights activist documenting the cases of lesbian suicides in Kerala, most women committing suicides are from Dalit, adivasi, working class communities, and have therefore been subject to multiple discriminations. . . . One explanation to the issue of women experiencing multiple discriminations largely committing suicide was that women-loving-women from middle class or more privileged backgrounds, while also experiencing a lot of suffering, have more choices with which to deal with their different sexual orientation. They have the option to move to an urban setting or have the resources to be able to maintain a secret same-sex relationship. (Khaitan 2004)

In the United States as well, LGBT youth are two to three times more likely to commit suicide than their heterosexual counterparts and may comprise up to 30 percent of all teen suicides in the country (Gibson n.d.; Morrison and L'Heureux 2001). One form of abuse of LGBT adolescents in the United States is forced institutionalization, especially of minors whose parents can commit them to institutions to undergo psychiatric torture to cure them of their sexual orientation.

A few years ago, I worked with Farida (a pseudonym, as are names of all survivors), a young woman in her early twenties who immigrated to the United States as an adolescent and whose family had recently discovered her lesbianism. Her father, mother, and brothers beat her and tied her up with the intent of forcibly taking her back to their country of origin. She fled to another state to escape the very drastic consequences of the discovery of her sexual orientation. Farida, like the majority of South Asian victims of homophobic family violence I have met, instead of feeling anger at the abusive responses of her family, felt much guilt for causing the family crisis. Some submit to arranged marriages due to physical coercion or guilt and are then subjected to another form of violence experienced by lesbians—nonconsensual sex within compulsory heterosexual marriage.

Relationship Violence

Intimate partner violence experienced by lesbian and bisexual South Asian women remains invisible and unacknowledged by many in the anti–domestic violence movement as well as the LGBT community. This form of violence may be experienced from a husband or husband's family, perhaps when they suspect or find out her sexual orientation, or within a same-sex relationship. The LGBT community often resists acknowledging same-sex intimate violence, as it fears further marginalization of an already marginalized community. This shame and fear of mainstream stereotyping is compounded for women, who are queer *and* South Asian.

People outside the LGBT community often resist acknowledging same-sex domestic violence because such recognition would have to be founded on the recognition of our relationships, and because it would threaten the theoretical model of domestic violence based solely on sexism. In the case of already marginalized community-based agencies, such denial of same-sex violence might be tied to an unwillingness to be further marginalized by the community's mainstream for associating with lesbian/bisexual women. Or, it may arise from the belief that heterosexual women from their communities would stop seeking services if they also serve lesbian/ bisexual women, thus prioritizing one group of women over another.

It is not uncommon for Asian activists and service-providers to say: "It's hard enough getting women to come to the [battered women's] shelter. Having . . . lesbians . . . there will only drive others away." Such a response reveals the flawed assumption that domestic violence occurs in a vacuum—unconnected to a woman's multiple identities. It assumes that identity itself does not become a weapon in the hands of a batterer. It assumes that how a woman experiences domestic violence is not linked to who she is in

society, or how she is perceived by her community, both of which contribute
to how she views her chances of escape, and whether she can imagine resistance. Even more tragically, there is an assumption that the decisions made
by advocates, activists and service-providers are not based on power and
privilege. (Poore 1997, 15)

Intimate violence in same sex relationships follows similar dynamics as those
in violent or controlling heterosexual relationships. The effects are also similar—
the destruction of a person's feeling of self-worth and self-efficacy, patterns of escalation of violence, the range of severity of violence, etc. Some studies of lesbian and
gay relationship violence indicate that the rate of violence and abuse in same-sex
relationships is the same as that in opposite-sex relationships (Merrill 1998).

Societal and familial violence provides the context for intimate partner violence: the more vulnerable a woman is in society, the greater the effects of violence
and the harder it may be to stop or escape the violence. Domestic violence is about
misusing power in a recurrent pattern to control one's partner. It is a form of per-
sonalized and individualized oppression, a microcosm of the oppression of groups.
Although this is overwhelmingly (but not always) perpetrated by the male partner
in heterosexual relationships, the fact that two partners are of the same sex does
not erase power differences or dynamics. However, that one of the partners is
engaging in battering behavior is not determined by her holding more socioeconomic power, but by her being disposed and willing to use whatever power she may
have in order to control her partner. The identification of the oppressor/batterer in
intimate violence between women is not clearly determined by social hierarchy.
Thus, one cannot assume that the wealthier partner in an interclass relationship,
or the white partner in an interracial relationship, is more likely to be abusive; nor
can this assumption be made regarding the poorer or nonwhite partner.

Some assume that if gender presentations differ in a same-sex relationship, it
must be that the more masculine, or "butch," partner is abusive. This is frequently
not the case. The power imbalance that exists between men and women in society
due to sexism and misogyny cannot be translated in toto and applied to women
with different gender identities or presentations. Assumptions about perpetrators
of violence cannot be based on gender presentation; instead, the dynamics of
power and control in the relationship must be examined.

Western cultural notions of women being the weaker sex perpetuate the belief
that women cannot be violent. However, as Yasmin Tambiah frequently observes: "If
South Asian women can use violence against their children and household workers,
then why is it surprising that women can batter the women they are in intimate relationships with?" (Poore 1997, 15). There is also a prevalent belief that a woman cannot rape or sexually assault another woman, although a penis is not the only possible
weapon of sexual violence. Even when abuse is recognized, the severity of violence is
often minimized when perpetrated by a woman. Many assume that abuse in a same-
sex relationship somehow poses a fair fight; therefore, no intervention is necessary.

If a battered heterosexual woman takes a self-protective, self-defensive, or reactive action, it is usually seen as such by domestic violence advocates. The same action by a battered lesbian/bisexual woman, however, is often construed as mutual abuse (Merrill 1998; Poore 1997). Such a belief ignores the systematic abuse of power and control that is at the core of domestic violence in any relationship.

Obviously, it is extremely dangerous to deny the potential lethality of any abusive relationship, gay or straight. The forms of abuse perpetrated—physical, emotional, financial, or sexual—are similar. Such violence may also include the manipulation of children, the abuse of pets, isolating the partner from friends and family, preventing the partner from participating in religious or cultural practices, or claiming that the violent or controlling behavior is simply an expression of the perpetrator's culture. Reasons for staying in an abusive same-sex relationship are often similar to those of heterosexual battered women who maintain their abusive relationships: love, children, property, fear, guilt, hopelessness, isolation, financial dependency, fear of losing friends and community support, and a belief in "making it work" despite all obstacles, among others.

While domestic violence can happen in any relationship, including relationships involving people who are out and part of an LGBT community, closeting often aggravates the effects of violence. When a woman feels that she is the only one with same-sex desires, her relationship with her partner becomes particularly isolating. Feeling that the two of them are vulnerable in the world as queer women of color may inspire a need to protect the battering partner from a society that would persecute her due to her race, gender, and sexual orientation. With no community support or models of healthy same-sex relationships, a woman may think that her partner's abusive behavior is normal, expected, or her only choice. Because domestic violence is conceptualized as a man abusing a woman, she may not even identify her partner's behavior as abusive. When the relationship itself is hidden, there is no one to identify or intervene in the violence, and no one to go to for support. The victim may be afraid that if she seeks help, the potential support person may revictimize her by applying stereotypes and attributing unhealthy or violent relationship dynamics to the race, culture, class, or sexual orientation of the couple, thus intensifying the isolation. She also may fear that if she does not do as her partner says or if she wants to leave the relationship that her partner may subdue her with threats to out her to her family, employer, immigration officials, etc.

Unfortunately, intimate partner violence experienced by lesbian and bisexual women continues to be invisible and unacknowledged even among many in the anti–domestic violence movement. Women experiencing such abuse frequently do not receive appropriate services, even when they *do* seek help. Survivors of intimate violence in same-sex abusive relationships face tremendous barriers to seeking, as well as receiving, help. Barriers to seeking assistance include not identifying the abuse; being afraid of homophobic or humiliating responses from service providers, family members, or law enforcement; and blaming themselves for the situation. In many states, "battered lesbians do not even have the option to press charges against an abusive partner because, in these states, domestic violence is explicitly defined as violence between members of the opposite sex or between spouses, former spouses, or family members who are related by blood or consanguinity" (Renzetti 1998, 124).

As domestic violence advocates are trained to believe the woman, those who are willing to help lesbian and bisexual women often end up serving whichever partner comes to them first for help. While it is important that both partners receive appropriate services in any situation of domestic violence, frequently an abusive partner in a same-sex relationship may seek out services *as a victim*. It is common for both gay and straight batterers to feel victimized, to maximize any self-protective behavior of their partner as being abusive while minimizing, justifying, or even overlooking their own violence. Evaluators who screen batterers and victims must collect a detailed history of the relationship and be familiar with the psychological tendencies of batterers (e.g., blaming their violence on others, emotional insecurity and dependence, need for control, fear of abandonment by the partner, etc.), as well as those of women who have been abused (e.g., self-blame, denial of the severity of abuse, excusing the violence, fear, hypervigilance, etc.).

Ending the Violence of Invisibility

As service providers, our first step toward better serving South Asian lesbian and bisexual women is to challenge our assumptions that they do not exist in the communities in which we circulate and work. Chances are, lesbian and bisexual women *are* in our community and *have* sought our assistance but have not disclosed their sexual orientation. We must ask ourselves, what are we doing to make these women feel safe enough to come out and seek help, particularly if they are still closeted? It is up to a service provider to actively convey to the LGBT members of our community that they will not judge, deny services, or otherwise violate or degrade someone for being lesbian or bisexual (which includes not degrading other communities with which lesbian and bisexual women may feel allied, such as gay men and transgender individuals). Without this basic level of trust, we cannot reach a significant sector of our community and thereby will continue to participate in the violence of silencing and enforcing invisibility.

In an attempt to ensure that a lesbian or bisexual South Asian woman seeking help receives services sensitive to her sexual orientation, a well-meaning social service provider at a South Asian agency may refer her to the local (mainstream) LGBT center. For the same reasons that straight South Asian women may be averse or uncomfortable seeking services at a mainstream agency, many lesbian and bisexual South Asian women also feel uncomfortable and may not want to expose themselves to the potential racism and lack of cultural understanding in a white agency. Manju, a victim of antilesbian discrimination in a medical setting, disclosed a particular incident during a videotaped interview: "I would not have approached [the local mainstream LGBT agency] to help me with this issue. I feel they are an extremely white and extremely racist organization at times. . . . Honestly, if I hadn't reported this through [the local South Asian agency], I would not have reported it. I wouldn't have reported it through a white queer organization" (South Asian Network 2005).

A South Asian organization in southern California, South Asian Network (SAN), has been taking proactive measures to become more inclusive of LGBT South Asians in their service provision and community-building activities. A Queer Advisory Board of LGBT and allied South Asian community members have been meeting to discuss the needs of the LGBT South Asian community and how SAN can better meet those needs. An initial needs assessment consisting of interviews of all staff and board members regarding their familiarity and comfort with the South Asian LGBT community was conducted. This process helped shape a series of agencywide trainings designed to raise awareness about the LGBT South Asian community, to discuss agency and community attitudes, and start creating a plan for inclusivity in the agency's day-to-day work.

The training involved a series of mandatory daylong workshops covering topics such as family issues, coming out, immigration, health, hate crime and discrimination, domestic violence, religious attitudes, and other topics. The staff and board members then strategized ways of being more inclusive of LGBT South Asian communities in each of their program areas of health, civil rights, immigration, and domestic violence. They also recognized the need to provide training on LGBT issues for all new staff and volunteers, as well as to intervene in instances of heterosexism and homophobia they observe in the South Asian and broader communities. This, they felt, was the only way to create a safer context for all members of the community to exist. There is a general understanding that this is an ongoing process of education and inclusion and not one that ends at the conclusion of the formal training. An exciting future direction for SAN's work with the LGBT community is that the organization has received funding to conduct a needs assessment of LGBT South Asians in southern California.

This work is still in progress and there are gains to be made, but the initial stage has been quite successful. Some key factors to success have been a leadership that staunchly supports the work of reaching out to the LGBT community (the executive director and board chair are active on the queer advisory board); the deep dedication of a few staff, board, and community members; and a willingness to meet people without judgment (including people with misinformed or heterosexist attitudes), allowing for frank and open discussions. It is important that this effort has been completely South Asian led and conducted, including all consultants, trainers, and advisers. In this process, strong ties have been built with the local South Asian LGBT social organization, Satrang, as a partner in this endeavor.

Seeing the transformation, growth, and healing among all parties involved in this project gives me hope that lesbian and bisexual South Asian women will no longer have to be isolated and hidden; that we will no longer feel that there is nowhere to turn when we are experiencing violence; that we will not have to choose between the racism of mainstream LGBT organizations, the homophobia of South Asian organizations, and the sexism of both if we try to seek help. It makes me hopeful that we will have a place in the community to come home to.

ACKNOWLEDGMENTS

Much appreciation goes to Fatima Jaffer and Vega Vahini for their time, contributions, and dedication, both to the community and to this essay.

NOTES

1. I use the terms *queer* and *lesbian, gay, bisexual, or transgender* (LGBT) interchangeably. *Queer* is a historically violent and derogatory epithet used to demean lesbian, gay, bisexual, and transgender people. However, in recent decades it has been reclaimed by (usually young) LGBT people as an inclusive and empowering term when used by members of the LGBT community.

2. I am reminded of a judge who in the 1980s proclaimed during a trial, "You mean it's illegal to beat up homosexuals?" I cannot remember his name, but the comment has stayed with me.

3. In a climate where multiple minorities become suspect, members of minority groups may try to escape suspicion by allying themselves with majority groups. After the events of September 11, 2001, many South and West Asian LGBT individuals expressed tremendous dismay at the racism they faced when seeking support/connection within mainstream LGBT communities and organizations (Dahir 2001).

4. Sexual orientation is not a protected class in federal antidiscrimination laws, which cover race, sex, color, national origin, religion, age, and disability. However, sixteen states *do* include sexual orientation in their antidiscrimination statutes, including Connecticut; Vermont; Washington, D.C.; and Wisconsin. Six states further include gender presentation (protecting transgender individuals) in antidiscrimination legislation. These are Minnesota, Rhode Island, New Mexico, California, Illinois, and Maine. In addition, several cities and counties nationwide have adopted local ordinances prohibiting discrimination based on sexual orientation and/or gender presentation (Lambda Legal 2005).

10

The Trap of Multiculturalism

Battered South Asian Women and Health Care

SUNITA PURI

Despite increasing scholarly attention to the social underpinnings of domestic violence in the diasporic South Asian community, there is a paucity of research on how medical treatment of battered South Asian women is informed by both politically grounded misconceptions about South Asian immigrants and a problematic version of cultural sensitivity in medical practice. The philosophy of multiculturalism links historically grounded stereotypes about South Asians with the medical treatment they receive, thereby politicizing health care in dangerous ways that result in unequal treatment of battered South Asian women.

In the health care sector, multiculturalism translates into cultural sensitivity in medical practice, a philosophy that claims health care can be improved and patients made more comfortable with treatment when providers are sensitive to cultural traits that clash with Western healing practices. In short, the hope is that consideration of a patient's background will help a physician provide health care that the patient finds acceptable. What goes unquestioned, however, are the politics of who is given the power to define a community, identify and name its different needs, and guide physicians and other social service providers to an assumed right course of action.

In this essay, I hope to explore some of the conclusions that have emerged from my research on the relationship between medical cultural sensitivity and domestic violence in South Asian immigrant communities. I am especially interested in the ways that multiculturalism in this context actually replicates structures of oppression within South Asian communities, resulting in unequal treatment of South Asian women patients on the grounds of respecting their cultural difference, a difference that is defined predominantly by male religious leaders. The propagation of specific imaginings of South Asian communities, as well as their presumed needs and sensitivities, is partly rooted in specific historical relationships between these communities and the British and American states. Such perceptions affect health care delivery to South Asian women by defining domestic violence either as a problem that does not affect the model minority South Asian Americans or as being best addressed within the confines of highly sensitive and protective South Asian communities. Viewed in this context, misapplied multiculturalism links caricatures of South Asians with health care provision that results in inequitable treatment of immigrant women and replicates the internal unequal power structures.

While the South Asian populations in Britain and America are socioeconomically and politically quite different, Britain still provides an extremely valuable example of the possible side effects of multiculturalism applied to health care settings. The philosophy of multiculturalism has been in place far longer in Britain than in the United States and has been far more influential there than it has been in America until recently. As the concept of culturally competent medical care gains momentum in the United States, it is important to consider its current and possible future effects on South Asian women by drawing on relevant information from Britain. Additionally, the South Asian women's movements in the United States and United Kingdom have remained rather separate, although they have much to offer each other. It is my hope in writing this essay to bring the struggles and differences of both movements closer and to encourage further trans-Atlantic collaboration and dialogue.

The British and American physicians I interviewed suggested that the concept of multiculturalism led them to provide medical care through assumptions about their South Asian patients, particularly women who wore *hijab, salwar kameez,* or *sari.* Some physicians, for example, did not feel it was their place to ask questions about possible violence because they did not want women to think that they were making assumptions about possible abuse based on their appearance or perceived religious affiliation. Thus, physicians based their decision to ask women clinically valuable questions largely on assumptions about a patient's possible reception of these questions, given her accent, choice of clothing, and immigrant status. The equation of apparent cultural conservatism with a woman's lack of desire to talk about sources of injury or her personal life was, the physicians made clear, not a set of assumptions that they would consciously extend to women from other ethnic or racial backgrounds such as white women. Such respect for women's loosely defined culture or religious traditions, based entirely on assumptions, actually resulted in unequal health care, which, in the case of battered South Asian women, proved not only deadly in some cases but also the largest possible source of their mistrust for physicians.

In this research, I draw on interviews with thirty South Asian women and fourteen American physicians (family practitioners, emergency room physicians, and gynecologists) in New York, Connecticut, and New Jersey. In England, I interviewed thirty-five South Asian women and fifteen general practitioners (GPs) based in Greater London and Southall. These interviews, along with reviews of primary and secondary literature on domestic violence among immigrant South Asians, form the basis of this chapter. All names of respondents and interviewees—women, physicians, and activists—have been changed. While the number of people I have interviewed is small, my analysis has been mainly ethnographic and makes no claim to be representative of a particular group of people or physicians in general. Nonetheless, the responses of the interviewees have indicated important consequences of dominant ways of dealing with and defining difference and have delineated important directions for future research.

The Origins of South Asian "Otherness" in Britain and America

Historical relationships between South Asian communities and the British and American states influence how these states perceive and deal with a wide array of social problems in these communities. In the United Kingdom, there is a better-developed research literature on the consequences of cultural sensitivity/multiculturalism in health care; thus, I will draw on important criticisms from British scholars and activists that have applicability to the American condition. In England, as many scholars and activists have noted, South Asians are seen as a problem (Prashad 2000), a group of people of color who are regarded as foreign and unwanted and whose presence in Britain is constantly threatened by right-wing white supremacist movements such as the National Front. At the same time, the British state has tried to promote cooperation with, rather than antagonism toward these communities by allowing them some autonomy in handling issues that they claim to be internal. Multiculturalism took hold in Britain primarily in the 1970s and 1980s in the education and service sectors and sought to promote and respect the distinctness of ethnic communities "based on the premise that their 'cultures' are decidedly different and ought to be left alone by the state so long as they are generally compatible, at least in public, with mainstream social norms" (Barai 1999, 5). This approach to dealing with ethnic, cultural, and religious diversity was generally regarded as an improvement upon the assimilationist tactic that Britain espoused before 1970. Multiculturalism has resulted in, for example, the creation of local level ethnic health units and funding for ethnic-specific community organizations that assist with issues that communities believe they can handle and contain independently.

This political aspect of social welfare provision makes the state more hesitant to intervene in highly sensitive issues that ill-defined communities claim as their business. These so-called communities, however, are problematically defined, and often by individuals within or outside of the group who have vested interests in painting specific portraits of these communities. Commonly, male religious leaders are called upon to speak on behalf of entire communities, many of whom suppress women's issues in order to improve the community's status in the eyes of the British state. As Nira Yuval-Davis (1997, 206) writes, "[State actors] regarded it as imperialist and racist for the West to intervene in 'internal community matters.' Women are often the victims of such a perspective, which allows the so-called male representatives and leaders of 'the community' to determine policies that ultimately concern women, their well being, and their physical safety."

In an interview, a prominent male community leader in Southall told me, "This country already thinks so low of our people. Why add to this perception by encouraging women to talk about issues that should remain within our community? Most of these concerns are misunderstandings that we can help to solve. I don't think we need intervention from others." His words reinforce mainstream perceptions that South Asians are family and community centered and are extremely sensitive to so-called incursions by outsiders into social issues that they claim to be internal.

The British state, as several critics of multiculturalism have noted, tends to comply with this internalization of community issues in order to avoid appearing intrusive, racist, and patronizing. But the questions of who defines the boundaries of and membership in a community, and whether these definitions are acceptable to all community members, particularly those most vulnerable, go unasked and certainly unanswered. While this approach to social welfare has grave consequences in all arenas, consequences are particularly deleterious for health care.

In contrast, the very different historical relationship to the U.S. state has produced the relative invisibility of South Asians—and domestic violence in their communities—on its political landscape, largely due to the perception of South Asians as a model minority. This political relationship has resulted in a different, but similarly problematic, community identity espoused and internalized at different moments by both the American state and South Asian communities. This community identity posits South Asians as economically successful, naturally hard-working, intellectually talented, and free of social problems such as gang violence, teen pregnancy, domestic violence, broken households, and drug abuse (Bhattacharjee 1992; Dasgupta 1998a; Prashad 2000). The motivation why South Asian community leaders in the United States want to hide problems from the larger community is thus the opposite of their counterparts in Britain. The South Asian American leaders wish to maintain an impeccable image of South Asian communities, as opposed to leaders in Britain, who struggle to rid themselves of the many negative sentiments directed toward the community by the British state and media.

Given this history, it is noteworthy that most of the American physicians I interviewed used terms such as "professional," "successful," "religious," and "spiritual" to describe South Asians. Among the physicians I interviewed in the U.K., the most commonly used adjectives and phrases were "religious," "troubled," "family oriented," "unable to adjust to life in the U.K.," and "sensitive about cultural matters." While the majority of physicians in the United States were surprised to learn of the magnitude of domestic violence in South Asian communities, British physicians were well aware of organizing around women's issues in the South Asian community, as well as the community's sensitivity toward outsider interference in its problems. Almost all physicians in both countries agreed that culture and religion most strongly distinguished South Asians from other ethnic groups and, they believed, was among the strongest forces shaping the outlooks and lifestyles of South Asian women. Interestingly, then, despite the different reasons behind and histories of such generalizations, both culture and religion were invoked by physicians as the concepts that best defined South Asians as a group.

When extrapolated to victims of domestic violence, this belief leads to certain assumptions about battered women. That is, perhaps more strongly than any other groups of battered women, physicians seem to presume that religion and culture structure South Asian women's responses to their abusive situations. Furthermore, to be sensitive to such assumed differences, physicians believe a laid-back multiculturalist stance is necessary.

The application of multiculturalist thinking to health care results in physicians being trained to be respectful of these essentialized cultural differences. Furthermore, it leads them to attribute some health problems of South Asian women to the culture and lifestyle that, in the minds of these physicians, South Asian women practice and defend. What results, then, is differential treatment of battered women based on a physician's interpretations of a woman's adherence to a particular culture, religion, or way of life. Despite very different American and British understandings of and relationships to South Asians, battered women in both countries received similarly inadequate medical attention. Physicians in both countries expressed a fear of inquiring about the nature of battered South Asian women's injuries on the grounds of appearing racist.

One of the most interesting findings in my study was that even though British physicians were more aware of issues of importance in these communities, their responses to South Asian women mirrored those of American physicians who had received far less training in multiculturalism, and certainly much less exposure to South Asians as a patient group, in medical school. What, then, is wrong with the version of cultural sensitivity that physicians are taught? Why has cultural sensitivity been conceptualized in a way that justifies a hands-off approach to women's health rather than active intervention, which is respectful of the relationship an individual woman has to her culture, ethnicity, and/or religion?

Experiences of South Asian Women in the United States

In speaking with doctors about domestic violence and South Asian women, I noted that physicians responded to questions in two layers: (1) the problems of meeting the health care needs of battered women in general, and (2) the challenges in caring for battered immigrant South Asian women. In this chapter, I will limit my discussion to the latter. I found that although physicians in the United States were familiar with some health problems and social issues of African American and Latino communities, the same was not true for South Asian communities. Physicians often asked for the definition of the term "South Asian" and overwhelmingly identified the community in terms of culture and religion. However, the most glaring assumption made about the community was its level of education, which physicians conflated with a woman's supposed responsibility to leave an abusive relationship. As one doctor stated, "So many Indians I know are educated and well-off.

It's quite a surprise to hear that there are so many Indian women in abusive rela-tionships. Don't they have the ability to leave? I would expect a more educated person to know that such situations are unhealthy."

The majority of the physicians I interviewed also pointed to the need to "maintain a cultural perspective" when addressing abuse. Another doctor stated, "I know that a lot of attention has been paid to culturally sensitive physicians. So I guess what I have tried to do is not assume that a woman is being battered because I don't want her to think I am insulting her culture or way it has affected her life. I'm not saying that it's a cultural thing to beat women, but my point is that I would rather the patient say something than have myself assume something incorrect and alienate her."

Obviously, this interpretation of cultural sensitivity is dangerous, for it pre-supposes that South Asian immigrant women interpret battery as a part of their culture. This particular physician believed that immigrant women are extremely protective of their familial and communal reputation, which is exactly what their abusive husbands wish them to be. Furthermore, such attitudes can potentially continue to widen the gap between health of whites and minorities in the United States, as physicians indicated that they would not make such assumptions about white women, and would, therefore, feel much more comfortable asking them routine questions that, in cases of South Asian women, would appear invasive. An important point to make, however, is that many physicians extended such beliefs to other Asian immigrant communities, simplifying the pan-Asian immigrant experience as one controlled and directed by ill-defined cultural norms.

Underlying American physicians' approach to South Asian women was ulti-mately a fear of losing them as patients. Physicians saw alienating and offending patients to the point that they may never return as their failure, which may jeop-ardize a woman's health to an even greater extent. Some physicians expressed a feeling of "being torn" between "wanting to jump in there and get these women out of their situations, no matter what their background" and "wanting to wait till the women themselves seek our help." This particular physician stated:

> You can't imagine how frustrating it is. I *knew* with one of my patients, who happens to be from Bangladesh, that her husband was beating her. I just knew it. But I honestly found it very hard to know how to start asking her about it. If I say that I know, she could never come back to see me. If I don't say anything, I feel like I'm not doing my job. So, what I did was document my suspicions in her records. But all that legal stuff aside, it's very hard. I think physicians are criticized left and right by women's groups, but they don't always know how hard a position we're in.

In addition to recognizing their own vulnerable position in such clinical encounters, most physicians also vocalized what they believed battered South Asian women might be experiencing. A gynecologist, told me, "It is difficult for me to imagine what that must be like, to be in a violent marriage when you are so far away from what you know." At her particular hospital, efforts were being made to organize grand rounds on dealing with and supporting battered immigrant women of all backgrounds, whom she recognized "are probably terrified of all kinds of authority, medical, legal, police, you name it. There has to be a way that we can meet their needs without being fearful of offending them or losing them as patients."

The physicians I interviewed, none of whom were South Asians, consistently mentioned their difference in background from South Asian patients. Many physicians vocalized a belief that, as one put it, their "cultural distance" from South Asian patients possibly prevented them from intervening most successfully in cases of domestic violence. "No, I do not understand the culture. But is that my job?" asked one doctor. It is also significant to note that while many non–South Asian physicians perceived their different ethnic background to be an obstacle in caring for battered South Asian women, their patients themselves did not share this perspective. One female patient described her experience, "I don't know that I would have wanted an Indian physician. I think what you mention is correct— American physicians may feel that they do not understand, so better that they should not be involved. But would I necessarily want a doctor who is Indian and Hindu, like me? I don't know! Would that mean that they would understand my situation and help me? I don't know! I just want some doctor to help me and treat me like he would treat other patients."

These interviews with American physicians and America-based South Asian women revealed the complexity of opinions and beliefs about providing culturally sensitive medical responses to battered South Asian women. In a health care system that is becoming increasingly consumer oriented and has to address the linguistic, cultural, ethnic, and racial diversity of its patients, U.S. physicians find themselves grappling with cultural sensitivity when such concepts were not necessarily part of their medical education or ongoing professional training. The physicians expressed a range of reactions to cultural sensitivity about domestic violence, ranging from a desire to understand and assist immigrant women to a feeling that dealing with domestic violence was simply not their job beyond the legal reporting requirements in some states. They cited the contradictions of cultural sensitivity, which simultaneously demanded understanding and proclaimed that doctor-patient differences in background and culture simply precluded true appreciation and sympathy. The frustrations around cultural sensitivity reflected physicians' general aggravations about dealing with battered women in clinical settings, fears of alienating patients in a highly politicized clinical atmosphere, and losing patients altogether due to lack of cultural awareness.

The expectation that American physicians will be able to accommodate diversity adds to another pressure, namely, that they will know how to handle complicated social situations in a clinical setting. The American Medical Association (AMA) has developed guidelines on appropriate clinical responses to domestic violence, outlined in the *Diagnostic and Treatment Guidelines on Domestic Violence* (2005). This publication includes statistics on the number of women who have been battered in the United States, how such cases present clinically, and what kinds of questions physicians need to ask to assess a woman's safety in the home. The handbook stresses that physicians "must be aware of their obligations in these cases, as well as their potential liability for failing to diagnose and/or report domestic violence" (17). In addition, it underscores the importance of handling each situation on an individual basis and paying attention to the factors that influence each woman's particular circumstances. Not once does the report suggest that a woman's cultural background should influence a physician's response to her; instead, it encourages physicians to be proactive, for ethical and legal reasons, in identifying and providing referrals and other assistance to battered women. Indeed, in some American states (e.g., California, Kentucky, New Mexico, New Hampshire, and Rhode Island), physicians are mandated reporters of domestic violence. In California, for example, physicians who have confirmed that a woman's injuries were sustained during a violent confrontation have forty-eight hours to send a formal report to law enforcement. However, reporting evidence of past abuse is not mandated. Due to such legal mandates, it is important to recognize physicians' discomfort in addressing domestic violence, as well as in dealing differently with patients of diverse backgrounds. It is crucial to allow physicians to express their own attitudes toward these issues and suggest how responses to vulnerable groups could be enhanced. My research suggested that physicians are unsure whether the rhetoric of cultural sensitivity around issues of domestic violence actually improves their ability to respond to South Asian women or simply introduces an array of paralyzing fears into clinical encounters with them.

The Experience South Asian Women in the United Kingdom

Unlike the situation in the United States, the British government has made considerable efforts to address South Asian health concerns, due to the community's status as the largest minority group in England. Yet, despite South Asians' visibility to health care providers and policy makers, a report of the Newham Asian Women's Project (NAWP) notes that the health needs of Asian women "is a subject that has been long misunderstood and marginalized by mainstream providers of medical and social services. Instead, it has been defined as a specialist area best left to the communities to address" (1998, 15). Thus, in Britain the recognition of diversity and the need for cultural sensitivity in the delivery of health care becomes reason for physicians to approach domestic violence with a stay-away policy, leaving women's well-being to their communities. Cultural sensitivity training, then, is useless if its exact implementation and limits are not problematized and discussed, and if it is not used to ensure that women receive quality, appropriate health care. This example of cultural sensitivity in the British health care system provides a crucial context in which to critically appraise cultural sensitivity in American health care.

In my research, I found that many more battered South Asian women in Britain than America were afraid of their general physicians' passing on information about their health to their families, precluding them from discussing the true source of their injuries. Additionally, even when women opened up to their health care providers about their injuries, physicians would use community leaders' vocabulary to advise women: telling them to go back to their families or to get married or remarried as a solution to their problems. The NAWP report (1998), in particular, demonstrated that while GPs were perceived as key players in the maintenance of community health, their potential to do so was limited by three factors: (1) concerns related to breaches of confidentiality, (2) lack of empathy, and (3) ineffective referral. A counselor at a prominent Asian shelter noted, "We obviously cannot expect full understanding from GPs, but the number of times they have breached confidentiality due to a faulty understanding that Asian families should know about a woman's problems in order to help her is absolutely unacceptable."

Other activists stated that such breaches of confidentiality occur because many GPs believe that complicated social issues are best addressed within South Asian communities. A woman's cultural background, therefore, exerts a disproportionate amount of influence on crucial medical intervention. A doctor who had practiced medicine for twelve years at the time of my interview declared that

> it doesn't feel right for me to interfere in problems I don't fully understand. I've always believed that it's probably best for someone else in the family to know. They are better connected with people that can actually help the woman. It's been hard to know when I should mention something, and to whom, but usually if I don't tell a family member, I don't know what else to do. Their situations are much more complicated. I will admit that white women are easier to serve than Asian women. They lack a certain cultural baggage that I just do not know how to handle.

This doctor's comments illustrate the greatest shortcoming of cultural sensitivity: reducing a patient to his or her religious, ethnic, or cultural background, and providing medical care in accordance to the limitations that a physician believes a patient's background imposes. Such an approach homogenizes members of an ethnic, religious, and cultural group, reducing them to a set of common behaviors that all of them supposedly practice, and giving primacy to the group characteristics defined by a handful of individuals. It does not recognize power differences within a community or the community's very heterogeneity.

Interpreting cultural sensitivity in such ways causes physicians to relate all aspects of an individual's health to their background, rather than to recognize the shared experience and common needs of battered women from many different backgrounds. Instead of seeing a battered woman as a woman in need of a particular kind of service and consideration, these physicians end up making a woman's background an obstacle to the provision of equitable medical care.

In fact, several British physicians, like American physicians, expressed a fear of treating South Asian women, citing the women's particular needs that physicians were not trained to properly address—which means that any exposure to cultural sensitivity training the physicians had received functioned to distance them from their South Asian female patients, based purely on the physicians' assumptions about these women's singular wants. One doctor apologetically explained, "Even though logically I may know that Asian women, like white women or black women, need to be treated a certain way, I also think that there is a much greater risk for the physician. If I ask a wrong question or word it improperly, I am always afraid that she will mistrust me or think that I have assumptions about her or her background."

Another physician allowed a woman's husband to sit in during physical examinations because family members stated that they were more comfortable with that arrangement. The doctor justified, "I realize that allowing them to stay in the room would place restrictions on my interaction with the patient, but if the family is insistent on staying, then I would oblige them. If Asians are used to this arrangement, then I must respect that."

The irony here is that the practice of multiculturalism forces physicians to make assumptions about how a woman's background will influence medical intervention, even though this approach initially militated against actions guided by such ethnocentric assumptions. However, as this example illustrates, (mis)applications of multiculturalism compromise a woman's right to confidentiality by accepting that South Asians require such ways of medical examination. These risky generalizations institutionalize beliefs that some sensitive issues fall under the purview of families and communities. Male leaders, then, enjoy the inadvertent cooperation of the health care sector in restricting South Asian women's ability to speak about, resist, and leave abusive and unhealthy situations. The welfare of South Asian immigrant women takes a back seat to these leaders' stated aim of combating racism, thereby, polarizing the struggle against gender and race inequalities.

Concluding Remarks

I initially began my research project questioning why increased attention to culture and ethnicity in medicine did not translate to South Asian women's increased faith in physicians and the medical system, particularly when dealing with sensitive issues such as domestic violence. How did South Asian women perceive attempts at enhancing cultural sensitivity? Were South Asians even consulted in researchers' and clinicians' attempts to understand what patients wanted from culturally sensitive medicine? How did physicians evaluate the efficacy of cultural sensitivity and multiculturalism in medicine? I quickly learned that there are no easy answers to these questions. Can philosophies of cultural sensitivity and multiculturalism improve health care delivery to minority battered women when negative perceptions of battered victims persist in clinical settings? Furthermore, when society, and the medical profession in particular, has not stopped to ask how cultures are defined, who gets the power to define them? As a result of these definitions, are entire communities being simplified and misrepresented in clinical practice? In endless attempts to remove biases from clinical encounters, why are increasing numbers of assumptions being made? In short, while I began my investigation with a number of questions I thought I could answer through interviews, I actually ended up with many more questions than concrete answers.

Despite the clear role that health care providers can and must play in the treatment of domestic violence victims and the physical, emotional, and mental ramifications of the violence, American and British health care sectors seem to approach patients in a way that deter individual physicians from interfering in the private family and community of South Asian women. Although the histories of multiculturalism and cultural sensitivity are very different in the United States and United Kingdom, especially with regard to South Asians as a group, the outcomes of such approaches to health care provision are eerily similar; that is, South Asian women rarely find the support and intervention that they need from their physicians.

Based on my research and my ongoing engagement with this issue, the following are a few suggestions for American physicians who are seeking to improve responses to South Asian battered women.

First, it is important to treat all women suspected of being in abusive situations with the same care and courtesy regardless of their backgrounds. The fear of offending a woman by asking about her physical safety should be replaced by thoughtful consideration of how to ask questions about possible abuse that reflect genuine concern for the patient. Most female consumers of health care I interviewed agreed that physicians *should* ask about possible abuse and that their responses would depend on the manner of questioning, level of comfort with the physician, and whether or not the physician was a mandated reporter. Prefacing a question about safety by stating its routine nature would help lessen a patient's feelings of being singled out. The American Medical Association notes, "A medical encounter may provide the only opportunity to stop the cycle of violence before more serious injuries occur" (2005, 8). In clinical settings where a woman's health and life could potentially be at risk, fear of offending her should not be a deterrent to asking necessary questions.

Research in this area supports the notion of open communication between physician and patient (Burge et al. 2005). In this study, 97 percent of the respondents that included both victims and perpetrators of violence believed that physicians should ask patients about family conflict and 94 percent thought that physicians could be helpful. Compassion, the ability to listen, and indication of an emotional investment in a patient's well-being were all listed by respondents as important qualities for their physicians to have. The same sentiments were echoed in interviews that I conducted with South Asian women. Studies such as this indicate that physicians need to focus more on embodying qualities that are conducive to patient comfort, rather than worrying about how routine questions central to patient health would offend them.

Second, on an individual basis, physicians must ask themselves how they define and handle difference in a clinical setting. Dr. Melanie Tervalon and her colleague have suggested that "cultural humility" replace the current ideas of "cultural competence" that largely structure physician responses to difference (Tervalon and Murray-Garcia 1998). According to Tervalon and Murray-Garcia, cultural humility encompasses a lifelong commitment to self-evaluation and critique, redressing the power imbalances in the physician-patient dynamic, and developing mutually beneficial and nonpaternalistic partnerships with communities on behalf of individuals and defined populations. In contrast to cultural competence, cultural humility invites physicians to abandon assumptions that they may have about how ethnic groups and cultures are categorized and defined, leaving it instead to the individual patient to describe and own their individual relationship to their ethnicity and culture. This approach both relieves physicians of having to know certain facts about people of different backgrounds and empowers patients to define themselves in ways they feel most comfortable.

The facts summarized in manuals and handouts about different ethnic and religious groups may not actually capture the realities of individuals' relationships to the different facets of their identities. For instance, a woman could be a Punjabi immigrant but might not conform to widely promoted ideas that South Asians prefer to handle domestic violence within their own families and communities. It is important not to restrict options of possible interventions based on assumptions about what a woman may want or value. Instead, giving her space to define what it is that she wants and believes is crucial in determining how best to be an ally in her healing.

Third, in the world of American medicine, increasing emphasis is placed on the proper protocols for handling various situations, both because of the growing strength of the evidence-based medicine movement and increasing fears of lawsuits. Therefore, many physicians have stated that some of their hesitancy and inaction around issues of family violence generally have to do with the lack of protocol of action that they should follow in clinical situations. It is, thus, imperative that settings of health care provision, be it hospitals or community clinics, discuss and develop protocols of action for dealing with domestic violence that are standardized, so that physicians feel more secure following the guidelines while paying attention to patients' individual circumstances. Although it is undoubtedly difficult to standardize medical responses to a phenomenon as complex as domestic violence, it is necessary to attend to physicians' concerns in addressing domestic violence. In addition, more room should be made in professional settings for physicians and medical students to discuss and receive training on responses to domestic violence.

Fourth, there should be greater collaboration between health care providing institutions and community based organizations (CBOs) working on domestic violence. The advice and experience of counselors and advocates at these CBOs should be given careful consideration, as they, far more than supposed community leaders, would be able to speak to the realities of battered women's experiences and needs. Their advice, stemming from their direct work with battered women of many different backgrounds, would be a trustworthy guide for physicians to follow when considering how to speak to women about their experiences of violence. In addition, seeking out translated materials on domestic violence and health care from CBOs can be a vital means of fostering partnership between health care groups and CBOs. It is also crucial to ensure that monolingual women of South Asian descent have access to important material about their rights as patient, issues of confidentiality and mandated reporting, and domestic violence resources within the community.

To what extent should difference matter and be codified in health care provision? To what extent should a battered woman be defined and treated as a South Asian woman, a Muslim woman, a Punjabi woman, or a Hindu woman? How could such sensitivity to a woman's background be carried out effectively, in ways that empower rather than marginalize her? To what extent does multiculturalism, despite possible good intentions, actually disguise racism and apathy toward South Asians? Clearly, cultural sensitivity and training on how to handle domestic violence must be improved if battered women—South Asian and non–South Asian alike— are to regain trust and faith in the British and American health care systems.

11

Ahimsa and the Contextual Realities of Woman Abuse in the Jain Community

SHAMITA DAS DASGUPTA AND SHASHI JAIN

In the mid 1980s, even as the South Asian anti–domestic violence activists organized to safeguard women, the mainstream of the diasporic community denied the very existence of woman-abuse. It has been particularly disinclined to acknowledge domestic violence based on four commonly held beliefs: (1) the class-based assumption that education and affluence protect against intimate violence; (2) the concept of unbreachable family privacy; (3) the shame associated with abuse perpetrated by intimates; and (4) the image of an impeccable immigrant group (read: model minority). When such violence occurred, South Asians were either oblivious to it or asserted that it was an anomaly perpetrated by a few sick individuals and therefore deserving of little serious attention.

However, domestic violence remains a significant issue among South Asians in America, an issue that has not yet been adequately addressed or investigated. This study was undertaken to attend to this gap in research and enhance understanding of domestic violence in South Asian contexts. It explores attitudes toward intimate abuse in one particular segment of the South Asian community, the Jains. The Jain community is distinguished by its adherence to radical nonviolence, *ahimsa*, and strict religiosity. Our goal in selecting this particular community was to assess the pervasiveness of woman-abuse among South Asian immigrants and test whether religious endorsement of nonviolence can erect a protective buffer against domestic violence.

Religion and Domestic Violence

Religion and women's movements have had sharp differences regarding their approaches to defining and dealing with intimate violence. Although both groups agree on a woman's right to live in safety in her family, they tend to diverge around the method of achieving it. Furthermore, they differ on the priority allocated to women's safety versus integrity of marriage (Cunradi, Caetano, and Schafer 2002; Merry 2001; Nason-Clark 2000). Battered women's movements have generally asserted that, above everything, women have the right to be safe in their homes. To this end, the legal system and community must support a woman's security, even at the cost of her marriage.

Feminist perspectives on domestic violence have connected violence against women with their secondary status in patriarchal societies and family structures (Bograd 1988; Dobash and Dobash 1979; McElvaine 2001; Pence 1999; Schechter 1982; Stark and Flitcraft 1996; Yllö 1993). The theory that imbalanced gender roles play out in woman-abuse has been corroborated by research in diverse societies, including immigrant ones in America (Ahmad et al. 2004; Boonzaier and De La Rey 2003; Bui and Morash 1999; Johnson and Johnson 2001; Yoshioka, DiNoia, and Ullah 2001). Thus, the focus of contemporary anti–domestic violence work has been on empowerment of women and social change toward gender equality (Angless, Maconachie, and Van Zyl 1998; Coker 2003; Pence 1999; Pence and Shepard 1999; Sharma 2001; Vijayanthi 2002).

Although most religious institutions readily share in the concerns of women's movements regarding battered women's safety, they have vigorously differed on the option of divorce as a viable solution to intimate violence. Instead of disintegration of marriage, religious institutions have generally promoted change in the conjugal relationship and perpetrators' hearts (assuming that behavior will follow) to ensure women's safety and well-being. For example, in most Eastern religions, such as Hinduism, Jainism, and Buddhism, the concept of divorce is absent altogether. Concurrently, many religions assume gender roles are divinely ordained and therefore beyond mortal alterations. Feminist efforts of social change, thus, have not always been acceptable to religious traditions. Despite such fundamental differences, in recent years, both religious institutions and battered women's movements are increasingly recognizing the need for collaboration to facilitate women's right to live free of domestic violence (Engelsman 2000; Fortune and Enger 2005; Holmes 2005).

Hitherto, most of the scholarly documentations and practical guides on domestic violence have focused on Judeo-Christian religions (Cunradi et al. 2002; Engelsman 2000; Fortune and Enger 2005; Holmes 2005; Merry 2001; Miles 2000; Moltman-Wendel 1978; Nason-Clark 2000). Studies on Eastern religious traditions and their relationships to violence against women are virtually nonexistent. This investigation strikes a break in this trend. The study was conducted in the Jain community, a community defined by its religion that originated and is still widely practiced in India. The keystone of Jainism is nonviolence, which makes the group particularly valuable as a milieu for research on domestic violence.

Jainism: A Primer

Jainism is an ancient religion, which is practiced mainly in the western parts of India. Although Jainism has strict behavioral guidelines for its followers, it does not believe in any omnipotent god. Jain gods are humans, *jina*, who have attained *moksha*, or liberation, from all worldly imperfections. *Jina* literally means the victorious, indicating a human, who has won over his or her earthly desires and characteristics. Jain teachers are known as *tirthankar*, humans who are not only *jina* but also social reformists and spiritual leaders.

Although the majority of Jains have not renounced society, their goal is to live a life of asceticism. Thus, Jains are required to live by five great vows of the religion, the highest of which is nonviolence (*ahimsa*). *Ahimsa* is the supreme doctrine of Jainism, which entails kindness and respect for all forms of life, regardless of its significance. *Ahimsa* entails not only nonviolence but extends to active compassion—that is, preventing others from committing violence as well as protecting all life forms from being subjected to violence. Jain scriptures forbid observants to injure, abuse, oppress, enslave, insult, torment, torture, or kill any creature or living being. Furthermore, Jainism maintains that violence can occur not only in acts but also in intentions and speech (Acharya Amrit Chandra Suri, as quoted in *Jain Study Circular* 1993). For example, an action that inadvertently causes harm is excused in Jainism, but a harmful thought, even when it has not been carried out, is considered unacceptable. Thus, Jains are exhorted not to eat root vegetables such as potatoes, onions, and turnips, as the act of pulling such vegetables out of the earth may accidentally cause harm to insects and microbes. To observe this religious directive, many Jains wear masks covering their nose and mouth so as not to inhale and cause small insects to die. All sects of Jainism endorse nonviolence as the basic tenet of virtuous conduct (Marrett n.d.). With such strong edicts of nonviolence, not only in action but also in thought and language (*man, vachan, kaya*), Jainism offers an excellent backdrop to investigate religion as a protective factor against domestic violence.

In addition to nonviolence, the role of women prescribed in the Jain tradition might also function as a shield against woman-abuse. Jainism recognizes both men and women can be *Jina*, and thus women are viewed as equal to men in spirituality and every other aspect of life. According to Jain scriptures, "Imagine the individual as a nut. The kernel hidden inside is the transmigrating soul or self, the essence of religious potential of the individual. The outer shell combines the circumstances of birth, personality, and all the existential trappings of a lifetime. Femaleness is evidently to do with 'existence,' not 'essence'" (C. Shah 1993). Consequently, Jain sects generally bestow equal religious and ritual status to women.

The Jain community is a significant presence among Asian Indians in the United States. It is a prosperous and financially successful business community. Although the U.S. census does not provide the exact number of Jains residing in the country, by one estimate it may be close to 50,000 (N. Shah 1998). According to the Pluralism Project, there are ninety-two Jain temples in the United States, five of which are located in New Jersey (Pluralism Project n.d.).

Description of the Study

No studies in the South Asian community have yet explored the population's attitude toward woman abuse, nor a specific religious context. Based on personal experiences as members of the community, we believe that the majority of our compatriots verbally condemn domestic violence and express genuine amazement at the occurrence of such incidents. Nonetheless, violence against women in the family continues to be a serious problem among South Asians (Abraham 1995, 2000b; Dasgupta 2000b; *Journal of Social Distress and the Homeless* 2000; Krishnan et al. 1998; Nankani 2000; Raj and Silverman 2002b; *Violence against Women* 1999). This study, aimed at assessing the attitude toward woman abuse in the Jain community, where it is most unlikely to exist, would allow us to understand the pervasiveness of such feelings and hence help us design more effective interventions and anti–domestic violence campaigns.

Since temples are integral to Jain religious and social life, we went to three temples in New Jersey to solicit participants. One of the authors, a Jain herself, facilitated entry into this community. Eighty men and sixty-five women agreed to complete the questionnaires. In addition, we conducted face-to-face interviews with eight individuals (four men and four women) to discuss the realities of religious beliefs and domestic violence. We also included a sample of Jains living in India to tease out the effects of immigration. We trusted that comparing and contrasting the two Jain groups, Indian and American, would yield insights into the changes that migration to the United States might have caused. The India-based Jain group consisted of twenty-five men and forty-six women.

Two separate questionnaires were constructed for the study. The first explored whether the participants were aware of any incident of domestic abuse in the Jain community and, if so, what was the nature of this violence: physical, verbal, emotional, financial, restriction of mobility, deprivation of food and water, isolation, harassment, ill-treatment for lack of dowry and/or sons, etc. The second presented an imaginary situation and four response options to gauge respondents' approval of violence against women. The hypothetical scenario was as follows:

> An Indian couple goes to a party in their friend's house. Although they do not drink alcohol usually, on this occasion the wife has a couple of drinks. She gets a bit tipsy and starts using foul language. When her husband tries to control her, she calls him an "old fool" in front of all the guests. As soon as they leave the party, the husband physically shakes the wife and angrily tells her never to behave like this again. She is terrified at his behavior.

The response options, from which the participant had to choose one, were the following:

(a) It is okay for husbands to teach wives a lesson once in a while.
(b) She humiliated him in front of all his friends. Under the circumstances, the husband's behavior is justified.

(c) The wife behaved disgracefully. She deserves to be shaken and terrified.

(d) Husbands should never physically chastise wives, no matter what the provocation.

Furthermore, each participant responded to a series of nine questions about their demographic background and strength of religious faith (religiosity). For the group in India, which was recruited from Punjab and Delhi, a local scholar translated the questionnaires to Hindi. For the group in New Jersey, although we offered individuals the option of translated questionnaires, all respondents chose the English versions.

At large gatherings in temples, we verbally explained the purpose of the study to potential participants. We described the study as looking into "attitudes toward women in our communities" and emphasized that participation was voluntary. We began by requesting the volunteer participants to complete all the questionnaires: (1) demographics and religiosity, (2) awareness of domestic violence incidents (Factual Q), and (3) addressing a hypothetical situation of spousal abuse (Situational Q). However, most participants complained about the length of time it took to finish the whole packet. Subsequently, we divided the packet into two, and half the participants responded to the Factual Q and half to the Situational Q. All participants completed the demographics and religiosity questionnaires. In the U.S.-based sample, forty-five men and thirty-two women completed the package that included the Factual Q and thirty-five men and thirty-three women completed the package with the Situational Q.

Only one of the authors recruited volunteer participants in India and followed a similar protocol. In the India-based group, fourteen men and twenty women completed the package with the Factual Q and eleven men and twenty-six women completed the package with the Situational Q.

Demographics of Participants

The Jain groups in both countries, India and the United States, were similar in many ways. The major distinction between them was the fact of immigration. For the U.S. participants the average age was approximately thirty-nine years, while for the India group the average age was a little over thirty-eight years. In the U.S.-based group, nearly 87 percent were married, while 93 percent of the Indian participants were married.

Education-wise, the U.S. group had completed at least four years of college, whereas the India respondents' average educational level was a year beyond high school. Furthermore, the U.S. group on average had received more than three years of education in a U.S. institution. Of course, the Jains in India did not have this opportunity available to them.

We recognized that it would be difficult to compare socioeconomic status (SES) of the India and U.S. based participants. Although evaluating SES by ranking occupations is a common method, the values different societies place on occupations and their remunerations are not equivalent. Between India and the United

States, this discrepancy might be so great that any assessment to compare the two might be rendered meaningless and invalid. Thus, we decided to utilize a slightly dated SES scale that is based on rankings of occupations in the United States (Duncan 1961). The Duncan SES index assigns a rank between 1 (lowest) and 100 (highest) to various categories of jobs: professional, technical, and kindred workers; farmers and farm managers; managers, officials, and proprietors (including salaried and self-employed); clerical and kindred workers; sales workers; craftsmen, foremen, and kindred workers; operatives and kindred workers; private household workers; service workers (excluding private households); farm laborers and foremen; and laborers. We felt that a scale that is dated in the United States might provide some understanding of socioeconomic status in Indian society, whereas a contemporary occupation-based scale might be quite inappropriate.

The participants' occupations were ranked according to the Duncan SES scale and each individual's socioeconomic status estimated. As expected, the results showed that the U.S. participants' average socioeconomic status was somewhat higher than their Indian counterparts (U.S.: 63.9; India: 44.9). The numbers might be better appreciated by relating them to actual occupations. For instance, the Duncan SES Index assigns a 64 to sports instructors and officials; advertising and insurance agents a 66; real estate agents 62; electricians 44; telephone operators 45; and professional nurses 46. In the U.S. group, men and women differed in their SES, the men being higher in their occupational index (67.39; compare to salaried managers, officials, and proprietors: 68) than women (59.54; compare to retail trade managers: 59). This gender difference in SES index was repeated in the Indian population (men: 50.2, compare to store floor managers: 50; women: 42, compare to photographic process workers: 42). We did not focus on family SES, as this was not the principal focus of our investigation.

Since the Jain identity is based on religious affiliation, we inquired how strongly the participants identified with their religion. To gauge religiosity, we administered a 4-point self-rating scale that varied between "Very" (3) and "Not at all" (0). The results indicated that the U.S.-based group believed it was moderately religious, with an average score of 1.9. The Indian participants also followed suit with a score of 2.2. For both groups, going to temple was not a priority.

These demographic characteristics point to the similarities between the participants from India and the United States. The dissimilarities between the groups seemed to be related to immigration, such as basic education level, U.S. education, and socioeconomic status. The Jain Americans in this study match the demographic profile of the post-1970s Asian Indian immigrants, who were required to be educated and technically skilled to secure visas to the United States.

Results

Religiosity

In addition to the self-report scale, we included nine separate items to measure which principles of Jainism the participants endorsed most (e.g., nonviolence, allowing

TABLE II.I

Participant Endorsement of Jain Religious Principles

Principle	U.S. Based N = 145	India Based N = 71
Nonviolence	.95 (95.1%)	.87 (87.3%)
Allowing children to make their own decisions	.71 (70.8%)	.76 (76.1%)
Giving money to charity	.82 (81.9%)	.63 (63.4%)
Visiting temples regularly	.59 (59%)	.41 (40.8%)
Respecting a woman's right to choose her own lifestyle	.79 (78.5%)	.77 (77.5%)
Vegetarianism	.97 (97.2%)	.93 (93%)
Standing up for the rights of the oppressed	.65 (65.3%)	.79 (78.9%)
Being helpful to all	.89 (88.9%)	.80 (80.3%)
Actively participating in social/community work	.67 (67.4%)	.62 (62%)

Note: Highest = 1

children autonomy, donating to charity, visiting temples, respecting a woman's right to choose her own lifestyle, vegetarianism, protecting the oppressed, being helpful, and participating in community work). From these nine key beliefs, the Jain Americans supported nonviolence (95.1 percent) and vegetarianism (97.2 percent) the most. In the India-based Jains, nonviolence (87.3 percent) and vegetarianism (93 percent) also received the highest approval rating. Within both groups, there were almost no gender differences.

In the face-to-face interviews we conducted, both men and women vigorously affirmed their allegiance to Jainism. Each of the eight interviewees asserted that they tried to strictly live by the rules of their religion, particularly *ahimsa*, while interacting with children, employees, coworkers, neighbors, spouses, and the environment. A forty-two-year-old man with an MBA degree said, "My colleagues at work laugh at me and say, 'Why do you keep going in an out of the building constantly'? It is because if I see a bug, I will catch it and take it out to release it. I will not kill even the smallest insects." A forty-four-year-old female accountant said, "I try not to hurt others, not take advantage of others, to control anger fully." However, they also recognized that the practice of their religion had to be compromised under the U.S. conditions. A thirty-seven-year-old male accountant said, "In America, we have to make adjustments in how we practice our religion. True Jains do not eat root vegetable such as potatoes, onions, and carrots so not to harm. Here, there is so little [vegetarian food] to eat anyway; I cannot be that strict [in my diet]."

Violence against Women

Thirty-three men and twenty-eight women in the U.S.-based Jain group responded to the hypothetical situation in the questionnaire by choosing one of four options. Except for one ("Husbands should never physically chastise wives, no matter what the provocation"), all the other options permitted violence toward women to varied degrees. Out of sixty-one respondents in this category, 36.1 percent supported the husband's use of violence toward his wife (51.5 percent men and 17.9 percent women). The overall score of the group was 0.36 (1 = highest approval of violence) with men scoring 0.52 and women 0.18. This difference between the genders was statistically significant at an extremely high level ($p > .0001$).

Eleven men and twenty-six women in India responded to the same hypothetical situation as their U.S. counterparts. Of the whole group, 45.9 percent supported abusive conduct of a husband toward his wife (45.5 percent men and 46.2 percent women). The average approval rating of spousal violence against the transgressing wife was nearly 0.46, with men and women responding virtually alike.

In the U.S. group, although religiosity and approval of spousal violence was positively correlated, the relationship was not statistically significant. Contrastingly, in the Indian group, the co-occurrence of the two variables was slightly negatively correlated; however, this, too, did not meet the requirements of statistical significance. Furthermore, among Jains in the United States, education, including U.S. education, and socioeconomic status had no statistically significant relationship with acceptance of spousal violence. In contrast, approval of woman-abuse and education was negatively correlated and statistically significant in the Indian sample ($p = .02$). That is, as the educational level went up, the approval of violence against women dropped among Indian Jains.

In the 111 combined participants from India and the United States who addressed the questions about their awareness of domestic violence incidents in the Jain community, some interesting findings emerged. In the U.S.-based group, over 58 percent admitted that they had heard of at least one form of domestic abuse being perpetrated against women. However, the response was marked by gender difference. Approximately 72 percent of Jain women claimed that they had knowledge of women being abused in the community compared to a little over 28 percent of men.

Both men and women claimed "insult and put-down" (emotional abuse) as the most common form of woman abuse. For female participants, the second most common form of violence against women that they were aware of was physical beating, while men believed verbal abuse (cursed and shouted at) was second most common. For women, verbal abuse, economic control, and restriction of independent mobility of women followed physical abuse. Women were also conscious of dowry-related criticism, disparagement because a woman lacked children and/or sons, and other unspecified harassments against women in the community. More men knew of women who were financially controlled, women being criticized because of lack of dowry as well as children and/or sons, but not of any other

TABLE II.2

Percentage of Participants Aware of Woman Abuse in Jain Community

| Type of Abuse | U.S.-Based (N = 77) | | India-Based (N = 34) | |
| | M = 45 | F = 32 | M = 14 | F = 20 |
	M	F	M	F
Physical (beating)	36.4	60.9	8.3	40
Verbal (cursed and shouted at)	59.1	56.5	25	80
Emotional (insulted and put down)	77.3	73.9	33.3	85
Economic (not allowed to have any money)	22.7	30.4	8.3	65
Restriction of mobility (not allowed to go out alone)	36.4	30.4	41.7	70
Deprivation of food and water	0	0	0	10
Locked in room	4.5	8.7	0	15
Criticized for lack of adequate dowry	22.7	17.4	41.7	75
Criticized for lack of sons/children	22.7	17.4	41.7	60
General harassment	0	17.4	16.7	0
Total	28.1	71.9	85.7	95
Overall total (both genders)	58.4		91.2	

harassment against them. Only two women and one man knew about situations where a woman had been locked up, but none could recall an incident where a woman had been deprived of food and water.

Of the eight men and women interviewed, only one man admitted that he had knowledge of a woman being abused in the Jain community. "My own aunt, my mother's sister, has been physically beaten and emotionally tortured by her husband for as long as I can remember. Everyone in the family knows about it, even her grown children. Many people tried to speak to her husband about it, but he does not listen to anyone. He keeps saying she has spoiled my life. My aunt is still living with him." Another man said that he has heard on rare occasions women being harassed for dowry but nothing else. He revealed that his sister's husband and in-laws had pestered her to get more [dowry] money from her family. But he had put a stop to it by refusing to comply. The other two men and four women all declared strongly that they had never heard of any incident of woman abuse in the Jain community. In fact, they were convinced that Jainism's firm stance on *ahimsa* in intentions, words, and actions left no possibility of any mistreatment of women.

In the Indian sample, awareness of women being abused in the community was quite high, as over 91 percent conceded such awareness (women: 95 percent;

men: 85.7 percent). Women stated that the most common form of abuse they were aware of was "women being insulted and put down" followed by cursing and shouting, as well as criticism for "not bringing enough dowry" in marriage. Limitation of mobility, economic control, and criticism for not having children and/or sons were also common, but fewer women knew about them. Interestingly, only eight women and one man indicated that they were aware of women being physically beaten in the community. However, women participants stated that they were aware of other women being locked into rooms and deprived of food and water. No man seemed to be aware of such mistreatment of women. Men were most aware of restricted mobility of women, criticism for not bringing in adequate dowry, and not giving birth to sons/offspring. They also had knowledge of women subjected to emotional, verbal, and economic abuse in their homes. Furthermore, 16.7 percent men, but no female, participants admitted to being aware of unspecified harassment of women.

Concluding Remarks

This study of domestic violence in the Asian Indian Jain community is significant at many levels. There are virtually no empirical studies of woman abuse in any South Asian religious contexts. Research on domestic violence in the South Asian immigrant community is a nascent field, to which this investigation contributes a unique cross-cultural perspective. By recruiting Jain participants in both India and the United States, the study allows us to disentangle the effects of immigration, even if in a limited way. However, due to the unequal and small number of India-based participants, we have to be cautious about generalizing the results.

The first lesson to be learnt here is that religion, however much it sanctions nonviolence and requires strict adherence to peaceable ethics, does not inoculate individuals against woman abuse. Neither does it add protective factors to women's lives. Although no religion directly encourages men to abuse women, Jainism takes an active stand against violence, thereby violence against women. Jainism's fundamental principle is nonviolence in every aspect of life and toward every life form. Jainism has zero tolerance for violence and requires all Jains to renounce aggression unilaterally. Thus, Jainism offers an extreme and ideal context to scrutinize the intersection of religion and violence against women. The results we gathered were startling.

Even though the U.S.-based participants declared overwhelming support for nonviolence as a religious code, they found a husband's harsh treatment of his recalcitrant wife appropriate. Furthermore, men showed much stronger approval of violent responses toward a transgressing spouse than women. Such gendered differences in response and the divergence between belief and behavior indicate that cultural nuances and patriarchal entitlements, rather than religious edicts, might be influencing treatment of women among Jains. Furthermore, in contradiction to the notion of gender equality advanced in Jain philosophy, almost all the interviewees acknowledged women's secondary status in the community.

The Indian participants also indicated that a husband's abusive conduct was an acceptable response to spousal conflict. Virtually no gender discrepancy emerged in this group. This is where we might be glimpsing at an effect of immigration. The heightened awareness of domestic violence in this country might have sensitized the Jain women to a woman's right to live free of violence. Hence, we see significantly lower approval of a man's abusive conduct toward his wife among Jain American women. Although awareness regarding domestic violence in India is increasing, the female participants there may not have been exposed to similar levels of anti–domestic violence messages. Without analogous social influences, the Indian women could still be nurturing the notion of husbands' entitlement to ill-treat their wives.

The high degree of approval of violence against women was substantiated by the participants' personal awareness of cases of domestic violence. More than 58 percent of the seventy-seven participants of both sexes in the U.S. sample admitted to being aware of actual incidents of domestic abuse in the community. Among the women, this number was nearly 72 percent. Among men, however, such awareness seemed to be quite low (approximately 28 percent). Among the eight men and women we had interviewed, except for one man (12.5 percent), all fervently maintained that they had never heard of any woman being abused in the Jain community. Although there were a small number of interviews, this stark disagreement between face to face and impersonal paper-and-pencil responses might imply the community's propensity to save face and avoid airing dirty laundry in public. These results are compatible with a recent study conducted in Michigan (Ramakrishnan 2005). Of the 212 South Asians surveyed there, 55 percent admitted that they or someone they knew had experienced domestic violence.

In addition to a general recognition of domestic violence, the U.S.-based participants were also aware of a variety of ill-treatments that women had experienced in the community, which included emotional, physical, verbal, economic control, restriction of mobility, harassment, criticism due to lack of dowry and children/sons. The only category of abuse that no one had ever heard about was a woman being deprived of food and water. A much higher percentage of participants in India acknowledged awareness of domestic violence than their U.S. counterparts.

These results indicate that there may be a necessity of myth-breaking in the immigrant Jain community. Although an overwhelming majority of Jain participants claimed that they clung to the most significant code of their religion, active nonviolence, nearly 52 percent men and 18 percent women viewed violence as a satisfactory method of treating "misbehaving" wives. These findings present an opportunity to examine the congruence between religious beliefs and behavior and encouraging internal modifications in the Jain community.

When we had presented the preliminary reports of this study in a Jain convention in the United States, many audience members challenged the validity of our findings and stated that since Jainism strictly enforces its code of nonviolence, woman abuse is just not possible in the community. A few others were sure that such negative changes in the community were consequences of immigration, perhaps due to contamination by other religious groups. The results from the India-based group dispute the latter argument. Over 45 percent of the Jain participants in India indicated their approval of woman abuse and 91 percent maintained that they knew such violence is a reality in their community. Thus, the claim that immigration has led to the deterioration of Jain traditions remains questionable. However, contradicting our expectations, being educated in the United States did not have any effect on one's acceptance of woman abuse.

This exploration of domestic violence in the Jain community indicates that even when religion foregrounds nonviolence, its intrinsic beliefs do not necessarily translate into protective factors for women. Acceptance of woman abuse has much deeper roots into the worldviews and lived cultures of communities. It is, therefore, important to critically analyze the individual, institutional, and cultural grounds of a community to understand, challenge, and deconstruct the nourishment it provides to domestic violence.

12

A Communicative Perspective on
Assisting Battered Asian Indian
Immigrant Women

MANDEEP GREWAL

Much has been said and written about the need to include constituents' voices in designing and implementing services and programs for victims of domestic violence. To ensure effective service provision, policy making, and planning, it is important to obtain input from the target population during decision-making processes (Flyvbjerg 2001).[1] Constituents' voices, however, can only be heard or taken into account when planners, policy makers, and service providers are able to correctly interpret their language use and communication patterns. In this essay, I argue that both understanding and taking into account ethnocultural communication differences is essential for effective policy making and planning.

Ethnocultural communication refers to communicative differences that arise from membership in a specific ethnic group. More specifically, ethnocultural communication refers to communication patterns and language usage influenced by and rooted in cultural norms. The issue of ethnocultural language and communication is critical, because it is not just the inability to speak English that is a barrier for battered South Asian immigrant women, but also when it is spoken, how this English is spoken. In fact, language may pose a more daunting hurdle for immigrant survivors who speak English, as service providers may assume that they understand what is being said, which they might literally but not contextually.

With regard to language and battered immigrant women, the majority of studies have focused on immigrant survivors' inability to speak English as the main obstacle to their seeking or receiving information and services (Dutton, Orloff, and Hass 2000; Kim 2002; Orloff 2001; Preisser 1999). The fact that a large number of immigrant women from India have the ability to converse in English, and yet they remain either unaware of existing domestic violence related services or unable to utilize them effectively (Domestic Violence Research Project 2001; Preisser 1999; Warrier 2000a) indicates that there may be factors other than language fluency involved in this problem. Since the majority of Asian Indians speak English, their narratives allow for a more nuanced exploration of why and how battered immigrant women remain unable to use available services.

All immigrants, in particular women, undergo a process of redefining themselves as they reconcile ethnic-specific ways of being with adaptive behaviors and roles expected of them in their host milieu (Espin 1999). One ethnic-specific factor, not unique but of foremost priority to immigrant Indian women is the need to keep their marriages intact (Abraham 2000b; Warrier 2000a). It is, then, not surprising that at least as a first step, Indian immigrant women overwhelmingly engage in passive resistance strategies such as silence and avoidance against their abusers (Mehrotra 1999). Even when they do seek assistance, mostly it is not to leave the marriage but to find ways to cope with the abuse or to change their partners' abusive behavior. Even though research finds that ethnic specific, sociocultural factors can result in communication patterns and language use divergent from those expected and practiced in the mainstream (Lull 2000), there is no examination of how ethnocultural communication impacts access to and use of services by immigrants. This chapter provides instances of immigrant Indian women's ethnocultural language use to articulate the linkage between their communication patterns and help-seeking behavior.

Drawing upon the narratives of twenty-five immigrant Indian women, I document how ethnoculturally specific language use and communication patterns impact the help-seeking behavior of battered women and effectiveness of service provision. My goal is to highlight this need for planners, policy makers, and service providers to both appreciate and understand the differences in immigrant survivors' language use and communication so that they may communicate with, and serve, their immigrant constituents more effectively.

Methodology

This essay is based on face-to-face, in-depth interviews with fifteen women over two separate one-hour sessions in Detroit, Michigan, and New Brunswick, New Jersey. In addition, structured telephone interviews were conducted with ten survivors residing in New Jersey, Connecticut, Illinois, Pennsylvania, and New York. At the end of their sessions, the face-to-face interviewees also completed the questionnaire used in the telephone interviews. Thus, a total of fifteen face-to-face and twenty-five structured interviews constitute the foundation of this study. I personally conducted all the interviews. The size of the research sample was not predetermined. Rather, I conducted the in-depth and structured interviews to the point when theoretical saturation of all relevant categories became apparent in the analysis of data that was conducted parallel to the interviews (Glaser and Strauss 1967). I recruited participants for face-to-face interviews in Michigan through a snowballing sample, and in New Jersey through the South Asian community-based organization Manavi. Telephone interviewees were also recruited through Manavi.

TABLE 12.1

Demographics of Interview Participants

Area of Residence	Years in U.S.	Age	Education	Marital Status	No. of Children	Religion	Profession
Midwest	17	40	M.A.	Married	2	Hindu	Teaching
Midwest	9	31	M.E.	Divorced	1	Hindu	Software engineer
Midwest	36	57	M.A.	Divorced	2	Hindu	Therapist
Midwest	3	49	11th grade	Divorced	2	Hindu	Administrative
Midwest	11	36	Masters	Divorced	0	Hindu	Health care
Midwest	7	50	B.A.	Divorced	1	Hindu	Administrative
Midwest	26	46	B.A.	Divorced	1	Hindu	Auto design
Midwest	29	48	B.A.	Divorced	2	Muslim	Physical therapist
Midwest	4	34	8th grade	Separated	1	Sikh	Administrative
East	2	28	M.A.	Separated	2	Hindu	Informal
East	6	29	M.A.	Married	2	Sikh	Computer consultant
East	12	22	B.A.	Separated	0	Hindu	
East	4	30	MBA	Married	0	Hindu	
East	1	25	M.A.	Separated	0	Hindu	Informal
East	7	33	B.Sc	Separated	1	Hindu	
East	5	30	B.A.	Separated	2	Sikh	Informal
East	8	34	High school	Divorced	2	Sikh	Administrative
East	2	35	LLB	Divorced	0	Hindu	Print shop
East	5	27	B.E.	Divorced	1	Hindu	IT consultant
East	3	49	B.A.	Separated	0	Christian	Nursing asst.
East	2	24	BA	Separated	0	Hindu	Computers
East	8	31	B.S	Separated	1	Hindu	Lab technician
East	6	40	M.A.	Married	1	Hindu	Administrative
East	4	38	B.A.	Divorced	2	Hindu	Administrative
East	19	36	High school	Married	2	Sikh	Quality control

The participants of the study were women born in India, who (1) at the time of the study or in the past were married to or lived with an Asian Indian male born in India or the United States; (2) had experienced domestic violence; (3) were in the age range of eighteen to fifty-nine years; and (4) were able to understand and converse in English. I defined domestic abuse as verbal, emotional, and economic abuse along with physical assault by a male partner and/or his family (Abraham 1999). However, I omitted sexual violence due to Asian Indian women's unwillingness to talk about this issue even more than other forms of violence.

The majority of existing research on domestic violence in the South Asian community has been conducted through South Asian women's organizations because of the relative ease in identifying and recruiting battered women. This, however, makes it difficult to examine the help-seeking behavior of those women who are unable or unwilling to access services offered by such agencies. This study engaged participants for the face-to-face interview phase in New Jersey, where a South Asian women's organization exists, and Michigan, where there is no such organization. Furthermore, there has been no published research conducted on South Asian or Asian Indian battered women residing in the Midwest, which made the inclusion of Michigan significant.

While the face-to-face interview sample provides a basis for comparing survivors who live with or without access to South Asian women's organizations, it does not include the population of immigrant Indian women who fall somewhere in between—those who use the services of a South Asian women's organization via telephone and email. Through Manavi's long-distance ex-client list, I was able to include such women in the telephone interviews. In order to triangulate (Hammersley 1992), the overall demographic profile of the telephone interviewees diverged from the face-to-face interview participants' profile, in that the former were from a lower income bracket and experienced greater language and employment difficulties.[2] Furthermore, a few resided in locations not serviced by either a South Asian or a culturally competent mainstream women's organization.

Participant Demographic

Each of the twenty-five women who participated in this study had a unique story of survival to share. The participants were significantly diverse. The average age of the women was thirty-six, ranging from twenty-two to fifty-seven years. The average annual household income of the women was $55,000, with a range of $8,000 to $225,000. Despite the wide spread in household incomes, the women were similar to each other in a number of ways. With the exception of three women, all had arranged marriages; twenty were either separated or divorced; all worked outside the home, except three who lived with their immediate families; and the majority (68 percent) entered the United States on dependent visas after marriage.

The Issue of Language

The majority of the twenty-five women were fluent in English, although there were some who preferred conversing in Hindi or Punjabi. "Sometimes, in this country, I really miss talking in my own language," lamented forty-nine-year-old Lata (a pseudonym, as are names of all survivors), who had come to the United States in 2000 on a visitor's visa and had successfully received gender-based asylum. Roughly one out of four women expressed a sense of discomfort about accessing social services due to differences in accents and language use. "I was not having confidence in my English," said Sarah, a middle-aged woman for whom the services offered by a South Asian organization were critical because of her lack of fluency in English. Women who spoke little or no English, after separation or divorce initially preferred to associate with their community members to help with the transition. "[The mainstream shelter] put me in touch with Manavi and I was so happy that there are Hindi-speaking people here also. With my own language I feel more comfortable," said Sonali (twenty-eight), who sought assistance after her husband abandoned her and her children in a Delhi airport. Her husband had taken them back to India on the pretext of a family vacation.

For survivors with limited or no knowledge of English, access to individuals who spoke the native language, especially at South Asian women's agencies, was essential. Nonetheless, 75 percent of women in the study did not consider language to be an obstacle in seeking help. For women with minimal English-speaking skills, finding out about South Asian women's organizations and accessing services could be "very difficult." An example is Parneet, a thirty-four-year-old woman, who was married in 1993 but lived with her in-laws and young son in India until 1999. When she came to the United States, she discovered that her husband was married to another woman and had children with her.

Sociocultural Context and Help-Seeking Behavior

Research indicates that membership in a given ethnicity influences survivors' help-seeking behavior and ability to effectively use existing services (Dutton et al. 2000). When the participants of this study were asked to identify and elaborate on ethnic specific, sociocultural factors that they believed influenced both their behavior and their experiences of seeking assistance, almost all of them mentioned the dependence of immigrant women on their sponsors (read: husband) for legal status. The women elaborated that such dependence is debilitating because, if withdrawn, it makes immigrant survivors not only extremely vulnerable to deportation, but also ineligible to work, get a driving permit, or otherwise acquire an independent status. Participants pointed to a general lack of information about their entitlements and available public benefits in their new environment as an impediment to seeking assistance or even talking about the abuse with friends and family. Other factors included inability to return to their home countries because of the stigma associated with being divorced and gender roles that discourage women from speaking openly with others, especially men, about personal issues such as abuse and sexually related problems.

For immigrant Indian women, as suggested by this research, help seeking is first and foremost impacted by women's unwillingness to leave their marriage. Sonali mentioned that if she had known, she might have called the hotline number, but "I would not have left the home; I would have asked their advice about what to do."[3] Many participants echoed Asha's sentiments: "Even when I took a stand, I wasn't ready for divorce." Instead, the women preferred imposing penalties on their abusers, physical and otherwise, to stop the violence. Monika (forty-six), who had come to the United States after her marriage in 1977 and had worked at blue-collar jobs for several years to repay her husband's debts recommended, "The one thing, I think, [that] scares most Indian men is that they don't want anything to be known at work. Even my husband did not want the child support money taken out from his paycheck because he thought if personnel knows, they'll put in his records that he must not be a regular payer. I think that would be very, very successful that if you [abuse your wife], we'll let your employer know." Jasvinder, a spirited twenty-eight-year-old mother of two, suggested that there "should be some compulsory punishment. This man did this, he should be penalized. He should be paying government $20,000 or $10,000. That way men will get scared that we are [being abusive] and if she goes to this organization or to INS I will be penalized for $20,000 or $10,000. That way [INS] will make money and they will spend the money on helping women who need shelter [and other related services]."

Patriarchally rooted sociocultural understandings held by the women also affect help-seeking behavior. The pervasive belief that the husband is their lord or god drove the participants to unquestioningly accept their spouses' authoritarian and dictatorial status. The women were socialized with the belief that "if husband says it's night, it's night, if he says it's day, it's day" (Harpreet). Even though most women did not believe this, sociocultural pressures required them to buy into the ideology. These patriarchal underpinnings contribute to the women's sense of being scared. For instance, Sanjana (thirty), who was unable to access many services because of her dependence on her husband for legal status, felt that the "law [would have] to be more stringent" before she could call the police or have her abuser deported without being scared. She elaborated, "My husband has been physically abusive toward me. I wanted to call the police but I'm scared if I take an action he will do harm to me and my parents."

The study indicated that abusers leveraged their partners' fears and discomfort in accessing services to control them. Ambika (thirty-three), a mother of one, had been separated for three months after almost seven years of marriage. She observed, "I don't trust police at all. My husband says they are very commercial. You hear girls are raped in police station, they touch boobs so I get scared." So, she did not contact the police for a number of years even though she strongly desired their protection and assistance. Kamal mentioned how her abuser "would always tell me about shelter. That I should go stay at the shelter—'you will get diseases there, you and your children.' I didn't know what I would do if he left me." Her abuser threatened that she would have to find a job, daycare for the children, and housing on her own without any access to public services or his finances. Parneet's statement captures the potency of the fear generated by the abusers: "I wanted to call the police but he said he will call and say things about me. I got scared."

These sociocultural understandings (e.g., husband is god) and structural beliefs (e.g., police are unhelpful to survivors) shape if and how battered Indian immigrant women communicate with service providers.[4] The result is the silencing of women. For example, Jasvinder stated that she did not realize she has the "freedom to talk. [When I spoke, he tried] to record my conversation. Later on I found out I have [the] freedom to talk. At that time, I thought I [had] said something wrong and so he is recording. He shouldn't be recording—I didn't think that then! He shouldn't be recording—I am free to talk." The women in this study had undergone a process whereby they were able to find their voices again, speak out against their oppression, and demand their rights. However, even as they began articulating their needs, they were sometimes not heard correctly.

Sociocultural Context and Ethnocultural Communication

The centrality of the issue of ethnocultural communication is captured by Kamal's experience of going to a university hospital for an abortion. She was unable to receive the services she wanted because of her inability to communicate the repercussions of possibly having a second daughter in a household where her partner and his family valued only boys. In order to get an abortion, she was required to speak with a hospital counselor. Kamal narrated how the counselor "was so upset [when I requested an abortion and] said don't do that, don't do any abortion. If it's a girl or boy, it's God-given. I spent two to three hours with her, she was convincing me not to do it. I kept it [pregnancy]." Instead of trying to understand Kamal's cultural context, why she was requesting an abortion, and how to address her needs, the service provider imposed her viewpoints and ideology on Kamal. Incidentally, after the birth of this child, a second girl, her partner became extremely abusive toward Kamal. Although Kamal stated to the counselor, "If you can do [the sonogram] now, I can decide [later]," she was not heard, because she was not forceful enough in demanding her rights. Kamal's communication style differed from that of the counselor, which may have led the service provider not to comprehend her situation.

Culturally specific use of language by the participants of this study manifested itself in various ways throughout their narratives. Malini, a forty-year-old mother of an adult son, had emigrated to the United States in 1997, leaving behind her son and abusive ex-husband in India. She observed, "Now I am able to talk a little. At the time I wasn't able to talk—I didn't want to discuss about this." By "not able to talk," Malini was referring not to her inability to converse in English but rather to her unwillingness to speak about personal issues. Similarly, Sonali elaborated, "We are taught from childhood [that] we are not able to get out of [a marriage]. There is so much depression [when a marriage breaks up]. They say you have lost your husband, lost your in-laws, that there is nothing without your husband, without your in-laws." By "losing," Sonali did not mean that she was not aware of the husband or in-laws' whereabouts, but she was without them.

Furthermore, the women spoke of their experiences of domestic violence, such as issues of control in an indirect manner. Sonali explained the motivation behind her in-laws' efforts to isolate her: "They had this in their mind, if we let her go outside, she will get ahead of us, that she will get out of our hands." Others justified such isolation as their efforts at being good daughters or wives. For instance, Uma (twenty-two), who had been separated from her husband for nine months and lived with her parents, noted, "I have very, very strict curfews and my parents don't like it if I go out. I am being a good daughter." The women showed discomfort and uncertainty regarding how to speak about abuse and domestic violence. It was not surprising, then, that most of the twenty-five women used euphemisms and referred to their abusive experiences as "the situation" that was "not good" or as a "bad situation." Similarly, abusive tactics were rationalized and explained by the women as stemming from jealousy and anger, which resulted in the abuser's use of "bad words" and physical violence.

Impact of Ethnocultural Communication

Help-Seeking Behavior

Not being able to explicate on the nature and extent of their abuse affected the participants' help-seeking behaviors. An example is Fiza, who had trouble communicating with the police, even though "they were very cooperative," due to an overwhelming sense of feeling humiliated. Since the police did not understand her shame, humiliation, and consequent communicative ambiguity, she was unable to access the counseling services she wanted. Additionally, the participants' unwillingness to name the abuse was tied up with their desire to keep their marriages intact, which also led to their preference for seeking assistance from familiar sources such as friends, family, counselors, and the Internet. "You create this persona of yourself and you want to keep it intact and you don't want it to leak out" that your marriage is not perfect, said Gitanjali, a mother of two who had reconciled with her previously abusive in-laws and continued with her marriage. In particular, the Internet provides a "most private place. You don't have to talk to anyone—you just go into the Net and look for stuff and you just get the right information and the right numbers, the right people who you can trust, who are [the] professionals," explained Aparna.

Isolation imposed by abusers also had a profound effect on how survivors spoke about their experiences, as well as how and when they sought assistance from outsiders. "Yeah, because I wasn't aware of anything. Even after seven years,

I didn't know how to open bank account," said thirty-one-year-old Suparna, who had been separated from her abusive spouse and his family for seven months. She finally left her abusers with the assistance of her parents and sister. Sonali observed that she "did not know anything [when living with the abuser(s)]. Only now I've found out that you call 911 when you have any such problem." In Swarna's case, due to her long isolation, she did not seek assistance because she "really thought it was my fault." In addition to isolation, women lacked direct access to information. "In this country, my mother-in-law would always be next to me. She won't let me turn on the computer even," remarked Sanjana. Some of the women observed that their abusers, who routinely micro-controlled their movements and behaviors, would not allow them to touch the home computer. This also restricted other options, such as going to a library to access the Internet or other services. Some survivors mentioned that their abusers did not allow them to watch certain movies or programs on television, especially programs on ethnic television.

Consequently, when survivors sought assistance, they were unable to respond to the requirements, both communicative and otherwise, of accessing services. For example, Sanjana did not call the police because she was not aware that the "police department and immigration department are independent of each other because my husband used to say that if you don't have papers, you can't do anything." Sarah lamented that she was not able to call the police for assistance because "I was thinking the police would ask for evidence; where I will get evidence?"

Approximately 85 percent of women considered the inability of service providers to understand their sociocultural contexts as a major barrier to both accessing and effectively using services. Sanjana observed, "In my case, I was with my mother-in-law for eight months. Twice I went to India in one year and my husband forced me to go. I told the lawyer and he couldn't understand how someone can force you to do something." Women, who tried to convey their culture-specific contexts, expressed frustrations because the service providers' understandings differed dramatically from their own. Payal, who was very proficient in her use of the English language, noted, "I told them that I would face extreme ostracism if I go back [to India]. This was my second marriage. [But] nobody understood why I couldn't go back. All the lawyers here kept referring to my marriage as a short-term marriage. It's not about a short-term marriage but my whole life." These situations left women frustrated and unable to communicate their realities across different cultural contexts, resulting in serious communicative failure. "They gave me the Manavi number but I told them I had that number. I wanted the information, more information. I thought maybe they will give me more information" (Kamal).

Perhaps because of such instances of communicative failure, the majority of the women in this study expressed a preference for seeking assistance, especially emotional support, from South Asian women's organizations. This preference was true for participants regardless of their length of stay in the United States, the extent of support from friends and family, and their fluency in English. According to Uma, who had resided in the United States for most of her life and had an extensive network of friends, she preferred relying on Manavi rather than American service providers: "We have the culture in common; [it's] just more comfortable because we can relate in the same way. We have the same reactions almost and we can understand what exactly is going on. Whereas I'm not sure the same would be true if it was a mixed community." Specifically, the women felt that they could speak openly about their issues and obtain immense benefits from the services of South Asian women's organizations. In addition, they did not face the risk of communicative failures because the service providers at South Asian organizations understood, without any explanation, dilemmas such as being unable to return to India after the breakup of a marriage, especially a second marriage. In fact, the women in this study made a clear distinction between "them" (American women) and "us" (Indian women). Monika maintained, "American women will shout back and kick her husband out. But Indian woman will never be able to kick her husband out. I was told that I should kick him out. The steps they think will work for American women will not work in Indian culture because we are hammered, hammered that your husband is always right. Now he is your heart and soul—that is so much put in our brain that we will never come out of it."

Without the risk of communicative failure and the assumption that personnel at South Asian women's organizations understand and appreciate their predicament and language use, the women feel more comfortable sharing their opinions, thoughts, and experiences. For example, Sonali was able to speak about the vulnerability of divorced or separated Indian women with me, also an Indian woman, because she knew she did not have to clarify the complicated sexual dimensions of her following statement: "[Asian Indians] who know that [a woman's] husband has left her try to take advantage. There are very few people who try to help. Mostly they think, there is no husband—like that. Maybe you understand what I am saying. It can be women also—they put you in wrong work. They are also Indian. If they have some humanity." Here "wrong work" refers to prostitution or sexual exploitation and harassment of women without a spouse. The phrase "taking advantage" similarly denotes sexual advances on (single/divorced) women by men.

Effectiveness of Services

The women in this study felt that the effectiveness of South Asian women's organizations stems from the fact that these organizations debunk and challenge the boundaries between staff and clients usually held sacrosanct by mainstream organizations (Kim 2002; Warrier 2000a).[5] The majority of women mentioned that the emotional and moral support provided by South Asian women's organizations was extremely valuable in helping them to cope with their problems. Jasvinder observed that when Manavi staff accompanied her to court, "They really made me feel they are with me. Even if I am wrong or something." Payal, who was fluent in English, noted, "At times, I did find it difficult to express my feelings, that is where Manavi helped me the most. I could call them and just let out all my feelings and cry." The opportunity to speak with someone who would listen and understand their social and cultural backgrounds was very important to the survivors. Kamal said, "I was looking for some guidance like what do you think I should do—he is hitting me, he is telling me that he will put immigration trouble for me, that he is trying to put me in jail. So [I spoke with a staff person] for two hours [the] first day [I called Manavi]." Seema, who is twenty-eight, divorced, and a successful professional, observed, "After I contacted Sakhi, they used to call me everyday until I moved out; they introduced me to New York Women's Center. They supported me with everything. That made it easier after leaving."

Of course, access to South Asian women's organizations was an even more significant issue for some women who were unable to speak English fluently. Sonali observed in Hindi, "I went to the American shelter, I felt like I was so subdued. I could not speak English [properly] so all my feelings were suppressed." When the inability to converse fluently in English was added to the lack of supportive family networks, survivors made statements such as "Without Manavi, there is nothing for me" (Parneet).

Survivors considered South Asian women's advocates as well as mainstream service providers, who were both knowledgeable about immigrant women's rights and sensitive to their cultural needs, effective. In fact, these service providers also had the ability to overcome other barriers to intervention. For instance, Mansi (twenty-four), who was separated from her husband for two years and did not speak English very well, expressed gratitude because the "police is very helpful in this country. And the lawyers, they did good in my case. Even [when] I don't have some witnesses also, they fight very well. Hardly it took seven months in the court." When mainstream organizations appreciated and accommodated the special needs of battered immigrant women, survivors found them valuable. "At the shelter a woman gets to stay for only thirty days and [under special circumstances] that stay is extended for ninety days. That means that normally her stay is only for three months and I was allowed to stay there for eight months until I got my asylum," noted Lata.

Survivors like Mansi were able to avoid the issue of language fluency because her service providers took the time to understand her intended meaning-system. Sonali, who was separated from her abuser and had two children, mentioned how "ten people would come to pick the children, ten people would come to drop them off. Then I started keeping contact with the police. I would tell them to come and they used to watch to make sure everything was okay. The police really helped me a lot." The idea of "ten people" coming to pick up and drop off the children means that not just the father, who shared custody, but his parents and other relatives were present during the exchange of the children. Even though Sonali was not fluent in English, she was able to brush aside language concerns because the police took the time to listen to her and ensure they understood her needs. "Even though we had a language problem, they used to understand me," she gratefully remarked.

For the most part, however, survivors pointed to mainstream service providers' ignorance about their sociocultural contexts as being the reason they found these services to be inappropriate or ineffective. Monika recounted her experiences of calling the domestic violence hotline, "I was so emotionally drained so they tell me why don't you go check into a hotel, stay in a hotel today? Not everybody in Asian community has that kind of money that they are going to go in a hotel. Then they told me why don't you go stay with your brothers or some relative? They will ask me fifteen questions—why are you here at this time. So, I think the hotline doesn't understand here that our culture is very closed about what to say and what not to say."

Sarah's case illustrates how access to services can be ineffective when service providers are unaware or insensitive to the sociocultural contexts of survivors. "My husband came [to the court] with so many letters, which are written by me but he forced me to write that says he is keeping me good. The judge was thinking, because I didn't go to the police, I was wrong. So, they have to understand that Indian women are not going out directly to the police. Second, if she is hurt in the breast, in the abdomen, or thigh, they will not [take a] photo of that and tell police." In Ambika's case, she was offended when "a cop [recently] asked me, did you sleep with the abuser?" Monika maintained that her counselor "did not understand the culture. I think I spent too much time explaining [that] what he [counselor] is telling me to do will not happen. Because he wanted me to talk to [my husband's] mom and sisters and stuff to see if they would help me. I was telling him that those things don't happen in our culture, the son is always right to their moms."

Service providers can be unsuccessful not only for their ignorance about survivors' sociocultural contexts, but also their lack of knowledge about immigrant women's rights. Lata said, "The thing is that when I went to the shelter, there the advocates never knew anything about immigration. Absolutely nothing! The advocates would come and talk to me if there were other foreign women in the shelter." Sanjana complained that she "was given contradictory answers by lawyers [about my legal status]. They scared me that I will become illegal, that [my husband] can deport me but that was all wrong information." Monika regretted that it was "just recently, two weeks ago, I found out that because I had a minor child, I could have stayed in the house without paying him anything. That would have really helped me but I didn't know that." Instead, because of an incompetent lawyer, she ended up paying her ex-husband half the value of the house, a financial burden she could ill-afford.

It is important to note that not just mainstream service providers can be ignorant of a survivor's sociocultural backgrounds and rights. South Asian women's organizations, due to the number of challenges they face, sometimes provide ineffective services to women. These gaps in services were apparent from such statements as the following one made by Lata, who had since managed to obtain legal residency with assistance from a community-based, nonprofit organization. "The picture that [a South Asian women's organization] gave me was very terrifying—that I would never be able to stay in this country because you are on a tourist visa and gender-based asylum cases are not very successful and it is very difficult to get that kind of status." Ethnic organizations, including religious institutions in the community that may be aware of survivors' sociocultural contexts, do not always provide adequate services to them. Some women explicitly mentioned their preference for mainstream service providers. They maintained that they were not very comfortable with Indian people because they tend to be judgmental.

Ultimately, neither mainstream service providers nor South Asian women's organizations were fully successful in reaching victims and providing them with full information about available services. Uma noted, "Manavi is there but it needs more exposure. Not many people know about Manavi." Further, in failing to advertise that their services are confidential, some service providers create a big obstacle for battered immigrant women. Maninder (thirty-six), who had recently separated from her husband after years of abuse, believed that the first thing battered women need is reassurance that the confidante will not "tell anybody—maybe then they will [talk and ask for advice]." Kamal observed that she had stayed with her abuser for three years because "I didn't know that everything would be confidential."

When service providers, whether mainstream or South Asian, appreciate the distinction in communication arising from ethnic and sociocultural differences, they are best able to assist battered women. Furthermore, service providers need to understand that even though a survivor speaks English, she may imbue her language with different meaning than a native speaker commonly would. A woman may use terms such as "bad situation" to suggest multiple possibilities. Lalitha, a fifty-year-old immigrant from India, provided an example of such complexity of meaning. She noted that when she came to the United States, she was "very shy, [but] you are supposed to talk over here. Now I know that and its getting better." Lalitha's use of the phrase "supposed to talk" does not imply the actual act of speaking, but the expectation in America of being explicit and forthright in one's engagement with a given issue or situation. Lalitha went on to say that in the past seven years she had learned that she could not be demure, speak in soft tones and indirect manner when asking for assistance. Instead, she had to articulate her needs very categorically.

Such language differences arise from an ethnic speaker's literal translation of native language words into English. For example, *maarna*, a Hindi word denoting physical striking, may be translated in English as "hitting," "striking," "punching," or "slapping." Thus, immigrant Indian women may use "hitting," "striking," "punching," and "slapping" synonymously, whereas mainstream Americans would interpret them distinctly (Tjaden and Thoennes 2000). Such language and communicative differences arising from a user's ethnicity can have ripple effects and culminate in the filing of incorrect police reports that subsequently jeopardize a survivor's case against her abuser(s). Such communicative failure has the potential to severely imperil the efficacy and utilization of services by survivors.

Likewise, service providers' use of simple language and, when necessary, elaborate step-by-step instructions may enable battered immigrant Indian women to overcome significant communicative barriers in accessing services and obtaining information. Kamal said, "[The service provider] told me what to do there, not just go there and sit. They told me you have to tell your situation, you have been thrown out of the house and then you have been beaten up and then you have no place to live; you don't have food, don't have diapers for your baby. So, go there and ask for aid. That was the help I needed. Otherwise I didn't know where I would have got milk. I got food stamps."

From the experiences of the twenty-five participants, it appears that South Asian women's organizations are most effective in meeting the emotional needs of survivors, while mainstream service providers, who take the time to listen and understand the needs of the survivors were most effective in providing services such as obtaining or implementing legal orders and safety planning.

Concluding Remarks

Even as this research confirms that language fluency is a significant issue for immigrant women, it problematizes the concept of language use and communication by documenting that certain words are privileged while others are taboo for South Asian survivors in relating their needs to service providers. Indisputably, those survivors who do not speak or speak very little English are most in need of multilingual services with a preference for ethnicity-specific service providers. Even the women who spoke English preferred community-based service providers because of differences in accents and language use. In cases where neither the language use nor the accent was an issue, the women still preferred to speak with female service providers based in ethnic organizations because of their culture in common. In other words, the women felt that other South Asian/Indian women were more likely to understand without elaborate explanation their use and context of such words and phrases as "taking advantage."

This study identifies numerous examples of survivors' ethnoculturally specific use of language and communication patterns. For instance, many of the women referred to "shouting" not so much in its literal sense of yelling, but to signify the inability of Indian women to answer back to their husbands. Abuse was never spelled out; rather, terms like "jealous," "angry," and "bad words" were used when speaking about tactics of violence. Controlling behavior was explained as abusers ensuring that survivors "did not get out of hand" and remained "good" wives and daughters. In the latter case, it would be important for service providers to understand the criteria of "good" that the women indicated. The study shows that South Asian battered women not only require translation services but also coaching in the use of the right words to obtain the desired responses and effective service provision in the U.S. context.

When service providers, both mainstream and South Asian, take time to listen and correctly identify survivors' needs, they can be successful interveners. The needs of battered immigrant women are unique, as is the manner in which they speak about them. Thus, service providers must move away from offering cookie-cutter interventions such as going to a shelter or getting a restraining order. When a survivor contacts them for assistance, service providers must be willing to take the time to first appreciate statements such as "divorce is not an option," then understand the context behind it before providing options and services.

Effective communication, which occurs when the receiver's interpretation is the same as the intended meaning-system of the communicator, requires a two-way dialogue between the service provider and survivor. Communication must be aimed at reaching a common understanding about the survivor's needs. Service providers, planners, and policy makers must take the time to listen to the voices of survivors so that their language use is interpreted within the appropriate sociocultural context. Only then will effective communication and effective service provision occur.

ACKNOWLEDGMENTS

I am deeply grateful to the twenty-five women who participated in this research.

NOTES

1. I have defined effectiveness of services as the ability of constituents to access and use the information source and/or service program in order to understand and/or access their legal and civil rights.

2. Triangulation "reflects an attempt to secure an in-depth understanding of the phenomenon in question. . . . Triangulation is not a tool or a strategy of validation, but an alternative to validation" (Denzin and Lincoln 1994, 5).

3. When the participants were asked which hotline number they called, many could not recall the exact number.

4. Certain barriers to access are independent of sociocultural and structural factors because some service providers minimize emotional or financial abuse.

5. Of the sixteen survivors who had sought assistance from South Asian women's organizations (e.g., Manavi, Sakhi, Saheli, and Apna Ghar), only four did not find them useful. The reasons behind these four women's dissatisfaction were primarily related to the lack of resources of these organizations, which made it impossible for them to provide certain services and facilities such as free legal clinics and housing.

PART THREE

The Body Evidence

Law and South Asian Battered Women

13

Law's Culture and Cultural Difference

SHARMILA RUDRAPPA

Feminist activists and scholars have deep ambivalence about the use of culture in legal cases when seeking state intervention in domestic violence (Coleman 1996; Volpp 2000a). We understand that violence is a gendered phenomenon—that is, inflected by culture (Bhattacharjee 1997; Dasgupta 2002; Rudrappa 2004b), yet we are profoundly uncertain about how the state should arbitrate on matters of culture with regard to domestic violence. My own ambivalence regarding culture's use in courtrooms arose when I served as an expert witness in Austin, Texas, in 2002, in the defense of a South Asian American woman, Sailaja Hathaway, who had tried to poison her children and herself. For the defense team, Hathaway's culture was ostensibly one of the reasons for her actions. While I recognized the necessity for using culture in understanding her feelings and state of mind, I was uncertain about what it meant to make cultural arguments in court in such a situationally expedient yet politically uncritical manner. The case that rose to my mind in stark contrast was that of another Texan mother, Andrea Yates. Yates had drowned her five children in the bathtub, and psychological arguments, not culture, were used to explain her homicidal act.

Building on my experience of providing cultural testimony in court, I note that given that the United States is a nation of immigrants we are compelled to use culture in understanding the defendant's state of mind when violence occurs. However, raising culture in the courtroom invariably raises questions on what we mean by immigrant culture, and whether cultural codes are thickly coherent—that is, have universal acceptance and adherence within a particular racial/ethnic group. Moreover, this also raises the question of law's culture. Stated more specifically, American law, too, has a culture that stands in authoritative judgment over its citizen subjects. I do not just mean the principle of whiteness, but also a law that individualizes and is set up as an adversarial system, demanding that real-life messy stories be narrated in teleological ways, with causal mechanisms in play.

I believe that we have to invoke culture in the courtroom, because ignoring difference means keeping silent on law's own cultures.

In addition, the law does not adjudicate on the principle of sameness. Because the defendant's state of mind, or mens rea, when the violence occurs is considered, psychological and cultural differences are admissible in court. Stated simply, individual difference matters. Not everyone is treated equally because the law attempts to consider each individual in his or her unique circumstances before calibrating and dispensing punishment. I conclude that for immigrant feminists there is no getting away from using culture when negotiating with the state. However, instead of allowing ourselves to be interpellated in ways that fix us, we need to take on law's culture on our own terms.

The Uses of Culture in Negotiating with the State

Feminists, especially women-of-color activists and scholars, profess ambivalence about using cultural arguments to justify state intervention into our lives on issues such as domestic violence (Volpp 2000a; Wu 2003). We agree that our cultures lead to widely varied familial arrangements and relationships; differences manifest themselves in gender norms, ways by which wives and husbands conduct themselves, children are mothered, and the responsibilities and expressions of love between parents and children. Yet, we are in two minds when it comes to allowing the state to use culture in arbitrating on family violence. Let me explain this ambivalence through making the four following observations:

First, persons working on domestic violence issues recognize that women too are compelled to violent crimes. Although women are perpetrators of violence, there has been, historically, very little attention given to such crimes. Since the 1990s, however, it has been impossible to ignore women's violence because of the marked increase in dual arrests as well as women-only arrests for domestic assault (Hirschel and Buzawa 2002; Martin 1997; Miller 2001). Dasgupta (2002) notes, for example, that family violence data from Connecticut indicates that "the percent of male victims increased from 16% of the total in 1987 to 21% of the total in 1997" (1365). The arrests of women who use violence against their partners have caused concern among advocates, not because they think women are becoming more violent than ever, but because they wonder at the appropriateness of the responses by law enforcement officials and the judicial system. Such concerns have led researchers to examine definitions of battering and the effectiveness of violence intervention programs. Feminist scholars and advocates argue that women-on-men violence is decontextualized from the cultures of patriarchal control and power exercised over women's everyday lives, which leads to flawed understandings and thereby inadequate treatment of women (Dasgupta 2002). Women perpetrators, we are beginning to understand, are different from men perpetrators, and therefore we need different approaches to such intervention. Cultures of patriarchy affect violence, and domestic violence advocates argue that the state has to acknowledge the differences between men's and women's violence.

The second way by which culture is acknowledged is the recognition that domestic violence is culturally specific and requires appropriate responses. For example, dowry demands can lead to violence in South Asian American families, or threats of deportation may be used as a means to keep a wife in an abusive relationship, all of which require culturally (and legally) specific intervention strategies (Abraham 2000b; Dasgupta and Warrier 1996; Narayan 1995). Hence, while American women, white or otherwise, can go to "mainstream shelters," ethnically/culturally specific organizations such as Saheli or Apna Ghar are crucial spaces for immigrant women (Vaid 1989). Battered women arrive here hoping to find a safe space where they can retain a sense of an ethnic-ness as they recover their selves. Over the past decade, a number of ethnic shelters and domestic violence intervention groups have emerged, allowing battered immigrant women to potentially recover a sense of an ethnic, gendered self once again. Almost all of these organizations exist because of state funding. They are eligible for state grants because they serve underserved women who may not use mainstream shelters because of cultural differences (Agnew 1998b; Rudrappa 2004b).

The state too recognizes the ways that violence can affect different women in different ways. Thus, the main purpose of passing the Violence Against Women Act (VAWA) in 1994 was to fund nonprofit organizations that address the needs of underserved populations such as immigrants, violence in same-sex relationships, and rural areas. In addition, VAWA provided a means by which immigrant battered women could circumvent laws that made the legality of their stay in the United States conditional upon their marriages to their abusive citizen or permanent resident spouses. To gain legality, the battered immigrant individual would need to prove that she entered her marriage in good faith, show evidence of abuse through police records, orders of protection, hospital records, and testimonies of social workers, mental health professionals, or shelter advocates. Furthermore, she had to prove that she could not return to her sending country because of the social/economic/political sanctions she might face for walking out of a marriage. To summarize, an immigrant woman needed to prove she was a victim of domestic violence *and* her cultural circumstances in order to become a legal, independent subject under the jurisdiction of the American state.

Activists and scholars note that tested methods of acting on violence issues will fail if we do not recognize the ways in which violence can differ across ethnic/racial groups, and they tend to use culture to legitimate to the state nonwhite immigrant women's injuries. Conversely, we are deeply troubled when abusive immigrant men argue in court that their culture exonerates their violence against family members. For example, in 1989, when Dong Lu Chen killed his wife with a claw hammer, his attorneys explained that Chinese men do not react the same way as American men when confronted with the possibility of spousal infidelity (Volpp 2000a). The cultural expert for the case, Burton Pasternak, noted that "casual sex, adultery, which is an even more extreme violation, and divorce" are perceived to be egregious deviations from Chinese social norms (396). Subsequently, the presiding judge, Edward Pincus, sentenced Chen to just five years' probation. One way to read the reduction in Chen's sentence from second-degree murder to second-degree manslaughter is that the life of the wife, Jian Wan Chen, was worth far less than other American women's lives because the perpetrator of her violent murder did not warrant greater punishment. In fact, Brooklyn Supreme Court Justice Pincus posited Dong Lu Chen, the perpetrator, as a victim: "Based on the cultural background of this individual he has also succeeded in partially destroying his family and his family's reputation. . . . There are victims in this case: The deceased is a victim, her suffering is over. The defendant is a victim, a victim that fell through the cracks because society didn't know where or how to respond in time" (Volpp 2000a, 398). Feminist activists and scholars ask that domestic violence, regardless of whether it is committed by a white or a nonwhite immigrant man, be judged by the harm it causes their women partners. It is not that feminists are against using culture per se, but instead, they are worried about how questions of power and control get effaced in cultural arguments. Focusing solely on race and culture, Judge Pincus ignored gender subordination. The murdered wife had completely disappeared from these trials, or if she did appear, she did so as "a reputed 'adulteress,' bringing a 'stain' upon her husband" (Volpp 2000a, 398). Moreover, culture is never used when American men batter their wives, and can potentially receive more severe sentences than did Dong Lu Chen. As a result, battered immigrant women are afforded far lesser protection by the state than are battered white women.

The fourth way by which immigrant feminists use culture in negotiating with the state is with regard to mothering. The practices of mothering are not universal; that is, the emotions and labors involved in caring for and raising a child are culturally specific. Hence, while corporal punishment is considered an anathema in some cultures, physical disciplining of a child may be acceptable in others. Because we see differences in mothering, we ask that cultural differences be acknowledged in court when mothers harm their children. While not all cases are so extreme, the examples that come to mind are the *Sailaja Hathaway v. Texas* and the *People v. Kimura* cases, where first-generation immigrant women were incriminated with crimes against their children—a form of domestic violence—and cultural explanations were used in criminal court cases in defending or explaining the women's actions. From understanding how culture explains the differential logic of violence among immigrant families, and bringing abusive men to justice, we are now using cultural explanations to account for women's violence against their children.

While structures of feelings and everyday actions are no doubt inflected by culture, justifying maternal violence in such a manner is analogous to immigrant men who beat their wives and use culture to defend their actions. Raising culture to explain maternal violence and give women lenient sentences leaves immigrant children more vulnerable than other American children. For example, Fumiko Kimura, a Japanese American woman, walked into the ocean with her two children upon hearing about her husband's infidelity. She survived her suicide attempt, but her children drowned to their deaths. Her defense argued that she was following the Japanese ritual of parent-child suicide, or *oya-ko-shinju*, and she received only one year in prison, five years' probation, and psychiatric counseling (Maguigan 1995; Sikora 2001).

Giving Fumiko Kimura a reduced sentence, the argument can be made, is similar to giving Chen a reduced sentence. She had power over her children, just like Dong Lu Chen had power over his wife. Both faced stress in their lives—she because of a troubled marriage, and he, one could argue, from the multiple oppressions resulting from racism and class disadvantages. Although the two cases are not necessarily equivalent, as Chen and Kimura would have wielded power in unequal ways within their own communities because of their genders, adjudication should be "more than a game of hierarchical rankings of 'who's most oppressed'; it means a serious commitment to the evaluating and eradicating all forms of oppression" (Volpp 2000a, 410). From this perspective, then, the two murdered Kimura children were left just as unprotected as was Jian Wan Chen, and the reduced sentence their mother received sent the message that the state affords lesser protection to immigrants' children than other Americans' children. Legal scholar Michelle Wu (2003) compares Fumiko Kimura's case to that of Susan Smith, the white woman who drowned her two sons and received life in prison. Wu notes:

> There is troubling disparity in the way the legal system has responded to the similar acts of the two women: Kimura is set free because her drowning her children is viewed as being consistent with her native cultural practices, while Smith is charged with capital murder for essentially the same act. Similarly, there is a disparity as well when shifting the focus on the child-victim of such crimes. The criminal system failed to vindicate the drowning of Kimura's children, and the message it sends to the Japanese-American children is rather dismal: that the cultural defense leaves them without the protection of the criminal law . . . the message sent in the Smith case is very different: that the legal system does value these American children's lives and the lives of others like them. (1010)

Upon examining the Chen, Kimura, and Smith cases one could argue that using culture in deciding mens rea undermines the rights of immigrant women and children (Sikora 2001).

But such blanket statements are not so simple with real life situations where people are hurt and end up hurting each other. When dealing with the reality of persons confronting life in prison or worse, the responsibilities cannot be taken lightly and it is not possible to dismiss the various factors, including culture, that affect the defendant's state of mind.

In the Hathaway case, the specter of state-endorsed violence hung over the defendant's head, and I had to explain in court what might have led to her actions. From the relatively safe space of solely intellectualizing about the American state and culture, I was thrust into a situation of bearing the weight of responsibility for the defense of someone. My cultural testimony carried the power of truth over

Sailaja Hathaway's life, and I was apprehensive. As a filicidal mother, she now faced the wrath of an avenging state; and as an expert witness, I became a vector of such a state.

Filicidal Tales: The Cases of Sailaja Hathaway and Andrea Yates

Married to Michael Hathaway after her first marriage to an Indian man had failed, Sailaja Hathaway's present marriage too was in trouble. To make matters worse, the Hathaways and their two sons had moved from Boston to Austin, Texas, where Sailaja Hathaway knew no one. She was socially isolated and had been undergoing psychiatric treatment. She had expressed homicidal and suicidal thoughts to her psychiatrist, whereupon her children were placed in protective custody with their father. Hathaway initially only had the right to supervised visits with her two sons, but upon improvement she was allowed unsupervised visits and her sons were allowed to stay overnight with her as well. On Valentine's Day, 2001, during the visit of her two young sons, aged three and six years, Sailaja Hathaway attempted to poison them. She did not try to mask the poison and offered it her boys in a cup, after which she consumed the pesticide herself.

Hathaway's team of lawyers wanted to prove that their client was driven to homicidal thoughts by mental illness, a manipulative former husband, *and* an Indian culture that does not accept divorced women into its fold. Culture, for this particular middle-class immigrant Hindu woman, was to be one of the extenuating reasons for her homicidal tendencies against her children. Hathaway was declared guilty of attempted homicide, and cultural and psychological expert witnesses were allowed to give their testimonies only in the sentencing stage of the trial. As Jason Spencer (2002) reported for the local newspaper, the *Austin American Statesman*: "With little defense against charges that she tried to poison her two young sons to death on Valentine's Day 2001, Sailaja Hathaway was not surprised that she was convicted Wednesday of attempted capital murder, her lawyers said. But as the jury of seven men and five women now considers a punishment of the 45-year-old West Lake Hills mother, Hathaway's lawyers said they plan to prove their client was driven to homicidal thoughts by mental illness, a cheating former husband, and an Indian culture that casts shame on divorced women."

As an expert witness on Indian culture, I argued that Sailaja Hathaway would have been anxious about what her community might have thought of her; she had one failed marriage behind her, and her present one to a white American was headed for failure as well. She felt that her shame and humiliation would adhere to her children. In addition, she would have worried that her children would be ostracized because they were biracial. While not justifying her actions, we would have to consider these cultural factors in understanding Sailaja Hathaway's state of mind, which led her to make her two sons ingest poison, which ultimately was not fatal to the young boys. Upon hearing psychological testimony in addition to my cultural testimony, Hathaway's sentence was reduced from the forty years the prosecution was asking to fifteen years in prison for attempted capital murder of her two sons.

I felt acutely uncomfortable about making these kinds of cultural arguments because I was intentionally participating in a ritual that bolstered stereotypical images and posited Indian culture as being singularly patriarchal. While patriarchy is no doubt extant, individual men and women, feminist social movements, and even state legislations have attempted to address gender inequities in India in countless ways. Using culture in this manner, I felt, set up Indianness as a formulaic, ahistorical set of practices that all Indians followed uncritically. While mothering and sense of self-other between a mother and her children are different, not all Indian mothers react in the way Sailaja Hathaway did when faced with marital difficulties or failure. Sailaja Hathaway herself requested that the jury be given information on her cultural background. She said, "the jury did not receive enough information about why this happened, about my background, about my state of mind. . . . I want the jury to hear my cultural background." As an expert witness in her defense, my responsibilities were toward explaining in court her structures of feelings, and those responsibilities included instructing the courtroom about Indian culture.

The obvious contrast that comes to mind when I speak of Sailaja Hathaway is Andrea Yates, the white, Roman Catholic, middle-class mother who killed her five children, between the ages of seven years to six months, by drowning them in the bathtub. Megan Stack (2002) of the *Los Angeles Times* wrote:

> A morbid mystery festers here in these sleepy, working-class streets cut like verdant tunnels between the Christian churches and gasoline stations: What happened to Andrea Yates? A woman without so much as a speeding ticket. A mother who delighted her children with American Indian costumes fashioned from grocery sacks and shepherd suits made of blankets. Docile, clever Andrea, the family's selfless caretaker, had battled depression for years and had attempted suicide. But this woman, a modern-day Medea? Talk to her neighbors, her family, her husband. They mouth the same words, over and over. I don't know.

As Huckerby (2003) notes, Christianity is a measure of superior motherhood: "Generally, in Western culture, a Christian mother will have a higher claim to motherhood than a non-Christian mother because the former is more readily seen as embodying the 'Christian' virtues of benevolence, forgiveness, and tolerance—virtues that are also perceived to be the hallmarks of good mothering" (152–153).

From all accounts, Andrea Yates seemed to have spent almost every waking moment with her five children. What's more, she and her husband planned to have more children. In fact, culturally she had all the makings of a good mother—docile, clever, and a selfless caretaker—who stayed home to raise her children, all below the age of seven. Eventually her satanic visions led her to drown her children to death; yet, in spite of all these extenuating cultural circumstances, psychology had been used to explain her state of mind. How could one look at culture when Christian, middle-class, white Andrea Yates, up until she killed her children, did all that a good mother was supposed to do?

Conversely, when immigrant women of color are charged with family violence, culture inevitably enters the courtroom. While Sailaja Hathaway is posited as a bad mother, to a degree because of her culture, Andrea Yates had all she needed to be a good mother, but instead killed her children because of mental illness—or, she was simply a mad mother. By popular descriptions, "she was nature's aberration" (Huckerby 2003, 152). On March 12, 2002, Andrea Yates was found guilty for the murders of three of her five children, and Harris County reserved the right to prosecute the murders of her two other sons, Paul and Luke, at a later date (O'Malley 2004). She was given a life sentence. On January 6, 2005, however, Yates's sentence was overturned. The Court of Appeals for the First District of Texas found that the state's expert witness, Dr. Park Dietz, had presented false testimony. Although five other expert witnesses had testified that Yates did not know right from wrong, Dr. Dietz had claimed that she knew what she was doing when she killed her children. As a result, Andrea Yates's insanity defense had been rejected in 2002. Upon discovering his false testimony, Yates's sentence was reversed.

Huckerby (2003) observes that bad mothers tend to receive worse sentences than mad mothers: "Although invocation of 'madness' as an explanation for infanticide does not guarantee exoneration, on the whole women who are perceived as being pathological are punished less severely than those who are deemed evil. The definition of the latter type of mother appears to be met if a mother is 'depraved,' that is, 'ruthless, selfish, cold, callous, neglectful of her children or domestic responsibilities, violent or promiscuous'" (158). The prosecuting team in Sailaja Hathaway's case argued "she had every right to be angry, bitter, upset. But she crossed a line. . . . Her intent to kill was obvious . . . don't give her credit just because she wasn't successful" (Spencer 2002). When asked if Sailaja Hathaway remained a danger, her psychiatrist Jay Fogelman said, "her illness and deceitfulness make her the most lethal weapon I have encountered in my 25 years of practice" (Spencer 2001).

The entry of culture in the courtrooms marks Third World immigrants as carriers of dysfunctional gender, familial, and social traits all attributable to their culture; they are more prone to being bad mothers. Not the individual woman, but her culture that made her act in a particular manner is put on trial. When Indian culture is evoked in the courtroom, such a culture does not stand alone, especially when a person's acts are to be interpreted according to the grids ostensibly set by this foreign culture; "the contrast in this usage is not between culture and not-culture," but between American culture and how people act within this cultural realm (Sewell 1999, 39). The abnormality of an act—such as mothers trying to poison their kids—is attributed to the immigrant's cultural difference, while such aberrations are assumed not to exist in American culture. Then how to explain the existence of white mothers like Susan Smith or Andrea Yates, who drowned their children to death? Theirs is a case of deviance and not American culture. Individual psychosis explains these women's acts of filicide. Huckerby (2003) states that white middle-class mothers are the poster girls for good motherhood. So positing women such as Andrea Yates as mad "prevents her acts from having wider significance. Rather than the acts being the byproduct of an insidious cult of motherhood, they are characterized as isolated and contained incidents that can easily be altered through medication and therapeutic treatment" (166). Hence, Andrea Yates's madness biologizes and individualizes filicide, thus preserving the myth of superior white motherhood.

Raising the problem of cultural testimonies does not mean I endorse psychological arguments, for these kinds of explanations can be equally problematic. While cultural explanations remove any kind of volition an individual may hold, psychological arguments are falsely individualizing, refusing to see the larger social contexts within which violence occurs. Psychological explanations render perpetrators of violence into *ur*-individuals, motivated wholly by personal choice.

Law's Culture

Many white feminists believe that asking the state to adjudicate with culture on its mind impinges on the liberal goals of gender equality and ends up harming women (Coleman 1996; Sikora 2001). An illustration of (white) feminism's overzealous suspicion of culture is Susan Moller Okin (1999), who observes that the defense of culture has "a much greater impact on the lives of women and girls than on those of men and boys, since far more of women's time and energy goes into preserving and maintaining the personal, familial, and reproductive side of life" (13). However, the situation is not as dire for white Western women because "though western liberal democracies also have cultures of patriarchy, women have the same legal rights and opportunities as men." Moreover Western cultures, "with the exception of some religious fundamentalists, do not communicate to their daughters that they are of less value than boys, that their lives are to be confined to domesticity and service to men and children, and that their sexuality is of value only in marriage, in the service of men, and for reproductive ends" (Okin 1999, 16–17). The same does not hold true for "women in many of the world's other cultures, including many of those from which immigrants to Europe and North America come" (Okin 1999, 17). Many immigrant cultures are more patriarchal than American or European cultures, and using an immigrant defendant's cultural background for establishing mens rea harms women's interests. Okin's (1999) conclusion is that attention to cultural differences is bad for women of color, "Indeed, they *might* be better off if the culture into which they were born were either to become extinct (so that its members would become integrated into a less sexist surrounding culture) or, preferably, to be encouraged to alter itself so as to reinforce the equality of women—at least to the degree to which this value is upheld by the majority culture" (22–23).

Aside from Okin's unashamed ethnocentricity and ignorance of the histories of non-Western feminisms, arguments such as the one above are premised on misreading of power and of mens rea. In spite of what we see as the misuse of culture in cases such as *People v. Chen*, we cannot do away with it when making claims on the state, because culture permeates all aspects of social life. Getting a handle on culture explains how power works in social spaces such as schools, workplaces, and homes; it is dispersed throughout social relations but remains naturalized. Hence, we almost always remain unaware of power's workings. Bringing culture to the state's attention, then, is a way by which feminists push for the formal recognition of the workings of power. While not being the sole causal factor, culture can explain the structures of feelings, ideas, and emotions we carry within ourselves, and why we act in the ways that we do. Given that law regards individuals in their particular circumstances when deciding on punishment, to ask that we exclude culture is politically untenable.

Good cultural analyses, Sewell (1999) explains, attempt to elucidate the articulation between the semiotic codes in culture (the system) and practice. The semiotic codes that people share are never all encompassing but have thin coherence. That is, not everyone within that cultural group unanimously agree upon symbols, the significance of symbols, norms, and values. Social actors give multiple meanings to symbols and often use the exact same set of symbols to justify very different social acts. Hence, the thinness of cultural coherence, together with the polyvalency of symbols and emergent practices continually subject cultures to transformation. The problem in many accounts of culture, according to Sewell (1999), is that they posit a high degree of coherence among various inhabitants of that cultural space. In addition, ethnographers seem to find a high degree of similitude among different cultural practices because they tend to focus on "clusters of symbols and meanings that can be shown to have a high degree of coherence or systematicity. . . . This practice results in what sociologists would call sampling on the dependent variable. That is, anthropologists tend to select symbols and meanings that cluster neatly into coherent systems and pass over those that are relatively fragmented or incoherent, thus confirming the hypothesis that symbols and meanings indeed form tightly coherent systems" (Sewell 1999, 47).

I will continue with the example that I have already presented—that is, the practice of Indian mothering. The argument I made in court in Sailaja Hathaway's defense was that Indian mothering is different because the boundaries between their self-identity and that of their children are far more nebulous than might be the norm among middle-class white women. When they are in bad marriages, Indian women such as Sailaja Hathaway see harm not only to themselves but also, as an extension, to their children as well. Hence, they attempt mother-child suicide. In their eyes, they are not committing homicide (by killing their children) but instead are committing suicide (as the child is part of them). Hathaway is neither a bad nor mad mother; she did not lack love for her children, nor was she psychotic. Instead, because of the ways by which she was shaped by her culture, she was doing what she thought was the best for her children. Thus, my argument was that Hathaway's Indian upbringing could perhaps be an independent variable affecting her understanding and, therefore, practices of mothering. Yet, to argue that a woman kills her children solely because of her cultural notions is thorny, given that the cultural precepts inherent in motherhood can play out quite differently.

I had hoped my testimony could raise questions about why the cultural symbols inhered in Indian motherhood and practices of mothering articulated in such a manner for Hathaway that the only option she saw as open to her was filicide. After all, there are millions of Indian mothers who are socially ostracized, lose face, and otherwise deemed misfits within their societies, yet do not harm their children. The point I wanted to make was that while culture may certainly influence the meanings we attach to motherhood, the act of mothers killing their children when they face difficulties is not necessarily a predetermined outcome. Filicide is one of the many choices that a victimized woman may make. Filicide is an overdetermined phenomenon that cannot be explained by culture or by psychology alone.

Yet, the format of giving witness in court, examinations by the defense, and cross-examinations by the prosecution meant that I had little narrative control, and inevitably my descriptions of Indian culture were rather simplistic. The narrative layout within which I was placed in court pushed me to focus on "a high degree of coherence or systematicity" (Sewell 1999, 47). Law demands strongly defined, teleological narratives, and anything that might threaten the idea of cultural consistency (when we speak of defendant immigrants' cultures) is excised from the narrative. If such complexity is presented, then it fails to make sense because law is incapable of dealing with internal contradictions that constitute cultural practices. The ambivalence one feels, the multiplicity of meanings in practices, the divergent interpretations of the exact same symbol, etc., all lie beyond law's comprehensive capacity.

When we make cultural arguments in court, the law sees immigrant cultures as being "logically consistent, highly integrated, consensual, extremely resistant to change, and clearly bounded" (Sewell 1999, 52). The notion is that immigrant culture is unchanging and ahistorical, and these immigrant "others" are incapable of reflexivity that allows an internal critique and contestations. In addition, actors do not have the ability to play on multiple meanings that symbols may hold. These immigrant others who stand to be judged feel no ambivalence about their own cultures. Indeed, their cultures can hold no polyvalent symbols that can be understood in various ways, thus leading to a multiplicity of practices. The understandings of the other in law is that there is thick, deep coherence to their cultures.

The truth of the matter is that cultures are inherently "contradictory, loosely integrated, contested, mutable, and highly permeable" (Sewell 1999, 53). Yet, how are the codes of law to make sense of these kinds of tumultuous multiplicity of meanings? Law has its own cultural conventions by which it operates, thus demanding its subjects to follow its codes. One aspect to law's culture is whiteness. Racial ideologies that permeate American society, permeate its legal configurations as well, for "law does not exist as a separate phenomenon distinct from society and concerned only with policing disputes, but is an integral part of society and an essential component in the social production of knowledge" (Lopez 1996, 123). The public sphere is structured by whiteness, which has tremendous power because even though it remains silent, it serves as a point of reference for measuring others. So, when Indian culture is brought into the courtroom, the silent contrast is American culture.

However, by law's culture I do not just mean whiteness alone, but also a culture that individualizes and one that is set up as an adversarial system, insisting that real-life narratives be recounted in teleological ways, with the establishment of causality. That is, we are asked to look at independent factor A, which causes dependent individual to behave in a particular manner. Law then takes factor A in drawing up the punishment for actor B. Writing on the narrative style of historians, Halttunen (1999) observes that they "enlist the same narrative conventions as fiction writers . . . inventively imposing the time frame of beginnings, middle, and end, organizing sequence to convey the sense of consequence, characterizing, scene-setting, emplotting, crafting the 'reality effect'—all in the voice of the omniscient narrator speaking from a single, unified point of view. . . . The function of historical narrative, like that of any other ideologizing discourse, is not transparently representational but moral and political" (166).

Law acts in precisely the same way in crafting the reality effect as it goes about establishing innocence or degrees of culpability so that decisions on individualized retributive justice can be made. By harking to law's crafting of narratives, I do not mean to say that it works on falsehoods, but "contingent and discontinuous facts of the past" are woven into coherent, intelligible stories (Halttunen 1999, 166). Legal narratives—here the cases of Sailaja Hathaway and Andrea Yates—take shape and emerge as coherent wholes when different episodes from the past are juxtaposed teleologically, illuminating and emphasizing each other. As defending lawyers, prosecutors, or expert witnesses, we make important choices on rhetorical forms. However, these choices are structured by causal mechanisms; that is, we seek cause and effect in our legal narratives, with one set of events or emotions (culture or psychology) explaining a particular outcome (filicide). This kind of ordering gives direction to legal narratives, making truths emerge. And the jury then sits in judgment of these truths.

Though some legal scholars (e.g., Engel 1998) may balk at positing a coherent legal culture, I hold onto such a notion. I see law's culture as being exceptionally consistent because the law is a codified system. And even if there is variability in the ways its effects are manifested, discrepancies are far more contained than in cultural systems that are more open and less codified. The court is a site where "potentially contradictory meanings [are] brought together and harmonized in ritual performances" (Sewell 1999, 53). The legal system, with the ritual space of the courtroom and law as ritual practice, attempts to bring together contradictory meanings and inhere some sense of social order. Law attempts to organize the messiness of real life, to bring "the semiotic sprawl into a certain order: to prescribe (contested) core values, to impose discipline on dissenters, to describe boundaries and norms—in short, to give a certain focus to the production and consumption of meaning" (Sewell 1999, 57).

Law is an authoritative voice of the state, and its business is the uniform application of justice. To do this it does not see everyone equally; instead, citizen subjects are observed in their individual circumstances, imputed with particular kinds of characteristics, judged, and punished accordingly. Law's cultural strategy is "not so much to establish uniformity as it is to organize difference. [It is] constantly engaged in efforts not only to normalize or homogenize but also to hierarchize, encapsulate, exclude, criminalize, hegemonize, or marginalize practices and populations that diverge from the sanctioned ideal. By such means, [it] attempt[s], with varying degrees of success, to impose a certain coherence onto the field of cultural practice" (Sewell 1999, 56). Hence, Andrea Yates and Sailaja Hathaway are different kinds of filicidal mothers motivated by psychological factors in one case and culture in the other, and we take into consideration their differences in passing judgment on them.

Organizing Individual Justice

Jerrold Seigel (1999) discerns three ways in which the self has been theorized. The first form of the self is what he calls the material; that is, the self is seen as nothing but the bodily expressions of the will to power. The second way by which the self is explained is what he calls the relational, where the social aspects to the self are emphasized. That is, the self is realized only within a social landscape, where cultural institutions, social hierarchies, personal and collective histories all inflect the way by which the self is expressed. The third way to think about the self is to see the self as reflexive; that is, to think about the abilities of individuals to transcend given contexts and make themselves anew.

In the case of Andrea Yates, the white woman, only the material is given emphasis in understanding her state of mind and her deeds. That is, her actions are seen as arising from her own biological being. She is the maker of her own destiny, with no sociality to her actions. On the other hand, when we use culture we focus only on the relational; that is, immigrant women's culture makes them commit acts of violence. They are incapable of acting outside the bounds of their cultural confines. However, regardless of the psychological or cultural explanations used to understand their respective states of mind, both Sailaja Hathaway and Andrea Yates (until her sentence was repealed in January 6, 2005) were declared guilty of their crimes, and they received prison sentences. Whether their selves were posited as being wholly material or wholly relational, what the law wanted them to do was be reflexive individuals. That is, the law demanded them to prevail over their life circumstances and transform themselves into stellar mothers, who are presented as the social norm. Hence, even if culture and psychology are used in assessing mens rea, the expectation for filicidal mothers is that they overcome their cultural or biological circumstances and fashion themselves anew into commendable mothers. Sailaja Hathaway and Andrea Yates are required to transcend their cultures and their bodies. However, there is silence on how these women can rise above the circumstances of their lives and become ostensibly normal mothers, for that is not the business of a differentiating, classificatory, and normalizing law.

Concluding Remarks

Law is an "authoritative cultural action, launched from the centers of power." Its effect is to "turn what otherwise might be a babble of cultural voices into a semiotically and political ordered field of differences. . . . [It] tells people where they and their practices fit into the official scheme of things" (Sewell 1999, 56). Through engaging in cultural arguments, whether to exonerate men who beat their wives or women who might harm their children, we are active participants in this semiotic field that is set for us. We orient our resistance, our sense of meaningful action, and our political struggles in these grounds that are already set. It is not possible for us to step out of these fields, because at present, there is no outside, and we have no choice but to pick fighting words in grammars that are not our own, using a lexicon that is not of our desires.

Audre Lorde (1984) may say that it is not possible to break the master's house with the master's tools, but what other alternatives do we have? Or, to ask an ominous question, is part of law's culture itself to make us believe that we have no option but to be ordered by the vocabularies that it sets for us? Fighting the good fight asks that we be creative, and it is only my lack of imagination that makes me post a critique of cultural arguments in court, without showing a way out. In my defense, all I can say is that this essay gives no road maps; it is only an invitation for us to collectively invent disruptions in the narratives that subject us into disciplined citizens. Our predicament is not about using culture, but instead the question is how do we constructively use culture, constantly changing yet all-encompassing, to explain people's differential behavior in the courtroom. The challenge we face is to make the narrative of culture, always contested and ever-changing, fit into the narrative of a strictly codified law, which presents itself as a rational, objective, independent, and unbiased mediator of justice amongst a nation's citizens.

ACKNOWLEDGMENTS

I thank Vivian Newdick and Sinikka Elliot for their critical insights, which greatly strengthened this article.

14

Middle Class, Documented, and Helpless

The H-4 Visa Bind

SHIVALI SHAH

Janice knew John for thirteen years before they married.[1] After college, Janice had been an accountant for several years in a large corporation. Their romance began after he moved to the United States to join a high-tech company. John was in the United States on H-1B visa; she joined him on an H-4 visa. Within two weeks of landing in the States, John's personality seemed to change. He scolded her for the slightest mistake, became increasingly suspicious of her, and would not let her leave the house alone. At least once a week he would sneak home during the day to hide in a closet to make sure she was not inviting men over while he was at work. John's verbal abuse escalated to physical abuse and almost daily threats of violence. He pulled her hair and made her do outrageous and embarrassing things in front of their friends. During her first trimester of pregnancy, he grabbed her head and forced her to drink four bottles of beer. Janice was at a loss as to what to do. She could not get a job legally or even pay for a plane ticket to return to India. Even if she did return, her family would not be able to support her and a young infant. Her own income as a junior accountant in Delhi would not be enough and, in any case, she would need time to take care of a newborn.

Unfortunately, Janice's situation is not unique. Well-educated, English-speaking South Asian women who come to the United States to join their H-1B visa holding husbands find that the American women's movement has no place for them. The legal strides that have been made on behalf of battered immigrant women in the United States have primarily favored those married to U.S. citizens or legal permanent residents. However, an unnoticed, yet substantial segment of battered immigrant women are dependent spouses of foreign nationals working in specialty occupations such as computer technology, health care, and academics. These foreign nationals are granted a temporary work visa, H-1B, which allows them to reside and work in the United States for up to six years.

Spouses and minor children accompanying H-1B visa holders to the United States are granted H-4 dependent visas. The legal and policy restrictions on the H-4 wife create a situation in which she must derive her entire legal and economic identity in the United States from her H-1B husband. The U.S. Citizenship and Immigration Services (USCIS) estimates that there are approximately 100,000 H-4 visa holders in the country at present and nearly half of them are nationals of South Asian countries.

For those H-4 wives caught in abusive marriages, U.S. immigration laws provide their batterers the opportunity to control them at every step of the immigration process. The law treats the H-4 spouse as an expendable appendage to the H-1B employee and, thereby, creates an inherent imbalance of power in the marriage. The H-4 spouse cannot work legally in the United States and thus is totally dependent on her husband for financial support.[2] Furthermore, she is dependent on her H-1B husband to obtain, maintain, and change her visa status. While an inconvenience to anyone on an H-4 visa, these constraints create and perpetuate an imbalanced relationship, which is most painfully felt by battered women. Given their limited options, women on H-4 visas often end up staying in the abusive relationship longer than they otherwise would. This often means enduring abuse until the green card comes through—a process which could take up to ten years after landing in the United States. Although the H-4 women have legal residency status in the United States and are in the middle-class income bracket, immigration and related laws create a class of women whose status is analogous to, and in some cases worse than, undocumented and indigent immigrants.

This essay draws upon legal research, a survey of current and former H-4 visa holders, and my own experiences with battered H-4 women through my work with Kiran and Sakhi, both domestic violence crisis centers for South Asians in North Carolina and New York, respectively. My arguments are based on in-depth interviews with H-4 visa holders, domestic violence advocates, immigration attorneys, and a survey of South Asian Women's organizations (SAWOs) in the United States.

The H-4 visa holders' relatively higher standard of living as compared to working-class and indigent women, as well as their valid immigration status obscures the fact that these women maintain their privileged status only at the pleasure of their husbands. Their apparent financial stability and valid immigration status make them a nonpriority for domestic violence service and advocacy groups. As a result, abuse victims on H-4 status are cut off from traditional channels of assistance available to other battered immigrant women.

At the end of this chapter, I have included suggestions for legislative change. In addition to granting H-4s work authorization, other legislative changes are necessary to normalize this visa status. Corporations that employ H-1Bs must also bear some responsibility for these families. Anti–domestic violence organizations must reconceptualize the H-4s as a subcategory of undocumented and indigent immigrants and provide services and advocacy appropriate for battered women.

Life after Separation

Immigration laws' failure to protect battered H-4 women is exacerbated by conditions in the United States and their home countries. The situation in the home country may make it difficult or sometimes even impossible to return if a battered woman falls out of status in the United States. For those who intend to remain in the United States unlawfully, living conditions of undocumented immigrants make it hard to stay away from one's abuser. Many battered H-4 women end up losing their immigration status as a direct result of an action or omission by their H-1B batterer; sometimes it is because she has left her husband, been evicted, or a combination of both. If an H-4 battered woman decides to leave the United States with no intention of returning in the future, then immigration status may be ignored.[3] Returning home as a separated or divorced woman, however, is often not a viable option for many H-4 brides.

Staying in the United States

Although here on legal visas, the law affords H-4 wives no more protection than undocumented immigrants. Like an undocumented immigrant, she may not have work authorization and either obtains unreported income or works using a false identity. In either case, she is committing fraud upon the state, which could prevent her from getting a visa or green card in the future. This may make her subject to deportation. Condemned to be without work authorization, H-4 wives usually end up taking on the same kinds of low-paying low-profile jobs performed by undocumented or illegal immigrants, such as maid service for motels, retail sales, and babysitting. Because H-4 women, on average, tend to be more highly educated than the average undocumented immigrant, some H-4s may also work at technical white-collar jobs on a cash basis for small private businesses. If abandoned by the batterer, an H-4 woman's lack of U.S. citizenship makes her ineligible for federal and most state and local public benefits as well.

> Farida was a doctor in Bangladesh before coming to the United States on an H-4 visa. To practice medicine in the United States, she would have to take additional courses and pass rigorous exams; both of which would require money that her husband refused to give. To save money towards getting her certified, Farida worked three days per week at a pathology doctor's office processing laboratory samples. She was paid one-third of what a regular lab technician's salary, did not receive benefits, and was at the mercy of her boss's schedule without notice.

Women like Farida, who are working in undocumented jobs while still with their abuser, know that they cannot subsist on their own income. Furthermore, those

H-4 wives who work on illegal cash-based jobs receive subminimum wages, no benefits, long hours, no bargaining power, and, in some cases, sexual harassment.

For H-4 wives, ineligibility to work also means that they do not receive social security numbers. Without a social security number, one cannot open a bank account, apply for credit cards, or, often, rent an apartment since many landlords require a credit check. The very fact that an immigrant does not have a social security number raises doubts in the average American's mind as to the validity of the person's immigration status. For example, a Bangladeshi immigrant woman had taken out a restraining order against her husband and had been granted the apartment by the judge. Because she did not have a social security number, she could not transfer the lease in her name.

In many states, H-4 status also means that individuals either cannot apply for a driver's license or they need their spouse's permission to apply. For a battered woman, not having a driver's license poses severe impediment to accessing help. In New Jersey, for example, an H-4 wife needs to not only produce all of her husband's immigration documentation, but also apply only at the Trenton office. Many states require proof of insurance, which an abusive husband may also withhold from his victim. Post 9/11, some states now refuse to issue driver's license to anyone without a social security number. Often employees of the Department of Motor Vehicles do not understand the intricacies of the various immigration statuses and refuse to grant licenses to H-4s altogether. One H-4 woman was told that she needed to produce not only her husband's immigration documents but also her H-1B husband in the flesh to vouch for her.

To many women on H-4 visas who prefer to stay in this country, there is nothing more important than maintaining their legal status. While with her husband, an H-4 wife has the same class and social standing as he does, and working in a blue-collar job under the table means a demotion in socioeconomic status. The trauma of this fall is sometimes the hardest to endure. Thus, when a woman realizes that there are no immigration options for her besides staying with her batterer until the green card is approved, she will decide to remain with the abuser and wait for the green card, despite the abuse.

Abandoned in the Home Country

Many battered H-4 wives end up returning to their home countries. Some may leave voluntarily; others are abandoned against their wishes. In many cases of abandonment, the couple goes back together to the home country on vacation. The husband returns first and then prevents the wife from coming back. He may convince her that she is not welcome back until certain conditions are met, withhold the paperwork she needs to return, or take away the documents she has in her possession and hold them hostage. Often, the batterer's family is complicit in such abuse.

After marrying Ayush, Aruna moved to California on an H-4 visa. Ayush was an executive in a Silicon Valley firm and had already applied for his green card. Right from the beginning, Ayush claimed she ate too much and used too much heat and electricity when he was at work. Aruna thought their vacation to visit family in India would settle him down. "But after he went back to [the] U.S.," Aruna said, "his parents went through my bags and took my passport, my [airline] ticket, and all my jewelry." When Aruna pleaded with Ayush over the telephone, he said his increased expenses were more than he could bear and he needed her to bear her share of the living expenses. Aruna asked, "On H-4, I cannot work; where do I get money from?"

In another case, Kriti's husband and father-in-law conspired to abandon her in India. In her affidavit, Kriti wrote, "[My husband] and his father forced me into going to India. Once we reached [an] Indian airport, he abandoned me and my son at the airport." After they passed through immigration, Kriti's husband took away her passport. "He did not bother to give me any money and went away," she said.

For South Asian women who have left their home countries to marry H-1B men in America, the pressure to keep the marriage together is especially acute. Many of these women depart for the United States with much fanfare, leaving behind envious family and friends. Marrying an educated man with a future in the United States is seen as a particularly good alliance and thus the women are expected to work extra hard to please their husbands. These pressures manifest in different ways for women from different backgrounds, but the underlying expectations are similar. Many of the women I have interviewed report being told, "He has a good job and he is educated, how bad can he be?"

Due to the social and economic impact, natal families are often unsupportive of women's return and disbelieve the abuse. Sometimes the family has spent a considerable fortune in wedding expenses and dowry for the daughter. Not only can they not afford to feed another mouth, but they might prefer that the daughter remain in the United States to avoid social embarrassment. The taint of a failed marriage may also affect a woman's ability to secure a job in her home country. A woman separated from a man living abroad is often viewed as unreliable, arrogant, and of questionable character. Alternatively, prospective employers may assume that she will eventually rejoin her husband in the United States and therefore would make an undependable employee.

Given these bleak options, it might be easier to endure the abuse, no matter how severe. Many battered H-4 wives, like other battered women, hope that their partners will improve with a change of jobs, more devotion from their wives, etc. Even those who feel that there is no long-term hope for their marriage might maintain it until they can convert their immigration status to an independent status or figure out a way to return to their home country without problems.

Women often prefer abandonment in the United States to abandonment in the home countries, because away from the U.S. jurisdiction the wife has less recourse to financial justice. For batterers, a divorce in the United States is more expensive and thus less favorable. Divorce and separation laws in the United States tend to be more equitable both legally and practically. Some women are reluctant to return to their home countries for fear that their legal rights will not be protected there. Abusers also recognize this. According to Kriti, her husband had physically forced her to sign divorce papers in the United States, "[but] later he tore the papers as he realized that getting divorce in U.S. would be expensive for him than in India."

Corruption in legal systems in South Asian countries is also cited as a reason women fear returning and filing for divorce there. Parminder is currently involved in an international custody battle for her ten-month-old son. Parminder's in-laws have a family business, which regularly uses the court system: "My mother-in-law knows all the tricks of the courts. When I was just married, she only was telling me how clever she is by bribing all the [court] officers every week to get her work done." In the affluent suburb of Bombay, in which her family and her in-laws live, there is no separate family court. So, her custody case is being bounced around the same courthouse in which her in-laws have deep connections.

In some cases, the women not only fear for their legal rights but also believe that returning will place them in lethal danger. Anu was physically and sexually abused in the United States for several years. Her husband is an attorney and before moving to the United States had practiced law in their home city in India. As a result, he had extensive contacts throughout the state. Whenever her family back home would intervene to assist her, they would get visits from the police or the local thugs in the middle of the night. Once when they were in India, Anu had reported him to the police after a particularly violent night. Later that afternoon, her husband returned home with the original police report and ripped it to shreds in front of her.

The Extent of the Problem

A common dismissal of the plight of H-4 women relies on the misconception that the numbers of battered H-4 women is insignificant. All South Asian women's organizations in the United States have had battered H-4 clients, some in alarmingly disproportionate numbers. Maitri in California reports that in 2001 between 25 and 33 percent of their new clients were H-4 visa holders. In 2000, the president of Maitri, Sonya Pelia, mentioned, "Three years ago, ten percent of our clients had dependent H-4 visas. Now, at least forty percent do" (Banerjee 2001). Raksha in Georgia reports that between 2001 and 2004, 30 to 35 percent of their new clients were H-4 visa holders. Manavi in New Jersey reports that in 1999 they had thirty-five new clients who were H-4 wives in domestic violence situations, approximately 20 percent of their total clients for that year. In 2000, 14 percent and in 2001, 20 percent of Manavi's clients were H-4 visa holders. According to Soniya Munshi, director of Manavi, the actual numbers might be even higher, because some women are on the verge of losing or have already lost their H-4 status, and many clients' immigration status was not recorded. Munshi estimated that the actual number of H-4 visa holder clients might be closer to 30 percent. Kiran, a domestic violence crisis service center for South Asians in North Carolina, stated that the percentage of H-4 clients they worked with increased from 25 percent in 2003 to a shocking 75 percent in 2005. The percentage of H-4 clients of Saheli in Massachusetts ranged from 50 to 75 percent between 2002 and 2004.

Legal Options for the H-4 Battered Wife

If an H-4 wife and her H-1B husband divorce, she no longer enjoys H-4 status. For the battered H-4 wife who wants to leave her abusive husband but remain in the United States, the options are limited. Although the services and legal provisions for battered immigrant women have increased, the currently available legal options for H-4 women are not only few and grossly inadequate but also have been decreasing post 9/11.

Options for Battered Women

The two main independent legal options available to battered immigrant women, the battered spouse waiver and self-petitioning, are closed to H-4 wives. Both these provisions only benefit immigrant women who are married to U.S. citizens or to legal permanent residents. While political asylum based on gender persecution is one option for battered H-4 wives, it is not viable for the majority. For an H-4 woman to receive political asylum, she must demonstrate that she has personally suffered gender persecution in her home country and that the government authorities are unwilling or unable to protect her. The burden of proof is quite prohibitive. The U and T visas, originally intended to include H-4 women, also fall short of providing them with safe havens. In their current forms, neither offers the kind of coverage that is required to protect H-4 wives.

The U visa was intended for noncitizen crime victims who fear that getting involved with law enforcement will undermine their visa status in the United States. According to the Immigration and Nationality Act of 2000, U visa was created for those noncitizens who have suffered substantial physical or mental abuse consequent to the perpetration of a crime, including domestic violence (Pendleton 2003). To be eligible, the crime victim must be helpful to the prosecution of the crime. In return, the immigrant victim will be granted a U visa allowing her to stay in the United States, work authorization, and the possibility of green card approval after three years. In theory, the U visa is a good step toward assisting domestic violence victims, but in practice it has not been very helpful for dependent-spouse visa holders. It was created primarily for undocumented women with no immigration status in hand. Due to the status and basic structure of the U visa, and the relationship between law enforcement and immigrant communities, women on H-4 are nervous about engaging in the process of applying for such a visa.

First, the most basic barrier with the U visa provision is that it requires the victim to rely on law enforcement. However, battered immigrant women in general, and H-4 women in specific, are less likely to rely on law enforcement intervention. A woman may come from a country in which local law enforcement is corrupt enough to be bought off by a persuasive abusive partner. Others may come from countries where curbing domestic violence is not a job for the police; instead, it is treated as a private matter. In both cases, law enforcement might be viewed as unhelpful, and such an action could enrage the batterer and heighten the victim's risk. For some women, getting her abuser entangled in the U.S. criminal justice system might carry dire consequences. A conviction on domestic violence charges could lead to the imprisonment of the batterer and termination of his employment. Many women on H-4 visas have to be dependent on their spouses, abusive or not, for economic support. Since H-4 women's immigration status is also dependent on their husbands, any conviction might result in deportation, which would leave the women without status and income. Even an arrest might inordinately anger the abuser, leading the women into financial and immigration problems.

> Jasleen, twenty-seven, had married Jaswant, thirty, a software engineer. Since her wedding, physical and emotional violence had become a weekly event for Jasleen. "If Jaswant wants to throw me and my son out on the street, there is nothing I could do about it," said Jasleen. She feared calling the police for several years because even if he was punished, what would become of her and her son? During a picnic with friends, they noticed Jasleen's fresh and visible bruises. "Seeing my red cheeks and swollen left ear, our friends enquired about it," Jasleen recalls. "I confided in them. [Our friends] asked me whether I wanted to call police or register a complaint against [Jaswant] in [the] police station. Due to my total dependency on him, I decided not to take any legal steps at that time."

Most of the women would not call the police or even tell their families about their horrible situation. The ones that do call the police generally are the victims of most severe abuses.

> Kenali came to the United States after marrying Kaushik, a software consultant on HI-B visa. Within the first week of her arrival in the United States, her husband beat her violently, bit her all over her body, and starved her. He justified the beatings as attempts to teach her proper housework. He broke several of her bones and burned her as part of her "training" to be a good wife. Kenali endured for two months without calling the police until the day he announced that his parents have given their approval to kill her.

Before 9/11, police and immigration authorities were generally unconnected and advocates asked even undocumented battered women to contact the law enforcement in crisis. After 9/11, the increasing collusion between police and USCIS has made South Asian and Middle Eastern women fearful of exposing their men to local authorities. Sensitivity to homeland security has increasingly led to detention of immigrants without legal charges. These new activities have been particularly focused on men of South Asian and Middle Eastern origin or those men who look, by their skin color, like them. Even legal immigrants have reportedly been detained, harassed, and stripped of their rights after the most innocuous of traffic stops. This has fractured what little trust these communities had of local law enforcement.

Second, by design, the U visa considers those crime victims who are in a valid immigration status at the time of application ineligible. This poses a problem for H-4 wives. A woman who has one year left on her H-4 visa must wait the year to be eligible for a U visa. Law enforcement officials are frequently not aware of these visa requirements, which make it difficult to exercise the U visa option for women on H-4 visa.

Employment- and Education-Based Residency Options

The only other option that a battered H-4 wife has to remain in the United States legally is to get a work visa, such as an H-1B, or student visa. While these are viable options for some women with skills and financial resources, it is not a solution for the majority. Women who are eligible must apply for jobs, interview, receive a job offer, and wait for the work visa to be approved. At an optimistic minimum, this process would take six months to complete. With the fall of the tech industry, women may find that it takes them up to two to three years to find a job with visa sponsorship.

Transferring to a student, or F-1, visa is another option. An F-1 visa is a good idea for those who would like to apply for an H-1B but may be lacking some of the requisite qualifications. While this is a legitimate option, there are obstacles as well. A foreign national without a green card must pay international tuition rate to enroll and may not be eligible for government or private student loans. Furthermore, foreign nationals on student visas, like H-4 visa holders, are not allowed to earn an income.

> Now separated from her abusive husband, Ananya is contemplating going back to school for a U.S. nursing degree. Her Indian nursing education is not sufficient to get an H-1B visa, but she cannot afford to stop working under the table and go to school full time. With two teenage boys to support, she is caught between keeping her immigration status and feeding her children.

The woman who has all the necessary education and financial resources to convert her visa to F-1 still faces another barrier. To change her status, the law virtually requires the battered H-4 wife to obtain her husband's consent. Because her immigration status is derived from her husband's, a battered H-4 wife is dependent on him to verify her legal presence in the United States. She must prove that she is in the United States legally when she submits the petition to change status. In addition, she must also show that her H-1B husband is still in status. Even if she is legally present in the United States, she cannot demonstrate this without her spouse's cooperation.

The Failure of Nonprofit Organizations to Serve and Advocate for H-4s

H-4 visa holders have consistently complained that they do not receive appropriate assistance from myriad social service providers, including those that provide

services to battered women, battered immigrant women, and indigent clients. Battered women's organizations and shelters, nonprofit organizations providing legal
services to immigrants, legal aid/legal service organizations, and immigrant advocacy groups tend not to recognize the needs of H-4 battered women. H-4 women
suffer from reverse classism in accessing services, which puts them in a particularly difficult bind.

The primary legal assistance an H-4 woman needs is an assessment of the immigration consequences of leaving her husband. Most service organizations are incapable of properly advising her of the intricacies of visas such as the H-4, H-1B, or F-1.
When an employer decides that it is appropriate to file a green card application for
the H-1B husband, a long process involving a large amount of paperwork commences.
A woman on H-4 needs an immigration attorney competent in employment-based
immigration to take care of her interests.

The critical issue for most battered H-4 women is how long one will have to
wait to receive approval for a green card through her husband. Each battered H-4
wife whose husband is likely to sponsor her for a green card will have to weigh the
time it will take to receive approval against the severity of the abuse she is suffering. After green card approval, her immigration status is no longer tied to her husband and she has work authorization. What an abused H-4 wife needs is advice
and informed estimates based on what little information there is on how long it
will take to complete the immigration process. With this information, she can make
a better judgment on whether she should wait for the green card or leave. Many
SAWOs commented that when an H-4 woman learns that she does not have any
viable immigration alternatives, they usually do not hear from her again. A few
might call back months later after a particularly violent incident.

Many nonprofit anti–domestic violence agencies and legal aid/legal services
organizations that provide services to battered immigrant women do not have the
competency to advise battered H-4 women appropriately. Most of these organizations concentrate on providing services to undocumented and low-income immigrant women. Their expertise tends to be limited to serving those eligible for relief
under the Violence Against Women Act (VAWA), the battered spouse waiver, the
U visa, and related provisions. Thus, an H-4 woman who may not be eligible for
any of these is often left high and dry. To most social service providers, there is no
overlap between the highly educated and marketable populations that qualify for
employment-based H visas and the indigent populations that seek help from nonprofit and legal aid/legal services. Furthermore, the terms of some funding sources
include restrictions against providing free legal services to employment-based
visa holders. The assumption is that those with employment-based visas are ostensibly documented and middle class and therefore have enough money to pay for
their own immigration attorney.

The experiences of Legal Services of North Carolina (LSNC) offer an illustrative example of the constraints under which legal service organizations operate.
Although LSNC was able to hire two immigration attorneys in 2001 and 2002, it

could barely meet the needs of in-state residents. Despite their specialization in immigration law, the focus of the attorneys was on undocumented immigrants. Jennifer Lee, attorney with the Domestic Violence Unit of LSNC, stated flatly that while she does go out of her way to give advice to those who are not official clients, "We are simply not equipped to deal with employment-based visas."

A nonprofit immigration attorney in a New England state had advised a battered H-4 woman that she should work toward getting an H-1B visa. This client spent the next four months applying for jobs in her field hoping to find an employer to sponsor her H-1B visa. When I met her, I learned that she had neither finished college nor had work experience; without a college degree or work experience to compensate, she was not eligible for an H-1B visa. Additionally, she was applying for jobs in areas in which H-1B visas are not typically granted. Her attorney confessed that she was not aware of the bachelor's degree requirement for H-1B visa.

Mainstream battered women's shelters also fail H-4 women by their lack of familiarity with immigration laws. Most battered women's shelters typically allow a woman to stay for only four to eight weeks. During this time, a resident is expected to get a job, get a place to live, and move out. However, an H-4 woman needs to get work authorization before she can find employment, a process that can take several months. Thus, this paradigm does not work for them.

Organizations that advocate for immigrants' rights do not always recognize the pressing needs of the battered dependent visa-holder spouse. Those that advocate for battered or indigent immigrants dismiss the issue, stating that organizations working with large numbers of employment-based immigration attorneys such as the American Immigration Lawyers Association (AILA) should be the ones advocating for this population. When AILA representatives were asked about advocacy for battered H-4 women, they declared that it is not in their scope of responsibilities, but that battered immigrant women's organizations should be advocating for the group. Consequently, the H-4 women fall through the cracks between documented and undocumented, indigent and middle-class immigrants. H-4 wives enjoy the privileges of their immigration status and class only as long as their husbands permit it. Once they have rejected or been rejected by their husbands, they are in a categorical limbo from which no one will retrieve them.

Intervention Options

Legal Solutions

There are three major legal changes necessary to improve the inherently unfair and imbalanced relationship immigration laws create between H-1B and their H-4 spouses. First is to grant employment authorization to *all* H-4 dependent spouses. Second is to allow H-4 dependent spouses who can demonstrate abuse to self-petition under the VAWA. Third is to change the requirement that for an H-4 dependent spouse to change her status, she must submit documents to which only her H-1B spouse has access.

EMPLOYMENT AUTHORIZATION The lack of employment authorization renders the H-4 wife completely dependent on her husband. While this imbalance causes strain in even compatible marriages, the consequences for a battered woman are severe. Although VAWA 2005 eases some of this onerous dependency by allowing battered H-4 visa holders to obtain work permits by demonstrating their conditions of abuse, the imbalance of power in the conjugal relationship is already set and reinforced by the basic structural injunction. Employment authorization is essential for all H-4 spouses to restore the possibility of economic independence. Without a job, an H-4 visa holder has no way to pull herself up by her own bootstraps and begin to live a violence-free life.

A popular argument against work permit for H-4 visa holders is that there already is a proper channel for foreign nationals to apply for work authorization. Dependent spouses should not seek to bypass this system but apply for an H-1B through the existing process. While a possibility for some, many would not meet H-1B visa requirements. The condition of H-4 women's lives in the United States is different than those of H-1B visa seekers, thus they must be treated differently. There already is a precedent for allowing dependent spouses to work. Since 2002, dependent spouses of temporary workers on the intercompany transfer visa (L-1 visa) and treaty trader visa (E-1/E-2 visas) are granted work authorization. Foreign nationals entering the United States on those two visas are mainly from European countries and Canada. This discrepancy in issuing work permits to dependent visa holders in first and third world nations is tantamount to institutional racism.

IMMIGRATION INDEPENDENCE Although economic rights would reduce the power imbalance in the H-1B/H-4 relationship, battered H-4 spouses need further protection. Immigration status is one of the most powerful weapons an abuser uses in creating and maintaining control over his immigrant spouse. To safeguard women from such control, battered H-4s should be allowed to self-petition for residency under VAWA. Some argue that VAWA protects only spouses of U.S. citizens and green card holders because these spouses would receive a green card anyway. However, it misunderstands the primary principle of VAWA, which acknowledges battered women's human rights. The violence that battered H-4 women suffer is exacerbated due to the constraints of the U.S. laws. Not only does the U.S. government render H-4 wives vulnerable to domestic violence by stripping away their independence, it refuses to provide reasonable means of protection when such abuse occurs.

RIGHT TO DOCUMENTS Frequently, batterers wield power over their spouses by restricting immigration information. To convert the H-4 visa status to an independent one, the dependent spouses need to demonstrate that they are in status through documents that their sponsoring spouses control. The application requires documents such as the H-1B husband's visa approval notice and his most recent pay stubs, which obviously are only accessible with his permission. In a battered wife's case, this access might be impossible to achieve, thereby perpetuating her dependence.

A potential solution would be to require the H-1B visa holder's immigration attorney to provide the dependent spouse with copies of all the documents she needs. However, this solution may be difficult since it violates the longstanding principles of privacy and attorney-client privilege. Another solution might be that USCIS uses other methods of verifying status that do not involve H-1B visa holders or their attorneys. A verification letter from an employer could provide the same information as a pay stub would. USCIS could look up H-1B work visa information in their own system instead of requiring the H-4 wife to extract the documents from an abusive H-1B husband.

Educational and Ethical Reforms

Educational and ethical reforms should close the information gap further. Employment-based immigration attorneys need to be trained on how to deal with the ethical dilemmas in a fracturing H-1B/H-4 marriage. Nonprofit immigration attorneys need to build competency in providing legal services for exploited employment-based visa holders, including battered women with H-4 visas.

Legal services, legal aid organizations, and nonprofit organizations must train their attorneys in providing appropriate advice to H-4 women. Alternatively, they should mark funds to compensate outside consultants to provide this service. Many cite not receiving calls from dependent spouse visa holders as a reason for not recognizing the need. If it is known that an organization can help the H-4 woman, she will be referred to the organization.

Currently, there is a lot of confusion and consequent abuse of authority among employment-based immigration attorneys caught between clients in a failing marriage. In theory, the immigration attorney represents all three parties: employer, H-1B employee, and H-4 dependent spouse. But, when there is dispute among the three, the dependent spouse is the most disenfranchised. The employer usually retains the immigration attorney, who processes the paperwork; when not retained by the employer, the H-1B employee retains the attorney. The immigration attorney also represents the H-4 wife so long as there is no discord between the husband and wife. Once there is conflict, legal ethics dictate that the immigration attorney withdraws from representing both parties. In practice, however, the attorney only ceases to represent the wife.

Two immigration attorneys I interviewed who asked to remain anonymous, stated that they have received calls from irate H-1B holders demanding that they not talk to their wives anymore. A third immigration attorney said that in her law firm, she has received files with the large warning "DO NOT TALK TO WIFE" posted on the outside. Battered H-4 wives routinely cite failure to communicate and being stonewalled by their immigration attorneys.

After her abusive husband kicked Parminder out of their house, her immigration attorney stopped returning her calls. She was waiting for a renewal of her H-4 visa, which the attorney had promised to send to her promptly.

"I didn't know what to do, how can she do that when she said she would put the renewal in the mail?" Parminder asked. The attorney continued to represent and advise her husband and did not even explain to Parminder the ethical issues and why she was not communicating with her anymore.

In such cases, the H-4 wife must retain her own attorney to sort out her immigration needs. However, since she has been prohibited from earning during her stay in the United States, her capacity to hire a competent employment-based immigration attorney is low.

Responsibilities of Corporations

Companies employing large numbers of temporary-work visa holders need to provide informational sessions on immigration for the employees and their spouses. Currently, immigration attorneys serving larger companies occasionally provide basic immigration information only to visa-holding employees. While these are useful to the employees, the dependent spouses are left out. This practice widens the information gap between the H-1Bs and the H-4s and contributes to the power differential. Corporations employing large numbers of foreign temporary workers should acknowledge their social responsibility toward assisting families acclimate to the United States. Families migrate to support the temporary worker and the employers benefit from their sacrifices. Reciprocity by corporations toward the families should be encouraged.

Social Reform

While legal and policy reforms are essential for the relief of battered H-4 women, social reform is the key element. There are many popular myths regarding domestic violence in the South Asian community that make women and their families ignore social realities. One myth is that the more formal education a man has, the less likely he is to be violent. Another is that the more educated a woman is, the less likely she is to get herself in an abusive marriage. Many families are lulled into a sense of security because they have found their daughter's partner in their own cultural community and class, and they have a high education. These myths prevent women from taking concrete measures to protect themselves when leaving their familiar environment on a visa status that officially fosters dependency.

Some of the most painful and severe accounts of abuse I heard were from women who were married to physicians, engineers, Ph.D.s, accountants, and teachers. The victims were equally well educated as the perpetrators. One H-4 wife's mother recounted to me her feelings before her daughter's marriage, "My daughter [was] marrying a master's in computer engineering, he has a big house in the United States, he has a car, this is not some uneducated, uncultured person, she will not have to worry." The idea that wealth, education, and a U.S. visa make a man nonviolent is a prevalent myth. I have met many women who believed that their own education and self-confidence would land them on their feet regardless of what their marriages brought them, and they were generally shocked to learn the realities of life under the H-4 visa. Sometimes the perception of self-confidence, emancipation, and urbanity places women in denial of their actual helplessness.

In a class-sensitive society such as South Asia, people tend to believe that class comes with not only financial benefits but also improved social norms. Such beliefs tend to prevent women and their families from preparing for survival when domestic violence occurs. Families marrying their daughters to H-1Bs must recognize the restricted nature of the visa on which they are sending their daughters to the United States. Even without the restrictive visa status, the speed at which many families agree to send their daughters thousands of miles away is alarming. Sociologist Lalita Pulavarti comments about the practice, "Innumerable number of women get married and come to the United States without even *knowing* whom they are marrying! I have known of 'meeting-greeting-wedding-leaving for U.S.' stories [in India] that take place in a week or less! And I never cease to be amazed at the tremendous amount of misplaced trust with which they put their lives in the hands of a stranger!"

Similarly, the optimism and naiveté with which many women choose to leave their full lives in their home countries to join partners already living abroad is disturbing. "I didn't know anything when I chose [my husband]," Chandrika says while laughing robustly. "My parents never told me what to look for in a guy. I saw their marriage was good, so how hard could it be? Sometimes I look back and think [about my parents] 'how could you send me to America with so little information about anything?'" Chandrika doesn't blame her parents for her failed marriage, but she recognizes that neither she nor those she relied on for advice had done the proper research and investigation necessary.

Concluding Remarks

Skilled and educated women, many of whom would be working professionals in their home countries, are turned powerless with the H-4 visa stamp in their passports. For many women, this increases the risk of domestic violence. Social reform is a long-term goal that our entire community must work on both in the United States and in our home countries. The legal reforms, however, are a more immediate goal, which can relieve the suffering of thousands of battered women and prevent abuse from taking place. We must organize as a community to highlight the consequences of imbalanced laws and demand protection for these vulnerable women. Appropriate changes in laws will also indicate respect and value for women who have come to support their husbands working to maintain the U.S. dominance in high-tech fields, research, and health care. If we truly believe in human rights and family values, we will not continue to ask a woman to make the choice between keeping her family together and having financial and legal autonomy.

NOTES

1. Names of all H visa holders and their family members have been changed to protect
    their privacy.

2. Since this article was written, the 2005 reauthorization of VAWA was signed into law
    (PL 109–162) on January 5, 2006, allowing battered H-4s to apply for work authorization
    on the basis of abuse by their spouses.

3. When an H-4 woman decides to leave the country but wishes to return to the United
    States, she must make sure that her immigration matters are in order. In some limited
    cases, abandoning one's status at certain stages of immigration may make it difficult to
    reenter.

15

Battered South Asian Women in U.S. Courts

SHAMITA DAS DASGUPTA

To end men's violence against their female partners, the U.S.-based anti–domestic violence activists paid special attention to modifying the criminal legal system (CLS) to prepare it to play a critical and sensitive role in the lives of battered women (McMahon and Pence 2003; Pence 1999, 2001; Weisberg 1996). Today, many advocates and policy makers consider the mandatory arrest and subsequent legal penalization in the courts (e.g., no drop prosecution) effective deterrents for batterers, as these evoke the formidable powers of the state. Regardless of the efficacy of these methods, domestic violence laws and policies differentially affect battered women who live at differing crossroads of race, class, sexuality, ability, and citizenship (Coker 2000, 2001; Dasgupta 1998b; Mills 1999; Ruttenberg 1994; Visweswaran 2004). Battered immigrant women of color, caught at the intersections of these various factors, often fall through the cracks of the legal and social service systems supposedly erected to protect *all* battered women.

In this chapter, I cull the experiences of nine advocates, three attorneys, and two academics who have assisted and, on behalf of South Asian battered women, represented and/or testified as cultural experts in U.S. courts.[1] Added to this is the knowledge that I have gathered over the past twenty-five years as a battered women's advocate, academic, community organizer, and South Asian cultural expert. The interviewees were all women and, except for two, of South Asian descent. Seven of the advocates I interviewed worked in South Asian community-based organizations and two in mainstream anti–domestic violence agencies. All the interviewees have supported, represented, and/or advocated for South Asian battered women engaged in the U.S. legal system. Through semistructured interviews, I attempted to explore the myriad problems South Asian battered women encounter when they seek justice in U.S. Courts.

Parameters of the Article

The purpose of this essay is to assess the complexities of and gaps in the legal safety net created for victims of battering in this country. My focus is specifically on battered South Asian immigrant women and the problems they face in dealing with the U.S. justice system. First, I contend that South Asian battered women in the United States have to negotiate their physical and psychological safety through antagonistic criminal and family courts, unsympathetic immigration laws, the push and pull of their social groups, as well as contradictions between the U.S. legal system and the legal systems of their native countries. Second, I discuss the ethical dilemma faced by advocates and cultural experts in facilitating South Asian battered women's petitions of residency and criminal legal dealings. Their conflict is created by the need to support individual women while recognizing that the best way to bolster their petitions in court is often to negatively stereotype entire nations and reinforce the notion that South Asian cultures are uniformly oppressive to women. I end by arguing that any individual benefits derived from such stereotyping are severely offset by collective repercussions of overgeneralizing a culture. Indeed, the utilization of such cultural stereotypes might actually endanger the possibility of justice for South Asian immigrant victims.

The scope of this essay is limited to the experiences of South Asian battered women who are involved in heterosexual relationships. Although there is a sizable community of South Asian American women who are involved in same-sex relationships, their experiences have remained largely hidden. Unfortunately, the majority of South Asian anti–domestic violence organizations has failed to centralize issues of lesbian battering in their programs and thereby added to this community's invisibility. Although I am one of the early anti–domestic violence activists in the South Asian community, to my shame, my awareness of same-sex intimate partner violence in my community is negligible. Thus, this paper remains constrained by the dearth of information on battered South Asian lesbians and their concerns about the U.S. legal system.

I have used the term *immigrant* regardless of an individual's formal residency status in the United States. An individual is deemed an immigrant in the United States not necessarily by his or her official papers, but by visible group (read: ethnic) affiliation. The immigrant category is thus a social construction rather than a legal one. For instance, the general populace may consider a young woman born and brought up in the United States but who traces her cultural roots to South Asia an immigrant, because she looks like others in the group who are immigrants. In contrast, even a very recent immigrant from England may not be regarded as a member of the immigrant class, especially if she is white. Therefore, I have used the term *immigrant* to denote South Asians who may or may not fit the category of legal citizenship.

South Asian Battered Women Seek Home

The term *domestic violence* succinctly foregrounds the space where women experience battering: home, supposedly a safe haven for its members. Furthermore, it highlights the context of intimate abuse, the everyday realm of women. The label "domestic violence" challenges the imagined safety and tranquility of home and family where women remain thoroughly vulnerable to violence perpetrated by intimates in their lives. Home continues to be the ground zero of battering, and inclusion in or ousting from it becomes a vital issue for women living in abusive relationships. Displacement is one of many, and debatably the most significant, nonlethal consequence of battering that women face, perhaps next only to loss of child custody. Not only do battered women often have to flee their homes in search of safety, but also they are evicted from their homes by abusers as a tactic of violence.

The issue of displacement turns even more complex and difficult in the lives of immigrant and refugee battered women. In addition to escaping war-torn conditions of their nations, battered women often run away from their abusers and their countries, where security may be elusive. Then again, many immigrant battered women are dislodged from not only their residences in their native countries but also their homes in the United States.

Since the passing of Immigration and Marriage Fraud Amendments (IMFA), South Asian immigrant women married to permanent resident or citizen men have been enduring tenuous residency status in this country. Under IMFA, without the sponsorship of the spouse the noncitizen battered woman becomes undocumented and thereby vulnerable to deportation. The threat becomes further complicated with the abuser's attempts to take the children away from the mother. In cases of many immigrant mothers, the immigration and family courts play into the hands of abusers by issuing contradictory rulings. For instance, while the immigration court may require a battered woman to leave the United States due to her expired visa or green card (and she is willing to do so), the family court may not allow her U.S.-born child, a citizen by birthright, to accompany her out of the country. Thus, a battered immigrant mother may be placed in serious conflict between leaving the country for safety and leaving her children behind with an abusive father. The following story may illustrate the point.

> After enduring five years of abusive marriage, Anuradha [pseudonym, as are names of all survivors] was thrown out of her home by her husband along with her infant son. He simultaneously sued her for divorce. During the divorce proceedings, she found out that her husband had never sponsored her for permanent residency since she had entered the country on K or Fiancée visa. The INS ruled that she must leave the country. Anuradha was eager to go back to her home in Nepal and prepared to leave the United States permanently with her son.

Anuradha's husband sued her for the custody of their child in the Family Court and claimed that as a U.S. citizen, the child must have the opportunity to grow up in this country. The Court agreed with him and ordered the mother not to take the child out of the country. Anuradha was placed in the dilemma of leaving the United States for the safety her family in Nepal guaranteed and leaving her child behind.

Despite frustrations due to such legal inconsistencies, many battered women continue to view immigration as a source of protection in their lives. Many choose to remain in or enter the United States in search of safety and well-being. In addition to escaping real and perceived strictures of tradition, retribution from the abuser's family, disapproval of the natal family, and unresponsive legal systems, South Asian battered women seek opportunities for developing autonomy through economic self-sufficiency and independent decision making in the United States. Lakshmy Parameswaran, an advocate with Daya, asserted, "[South Asian] women are attracted to the [U.S.] life even when they are unhappy here. There is the potential for freedom and opportunities to make their own way. Often, after their marriage breaks up, there is shame—failure written on their faces. There is also anger at parents [for] making arranged marriages for them."

According to attorney Suneeta Dewan, "Women feel liberated here, without the shackles of tradition. They create their own world without in-laws and mandatory household duties. Even women from wealthy families feel their societal chains have been removed." Margaret Stock, an attorney and law professor who has provided legal representation to several battered South Asian women, reflected, "It takes time for battered [South Asian] women to recognize that they are in a new paradigm. Women slowly learn husbands can't have them deported, a threat that has kept them intimidated. It is amazing to watch the moment of empowered transformation—women become powerful at this revelation. It doesn't happen with U.S. [citizen] clients." Thus, immigration can be a source of conflict and tyranny but also emancipation and safety for many battered South Asian women.

Realities of Immigration Abuse and Intervention

The Immigration Marriage Fraud Amendments (IMFA) of 1986 created a new category of abuse that helped batterers wrest further power and control from their foreign-born wives. Consequently, battered immigrant women became even more trapped in abusive relationships. The only relief for battered women in IMFA was a hardship waiver, which required them to prove that extreme hardship would result if they were deported. The proof of extreme hardship had to be supported by affidavits from experts, who discussed the adverse cultural conditions of a battered woman's native country and upon return the difficulties she and her children might face there.

IMFA was revised by the Immigration Act of 1990 (IMMACT). Under IMMACT, battered women could circumvent their citizen or permanent resident spouses' sponsorships through a battered spouse waiver. To achieve this waiver, women had to prove their victimization by offering expert evidence of physical abuse or extreme cruelty. The evidentiary requirements for the waiver were complicated and impossible for many immigrant women to satisfy. Albeit the modification to ease immigration issues, IMMACT remained onerous and a bane in battered women's quest for permanent residency. The Violence Against Women Act (VAWA), title IV of the Violent Crime Control and Law Enforcement Act, was passed in 1994 and addressed immigrant battered women's vulnerability to threats of deportation. VAWA offered the option of self-petitioning to battered women. Self-petitions required battered women to substantiate their claims with affidavits of extreme hardship, which deportation would produce. Again, cultural experts founded their extreme hardship testimonies on nationwide cultural conditions that would be unfavorable to the well-being of the battered applicant and her children. VAWA II, passed in 2000, has eliminated the extreme hardship affidavit requirement for self-petitioning and added the relief of the U and T visas.[2] Regardless, the responsibility of substantiating abuse for self-petitions and meeting other evidentiary requirements still rests on battered women.[3]

For women living with abusive spouses who are neither U.S. citizens nor permanent residents, the only option for residency in the United States may be petitioning for U visa or gender-based (or gender) asylum.[4] Gender asylum is also the only option available to women who are fleeing their native countries to escape domestic battery and persecutory violence. The requirements for gender asylum are gravely prohibitive.

Clearly, South Asian battered women's pursuit of permanent residency in the United States is fraught with difficulty and complications. Even this tenuous situation deteriorated noticeably after September 11, 2001. A number of changes that occurred in the name of homeland security affected South Asian women's community cruelly and set advocacy on behalf of battered women drastically behind.

Immediately following 9/11, a new set of obstacles to accessing the legal system emerged for battered South Asian women. Public suspicion became aimed at South Asians and many became victims of hate crimes. South Asian women, who are often readily recognized by their distinctive clothing, became frightened for not only their sons and husbands but also for their own safety. Many women experienced increased racist attacks in the weeks and months after 9/11 at the connivance of the local law enforcement.

South Asian men, especially from certain nations such as Bangladesh and Pakistan, were required to appear for special registration by the government.[5] The reasons behind this obvious profiling was not lost on the women and community. In addition, many South Asian men were detained for indeterminate lengths of time without due process and notification to their families. Such selective oppression sent alarms though the community and placed South Asian battered women, particularly from the Muslim community, in a tricky situation. If they sought outside help, especially from the police, chances were that not only their abusers would be detained but also their sons and other male relatives. Furthermore, they would certainly expose their spouses and relatives to prejudicial harassment by the police and other officials, as well as let ill treatment into their own lives.

As many South Asian men were summarily deported for minor infractions of their visas or other violations of the law (including domestic violence), their wives either had to accompany them or stay behind as undocumented immigrants without minimal resources or support. Such deportations increased battered women's threat of danger from their abusers and communities. By inviting immigration scrutiny into the community, battered women ran the risk of being ostracized by friends, neighbors, religious and community leaders and being labeled as traitors. As a result, many South Asian anti–domestic violence agencies reported that post 9/11 they experienced significant decrease in the number of women seeking assistance.

The H.R. 4437 of 2005 and CLEAR Act proposed in 2003 further threatens to thwart battered South Asian immigrant women's inclinations to call the police in an emergency or rely on any sort of legal recourse (Almjeld, 2003/2004; Hing 2004).[6] The passing of these acts would ring death-knell for many battered immigrant women.

Complications in Legal Recourse

The legal difficulties in a South Asian battered woman's life are certainly not confined only to U.S. immigration laws. Her life as an immigrant generally spreads across two continents, between her country of origin and residence. Thus, the sources of complications and contradictions in her life are two legal systems that are often at odds. In addition, various extralegal influences affect her decision making and the legal actions she takes.

Contradictions from Different Shores

Although the legal systems in South Asian countries and the United States are supposedly reciprocal, local courts often act independently and contrarily to the frustration of battered women. The courts in a South Asian woman's native country may ignore all legal decisions she struggled to receive in the United States and hand out new sets of contradictory judgments related to divorce, custody, and property settlement. For example, a batterer whom a woman has successfully divorced in the United States may go back to their native country, India, and petition the courts for "Restitution of Conjugal Rights" (Gour 2003).[7] Simultaneously, he may successfully seek full custody of their children in Indian courts. Until very recently, Indian courts routinely upheld the tradition of the father's right to full legal custody of his children, while separated/divorced mothers could have temporary physical custody, especially if the children were very young. Under Islamic law, the father is still considered the legitimate custodian of his children, although mothers may have physical custody of sons up to seven years and daughters up to adolescence. Such disagreements between courts in countries of origin and residence may occur in all areas of family law and settlement of property.

In matters of property settlement, such discrepancies are particularly problematic. As an advocate of Manavi, I have noticed that U.S. courts routinely ignore dowry and *mehr* issues that South Asian battered women frequently raise in their divorce proceedings.[8] These issues in the courts of South Asian women's home countries might be treated quite differently. Anti–domestic violence advocate Sonya Pelia concurred with my observations, "The U.S. courts see these [*mehr* and dowry] as [joint] possession or jewelry issues. A woman may submit her wedding pictures with jewelry and gifts all around her and end up with nothing. The courts don't care and do not appreciate the significance of these items for the woman." Sabena Khan, legal advocate for Sakhi for South Asian Women (Sakhi), succinctly highlighted the problem:

> Dowry is not marital property; it is *stree-dhan* [a woman's assets]. The courts and attorneys [here] don't understand this. So, women lose jewelry and money given in marriage and attorneys won't ask for it because they don't understand and believe this. The courts don't understand *mehr* either; so, women lose money that is rightfully theirs. Courts might understand *Nikah*, but not *Talaq*.[9] Courts view all marriages after the first as invalid. Marriages of Muslim women, who are second, third, or fourth wives and were married in their native countries, may be canceled here. As a result, all women lose and suffer.

To complicate matters, a battered woman's family members and community may ignore all legal rulings and demand her compliance to a very different set of emotional decisions. They may want her to go back to her abuser so as not to jeopardize the family's reputation in the community, their own physical and/or economic safety, and/or the possibility of contracting good marriages for her siblings. I have known the powerful family of an abuser to campaign against a victim's father in India to ruin his business, until her family forced her to reconcile. Abusers' families have contracted local thugs to murder victims' family members and/or victims themselves during their visits home, or harass them in various other ways to bring about reconciliation. Often, parents and grandparents of women have pressured them to reunite with their abusers because the family astrologer or guru had predicted imminent shifts in planetary configurations that foretell everlasting happiness for the couple. In these situations, a battered woman has few viable choices to elicit harmony in her life except through the sacrifice of her own safety.

Many battered women in the United States use law enforcement as a viable resource when in crisis. For South Asian battered women, impediments to legal recourses emerge from two sources: internal and external.

Problems Internal to South Asian Battered Women

Within the South Asian community, seeking assistance from outside sources, especially law enforcement is generally a taboo (Dasgupta and Warrier 1995). The postcolonial experiences of South Asians often prompt them to view the police and the legal system as oppressive, alien, and arbitrary. In South Asian countries, women in particular are taught to fear the law enforcement as a source of personal danger and embarrassment to the family. The record of custody rape and torture of women by members of the law enforcement (Human Rights Watch Women's Rights Project 1998; Joshi 1995; Kumar et al. 2003; Sengupta 1989) has led many South Asian women to nurture deep distrust of the police. The immigrants transfer this attitude of suspicion and antipathy toward the law enforcement and legal system to the United States. Furthermore, when South Asian battered women have sought help from law enforcement and the legal system in the United States, their experiences have not always been positive. The community's negative encounters with the police in situations unrelated to domestic violence (e.g., while driving) also contribute to battered women's wariness.

In addition, some South Asian women's lack of fluency in English becomes a serious hurdle in accessing the legal system. Although courts are supposed to provide translators for non-English speakers, South Asian women speak not only a variety of languages but also numerous esoteric dialects, making it difficult to find suitable interpreters. Thus, courts and first responders are often at quandary as to how to communicate with women and frequently take the easy way out—that is, they speak with the abuser or use children and friends of the family for interpretation. According to Anindita Chatterjee Bhaumik, the legal intake coordinator of Sanctuary for Families, "Even educated women don't have enough English to deal with the legal system. [Because they don't speak English] the resources that are given to women don't make sense to them. What good are Rights cards if you can't read them? They are at the mercy of officials who are dealing with them."

A byproduct of the language barrier is that South Asian women often remain ignorant of or misconstrue how the legal system works in this country. All the interviewees unanimously said that South Asian women need education in the U.S. legal culture and processes. Both Sonya Pelia, advocate, and Professor Margaret Stock, attorney, claimed that South Asian women go to court with unrealistic expectations. They seem to view the judge as omnipotent, an authority who can impartially dole out justice. Manavi's executive director, Soniya Munshi, echoed this opinion and maintained that women viewed courts as a place where truth and honesty would be validated. "They do not quite recognize that a court is an artificial area where truth is often lost as it gets translated into evidence," said Munshi. Thus, women are shocked when judges allow attorneys to be adversarial, question women's stories, and/or deny women's petitions. The length of time it takes the courts to settle a case also disheartens women.

Issues External to South Asian Battered Women

It is important to understand that when South Asian women call the police, they have had to circumvent many psychological and cultural inhibitions. Thus, the nature of the initial contact with first responders becomes a significant predictor of women's trust in the system and help-seeking behavior in the future. Often, a few women's negative experiences with the legal system are passed around in the community and inform other women's decisions to call the police and seek legal assistance. Unfortunately, in many instances, responding police officers have shown little sympathy to South Asian battered women for their inability to speak English and hesitation to press charges. According to Anindita Chatterjee Bhaumik, "The courts and police are reluctant to deal with women who don't speak English and are not knowledgeable about the system." In a number of cases, police officers, responding to women's calls, have gathered information from the husbands due to their fluency in English and have left women high and dry. At times, officers have made xenophobic comments to women and seemingly sided with abusers.

Soniya Munshi remarked that often the police, attorneys, and judges have little grasp of domestic violence in the South Asian context. Thus, they frequently minimize domestic violence issues and pressure battered women to settle for less safe procedures such as mutual orders for protection (OFP). Munshi had also observed that judges were more abrasive with South Asian women than South Asian men or whites. She elaborated, "[South Asian] women's credibility is routinely questioned in courts, and when women try to talk about threats to their families, they are just ignored. Often, women's stories are silenced, or presented in court in such a way that leaves them dissatisfied. [Women] are seen as irrational and inconsistent." Vartika Mathur, legal advocate of Manavi, asserted that in her experience, prosecutors viewed individual South Asian women by their stereotype, indecisive and submissive, and felt that it was a waste of time to work with these women, as they would be back with the abusers in no time. Tanvi Tripathi, of Sakhi, claimed, "The police are not helpful to women, and attorneys hardly spend any time to understand the [South Asian] women or domestic violence." According to her, South Asian women are often pushed not to be truthful but to conform to the images that attorneys know and are comfortable with.

The advocates and attorneys I interviewed repeatedly stressed the problem of the perception of South Asian women's credibility in courts. Most declared that the U.S. legal system perceives South Asian women as untrustworthy. Professor Kamala Visweswaran affirmed, "Women are not believed by the community and the legal system. The institution of law is used to shame them." Professor Margaret Stock suggested that [South Asian] women look deceptive because they keep their eyes downcast. According to her, "Direct eye contact is an important issue in this country. It is a cultural signal for honesty. But, South Asian women tend not to look directly at authority figures in court. They are intimidated easily, so when judges ask them questions, women become flustered. They are more distressed by the adversarial legal process than other Americans, as they are generally noncon-frontational. All of this subtracts from their credibility."

Interestingly, in a meeting on domestic violence related legal issues in New Delhi, India, in 2004, a group of activists and attorneys informed me that they teach women to keep their eyes downcast in court lest they be considered arrogant and controlling by the judge. Such contradictory expectations in the two cultures, U.S. and India (perhaps all of South Asia), are sure to confuse battered women and land them in trouble in both. To deal with the issue of trustworthiness, the interviewees strongly recommended that the U.S. courts become educated in South Asian cultural nuances.

Officials in the legal system and law enforcement approach South Asians with strong biases and stereotypes and become frustrated when individuals do not fit their preconceived models. South Asian batterers, who seem to be much more conversant with the U.S. legal culture, often play these stereotypes to their advantage. Consequently, battered women end up being identified as bad or mad.

Professor Kamala Visweswaran gave the example of a severely battered woman who had thrown hot curry at her abuser in an act of resistance. Not only did the community immediately side with the man and dub her crazy, she was incarcerated, put on antidepressants, and prevented from seeing her children. Pelia gave details of a woman who lost her children's custody to her abusive husband, as the court believed that she was suicidal because of the apparent cuts on her wrist. "The cuts were made by the glass bangles she wore, which he [her husband] had broken by grabbing her forcefully by the wrists. Something as simple as that; but the judge just could not comprehend it." Furthermore, the attorneys and judges seemed not to comprehend the complications of living in a joint family where husbands did not directly abuse their wives but passively endorsed such behavior by other family members.

Most interviewees felt much of these problems were the by-product of racism and xenophobia that are integral to the U.S. legal system. Soniya Munshi described a case when she had accompanied to court a young South Asian woman who had petitioned for an order for protection against her parents. She stated that although the judge's attitude favored the young woman, as a South Asian community member it was difficult for her to stomach the racism that spewed forth toward the woman's parents. Even though the parents did not speak English very well and had no legal representation, there was no effort to stop the proceedings to find an interpreter or tone down the legalese for them. Anything the parents said was perfunctorily dismissed and they were plainly disrespected as "uneducated boors." Munshi also claimed "when judges talk to South Asians in abusive situations that they are seen as representatives of a barbaric culture."

Many of the interviewees discussed the racist, classist, and xenophobic attitudes that pervade the legal system and the increase of all after 9/11. Bhaumik mentioned that the situation is exacerbated for Muslims as every person is regarded as related to Osama bin Laden. The following incident in a New York traffic court corroborates her observations. A judge in Tarrytown, New York, asked an Arab American woman who was there to contest two traffic tickets if she were a terrorist. The judge then proceeded to comment that she had money to support terrorists but did not want to pay traffic tickets. Later, the judge admitted to the remarks but said that he was being lighthearted (Bandler 2003).

A Dilemma of Advocacy

More and more advocates and activists are coming forward to facilitate South Asian battered women's struggles to escape abuse, secure residency, and find autonomy. For these advocates and activists, conflicts arise from the need to support the individual woman and the knowledge that such support might be most successful when her whole culture is universally degraded. This issue of benefiting an individual woman at the cost of an entire culture often proves heavy for advocates.

Putting Culture on the Stand

The deprecation of South Asian cultures is evident in this Op-Ed piece:

> So although I did not find Osama, I did encounter a much more ubiquitous form of evil and terror: a culture, stretching across about half the globe that chews up women and spits them out.
>
> We in the West could help chip away at that oppression, with health and literacy programs and by simply speaking out against it, just as we once stood up against slavery and totalitarianism.[10]

Immigrants of color, especially Asians, have historically been viewed by mainstream Americans as imprisoned in their cultures. Professor Leti Volpp of American University maintains that Asians are considered to be burdened with an "excess of culture" (2003). Furthermore, violence against women is deemed a marker of Asian cultures. Asian cultures are taken as unchanging, oppressive, and retrogressive as opposed to American or Western ones that are considered flexible, egalitarian, and progressive (Narayan 1997; Razack 1998; Said 1978; Visweswaran 2004). Among Asians, culture is deemed a co-respondent in woman abuse.

Likewise, South Asian cultures are believed to provide tacit, if not explicit, support to violence against women. Contrarily, battering in the United States, especially among whites, is seen as a product of individual bad behavior or predicament—thereby culture escapes culpability. Professor Uma Narayan (1997) writes, "'Culture' is invoked in explanations of forms of violence against Third-World women, while it is not similarly invoked in explanations of forms of violence that affect mainstream Western women. . . . [W]hen such 'cultural explanations' are given for *fatal* forms of violence against Third-World women, the effect is to suggest that Third-World women suffer 'death by culture.' . . . [F]atal forms of violence against mainstream Western women seem interestingly resistant to such 'cultural explanations'" (84–85).

Perceiving violence as a cultural phenomenon means that its causes are considered internal and stable to a nation, whereas attributing violence to individual conduct makes it merely temporary and external to a group and thereby easily fixable. This perspective has also seeped into the U.S. legal system (Dasgupta 1998b; Volpp 2000b).

The perception that Asian cultures are surfeit with vicious patriarchy and consequent brutalities against women complicates the legal status of batterers and victims alike (Chiu 1994; Dasgupta 1998b; Razack 1998; Sinha 2001; Visweswaran 2002; Volpp 2000b). Depending on the individual perspectives of law enforcement officers, judges, and attorneys, a South Asian battered woman may find her petition to fall on patronizing or disbelieving ears. For example, judges and attorneys may view South Asian batterers as vicious monsters or behaving in a culturally acceptable way; while victims may be perceived as scheming harridans or long-suffering broken women in need of rescuing. Both extremes attempt to fit the individual to racial/cultural stereotypes and reactions to it are often disproportional to the situation at hand.

The issue of putting the entire culture on the stand came to the foreground for advocates and activists when they needed to support individual battered women's residency petitions under IMFA, VAWA, and gender asylum. To prove extreme hardship under IMFA and VAWA, a cultural expert had to provide written testimony detailing why deportation would be cruel to the battered petitioner and her children. To be successful, affidavits had to elaborate individual harm in the context of a culture. Fortunately, VAWA II in 2000 eliminated this requirement. However, such testimonies or affidavits from cultural experts are still central to asylum petitions. The success of the asylum affidavits hinges on explaining the petitioner's victimization and persecution by "unusually patriarchal and culturally dysfunctional cultures" (Razack 1998, 20). Knowing that overgeneralizations about cultures bring results, the stipulations of affidavits lay contrary burdens on South Asian activists by compelling them to choose between individual benefit and collective cost.

Gender-based asylum, charted by United National High Commissioner for Refugees, is approved when an applicant has convincing evidence that her membership in a particular class (i.e., gender) makes her vulnerable to harassment and violence. This acknowledgment of gendered violence as targeted persecution shifted battering from idiosyncratic actions to systematic misogyny. Although the United States is not a signatory to the related UN convention, immigration services heard and often approved gender-based asylum petitions for battered women. Unfortunately, the foundations of these decisions frequently seemed arbitrary, and the best possibility of success came when asylum claims were supported by affidavits that contextualized the petitioner's risks of abuse, systematic persecution, and danger in her natal culture (Razack 1998; Sinha 2001; Visweswaran 2002). That is, to prove gender-related persecution, affidavits have to present a culture as injurious to women in general and, thereby, the applicant in particular. This evidentiary requirement for gender asylum places cultural experts and advocates in the unenviable position of supporting a battered woman's residency claim at the cost of reinforcing negative stereotypes of a culture and nation.

Struggles in Double Bind

Most South Asian advocates, immigration attorneys, and cultural experts comprehend that the content requisites of a cultural affidavit nest at the intersection of race, nation, and ways of life that makes a culture the bizarre "other" (Sinha 2001; Visweswaran 2002; Volpp 2000b, 2003). Menaka Guruswamy, a South Asian attorney who has won a number of asylum cases for South Asian battered women, stated that asylum work is distasteful to her. According to Guruswamy, "In asylum work, you have to hit the stereotypes that immigration adjudicators hold. For example, honor killings in Pakistan. They have to fit the battered woman in a box—the country and the victim. It is hard to work with people here—to break stereotypes and at the same time advocate for battered women." Anita Sinha (2001) echoes similar sentiments, "Asylum applicants who flee from non-western countries because of gender-related violence find that their cases often turn on whether they can show that the persecution they suffered is attributable to the cultural 'backwardness' of their home countries" (1578).

This "othering" of non-Western cultures is evident in the value given to types of abuse in immigration decisions. Violence that seem foreign to the U.S. culture, such as female genital mutilation (FGM), dowry harassment, honor killing, stoning as punishment, and religious persecution, hold sway more than domestic violence even in its severest form (Sinha 2001; Visweswaran 2002). The minimization of domestic violence, the most common abuse women systematically suffer due to their membership in a group, clearly indicates the racist slant of U.S. immigration services. "Domestic violence cannot be coined a 'practice' or 'custom' attributable to a particular nonwhite race because it frequently happens within the United States's [sic] own borders. Granting asylum in In re Kasinga but not in In re R-A- is consistent with the colonialist feminist agenda of 'saving women from primitive cultures'" (Sinha 2001, 1589). In the former case, a woman from Togo had applied for asylum in 1996 based on her fear that she would be coerced to undergo FGM if she returned to her country, while, in the latter, a woman from Guatemala had applied for asylum in 1999, based on ten years of severe abuse by her politically powerful husband.

Racism becomes even more blatant in cases where cultural experts are required to testify in person. Defense attorneys, who often seek experts to explain the cultural background of a battered woman charged with crime, recognize the biases in court and tend to reject nonwhite immigrant witnesses. According to Professor Visweswaran, "White males providing cultural information about South Asia are believed more than South Asians, and South Asian women in particular." Professor Sharmila Rudrappa, who testified for the defense in the case of a South Asian mother charged with attempted murder of her children, described how the symbols of progressiveness (read: Western and rational) and archaic oppression (read: South Asian and tyrannical) were created during the trial. "I was asked to wear western clothes while the woman [defendant] was supposed to wear a sari. They were mediating South Asianness in court and wanted to symbolize modernity with these accoutrements. Culture was put on the stand." In the case of a South Asian woman charged with killing her batterer, although the defense team consulted with me in the early stages, they told me brazenly that they needed to find an American (read: white) cultural expert to testify in court.

Whether it is in relation to asylum or criminal legal issues, the burden of explaining culture to the courts to support battered women generates profound conflicts for South Asian advocates and cultural experts. On the one hand, they accept the responsibility of translating the meaning of battered women's needs to the legal system; and on the other hand, they guard against universalizing one woman's experiences to characterize the whole culture. As most experts and advocates appreciate, in the vast region of South Asia and its constituting countries, diversity is the rule rather than the exception. However, asylum adjudicators and defense attorneys hardly seek nuanced explanations of a culture. Successful petitions carry the implicit message that blanket vilification of a culture is necessary to win approval. "Culture is used as a means to specify the qualitative nature of violence, so that heterogeneity and diversity within communities is downplayed in order to establish evidence of persecution" (K. Visweswaran, pers. comm.).

Concluding Remarks

There are no easy solutions to the myriad problems battered South Asian women face when they tangle with the U.S. law enforcement and legal system. Both personal and institutional hurdles impede victims' search for justice and redress. On the individual level, South Asian women need to be educated in the U.S. legal processes and learn to negotiate the legal system competently. This, of course, is not going to be easy with the racism, xenophobia, and various other biases inherent in the institution.

For advocates and activists who undertake the task of culturally contextualizing women's experiences of battering, the problems are no less complicated. The debate whether to stereotype a culture to be successful or present nuanced cultural descriptions and risk rejection of a woman's petition (dealing with asylum and criminal legal issues) has not yet been resolved in the advocacy community. Generic and wholesale accounting of culture that asylum adjudicators and courts seem to require might endanger South Asian women who engage with the legal system in the future. By reinforcing biases against a nation and typecasting individual experiences, advocates might actually increase legal hazards for those South Asian battered women who do not correspond to a cookie-cutter paradigm. The effects of such stereotyping, of course, extend beyond battered women's lives to mass perceptions of the South Asian community and U.S. foreign policies. Thus, in explaining cultural contexts of battering, South Asian activists truly have to walk the razor's edge.

Many activists have suggested that explanations of cultural contexts need to end so that individual cases are judged on their own merit. It is my belief that culture cannot be overlooked if we are to fully understand human conduct. Culture envelops life and permeates living. It affects the ways we experience and react to battering. Yet, the assumption that battered women experience culture homogenously and react to it generically is misleading. Although there are common motifs of a culture that characterize a country or region, it is culture at the micro level of province, village, class/caste, and home that influences an individual woman's perceptions, experiences, and behavior. It is not the use of cultural explanations but the misuse and misrepresentation of culture that becomes a problem for South Asian anti–domestic violence advocacy. Visweswaran (2002) asserts that governmental unwillingness to protect women and religious/cultural practices are often confounded in the expectations of cultural testimonies and affidavits. That is, in cases of woman abuse, whether it is in relation to asylum or criminal legal issues, a nation or community's political reluctance to protect women is often subsumed under the rubric of culture.

The success of nuanced presentations of a culture is predicated upon the U.S. legal practitioners and law enforcement officials' knowledge about South Asia and its cultural diversity. In fact, there must be an overall increase in the understanding of how culture affects battering, batterers, and battered women in general. The tendency of the dominant community to assume that "others" have culture but it is devoid of any impact must be altered. The advocates I interviewed collectively emphasized the need for continued education for legal practitioners, judiciary, and law enforcement in this area.

While it is important to abort the notion that culture is the petri dish of domestic violence in some cultures, it is vital that we do not throw the baby out with the bathwater. Culture does affect our perceptions, reactions, and responses to domestic violence. It does influence our help-seeking behavior and must be taken into account in developing successful intervention programs. Professor Rudrappa succinctly addressed this issue by noting, "We have to understand the meaning she [a battered woman] makes of her culture." It is by scrutinizing this that we begin to understand the complex political relationships among women, communities, states, and the legal systems that affect battered women and, ultimately, all of us.

NOTES

1. The cultural expert's job is to describe/explain to the court the modal characteristics of a particular culture as it affects the victim/perpetrator. That is, a cultural expert occupies the position of a native informant.

2. Both U and T are legal visas created with the passing of Victims of Trafficking and Violence Protection Act of 2000 (TVPA), which includes VAWA 2000. T visas are available to individuals who are victims of severe forms of trafficking in persons, specifically for the

purposes of sexual or labor exploitation. U visas are available to immigrants who are victims and/or have information about serious criminal activities and are essential for the successful prosecution of a felony.

3. See, §204(a) of Immigration and Nationality Act (INA) for VAWA provisions regarding immigration and the Code of Federal Regulations at 8CFR§204 for the rules.

4. See UNHCR's Guidelines on International Protection: Gender-Related Persecution within the context of Article 1A(2) of the 1951 Convention and/or its 1967 Protocol relating to the Status of Refugees. HCR/GIP/02/01, May 7, 2002.

5. Arab and Muslim male students, tourists, and immigrants over sixteen years of age were and are required to register themselves by the decree of the Department of Homeland Security. This registration and interrogatory is mandatory to obtain proof of innocence. See http://www.whitehouse.org/homeland/arab-registration.asp.

6. The CLEAR Act of 2003, sponsored by Representative C. Norwood (R-GA) proposes to extend the authority and duties of local and state police departments to "investigate, apprehend, detain, or remove aliens" (presumably individuals with legal violations) discovered in the course of their normal activities. States would be encouraged to institute this act or risk the withdrawal of federal funds they would otherwise receive. H.R. 4437, sponsored by Rep. F. J. Sensenbrenner Jr. (WI) and passed in the House on December 16, 2005, proposes to criminalize even minor violations of immigration law, providing aid to undocumented immigrants, broadens mandatory detention policies, and restricts judicial review.

7. Under Indian law, when one spouse withdraws from the marriage without "reasonable" excuse, the aggrieved party may petition the court for restitution of conjugal rights. The expectation is that the couple must give the marriage another try by living together in their matrimonial home. The burden of proof that the withdrawal from marriage was reasonable rests with the party who withdrew from it.

8. For a detailed analysis of dowry, see Veena T. Oldenburg's *Dowry Murder*. Islamic law dictates that at marriage the husband must pay a contracted dowry or *Mehr* (also known as *Haq Mehr*) to the wife. Half of the dowry is to be paid at the time of the marriage and the other half on divorce, separation, or on demand. *Mehr* is considered a woman's personal property.

9. In Islamic law, *Nikah*, or marriage, is a contract between husband and wife. It is not a sacrament but revocable. The written marriage contract is known as *Nikah Nama* or *Kabin Nama*. *Talaq* is the dissolution of marriage or divorce that is generally a husband's prerogative. A wife may also seek divorce under certain conditions stipulated in their *Kabin Nama* or *Nikah Nama*.

10. Writing on meeting Mukhtaran Bibi in Pakistan, op-ed columnist Nicholas Kristof (2004) makes the comparison between the evil of Osama bin Laden and the toxicity of Pakistani and perhaps all South Asian cultures. Mukhtaran Bibi was gang raped on the orders of a Pakistani village council in June 2002. Here Kristof ignores the successful prosecution of her rapists in Pakistan and the compensation sanctioned to her, as well as the many sexual assaults and gang rapes that occur in the United States. Unfortunately, on appeal, the Lahore High Court in Pakistan overturned the sentences of all six convicted men based on insufficient evidence and acquitted five of them (Kristof 2005). In June 2005, the five freed men were rearrested to await a new trial.

Interviews for this essay were conducted by the author between September 17 and November 2, 2003.

PART FOUR

The Body in Action

Activism and Transnational Anti–Domestic Violence Work

16

Navigating Gender, Immigration, and Domestic Violence

Advocacy with Work Visa Holders

RUPALEEM BHUYAN

The topic of domestic violence advocacy with South Asian immigrants on temporary visas raises more questions than answers. In general, women who seek support from domestic violence agencies have a complex set of needs when responding to the abuse in their lives. Many immigrant women further contend with limited access to services due to language barriers, institutional racism within domestic violence and other social services, and pressure not to seek help outside their cultural community (Acevedo 2000; Bui and Morash 1999; Raj and Silverman 2002a). In addition, immigration history and residency status powerfully shape an immigrant woman's responses to abuse, as these determine her eligibility for public benefits, options to maintain a legal presence in the United States, and the right to seek legal employment. Although federal legislation through the Violence Against Women Act (VAWA) provides substantial immigration relief to some battered immigrants, the safety net it erects remains permeable and leaves out many groups of immigrant women who have few, if any, options to find relief from abuse.

This essay discusses the barriers to safety encountered by South Asian victims/survivors of domestic violence who reside in the United States on temporary dependent visas. The most recent wave of immigration from South Asian countries occurred as a direct result of the boom in the computer industry in the 1990s and early 2000s. Under the auspices of U.S. economic growth, thousands of South Asians, primarily Indians, were granted H-1B or temporary work visas, allowing them to enter the U.S. workforce for up to six years if sponsored by an employer. However, the conditions of immigration under the H-1B program potentially exploit temporary workers and their families while exacerbating power dynamics, which contribute to women's vulnerability to domestic violence. The dependent nature of the H-4 status enables abusers to maintain control through financial and legal means with severe consequences for the safety of victims/survivors of battering. For example, while the

H-1B visa program permits individuals to sponsor their spouses and children on H-4 visas, it reinforces dependence by allowing the sponsor control over his family's immigration status.

This chapter is a critique of current legal and social policies from the intersections of gender, immigration, and domestic violence. It combines analysis of national reports on immigration and violence against women policies with information gathered from interviews with advocates of South Asian battered women. Because domestic violence advocacy in the United States has become nearly synonymous to legal advocacy, options explored here are mainly based on legal redress. Furthermore, the essay addresses how current trends in economic growth and immigration influence the makeup of the South Asian community in the United States and illustrates some of the contexts in which H-4 visa holders experience domestic violence.

Given the heterosexual bias in immigration laws, H-4 visas are only offered to legal spouses, which in the United States refers to heterosexual couples (i.e., same-sex marriage and domestic partnership are not yet recognized by U.S. immigration law). While the temporary visa program for H-1B and H-4 is technically gender neutral, nearly three-quarters of all H-1Bs are issued to men, while H-4s are issued primarily to women and children. Lastly, although I principally discuss the H-4 visa, other nonimmigrant dependent visas—namely, spouses of student visa holders (F2) and intracompany transfers (L2)—face similar issues when experiencing domestic violence.

In this essay, I have drawn from my professional knowledge of domestic violence and sexual assault prevention work, volunteer services with Chaya, and my own experiences as a second-generation immigrant woman from Assam, India. Here I elaborate some of the strategies used by Chaya's advocates to support women on temporary visas and the struggles in advocating for the well-being of women on H-4 visas, given the current social and political context.

Responding to a Growing South Asian Community

Over the last fifteen years, Seattle and other parts of the United States have experienced a dramatic increase in the South Asian population, in part due to the technology boom of the 1990s. Similar to other periods in U.S. history, this wave of immigration reflects both limited economic opportunities in postcolonial South Asian countries, as well as demands from the U.S. technology industry for highly skilled workers. Between 1990 and 2000, Seattle's King County witnessed a dramatic increase of 650 percent in the South Asian population, a jump from approximately 5,000 to 30,000 South Asian people (U.S. Census Bureau 1990, 2000a). Indubitably, the single major reason behind this unprecedented surge is the location of a number of information technology (IT) companies in the Seattle area, including the Microsoft Corporation and dot-com companies like Amazon and Adobe. Other IT centers around the country have experienced similar explosions in South Asian populations; for example, California's Silicon Valley just north of San Jose and North

Carolina's Research Triangle Park, which links Duke University, North Carolina State University, and the University of North Carolina at Chapel Hill (Armas 2004; Tanneeru 2001).

As the South Asian population increased in Seattle and other areas around the United States, the need for culturally sensitive services to support the community also swelled.

As several authors have noted, ethnic and racial minority women have continued to be underserved by mainstream anti–domestic violence agencies (Dasgupta 2000a; Merchant 2000), and even when they engage with mainstream domestic violence interventions, they often face racism (Kasturirangan, Krishnan, and Riger 2004). In an effort to attend to these gaps in services, Chaya was founded in 1996 to directly serve South Asian women and raise awareness of the problems related to domestic violence in South Asian communities.

Before focusing on battered women on dependent visas, it is important to understand the terminology used in this area of work. Both domestic violence and immigrant advocacy groups use the term *immigrant* to refer broadly to persons who have migrated to and settled in the United States for work, refuge, or to join their families. U.S. immigration law, however, has a more narrow construction, designating the term exclusively for persons whose status potentially permits them to reside in the United States as legal permanent residents (LPR) or naturalized citizens (USC). Everyone else who comes to and resides in the United States is considered an alien.

The label *nonimmigrant* refers to anyone whose status cannot be adjusted to legal permanent resident status in the United States, including temporary workers, students, company transfers, and visitors. Refugees and asylees form a special class of immigrants because they are granted visas based on political persecution in their native countries and thus are eligible to adjust their status to LPR within one year of residing in the United States. Others who are in the United States without official documentation or whose legal documentation has expired are considered illegal immigrants or illegal aliens.

The H-1B Skilled Worker Program

The U.S. Department of Homeland Security (USDHS) states, "An H-1B temporary worker is an alien admitted to the United States to perform services in 'specialty occupations,' based on professional education, skills, and/or equivalent experience" (Office of Immigration Statistics 2004, 3). Approximately one-third of H-1B visas are issued to workers in computer-related fields, while other specialty occupations included architecture, engineering, education, and medicine (Office of Immigration Statistics 2004). Based on DHS annual reports on the characteristics of H-1Bs, workers from India and Pakistan combined, received on average 44 percent of all H-1B visas since the program started in 1990 (see annual reports of Immigration and Naturalization Service [INS] and Office of Immigration Statistics [OIS] for FY 1999 to FY 2003).

The H-1B status requires a sponsoring U.S. employer to petition for the prospective employee. Once issued, the visa is good for three years, with the possibility of one renewal. The H-1B visa is portable; their holders can switch employers provided they follow certain procedures, including not getting out of status. H-1B holders who are laid off have no grace period; that is, their status expires the last day of their employment (Jorgensen 2002). An H-1B visa holder may apply for H-4 visas to allow his spouse and dependent children to reside with him in the United States. During their stay, H-4 visa holders, as dependents on their spouse's status and employment, are permitted to attend school but prohibited from legal employment.

Although the H-1B program is designed for temporary work, scholars and industry analysts agree that many H-1B applicants have hopes of immigrating to the United States permanently (Matloff 2003; Ngyuen 1999). H-1B visas are particularly desirable because they are classified as dual-intent visas. The dual intent doctrine permits an H-1B visa holder to apply for permanent residency under sponsorship of his or her employer without repercussion on the current visa status (Martin, Lowell, and Martin 2002; Vaughan 2003).[1] Nevertheless, applying for a green card can take up to six years. During this time, H-1B visa holders are veritably tied to their employers in a situation some liken to indentured servitude; that is, H-1Bs may be potentially exploited by employers while they are in immigration limbo (Matloff 2003). Still, as many as 40 percent of H-1Bs eventually adjust their status to permanent residency (Ngyuen 1999). In 2002 alone, 89,930 people who originated from South Asian countries and initially entered the United States as temporary workers or trainees, successfully adjusted their status to legal permanent residency (USDHS 2003).[2]

The H-1B visa program was created in 1990 to respond to the growth in the U.S. technology sector. Many of these temporary workers held graduate degrees from outside the United States, but a large portion also consisted of foreign graduates from U.S. schools. An annual numeric cap of 65,000 for new H-1Bs was imposed to protect domestic workers. However, lobbying from software and hardware companies pressured Congress to raise the annual cap for H-1B visas to 115,000 in 1999 and again to 195,000 in 2000 (Jorgensen 2002). At its peak in 2001, 331,206 H-1B petitions were approved for initial and continuing employment (USDHS 2003).

In 2001, the H-1B program declined sharply because of large-scale layoffs in the dot-com industries and elsewhere (Martin et al. 2002). The number of H-1B petitions approved dropped by 40 percent between fiscal years 2001 and 2002 (INS 2002b). The H-1B program was further reduced when the raised cap expired in 2004 and was lowered back to 65,000. Despite the reduced number of available H-1B visas, employers' interests in foreign temporary workers remain high, as illustrated on October 1, 2004, when the cap of 65,000 was filled the first day of FY 2005 (Thibodeau 2004).

While some women apply for and receive their own H-1B visas, an overwhelming 74 percent of all H-1B visas are issued to men. In comparison, 75 percent of H-4 visas are issued to female applicants. Considering the employment restrictions that the United States places on H-4 visa holders, these statistics provide an inkling to the differential access to resources available to men versus women who enter the United States on temporary visas. This imbalance is compounded when spouses of H-1B visa holders lack work authorization while they reside in the United States.

Not having the right to work is problematic for all H-4 visa holders, not only those facing domestic abuse. Most South Asian H-4 visa holders are young educated women, many of whom have left behind professional careers to join their spouses in the United States. Once in the United States, H-4 visa holders are prohibited from working by law and are thus rendered reliant on their spouses' incomes and immigration status. Many H-4 visa holders with marketable skills, or those who go to school to gain skills, may seek their own H-1B visas as a way to get work authorization. Others may look for work under the table, unpaid or volunteer work, or simply not work while living in the United States. These conditions potentially exacerbate power dynamics in any relationship and are powerful instruments that an abuser can use to control his partner (Raj et al. 2004).

Immigration and Domestic Violence

Recent studies have shown that immigration often increases women's economic and legal dependence on their male spouse and is associated with vulnerability to abuse (Raj et al. 2004; Salcido and Adelman 2004). General factors that prevent or impede South Asian immigrant women from resisting, mediating, or leaving abusive partners relate to economic dependence on their spouse, gender role socialization, pressure to keep problems in the family, fear of losing custody of children, and social isolation (Abraham 2000a; Warrier 2000b; Yoshioka et al. 2003). The ability of abusers to exert power and control over their immigrant spouse is compounded by the precarious conditions of legal immigration status, including work prohibitions and the threat of deportation (Narayan 1995; Raj et al. 2004).

The criminal justice response, access to housing, employment, social services, and right to stay in the country are all affected by one's immigration status. Many women on H-4s are reluctant to call the police and engage the criminal justice system, because they are worried about being deported or risking deportation of their spouses. Women from Muslim communities are particularly aware of the increased detention of Muslim men after September 11, 2001, and thus fear calling the police, even during crises. Housing is also an issue for H-4 women seeking relief from abuse. Both temporary and long-term housing are restricted for nonimmigrants. Although emergency shelter is available to everyone for at least thirty days and up to three months, women on H-4 visas as nonimmigrants are generally ineligible for longer-term housing assistance. Moreover, many transitional housing units require residents to work, which may offer a limited option for H-4s, as they generally lack work authorization.[3]

Furthermore, immigration status itself is a tool that abusers use over their spouses. The H-1B visa holder is the legal sponsor for an H-4 and thus has control over the H-4's documentation. Some abusers use this leverage to threaten their spouses with withdrawal of sponsorship. An abuser may also destroy or hide official documents, withhold information about the immigration process, or simply allow the spouse's H-4 legal status to expire. This mechanism of control exists for other immigration statuses that are sponsorship driven, including a conditional green card and a fiancée visa (K). Other temporary visa categories with similar dynamics include the F-2 visa, for dependents of student visa holders (FI), and L-2, for dependents of intracompany transfers (LI).

Social isolation is also a big concern for newly arrived H-4s, who may not know people outside their husbands' social networks. In her research on the role isolation plays in marital abuse among South Asians, Margaret Abraham defined isolation as "the individuals' perception and reality of being emotionally and socially alone, economically confined, and culturally disconnected" (2000a, 222). Immigrant women are geographically isolated from support in their communities of origin, increasing their dependence on their spouses to develop social networks within the immigrant community and the country of immigration. Over time, severe isolation can hinder a woman's ability to cope with abuse. Isolation can also cut a woman off from emotional support or support to get health care when dealing with physical abuse (Abraham 2000a; Hass, Dutton, and Orloff 2000).

Chaya's Advocacy with H-4 Visa Holders

Within the last two decades, South Asian activists and scholars have increased the visibility of domestic violence in South Asian communities (Abraham 1995, 1998; Dasgupta 1998a; Nankani 2000; Narayan 1995; Raj and Silverman 2003) while highlighting the strengths of and challenges facing South Asian–based domestic violence services (Agnew 1998a; Dasgupta 2000a; Merchant 2000; Rudrappa 2004a; Warrier 2000b).

When considering immigration status or advocacy work, it is important to note that not all H-4 visa holders are alike. In addition to differences in education, cultural values, religion, family of origin, and degree of abuse, H-4 visa holders also vary in the length of time they have lived in the United States and the specifics of their H-4 status. In some cases, H-4 visa holders and their husbands share children, who may be U.S. citizens. Furthermore, the type of support a woman seeks varies, based on whether she wishes to leave or stay with her husband. There are also distinctions between women who want to remain in the United States and those who wish to return to their country of origin.

The following scenario provides an illustration of how domestic violence can unfold for an H-4 visa holder. This scenario is one of several written by Chaya advocates as a composite of clients' experiences for their volunteer training.

Farah is a young Pakistani woman with three young children. Her husband is a software engineer. Farah has been in the United States for almost two years. Her youngest child was born in the United States and is a U.S. citizen. Before her marriage, Farah worked as an accountant in Pakistan.

Farah's husband is here on a work-visa (H-1) and her visa is dependent on his (H-4). Her husband will only allow her small amounts of money for groceries and insists that she give him receipts to account for every cent. Farah's husband is very suspicious and will only let her call her family and friends when he is in the room to listen to her conversations. She wants to take courses at a local university to gain new skills, but her husband complains that it will cost too much money because she will have to pay international student rates instead of in-state tuition. He also says it's pointless for her to gain new skills since she isn't allowed to work in the United States anyway. Her husband often beats her and tells her that he will divorce her and send her back to Pakistan.

The beatings eventually get bad enough that Farah begins to fear that he might hurt her very badly and threatens to call the police. Her husband tells her that if she calls the police, not only will she shame her family, but he will get in trouble with immigration.

One night while Farah is being beaten, her oldest child, a six-year old, calls 911. When the police arrive, they arrest her husband and tell Farah that she should go to a battered women's shelter with her children. Farah refuses to give the police a statement because she is terrified her husband will be deported if she tells the police anything. Her husband is arrested anyway and Farah is taken to a local shelter.

The shelter staff tells Farah she will have to leave after three weeks, but don't have many suggestions for her, as she's not eligible for most programs such as food stamps, medical coupons, or other support from the Department of Social and Human Services because she is in the United States on a temporary visa. An immigration lawyer she consults tells her that she is not eligible for work permit because her husband is on H-1B visa. When Farah's shelter stay is up, she decides to return home instead of transferring to shelter after shelter.

Farah's story highlights issues that have specific consequences for a temporary visa holder, including financial dependence on the abuser, fear that calling the police will lead to deportation, fear of losing children if deported, misinformation from domestic violence service providers, and limited access to public benefits. Limited financial resources also affect her ability to pay for a lawyer, filing fees, childcare, and a host of other expenses.

Safety Planning

Advocates at Chaya recognize that they cannot guarantee women's safety; thus, they focus their work on helping a woman manage risks and build support systems. "In some respects I'd consider a lot of what we do to fall under the purview of safety planning even when it's public benefits advocacy. In the sense that those public benefits may be critical for maintaining a stable home, a roof over your head, or food on the table." Safety planning also involves minimizing isolation as a preventive measure, although in some cases physical safety may not be a woman's priority. However, Chaya advocates try to assist a woman find ways to stay connected or build connections outside her abusive relationship. Advocates stress that building a supportive community of friends and family can be an important way for a survivor to sustain herself beyond the support offered by a social service agency.

Chaya advocates believe that safety planning is an ongoing process and many life circumstances affect how safety planning occurs. Safety planning with women on H-4 visas takes into account what options are available to them, given the constraints of their immigration status that limit access to public benefits. For example, Sandra, a Chaya advocate, said, "If it's someone's desire to stay in the United States then I think the safety planning comes in when someone is examining those options and thinking about the consequences or implications of making certain decisions. Whether it might make her abusive partner more aggressive and escalate the situation, or regardless of her abusive partner, [whether the decision] might somehow put her at greater risk for having to leave the country."[4]

Advocates state that battered South Asian women's fear of calling the police is particularly troubling, because the police are often the first responders to a domestic violence incident. Amber, another Chaya advocate, discussed the challenges of balancing potential risks associated with help-seeking options like calling the police: "I think it's a really hard topic, because for a lot of people there is a physically violent situation and you don't have family or friends who you're comfortable with or are able to or want to respond to those situations. The police are kind of the first responders to those severe physical situations. And yet, some women feel more unsafe at the possibility of their husbands' immigration status being possibly affected than experiencing physical abuse with nobody to turn to."

Chaya advocates seek to talk honestly with their clients about the potential risks involved in calling the police while also emphasizing that calling the police can be a life-saving option. In situations where calling the police may impact a woman's immigration status, an advocate might advise, "I know you're concerned about this and I recognize that it's a very real and legitimate concern. But if the degree of risk or safety is so severe, when it comes down to it, if you are in serious fear of your safety or your life, call the police."

Economic Advocacy

Economic advocacy varies depending on if the battered woman is living with her husband, has children, or is separated or single. For example, if a woman is living with her husband and relying on his income, the advocates would explore possibilities of putting money aside or, if possible, opening a bank account for the woman's exclusive use. In some cases, women who get an allowance from their husbands can save some money, just to have a little financial security in case of an emergency.

Advocates also discuss options for getting financial support from family members in the United States or in their home countries. However, since financial control is a common form of abuse in domestic violence situations, many women have little or no access to money.

Economic advocacy can also take the form of financial planning with a woman who has limited experience in managing her own finances, or whose husband has kept them in the dark about finances, as a means to exert power and control. As one advocate described, "If you've been in a relationship that's very financially controlling and you've never lived alone, you may not have a sense of how much it costs to live. [An advocate might] say, 'This is how much you have in savings, let's sit down and see what's the minimum you could survive on.'"

The need for economic advocacy also arises when a woman is going through divorce or legal separation and might request maintenance and/or child support. However, securing payment of maintenance monies after divorce can cause more strife while providing an abuser with the opportunity to continue his control. Even though there are government agencies that can help with the collection of child support, it is very difficult to enforce. Such collection becomes nearly impossible if he or she returns to the country of origin. In some instances, if the abuser has assets it may be possible to request the judge to order maintenance to be paid in lump sum. This can be helpful in giving a woman some funds to get her life in order and minimize contact with her abuser.

Until VAWA 2005, H-4s had no legal right to work even when they were abused. Thus, some women looked for undocumented or illegal work that pays under the table. While this option is less desirable, it may be the only way a woman on an H-4 can find economic independence. Undocumented work poses its own risks, as workers who have no legally recognized rights may be subjected to economic exploitation or physical and sexual abuse by their employers. Although Chaya advocates do not encourage their clients to seek undocumented work, they do talk with their clients about the potential risks involved. For example, Chaya advocates discussed working with women who have been sexually harassed: "We had so many women working in South Asian restaurants who experienced sexual harassment. And the labor laws don't apply. Like the owners don't follow at all and there's very little recourse that people feel they have." Thus, survivors who work under the table can expose themselves to workplace abuse, which is shielded by the undocumented nature of the work. Working under the table can pose an additional threat, should a woman's partner find out. Although VAWA 2005 includes the provision of issuing work permits to women who can *demonstrate* that they were subjected to battery and/or extreme cruelty by their spouses, it is too early to gauge its connotation and effectiveness.

Legal Immigration Options

Immigration may or may not be the most pressing concern for a woman who calls Chaya for support. However, advocacy with H-4 visa holders inevitably addresses how their options to cope with or respond to abusive situations will impact their immigration status and vice versa. Advocates at Chaya do not give legal advice, and as a standard practice they refer their clients to immigration lawyers to discuss specifics related to their immigration options. Nevertheless, the advocates have found that women on H-4s are often aware of their unstable immigration status and look to them for help and hope. Amber said, "Most women call us hoping there's something that we know that they don't. Since we're an organization for abused women, they think we must know of some option that's out there. Unfortunately, although we may know of a few other options, they're usually unlikely to be applicable to that woman's situation. So it's also part of our work, when we share those options, to try and be really responsible in letting them know how realistic these other options are for them and the potential risks and benefits."

Advocates also discussed immigration options as a way of helping women buy into other options. As Sandra stated, "I think something that I've heard a lot, around buying time, buying time to find a more permanent solution. Also, I think buying more time is just to think about what you really want. People aren't sure. Maybe you have completely distanced returning to your country of origin [as] an option. And maybe [you] are scared and haven't really thought about it. And maybe [you need time] to figure out what it would be like."

Advocacy around immigration can also support the rights of women who want to return to their native countries. Many women who want to return to their native countries might settle for a fair share of marital property, child support, and/or visitation rights to children. Complications can arise when a woman is forced to return to her native country by her husband, family, or when her husband initiates divorce either in the United States or their native country. Because divorce laws in the United States are generally more favorable to women concerning child custody and division of property, many women try to settle their legal disputes and secure custody of children in the United States.

At present, if a woman is considering leaving her spouse and would like to continue residing in the United States, there are only a few available options, many of which are either difficult to access or undesirable. "Even if a woman doesn't want a divorce, but wants to separate for a while, she might fear that by separating, the husband might initiate a divorce," which would cause her H-4 status to expire. In some cases, women do not necessarily want to separate from their husbands, but want to explore options to change their immigration status, so they may work in the United States or have more security in their abusive situations. Thus, discussing immigration options is a strategy for safety planning, whether a woman leaves or stays in the abusive relationship. The following are some immigration options that Chaya advocates offer battered women on temporary and dependent visas.

APPLYING FOR F1 or H-1B VISA If a woman has sufficient resources and/or marketable skills, it is possible for her to apply for her own F-1 student or H-1B visa. Getting an F-1 or H-1B can provide temporary support to a woman who wishes to leave her abusive spouse or have some source of income and/or social support outside her marriage. Nevertheless, advocates at Chaya consider both the F-1 and H-1B visas as improbable options for women on H-4s who are contending with domestic violence. Student visas require that applicants have financial resources for support. Many women in abusive marriages may not be able to access the necessary funds or document their finances. Obtaining an H-1B work visa may also be difficult to realize, given the cutbacks in the H-1B program and growing competition in the technology field. Anita, a Chaya advocate stated, "The H-1 visa is often difficult or impossible for the women we work with to obtain. Especially since the cap on H-1 visas has been cut back, it is very difficult. Even women, who are very educated and may have had work experience in India, usually have been in the United States for some time, so their skills are not up to date. Depending on the industry, that may be more or less important; but a lot of industries that sponsor people on H-1 visas are in technology or biotechnology, so being two or three years out of date doesn't make as strong of a candidate." Furthermore, F-1 and H-1B are temporary visas that come with their own restrictions. For example, student visa holders can work but are limited by hours and places of work. They must also be enrolled full time to maintain the student status and have the resources to pay out-of-state tuition.

WAITING FOR THE APPROVAL OF SPOUSE'S PERMANENT RESIDENCY STATUS Self-petitioning through VAWA may be an option for securing more stable immigration for battered women on dependent visas. If a woman's spouse is in the process of applying for a green card, she may decide it is worth waiting for the application to be approved, after which she would be eligible to self-petition independently for her own green card through VAWA. Even if the H-4 visa holder divorces or is divorced from her spouse prior to his obtaining a green card, she may self-petition within two years of the divorce, if she can demonstrate that the divorce was directly related to domestic violence. However, depending on the severity of the abuse, waiting in an abusive relationship can carry its own risks.

INTERIM RELIEF THROUGH U VISA U visa is a provision of VAWA 2000, designed to offer relief to crime victims with the condition that the applicant cooperates with the prosecution of a crime committed in the United States. Although some acts of domestic violence do qualify as crimes under U visa specifications (e.g., physical violence but not financial or emotional abuse), many women are unwilling to adhere to its requirements, lack the necessary documentation to qualify, or are reluctant to pursue a U visa as long as it remains unregulated.

At present, some women may receive interim relief by applying for a U visa. In November 2003, local district INS offices began giving temporary work permits to U visa applicants who made a prima facie showing, or preliminary approval. In May 2004, the USDHS finally gave authority to the Vermont Service Center (which adjudicates VAWA petitions) to grant interim relief that allows applicants to stay in the United States and apply for work permits on an annual basis until the U visa regulations are issued.[5]

Regulation aside, the U visa is only a viable option for survivors who are willing or able to cooperate with law enforcement. When a victim/survivor of domestic violence wants the abuse to end or wants to leave her abuser, it does not imply that she wishes to cooperate with the police or prosecution.

Finally, not all women are in positions to accept the risks associated with immigration options. For example, "A young single woman might be more comfortable taking the risk of beginning with a short-term solution, like U visa or interim relief, while she can plan what the next step will be." In many cases, women on H-4s who call Chaya recognize that they do not have immigration options and thus seek support for ways to cope with their abusive situation.

Concluding Remarks

In writing this essay, I found the topic of H-4 advocacy filled with uncertainty, raising feelings of helplessness and frustration in advocates and H-4 visa holders alike. Yet, despite some trepidation to raise a topic with few answers in hand, there is a need to dialogue and for practitioners, advocates, and policy makers to work together to develop strategies for change. In the past twenty years, a surge of activism, community organizing, and writing has brought various forms of violence against women in South Asian communities into focus. This body of work illustrates how domestic violence in the context of immigration intersects with axes of power and control, both within and outside intimate relationships (see Abraham 1998; Dasgupta 1998a; Nankani 2000; Narayan 1997; Raj and Silverman 2002a).

The circumstances of immigration increase a woman's dependence on her spouse, especially if she is reliant on him for her legal residency. Consequently, immigration is a particularly powerful mechanism available to an abuser to maintain power and control over his spouse. Studies with immigrants from different countries demonstrate that many issues facing immigrant women are common across ethnicity and national origin (Bui 2003; Erez and Bach 2003; Hass et al. 2000; Salcido and Adelman 2004). However, the differing patterns of immigration from region to region necessitate an understanding of how particular immigration statuses, in this case the H-1B and H-4 temporary visas, contribute to immigrant women's vulnerability to domestic violence.

VAWA brought needed legislative support for immigrant women. However, we must continue to improve upon VAWA while ensuring access to existing provisions. A possible change may be to broaden the scope of immigration relief to include those not married to U.S. citizens and LPRs. Issuing work authorization and making public benefits available to *all* who legally reside in the United States, including temporary visa holders, is another way of providing basic support for preventing and/or minimizing the risk for domestic violence.[6]

Whether or not a woman wishes to leave her abusive spouse, economic autonomy is an important step toward self-determination. The marked value of obtaining the right to work becomes evident in the clients of Chaya, who gain eligibility for work authorization through VAWA provisions or as asylum seekers. "Most of the women that I've worked with are so excited when they got their working papers. It just seems kind of ridiculous that they couldn't get them quicker, you know, when they were ready to move out of this abusive situation and work to take care of themselves and their kids. It doesn't really seem fair, seem right."

Efforts to extend work authorization to new groups of immigrants draws criticism from those who contend that jobs are growing scarce in the United States and need to be reserved for "Americans." Such nativist arguments are not new and pose a substantial political barrier. Nevertheless, the actual number of people who would qualify for work authorization, though significant in the context of domestic violence prevention, remains marginal considering the hundreds of thousands of immigrants who legally enter the United States to work each year. Furthermore, advocates at Chaya point out that many of the women they work with seek low-wage service level jobs to help them make ends meet while deciding how to move forward with their lives. These potential job seekers pose an unsubstantial threat to the U.S. economy.

The focus on H-4 visa holders is an attempt to bring focus to a group of immigrants that continues to occupy a space on the outskirts of domestic violence advocacy. I refer to this space as "on the outskirts" to acknowledge that with so few available legal solutions, advocacy for H-4 visa holders appears outside most of the strategies available to domestic violence advocates. Given the upward mobility of many recent South Asian immigrants, social service providers and the public at large view this group as privileged (at least economically) and thus less troubled. The affluence of this group may obfuscate the particular form of vulnerability to domestic violence created by dependent immigration status. Furthermore, since South Asian immigrants generally enter the United States legally, underground networks to support women who fall out of status while attempting to escape abuse have not yet firmly developed.

Advocacy for H-4 visa holders and other marginalized social groups has also been weakened by the growing reliance on legal interventions as the most significant means to hold abusers accountable and offer protection to victims/survivors. While the criminal justice response to domestic violence has improved, the necessity of relying only on the criminal justice system to account for batterers' behaviors carries its own consequences. Even as legislative progress has occurred on state and federal levels, battered women have been continually ignored or revictimized by police and court practices, while battered women and batterers in marginal positions in society have been made increasingly vulnerable to inequalities in the system (Shepard and Pence 1999).

Systemic inequality is particularly salient for immigrants who are abused by their partners and remain reluctant to seek police intervention because of the already disproportionate levels of incarceration of men of color and racism inherent in the criminal justice system. For example, immigration reforms in 1996 made some misdemeanors such as a violation of a protection order possible grounds to detain and eventually deport nonimmigrants or even legal permanent residents (Espenshade, Baraka, and Huber 1997).[7] Additionally, South Asian immigrants who have witnessed the escalation of policing and detaining of immigrants after 9/11 are even more reluctant to seek any intervention from the state. After the 1996 immigration reform and the Patriot Act of 2001, up to 300,000 immigrants have been detained each year since 2001. The detention of immigrant women also doubled between 1996 and 1998 (Bhattacharjee 2001). The increased policing and detention of immigrants have had a chilling effect on battered women on temporary visas who may now be too afraid to call the police even when in grave danger.

Community mobilization and community outreach programs at Chaya and across the country have been integral to generating dialogue in South Asian communities and developing networks that stand up against domestic violence. Advocates at Chaya and sister organizations around the country routinely grapple with numerous issues of advocacy at the intersection of gender, violence, and immigration. With few legal options for supporting the autonomy and safety of immigrant women, it is imperative that we generate further dialogue toward policy reform and community mobilization, to protect all groups of immigrant women and ensure their right to live free of violence.

ACKNOWLEDGMENTS

I gratefully acknowledge the support and contribution of Chaya's staff and advocates, Amber Vora, Anita Prasad, Aaliyah Gupta, Vega Subramaniam, Sandra Gresl, and Anita Sinha.

NOTES

1. Despite the dual intent of the H-1b visa and the possibility of getting a green card, the United States operates as if these guest workers will return home.

2. This number includes H-1 Bs as well as their spouses and children on H-4 visas.

3. The 2005 reauthorization of VAWA, signed into law on January 5, 2006 (PL 109–162), extends work authorization to some groups of temporary visa holders, including H-4s, who can establish that they are victims of abuse by their spouses.

4. Names of interviewees have been changed to protect their privacy.

5. VAWA 2005 requires the USDHS to issue regulations for provisions passed in 2000 and 2005, such as U visa, within 180 days of its signing.

6. Temporary visa holders (officially referred to as nonimmigrants) are ineligible for public benefits such as Supplemental Security Income, Temporary Assistance for Needy Families, Medicaid, and food stamps (National Immigration Law Center 2005).

7. In Washington State, a violation of a no-contact order can be charged as a felony or misdemeanor, depending on the circumstances.

17

Local and Global Undivided

Transnational Exploitation and Violence against South Asian Women

SUJATHA ANBUSELVI JESUDASON

Setting the Stage

The story of Lakireddy Bali Reddy, a Berkeley, California, landlord from India who was sentenced to eight years in prison for trafficking and immigration fraud, is resplendent in the *filmi* drama of more than a couple of Hindi movies combined. There is sex, money, death, fraud, fake parents, a dead fetus, smuggling, and a huge media scandal around a multimillionaire landlord and his two sons exploiting and sexually assaulting vulnerable, lower caste girls. And all this takes place in two exotic locales—Berkeley, California, U.S.A., and Velvadum, Andhra Pradesh, India. All the drama notwithstanding, this is a case of many stories rolled into one. There is the story of sex and labor trafficking between Berkeley and Velvadum, immigration fraud, the U.S. Immigration and Naturalization Services (INS) and H-1B visas, caste exploitation, patriarchy, familial obligation, and sexism; the involvement of South Asian American activists, South Asian American domestic violence organizations, white American feminists, philanthropy in the Bay Area and Velvadum, and the Bay Area South Asian community; and a curiously contradictory tale told by the Velvadum community and Reddy's family.

For many people this was an easy case to resolve—Reddy did some bad things to some innocent young women and deserved to be punished. For others, this case raised many difficult and disturbing questions. The central characters in the legal case, the Reddy family and the nine victims that Reddy brought to the United States, were individuals embroiled in a transnationally dangerous situation. The exploitation and violence in the case crossed national and cultural boundaries of a small village in Andhra Pradesh in India and entered, from an American perspective, into our own backyard in Berkeley, California.

The violence occurred on many levels. There was the interpersonal violence and rape of young women and girls by older and more powerful men. But there was also violence at a structural level. Violence on a global scale, where the inequalities between two countries rendered even exploitation in Berkeley a better life

243

(Yi 1999); the violence of an age-old patronage system that tied vulnerable lower caste families to a large landowner in India; and the violence at the level of the United States' strict immigration policies, high demand for labor, and weak labor laws allowing an exploitative situation to take place.

Everybody was caught flatfooted. Nobody, including law enforcement, lawyers, social service providers, activists, or the media was prepared to deal with the transnationality of the Reddy case. Indeed, each of these groups framed the fundamental problem and, thus, the solution differently. The Reddy case erupted in two cities and two countries that were not ready to deal with their own global interconnections. Furthermore, it brought a few extremely significant issues to fore. Given these transnational flows of bodies and cultures, how can we understand and articulate cases of transnational violence and exploitation against South Asian women, and perhaps even more importantly, how can we imagine and enact new forms of transnational justice? In this new era of globalization and transnationalism, we can no longer rely on our old imaginations of violence and justice, but instead must develop new perspectives that will help guide us in this shifting, complex, and interconnected world of thoughts and actions.

Instead of retelling the "shabby" (Herron Zamora & McCormick 2000) and "lurid" (Herron Zamora & Yi 2000; Yi 1999) details of the "sex-slave case" (Richman 2004), I will focus on the heartbreaking and complicated story of transnational sex and labor exploitation that is at the heart of this incident. I will describe some of the multiple standpoints involved in this case and describe in depth how two actors, South Asian domestic violence organizations and several South Asian political activists, addressed the situation.

During the first year of this case, I was in a unique position. At the time, I was working for Narika, a South Asian domestic violence prevention organization and later became one of the founding members of the Alliance of South Asians Taking Action (ASATA), a South Asian political activist organization. I share these stories here in an attempt to document the mobilization, activism, and courage of South Asian women in the United States in responding to labor and sexual exploitation and violence against South Asian women.

Often, when we talk about violence against South Asian women in the United States, we focus primarily on the interpersonal violence of family and domestic abuse. Beside this secret private violence, South Asian women in America are generally represented as successful immigrants—doctors, lawyers, academics, and entrepreneurs. However, this particular case of sex and labor exploitation is also a secret and unspoken part of our community and immigrant life. The Reddy case raises deeply troubling questions about the nature and dynamics of violence against and exploitation of South Asian women and violence in and against immigrant communities and across national borders. The Reddy case reminded us that violence against South Asian women in the United States is not confined to the family; it is more expansive and structurally embedded.

In addition, for those of us who are vigilant about these trends in immigrant communities, I want to make sure that the history of South Asian American women's resistance is not lost, forgotten, or rendered invisible. My aim in documenting this event is not only to challenge us to confront and engage with the dark underside of transnationalism, but to also remind us that South Asian women are not always the victims. We act out against violence—we resist it, we speak out, and we mobilize against it.

The Play

On November 24, 1999, the night before Thanksgiving, a passing motorist in downtown Berkeley, California, noticed some "men carrying what appeared to be a body" out of an apartment building. "These men were also dragging a screaming woman out. It appeared that they were getting ready to load both into a waiting van owned by Reddy Realty" (Yi 2000a). When she asked if they needed any help, the men dismissed her with, "It's none of your business!" (Sundaram 2000). The motorist called 911 anyway, and when the police arrived the men scattered, leaving a girl on a side exit landing (Yi 2000a). The girl turned out to be Sitha Vemireddy, who along with her sister, Lalitha Vemireddy, were found unconscious by a third roommate, Buji, in the one-bedroom apartment they shared. Sitha was pronounced dead from carbon monoxide poisoning, while Lalitha was treated at the local hospital and released. After preliminary investigations, the problem appeared to be a faulty heater and the police declared that they would not pursue the case any further.

Lakireddy Bali Reddy, the owner of the building, stated in interviews that the two sisters came to Berkeley from South India two months ago to be with their parents, Venketeshwara and Padma Vemireddy, who had come to Berkeley looking for better work. According to him, because the girls were used to the warm south Indian weather, they had turned the heater up to full blast and closed all the windows. Of Sitha he said, "She was such a wonderful girl. She was so charming. This is just shaking everyone in my family. It's just disastrous" (Levi Holtz 1999, 25).

But that was not all there was to this tragedy. The Berkeley Police Department received several anonymous letters that Venketeshwara and Padma Vemireddy were not in fact the girls' parents; they were not even husband and wife, but siblings. The letters also stated that there was H-1 visa "dooping" [sic] going on at the "Pasand Hotel." The Berkeley Police Department took the letters and the case to Manuela Albuquerque, Berkeley city attorney. Albuquerque, an immigrant from India, began acting as a cultural adviser to the police department and a liaison with two South Asian women's agencies, Narika and Maitri, consulting with them on various issues in the case. "It seemed very suspicious for these two young girls to be left alone in that apartment by their parents. That seems out of character for a family from India," stated Albuquerque (Herron Zamora 2000a). Up to that point, Lakireddy Bali Reddy and his son, Vijay Lakireddy, had served as translators for the police. Lalitha and her roommate only spoke Telugu, as did the Vemireddys and all other Reddy workers. With the help of an independent translator, the picture began to change.

On January 14, 2000, Lakireddy Bali Reddy was arrested and charged with "importing aliens for the purpose of prostitution and for other immoral purposes" and "encouraging and inducing immigrants to illegally enter and reside in the United States" (Yi and Delgado 2000). The arrest affidavit charged Reddy with bringing people into the United States on twenty-one fraudulent H-1 visas to work in his restaurant, property management, and construction companies. It also accused Reddy of making a deal with Venketeshwara Vemireddy to pose as the girls' father to bring them to the United States on dependent visas so that he could continue to sexually exploit the girls. Vemireddy claimed that Reddy paid off his debts for him in India and gave him a loan of $6,500 for airline tickets for him and his sister in exchange for posing as the sisters' parents, bringing Sitha and Lalitha over at Reddy's request, and working at his Pasand restaurant. The affidavit claimed that Reddy "bought the girls from their parents" for Rs.10,000 (approximately $250), had started "having sex with" the sisters in India when Lalitha was twelve years old and Sitha fourteen, and continued "sexual relations" with them once they arrived in the United States. Eleven days later, on January 25, Reddy was released on a bail of $10 million. His two sons, Vijay and Prasad Lakireddy, were released on $500,000 bail each.

In the end, all six Reddy family members, Lakireddy Bali Reddy, Jayaprakash and Anapurna Lakireddy (Lakireddy Bali Reddy's brother and sister-in-law), and Vijay and Prasad Lakireddy (sons), pled guilty by way of plea bargains. On March 5, 2001, Jayaprakash and Anapurna Lakireddy pled guilty to conspiring to commit immigration fraud and were sentenced to six months' detention. On March 7, 2001, Lakireddy Bali Reddy pled guilty to one count of conspiring to commit immigration fraud, two counts of transportation of minors for illegal sexual activity, and one count of submitting a false tax return. On June 21, 2001, he was sentenced to ninety-seven months in federal prison. Eventually he paid $2 million in criminal restitution and $8.9 million for the wrongful death of Sitha and an undisclosed amount in a workers' class action suite (Artz 2004). Vijay and Prasad Lakireddy, Lakireddy Bali Reddy's sons, also pled guilty. At the time of writing this article, Vijay Lakireddy was serving a twenty-four-month detention sentence in a Nevada drug treatment center. Prasad Lakireddy was finally sentenced on June 8, 2004, to five years' probation, one year under house arrest, and a $20,000 fine for his role in the sex and labor exploitation (Artz 2004).

Characters and Players

For the most part, people responded to the Reddy case with outrage, sadness, and disbelief. However, the most shocking part to many people was not the labor exploitation; in fact, many people said that they were not surprised by those allegations. One of Sitha's neighbors said, "We know they bring them back from villages in India and really make them work" (Yi and Delgado 2000). Lakireddy Bali Reddy had the girls paint the exterior walls of a couple of three-story buildings in downtown Berkeley standing on scaffoldings in saris. What was shocking was the sexual exploitation of the two young women. As the lead investigator, Captain Bobby Miller stated at the first press conference, "The worst part of all is that some of the women, including some minors, were sexually molested by Mr. Reddy" (Sundaram 2000). During this first press conference, most of the questions were about the young girls, sex, trafficking, and prostitution. Captain Bobby Miller kept reiterating the word "molesting" in a deep voice and imbuing it with immense meaning and a sense of disbelief.

In addition to the police focusing on the sexual aspects of this case, the media found it vastly titillating. Repeatedly the headlines read, "Sex scandal," "Sex case," and "Landlord sex charges" (Yi and Delgado 2000). Similar headlines such as the following appeared in local papers on an almost daily basis, "Cops Hunt Victims in Landlord Sex Case" (Yi, Herron Zamora, and Wadhwani 2000); "Lurid Charge in Berkeley Sex Case" (Herron Zamora and Yi 2000); "Berkeley Landlord Depicted as Overlord of India Village" (Levi Holtz and Squatriglia 2000); and "Sex Case Landlord's Shabby Past" (Herron Zamora 2000b).

Despite, or maybe because of the sexually sensational portrayal of the case, many Americans responded with outrage. In the first two weeks after the story broke, the four phone lines in the Narika offices, a Berkeley-based South Asian domestic violence prevention organization, rang off the hook. Narika was listed in the newspapers as one of the places for additional victims and witnesses to call. Few called with actual information; most called because they wanted to help the victims and punish the perpetrator. When a victim relief fund was set up, thousands of dollars poured in. People called with all kinds of recommendations for lawyers, suggestions for civil suits, psychologists for the girls, ideas for boycotts, and additional criminal charges. At least fifteen lawyers offered their services and advice pro bono. People were infuriated with Reddy, and they wanted to do something about it.

In the South Asian community, it had been well known for many years that Reddy brought in improperly documented workers to use cheap labor in his restaurants and construction and property management companies. There was no other way he could have such large number of Indians working for him. These workers often lived in concentrated housing and Reddy-owned buildings in downtown Berkeley. One of the most well-known places where the workers lived was at the corner of Durante and Dana Streets, in an apartment building with an engraved sign over the doorway, "Indra Bhavan" (House of *Indra*, the king of gods).

While some members of the South Asian community responded with sadness and shame over the deplorable situation, others responded with disbelief that Lakireddy Bali Reddy could have actually done what he was accused of doing. They were "shocked by these criminal allegations" and thought that these charges "might be the result of cultural misunderstandings" (Yi et al. 2000). Many believed that they should reserve judgment until he "has his day in court, then all these charges will be dropped." Others were caught completely by surprise and hoped "it's all wrong" (Herron Zamora 2000a).

What were the reasons behind these differing reactions to the same case? Why have some responded with sadness and shame, others with shock and disbelief, and yet others with outrage and anger? These differing opinions point to the uniquely transnational character of this case; it was unclear who were the victims, villains, and heroes in the situation. This in turn confused the case in terms of political, legal, and activist strategies, as well as community responses.

In the first couple of articles in November 1999 that reported the death of Sitha Vemireddy, Lakireddy Bali Reddy was portrayed in a very sympathetic light. He was shown as a caring and distraught landlord who was saddened by the death of this young woman from his hometown. However, once the story broke the headlines declared "Sex case landlord's shabby past," where he was described as "one of the most complained-about landlords" (Herron Zamora 2000b). An article by Herron Zamora (2000b) declared that Reddy had "faced hundreds of lawsuits and complaints" and he was "ranked as one of the worst landlords in the city" (1). Given that Reddy was the largest landlord in Berkeley and owned nearly half the rental units in the city, perhaps it is only logical that he received the most complaints.

As people began to know about the case, there were a number of calls to picket in front of Reddy-owned Pasand restaurant, particularly by Diana Russell, an activist, feminist, and professor emeritus at Mills College. She began picketing the restaurant and carried signs that read, "Prosecute Reddy for Negligent Homicide" and "Sex Slavery in Berkeley. Boycott Pasand!" (Russell 2000a). She handed out flyers entitled, "Fight back against sexual slavery, illegal rent increases, slave labor and death trap apartments! Help close down the Pasand restaurant!" (Russell 2000b). In a press conference held on January 19, 2000, at the Berkeley City Hall, Reddy was characterized as one of the "evil people in the world who abuse and exploit those less fortunate."

As portrayed by the media and others, the victims in this case were the sexually exploited women in Reddy's employment, particularly the two sisters, Sitha and Lalitha Vemireddy. However, there were more trafficked individuals involved. Eventually nine victims were identified out of a potential pool of twenty-five young women and girls and 150 individuals sponsored on work visas.

ASATA called for a defining of "More Than Just Two Victims" in the Reddy case (ASATA 2000a). They worked to redefine the "sex scandal" to "sexual exploitation" by focusing on "the power differential that exists in the situation" (ASATA 2000a) and also to bring attention to the rights of the other undocumented workers involved in the case. ASATA advocated against the deportation of any workers who stepped forward to complain about working conditions with the Reddys and developed a strategy of outreach to encourage more employees to come forward. It tried, with limited success, to create safer conditions for the victims of both sexual and labor exploitation.

In contrast, Professor Diana Russell focused specifically on the young women as victims. In her flyer, she wrote, "He used these young girls as sex slaves, and forced them to work in the Pasand restaurant and to clean and paint some of his numerous buildings. The 15-year old sex slave who Reddy housed with her now deceased sister and another young Indian sex slave in one of his apartments told the police that Reddy had sex with her in India when she was 12 years old" (Russell 2000a). However, according to the civil depositions, during their time with Reddy, the young women traveled back and forth to India to visit their families. They were paid for their work on his buildings, anywhere from $100 to $1,000 a month beyond their expenses, which included meals and groceries from the restaurant, rent-free apartments, and utilities. Their pay was raised in increments from $100 to $200, $400, $800, and $1,000 depending on the time they had been in the United States. While they did not pay for their initial trip to the United States, subsequent trip tickets were subtracted from their wages.

Reddy's legal team contested the portrayal of the social conditions of these women's lives and the claims that the women were kept as sex slaves and virtual prisoners to the Reddy family. According to the depositions, the women would go shopping or rent movies after work, one woman got her driving license and bought a car with the money she earned, and that they had telephones and televisions. In the words of one woman, "nobody ever beat—did beating or scolding or any such thing to any one of us" (Pinto 2004). Based on these facts, the Reddy legal team argued that these women and workers were not in a coercive arrangement but had the freedom to come and go as they pleased.

The Berkeley Police Department and the Immigration and Naturalization Service (INS) were portrayed as the heroes in this case. According to the media, by arresting Reddy, the Berkeley Police Department saved the girls from exploitation and abuse. By following up on the anonymous letters and investigating Reddy, they broke this prostitution and smuggling ring. At the January 19, 2000, press conference, which I attended, Berkeley Police Captain Bobby Miller said, "This could be the tip of the iceberg. We do believe that there are more victims out there that we don't even know about. It might be too big for the Berkeley Police Department to handle. It could touch several cities, several counties, even other states." And since it was too big for the Berkeley Police Department, they brought in the INS. Chuck DeMore, the San Francisco director of the INS, commented at the press conference, "Clearly this is one of the most egregious cases that we have come across in Northern California in a long time. It's as if these individuals were almost sex slaves." Both the police and INS repeatedly offered assurances that they were "really interested in going after the perpetrators of this exploitation, not after the innocent victims"; they just wanted justice done and the bad guy (read: Reddy) punished.

However, for many people, particularly the South Asian activists involved in the case, this framing of villains, victims, and heroes did not resonate well. And this is where the transnationality of the case became apparent. While to some, Reddy was the evil abuser of innocent victims, to others in the South Asian community, he was a "father figure" (Reddy 2000, 4). In the Bay Area South Asian community, Reddy was a well-respected businessman. He had immigrated to the United States in 1960 to pursue a master's degree in chemical engineering at the University of California at Berkeley. He received his degree in 1963, and by 1971 he began purchasing apartment buildings around the Berkeley campus. His business holdings included the alleged high-tech firm Active Tech Solutions and Reddy Realty, of which he was the principal partner. In sum, Reddy owned more than 1,000 rental units in Berkeley, as well as two branches of the Pasand Madras Cuisine restaurant, one in downtown Berkeley and one in Santa Clara (Levi Holtz 1999). His personal wealth was estimated between $40 and $60 million. He was the second largest landlord in Berkeley, with holdings second only to the University of California. He was described as one of the largest property owners in Berkeley, collecting over $1 million per month in rental proceeds (Wang 2001).

Reddy was actively involved in a variety of community improvement organizations and temples. As another restaurant owner described him, "He is like a father figure to the community. He is very well-respected" (Reddy 2000, 4). Quite consistently, South Asians, particularly men, expressed disbelief about the accusations and charges leveled against Lakireddy Bali Reddy. As one man said, "It is not a black or white issue. When we go to India, a lot of poor families approach us and ask for money. A lot of people want to get over to the U.S. We give them money if we can, and sometimes we help their children come over here. Reddy probably gave money to the girls' father but that doesn't mean that he bought her. Buying is not the issue, its helping poor people" (Yi et al. 2000). In addition, at least thirty individuals credited Reddy with giving them the support and experience to own and operate their own restaurants in the United States. They had learned the trade in Reddy's restaurants as cooks and waiters.

In fact, many in the South Asian community felt the prosecution of Reddy was a witch hunt. They saw him as the victim in the case. To them, these accusations were a part of a pattern of persecution. As one Indian man wrote in a letter to the editor of *India Currents*, "I am very sad and angry because of all the wild accusations leveled against Mr. Reddy, because he is the largest landlord in the city of Berkeley. Some officials are using the media to portray him as a monster in order to advance their political ambitions. Berkeley officials and media have labeled his philanthropy as buying people" (Reddy 2000, 4).

And beyond being a victim of the media and Berkeley officials, in his hometown of Velvadum in Andhra Pradesh, India, Reddy was "like a god" for all the help he had extended to others. "To many people [in Velvadum] Lakireddy Bali Reddy is a god, a hometown hero who made millions in America and brought some of it back to his home village, building schools and a new hospital wing" (Nisperos and Levi Holtz 2000, A1). In Velvadum, Reddy had built elementary and high schools, a temple, a bus station, a 400-seat technical college, and a groundwater pump and storage facility to provide potable tap water in the village. In Velvadum, police investigators were "getting little assistance from the local people" because he was so trusted and revered (Yi 2000a). According to police in India, Reddy had helped between 500 and 5,000 people through assistance with emigration and financial assistance; he had done "wonderful things" for the people of Velvadum. When American reporters went there to cover the story, signs went up that read "Bali Reddy is our God's gift," "Bali Reddy is innocent," and "Lakireddy Bali Reddy is our God" (Yi 2000b). The villagers believed that Lakireddy Bali Reddy could do no wrong.

Transnationalism added a completely different and unexpected dimension to this case. In India Reddy was a god and in the United States he was a villain and a victim. The young women were defined as victims in the United States, but in their hometown of Velvadum they were probably seen as young women who left to make a better life for themselves and their families. They were seen as agents in their lives. In the United States, the criminal justice system and the INS were seen as the heroes and saviors who had caught the villain and made things right for the young women; but in India and in parts of the South Asian immigrant community, they were viewed with suspicion and characterized as the villains from whom they needed to protect Reddy. In this case of such diametrically opposed characterizations, what does justice mean, and who gets justice and who is deprived of it?

Actors and Activists: South Asian Anti–Domestic Violence Organizations

In addition to the disparate reactions from populations in India and the United States, and the United States media and law enforcement, it is important to explore the responses of two major players in the case, South Asian domestic violence organizations and South Asian activists. Each group mobilized around and responded to different aspects of the case, reacted differently to its criminalization and legalization by the police and immigration officials and the sensationalization by the media.

Even before the story hit the news media, flags were raised for the law enforcement during the investigation into the death of Sitha Vemireddy. Berkeley city police contacted the city attorney and she contacted the two local Bay Area South Asian domestic violence prevention organizations to consult on the case. As soon as it became apparent that monolingual South Asian young women and girls needed shelter and protection, both organizations stepped in to support and protect the victims. Their first step was to provide adequate translation and interpretation services, as well as confidential and safe residence. Then they worked with the police and city attorney to secure legal representation for the women and determine a strategy for how best to keep the victims safe. In addition, one of the organizations, Maitri, immediately activated their contacts in India to help with the investigation and organize protection for the girls' families in India. From then on, they were somewhat limited in the kind of public demonstrations they believed they could participate in or organize. Maitri did not want to alienate the mainstream

South Asian community and felt that this was imperative to protect the confidentiality of the young women and the legal case being built.

However, once the young women were protected, there was a growing sense that some kind of public statement was needed from the South Asian community and antiviolence activists. Both Maitri and Narika wanted to hold off on any public demonstrations against Reddy because they wanted time for other victims to step forward and for the women in custody to feel safe and stabilized. However, it became clear that there was increasing pressure from the mainstream community, activist groups, and some sections of the South Asian community for some kind of a public statement. There was a need for space to express support for the young women and outrage against what had happened to them.

A coalition was formed spearheaded by a few South Asian activists, including me, to organize a public response and provide a community presence at Reddy's bail hearing. We called ourselves the Coalition to Support South Asian Survivors of Sexual and Labor Exploitation (Coalition) and identified as a "loosely formed coalition of South Asian community groups, activists, students and concerned citizens" who were there to "seek justice for the victims of sexual and labor exploitation" (2000a). In this loose coalition, there were representatives from organizations such as Narika, San Francisco Women Against Rape, National Network for Immigrant and Refugee Rights, South Asian Student Union at Berkeley High School, Coalition against Trafficking in Women, Asian Law Caucus, Women's Health Rights Coalition, Asian Health Services, South Asian Bar Association, Middle Eastern and South Asian Women's Association, Woman, Inc., and the Center for Digital Storytelling. Almost all the representatives from these organizations were of South Asian heritage. We placed the Reddy case in the context of global violence against women and girls and called for (1) bail to be denied in Reddy's case, (2) other victims to step forward and know that we supported them and were available to provide assistance, and (3) the "complete immunity from deportation" for all victims who came forward (Coalition 2000b).

Working in alliance with Maitri, the Coalition and Narika organized a candlelight vigil and demonstration on January 29, 2000, in front of Reddy's two most public holdings, his Pasand restaurants in Berkeley and Santa Clara. In Berkeley, the coalition decided to hold this vigil to show its support for the women and workers and not to turn it into a confrontational event with chanting and protest. We wanted to connect this case to the global issues of exploitation, violence and trafficking of women and children, and not just target Reddy (Coalition 2000c). The East Bay flyer called out "to show support for South Asian survivors of sexual and/or labor exploitation, and to honor the memory of those who did not survive" (Coalition 2000d). Along with candles, flyers handed out at the vigil read: "We gather today in solidarity to remember a woman who died young. She was a daughter, a sister, a friend and now a symbol to us all who deplore the oppression of women, girls and workers. This vigil honors her memory . . . We come together as a community to: express support for victims of sexual and labor exploitation, seek immunity from deportation for victims, end violence against women and express our outrage against abusers" (Coalition 2000e).

The Maitri demonstration in Santa Clara was framed as support for "victims of abuse and exploitation. Show your solidarity with community organizations. There is no shame in being a victim. There is no stigma in blowing the whistle" (Maitri 2000). The main goals of their demonstration were to "mourn the death and honor the memory of Sitha; set up a special fund to help resettle the victims; urge others to blow the whistle; assure investigating authorities of community support; and request permanent residency for the undocumented workers involved" (Maitri 2000). Publicity for the events spread through the social and racial justice activist networks, student networks, and through the media.

At the two events, several hundred people showed up. Silence was observed in memory of Sitha, and songs, speeches, and poetry were shared. Both events took place over a couple of hours and received substantial press coverage. The crowd was primarily South Asian at both events and was a diverse gathering of South Asian activists, students, and community members. There was also a visible presence of non–South Asian allies and supporters at these vigils.

After these events, both Maitri and Narika focused their energies and resources on protecting the young women and providing them with support services and legal representation. They worked tirelessly to ensure safe and confidential shelters through the Bay Area network of domestic violence shelters. This task became particularly challenging in the face of numerous threats from the community: Indian men showing up at the confidential shelters asking for the women and serious threats targeting the women's family members in India. Eventually, these organizations worked to help the family members of two of the victims migrate to the United States. They worked closely with and met endlessly with lawyers, immigration officials, and police investigators to strategize for and solidify the case, bring the young women to deposition hearings, and ensure that they understood what was going on.

Narika and Maitri also worked to meet the emotional needs of the victimized women. They provided a sisterly shoulder throughout the trauma of the investigation, the isolation of being away from the community, and the terror of anonymous threats to them and their families. The organizations labored to ensure the emotional, physical, and legal safety of the women and their families with their extensive volunteer networks and alliance with the police and legal teams working on the case.

Shortly after the candlelight vigil, tensions between the need for continuing public response and the need to ensure safety and confidentiality of the victims became even more apparent. It became clear that both public and private responses were needed and a division of labor necessary. Narika and Maitri focused on providing and securing the legal and supportive services for the women, and the coalition morphed into an activist organization seeking to shape the public debate and demands in the case.

As a coalition, we realized that one of the biggest challenges we had to grapple with was organizational constraint ensuing from accountability structures of individual agencies in terms of liability and the board of directors' review of public statements. Ultimately, we decided to form our own independent organization to bypass such limitations and be a stronger political voice. As an independent, volunteer organization, we did not have to worry about liability issues or the fear of alienating the mainstream South Asian community.

A relatively modest group of fifteen to twenty women formed the Alliance of South Asians Taking Action (ASATA) to articulate a strong South Asian progressive voice. We developed a list of short-term goals in relation to the case such as organizing and educating the Reddy workers about their rights, protecting them from deportation, holding an education and discussion forum for the South Asian community on the multiple issues raised in the case, and shifting the media coverage from blaming culture for Lakireddy Bali Reddy's behavior to recognizing the global forces at play. We envisioned ASATA as working to deepen the progressive sector of the South Asian community and engaging in campaigns to change South Asian perspectives, attitudes, and beliefs around issues of race, gender, class, caste, violence, and immigration.

While frantically responding to the media and other activists, we worked to develop organizational structure and value statements. We defined a mission for the organization: "The Alliance of South Asians Taking Action (ASATA) works to educate, organize, and empower the Bay Area South Asian communities to end violence, oppression, racism and exploitation within and against our diverse communities" (ASATA 2000b). We worked in small groups to develop political position papers on issues of trafficking of women and girls; immigration and the INS; labor exploitation in the context of poverty; race relations and cultural understandings between South Asians and the U.S. mainstream; and casteism, classism, racism, and sexism in the South Asian community.

Ours was an interesting collection of people; mostly 1.5 and second generation Indians, with a few folks from Sri Lanka and Pakistan along with some mixed-heritage people from the diaspora. Our ages ranged from early twenties to mid-thirties, and the group size fluctuated between ten and thirty people attending any given meeting. There were students, nonprofit workers, environmentalists, lawyers, teachers, and corporate employees. A few of us had some previous activist histories of organizing and political education, but for most of the members this was their first experience with political activism. Interestingly, in the initial organizing meeting, several South Asian men came. However, by the fourth meeting, most of them had dropped out. When pressed about why they were no longer participating, some said that they felt ASATA was a woman's space and wanted to respect that. They supported our work by providing meeting space and some financial support, but for the most part they abstained and/or cheered from the sidelines.

The diversity of our group's experiences was our biggest challenge. While we developed this amazing list of goals for our work, in no way did we share a common understanding of the issues involved or strategies for change. While we spoke the same words of "sex and labor exploitation, trafficking, racism, and casteism," we had very different analyses of the sources of problems and solutions. This gap became apparent only after we started discussing the position papers. There were those who believed that Reddy was an anomaly and a "bad man who did bad things" and others who saw him as the result of global systems of inequality and exploitation.

The most painful part of these political educational debates was that they were occurring in the context of extreme urgency to act and respond. We were constantly confronted with several different challenges. First, there were the constant demands of the case. We were getting numerous calls from the media for comments and background stories. Given the extensive national and international coverage, journalists were on the lookout for new and interesting angles. We were in regular contact with them, trying to give the story a broader context and an alternative frame, other than a cultural explanation or a demonization of Reddy. Where the media framed it as a case of immigration fraud and sex scandal, we tried to (re)frame it in the context of labor and sex trafficking; immigration flows; cultural stereotypes; the transnational migration of people, culture, and resources; labor exploitation in the context of poverty; race relations and cultural understandings between South Asians and the U.S. mainstream; and issues of casteism, classism, racism, and sexism in the South Asian community. In addition, we had decided to organize a South Asian presence at all the court hearings. We wanted to ensure that there would be a visible presence in support of the young women and the workers. We also wanted to circulate a public and political statement that as a community, we did not condone Reddy's behavior. We recruited people to attend the court hearings and trained ourselves to be media spokespeople with clear messages.

Some ASATA members, in collaboration with the Asian Law Caucus's Worker Outreach Project, did door-to-door outreach in the neighborhood of the Pasand restaurants. They tried to make contact with other Reddy workers. We hoped to create enough safety and resources to encourage other workers to come forward, if they had not already been sent back to India.

In the midst of these external activities, ASATA members were also struggling to build an organization and set its direction. We worked to establish a decision-making structure, recruit and follow-up with new members, diversify the membership base, and debate the political analysis and strategy for handling this particular case. Two strategy issues that were deliberated over a sustained period were whether to build a campaign to picket and boycott the Pasand restaurant in Berkeley, and how to balance the simplistic demonization and criminalization of Reddy with a nuanced interpretation of the case and condemnation of his behavior. A group of white feminists headed by Diana Russell called for a boycott and picketing of Pasand restaurants. We debated the merits of a boycott and picket in light of trying to create the conditions for other workers to come forward. Furthermore, while we denounced Reddy's behavior, we were not comfortable with the framing and demonization of Reddy as a murderer and sex-slaver. We also pondered the impact the label "sex slave" would have on the women involved in the case.

Perhaps one of the biggest challenges we faced in formulating our strategies was the lack of accurate information about what was going on in the legal case. Both Narika and Maitri were bound by confidentiality and legal liability for the criminal and civil cases that were going to be brought against Lakireddy Bali Reddy. And since we had no access to the young women, we spent a lot of time debating what they could need and want.

Internally, we were constantly discussing where to put our attention; should we focus on trying to change the South Asian community, change the framing of the issue with the mainstream media, downplay the scandal, highlight Reddy as a bad man, use direct action strategies, educational forums, or media campaigns? We struggled to fathom our relationship with the mainstream South Asian and American communities. We were passionately and determinedly engaged with many unresolved questions, organization building requirements, options, and strategies.

We went through a few issue identification processes and brought in outside consultants and allies to help us define our strategies and demands. In one memorable meeting, an experienced racial justice organizer took us through a campaign identification process, whereby at the end of the meeting we were contemplating a campaign to get Berkeley businesses, and particularly South Asian businesses, to sign on to a statement of ethical business practices. However, on deeper thought we remembered that we wanted to work with the South Asian community, not just the Berkeley business community.

Ultimately, while we were not able to figure out a clear organizing campaign, we were successful on several fronts. We created a visible and organized South Asian progressive voice and managed to complicate the media portrayal of Reddy and the South Asian community. We were able to reframe the case from immigration fraud, bad guys, and sex scandals to complex transnational flows of labor and sexual exploitation.

Concluding Remarks

At the end of the Reddy case, we are left with the following outcomes: Reddy and his family members are now serving between ninety-seven months in prison and twelve months under home arrest; they have paid out more than $11 million in restitution; although nine victims were identified, only four women received permanent residency in the United States and two of them have their families with them for safety; Sitha's sister, Lalitha, was awarded millions in the wrongful death civil case; there is increased awareness of the issues of violence, exploitation, and trafficking in the South Asian community; Narika and Maitri have increased their capacity to respond to violence against South Asian women in the United States, particularly in cases of sex and labor trafficking; and the San Francisco Bay Area has a progressive South Asian voice and organization that is stable enough to mobilize rapidly and efficiently against injustices such as the racial profiling and hate crimes against South Asians that shook the community in the wake of 9/11.

Ultimately, South Asian domestic violence service organizations and South Asian community activists complemented each other to meet the needs of individuals violated and exploited, and to express community concerns. Moreover, they worked to increase community awareness of the dangers and injustices of the underside to the transnational flow of people, economic and political forces, and culture.

However, the troubling question of transnational justice remains open. While the Reddy family was punished, and one hopes deterred from engaging in such exploitative activities in the future, the transnational trafficking, violation, and exploitation of women, men, and children continues unabated. According to the U.S. Department of Justice, at least 700,000 people are trafficked within and across international borders, with approximately 50,000 women and children annually trafficked into the United States (U.S. Department of Justice 2001). How do we as activists and service providers, operating in transnational communities, develop responsive and proactive strategies to intervene in such flows of people, cultures and relationships, and the political, economic and social forces of globalization and capitalism?

In the Reddy case, when the exploitation became public, South Asian women were successful in assisting the victims and organizing a South Asian voice of resistance. We provided effective representation and permanent legal status for the victimized young women and helped them to be free of financial hardship. We built a new organization and reframed the media portrayal and public understanding of the case. Given the inordinate complexities of the case, the collision between the local and global, the nexus of violence, gender, race, class, caste, immigration, and ethnicity, these certainly are major successes.

And yet there is a lingering sense of dissatisfaction. Could we have dreamed of more and fought for more? Could we have worked to have some of Reddy's millions go toward building community capacity to prevent and respond to trafficking? Could South Asian community members been held more accountable for turning a blind eye to Reddy's behavior? In this rapidly globalizing world, how do we understand and engage with transnational political forces that play a central role in nations' migratory flows? How do we not let such knotty problems wash over us and rip through our communities?

While this particular case of transnational labor and sexual exploitation has met its legal end, it leaves many open wounds in the women, workers, Reddy family members, and the South Asian community. The South Asian community has lost a particular innocence as model minorities in the United States, and we now know how deeply implicated we are in the dark underside of the forces of globalization. And as activists we are left with challenging questions—what would transnational justice look like in similar cases and how can we work more effectively to achieve it?

18

From Dhaka to Cincinnati

Tracing the Trajectory of a Transnational Violence against Women Campaign

ELORA HALIM CHOWDHURY

In September 2000, I received a phone call from Bina inviting me to an event honoring television journalist Connie Chung and her ABC 20/20 team for the Amnesty International Media Spotlight Award.[1] Chung and her team were receiving this award for the report "Faces of Hope," which had aired nationally in the United States in November 1999 and featured the experiences of two young Bangladeshi women, Bina Akhter and Jharna Akhter. The event was hosted by ABC producers and would take place at the Yale Club in New York. A number of Bina's friends had been invited. "It would be my pleasure," I told Bina, "to see my old friend, and to witness such a momentous occasion honoring her story." Bina and Jharna (no relation to each other) would be flying in from Cincinnati, Ohio, where they lived with their American host family.

"Faces of Hope" had reported on a growing epidemic of acid attack on women in Bangladesh. It informed the American prime-time viewers that the incidence of acid throwing had become highly prevalent among lower socioeconomic groups in both Bangladeshi urban and rural areas. The reporters also noted that the perpetrators were mostly young men and adolescent boys, whereas the targets were primarily females between twelve and twenty-five years of age. While this profile of targets and perpetrators was accurate in the late 1990s when ABC produced its report, in early 2000 there had been a dramatic change. By 2003, acid throwers of both genders were attacking women, children, and even men. Nonetheless, in the late 1990s as well as 2003, females were overwhelmingly the victims of acid throwing, attacked for reasons ranging from rejection of sexual advances, refusal of marriage proposals, family or land disputes, vengeance, and unmet dowry demands (UNICEF 2000).

"Faces of Hope" had an angle expected to give it immediacy for the American viewers. The 20/20 report focused, in particular, on the compelling story of a courageous young girl, Bina Akhter, whose strength and tenacity facing unimaginable trauma left the television audience stupefied. The story also peripherally focused on Jharna Akhter, another young girl who had acid thrown at her face. Connie Chung's visit to Bangladesh preceded only by a few days Bina's and Jharna's coming to America, sponsored by a U.S.-based organization called Healing the Children. It had arranged for the Shriner's Hospital in Cincinnati to donate surgery for the seventeen- and fourteen-year-old acid violence survivors. The narrative culminated in the momentous journey from Dhaka to Cincinnati, leaving its intended American viewers with the promise that the girls, extricated from the oppressive lives in Bangladesh, were being transported to good hands and on their way to recovery.

I arrived at the Yale Club promptly at 2 P.M. The plush interior and leather sofas were in stark contrast to the surroundings and circumstances in which we, Bina and I, had met last. Bina was a strong, vocal leader in the campaign against acid violence in Bangladesh. When I had last seen Bina in 1998—then fifteen—in Dhaka, she was helping to create a network of female survivors of acid attacks, women's rights advocates, local journalists, doctors, lawyers, and even members of the Bangladeshi government. Two years later, following her medical treatment and residence in Cincinnati and the showing of the 20/20 report, Bina held center stage in New York in a gathering of Western philanthropists, international journalists, and human rights actors. Amid the Yale Club's plushness, Bina alone represented, very skillfully, a cause that had always been hers, but now with a slightly different twist and for a different set of actors and audience. Indeed, she alone was presented to this room of New York influentials as the spokesperson of an *issue* that had a complicated genealogy involving the efforts of manifold collaborations and institutions that spanned the divides of time, geography, and history.

Several speeches were made during the course of the afternoon. In her speech, Bina profusely thanked, first, ABC Television for drawing the attention of the international audience to such a crime against humanity; second, Healing the Children for sponsoring her and Jharna in their road to a new life; third, Shriner's Hospital for nursing them back toward a healthy existence; and, finally, the development workers and the journalists for their humanitarian work. She assured her listeners that the combination of efforts of everyone in the room had truly changed her life. Bina was the quintessential grateful recipient of her patrons' benevolence.

I left the Yale Club that afternoon with mixed feelings. It is true that I was happy for Bina and Jharna, who had been sponsored by international agencies and voluntary organizations to undergo reconstructive surgery in a reputable burns hospital in the United States. Particularly in the context where medical and reconstructive treatment for victims of acid attacks in Bangladesh was still inadequate, despite increasing activist work to develop such services. I was in awe of the strength demonstrated by two teenaged girls who had left their families and everything familiar in search of restoring some semblance of normalcy to their physical and emotional well-being. At the same time, however, I was disappointed in the tone of the events of that afternoon, which advanced a too simple, too self-congratulating progress narrative crafted by the sponsoring institutions.

For these institutions were supporting Bina's and Jharna's recoveries in a way that was yet erasing another crucial element of the struggles to reconstruct their lives. That element was the anti-acid violence campaign mobilized in the mid 1990s primarily by Naripokkho, a women's advocacy group in Bangladesh. It was the efforts of this group that had created both the conceptual and organizational groundwork for placing acid violence against women and girls in Bangladesh into the global landscape of gendered human rights violation and, concurrently, had mobilized attention of both national and international actors.

Even as I left the Yale Club that September afternoon, it did not seem accidental to me that this event was being held not at a Bangladeshi women's center in Dhaka, but at the exclusive club of an elite U.S. university. The choice of location for the celebration of two young Bangladeshi women's courage, the hosting of it by a powerful Western television corporation, the choosing by a Western-based human rights group, Amnesty, of a U.S. media corporation for an award seemed to reinscribe imperialist rescue narratives.

According to feminist legal scholar Mutua (2001), the Western human rights discourse, which shapes rights-based development programs, is "marked by a damning metaphor" pitting "savages" against their "saviors" and "victims." She states:

> The predominant image of the savage in the human rights discourse is that of a Third World, non-European state, cultural practice or person. The second dimension of the prism depicts the face and the fact of a victim as well as the essence and the idea of victimhood. That is, a human being whose "dignity and worth" have been violated by the savage is the victim. Many are women and children twice victimized because of their gender and age, and sometimes the victim of the savage culture is the female gender itself. The third dimension of the prism is the savior or the redeemer, the "good angel who protects, vindicates, civilizes, restrains, and safeguards." (202–203)

The savior promises freedom from the tyrannies of the state, tradition, and culture. In the human rights story, the savior is the human rights corpus itself, with the United Nations, Western governments, international nongovernmental organizations (INGOs), and Western charities as the actual rescuers, redeemers of a benighted world. Mutua posits that in reality the institutions are merely fronts. The savior is ultimately "a set of culturally based norms and practices that inhere in liberal thought and philosophy" (Mutua 2001, 203). Together, the three dimensions of the triangularized metaphor maintain the human rights corpus.

This metaphor continues to infuse the doctrines of powerful first world based institutions that profess to do humanitarian work in third world nations. Hence, Mutua's three-sided metaphoric narrative helps us understand the discourse of human rights as a space for the systematic creation of concepts, theories, and practices that reinscribe inequalities even after the dismantling of formal domination with the end of colonial rule. That is, human rights discourse even as it claims to protect the rights of the oppressed has simultaneously served to natu-ralize the control of the "savage" or the "underdeveloped" world by the West after the so-called demise of formal colonial rule.

Meghna Guhathakurta (1994) states that the issue of gender discrimination and exploitation in Bangladesh has been initiated through and featured more in the developmental discourse rather than in mainstream politics. In Bangladesh, where the development budget is largely dependent on foreign aid, it is natural to expect that much of the discourse on women and development will be donor ori-ented. That is, such discourses and projects will be couched in neoliberal economic policies, modernization, and integration of the underdeveloped (Lind and Share 2003). Some of the demands for social transformation, however, also stem from women themselves, whether through mass based national movements or parallel and autonomous women's movements expressed through small local NGOs.

While ABC News, Healing the Children, Shriner's Hospital, and UNICEF had contributed immensely to help Bina and Jharna receive medical treatment in the United States, there were critical "others" whose names and efforts went unmen-tioned that afternoon at the Yale Club and who, in fact, had enabled the better known, better financed, better connected institutions to make critical interven-tions in supporting survivors of acid violence in Bangladesh. The compelling story of Bina had another side that involved actors who had built an international cam-paign against gendered violence in Bangladesh. Without that story, Bina's would remain incomplete.

The story is of contesting narratives of the anti-acid violence campaign in Bangladesh from 1995 to 2003. Today, the achievements of the campaign against acid violence in Bangladesh are measured by the creation of an independent coor-dinating service providing body called the Acid Survivors Foundation (ASF), estab-lished in 1999 and financed by an international donor agency, UNICEF-Bangladesh. I contend that by ignoring the complex genealogy of the anti-acid violence cam-paign, the dominant narrative presented by ASF, UNICEF-Bangladesh, INGOs based in the United States, and the international media such as *20/20*, erased the contri-butions of the Bangladeshi women activists, including Bina herself, whose ground-breaking work made the campaign possible and eventually successful. Thus, this chapter is a story that makes central and visible those women activists who launched the acid campaign in the mid 1990s, yet whose contributions by 2003 were forgotten by powerful institutions benefiting from the activists' work.

Naripokkho Launches the Acid Campaign

Naripokkho (literally meaning pro-women), founded in 1983 in Dhaka, is a membership-based women's activist organization in Bangladesh. Naripokkho's work is clustered under four themes: violence against women and human rights; reproductive rights and women's health; gender issues in environment and devel-opment; and representation of women in media and cultural politics.

Naripokkho embarked on its work on acid violence against women and girls in August 1995. Although no systematic study or records documenting incidents of acid throwing on women and girls in Bangladesh existed at the time, media recorded this violence since the early 1980s. Naripokkho's investigator, Bristi Chowdhury, believed that as early as the 1980s, with the growth of the auto-mechanic industry, which used car battery acid, the weapon of choice became easily obtainable by the public. However, increase in gendered violence in recent decades must be understood in the context of socioeconomic, political, and cultural changes in Bangladesh.

Since independence, Bangladesh has witnessed economic devastation, rising landlessness and unemployment, rural to urban migration, and transitioning from an agrarian to monetized economy. These shifts have affected the rural and urban poor, particularly women, as they have had to diversify their livelihoods in search of work. Governmental, nongovernmental, and international aid agencies have intervened by promoting income-generating programs that have tried to integrate women. International financial institutions have implemented economic liberalization programs and export-oriented manufacturing—namely, the garments industry. Increasing feminization of labor has occurred because of these changing socioeconomic dynamics, albeit in the absence of structural change in the asymmetrical gender relations in Bangladesh (Feldman 1998; Kabeer 2000; Rozario 1998). In particular, young women transgressing social norms of female seclusion, disrupting the gendered social order, and occupying a more visible presence have been targets of male violence in the home and outside. Naripokkho's work in the mid 1990s focused specifically on acid throwing as a gendered crime within the larger context of women's oppression, whereby men attempting to put young women in their place punished those who dared to say "no."

Looking back at Naripokkho's strategic planning phase in 1996 and reassessing their work, Bristi Chowdhury explained in an interview, "Acid violence was not yet a buzzword. Nobody had drawn serious attention to it. It was overlooked in the national and international arena. It was not as huge as dowry killings or honor killings, which are commonly cited as 'barbaric southern practices' by foreign donors and the media. Acid violence was not attention grabbing, nor fund grabbing. The discourse had not been created yet to make it so."

So, for Naripokkho members to turn any occurrences of violence against women into an issue required not just national media coverage but also outside donors' recognition that would eventually generate funds for necessary programs. Thus, it was a strategic goal on the part of Naripokkho to help in the creation of a discourse on acid violence that would put the issue on the national and international map. In the mid 1990s, Bristi Chowdhury developed a log of acid attacks by visiting various libraries, NGOs, hospitals, and police stations and recording information that appeared in newspapers. This gave Naripokkho activists an inkling of why, when, and how acid attacks were taking place. Simultaneously, with other Naripokkho staff, Bristi Chowdhury visited the burns unit of Dhaka Medical College Hospital (DMCH) regularly and provided emotional support and friendship to the young girls being treated there who were victims of acid attacks. Bristi Chowdhury's careful documentation allowed Naripokkho to demonstrate that acid throwing was not random; rather, it had a pattern and a set of causes. Showing this pattern and proposing the causes enabled the group to argue that acid throwing should be seen as a concern of public importance.

According to feminist scholar Chandra Talpade Mohanty (2003), UN conferences on women such as the one in Beijing in 1995 shifted earlier discourses of "sisterhood is global" to the "human rights" arena in the mid 1990s. This shift has marked the "mainstreaming of the feminist movement," successfully foregrounding issues of violence against women on the world stage (Mohanty 2003, 249). Some feminist scholars have attributed the 1990s as the period in which the culmination of UN summits provided women's movements and their representatives from the North and the South, an active transnational platform to craft and influence development policies attentive to gender discrimination (Alvarez 2000; Basu 2000; Molyneux and Razavi 2002). Naripokkho, a women's advocacy group, framed their own organizational work on violence against women in Bangladesh within the mandate of an international platform and thus hoped to leverage this issue onto the stage of international women's rights and affect policy changes in the home front.

Naripokkho activists' work in transforming the occurrences of acid violence into an issue had several objectives. First, as part of the organization's larger work on violence against women, they undertook a research study investigating newspaper reports as well as records from NGOs, government documents, hospitals, and police stations. The objectives of the study were to identify the service gaps in addressing survivors and victims of violence and their coping strategies. Naripokkho networked with 250 local women's organizations and intended to collectively analyze and respond to cases of violence nationwide. Their research indicated that since 1983 eighty cases of acid violence on women had been reported (Violence Logbook 1996). Nasreen Huq, coordinator of the acid violence work at Naripokkho said, "The focus on acid burns is part of an overall campaign on violence against women, which draws on the government's mandate to address specific forms of violence articulated in the 1995 UN Beijing Conference on Women and the Program of Action of the International Conference on Population and Development (ICPD) in 1994."

Second, the specific work on acid violence was undertaken by a smaller group of Naripokkho staff members who visited the survivors of acid violence, mainly young women and girls, regularly, provided them with emotional support, and assisted them in legal and medical matters. Third, the group tried to raise social awareness around violence against women by promoting an understanding of the root cause of such violence. The slow but gradual mobilization of journalists, members of the government, DMCH staff, and local police accomplished this.

Eventually, in 1997, Naripokkho activists, armed with the information gathered in the previous two years, organized a three-day workshop that brought

together a group of teenaged survivors of acid violence to highlight the phenomenon and bring it to the attention of government, medical professionals, law enforcement agencies, donor community, activists, and journalists. The workshop generated
much interest and support from national and international groups. Private donors
offered support, and various international print and television media published
feature stories on acid throwing in Bangladesh. Due to the increasing international awareness, medical teams from India, Spain, and Italy offered to donate free
reconstructive surgery as well as participate in projects to train local medical staff
in caring for acid burnt patients. Bina Akhter, an acid violence survivor, was hired
by Naripokkho to continue the research and networking. Several years later, Bristi
Chowdhury noted in an interview, "Bina was brilliant at this work." Within a few
months, Bina had contacted over forty survivors around the country, often visiting
them in their hometowns. She connected with journalists, heads of organizations,
philanthropists, and even gave interviews in leading daily newspapers and TV
programs. The campaign took on a life of its own.

The 1997 workshop achieved its goals. However, the success led to the diversification of participants in the campaign, and as a result Naripokkho's involvement
began to change. In 2003, Nasreen Huq stated, "We wanted to maintain the energy
generated at the workshop and build on it. The network of survivors incepted at
the workshop had to be developed further so that there would not be a vacuum
when Bina left. There had to be continuity because we knew that there would be
others [survivors of acid violence and potential leaders]." Huq continued on Bina's
performance as leader of the survivors' network, "She was critically involved. Bina
handled the press, she developed a wide network; she did so much work. In her, we
saw the whole spectrum unfold—from victim to survivor to activist. This was what
we had dreamed of—the transformation." The following summer, Bina Akhter won
the UNICEF Young Leader Award to attend the Amnesty International Youth Forum
in New York.

The April 1997 workshop was significant because for the first time Bangladeshi
civil servants and several international organizations' staff came face to face with,
and listened to, young Bangladeshi girls and women who had survived acid throwing, and their families. The Naripokkho activists had broken through an existing
wall of official denial and trivialization of the problem. This breakthrough initiated
acid-violence against women in Bangladesh as an issue that needed instant and systematic attention from the state, media, donors, and the medico-legal establishments. The campaign coordinators believed it was important for those girls and
women who had experienced the violence to be at the forefront of shaping the
movement. This philosophy motivated Naripokkho's decision to hire Bina Akhter,
Nurun Nahar, and Nargis Begum to continue developing a nationwide network with
other survivors by visiting them at DMCH and in their homes, as well as encouraging survivors to speak in public.

The workshop also allowed survivors to share experiences with one another,
which enabled recognition of their experiences as political and transformative

(de Lauretis 1986). Such visibility is particularly important in cases of acid violence because it challenges the motivation behind the crime, which is to force women into isolation and end their social lives (Del Franco 1999). Naripokkho was a catalyst in the process of building a critical consciousness among the survivors and encouraged many to become part of the campaign and even take on leadership roles.

The second stage of the acid campaign emerged upon the official entrance of various actors such as the medico-legal establishments, the state, and UNICEF-Bangladesh. A combination of Naripokkho's successful efforts in exposing and launching acid violence as a national and international issue, as well as the UN headquarters' decision to act upon what by the late 1990s was perceived by an international audience as an assault on women's human rights, set in motion the activities toward creating the Acid Survivors Foundation (ASF) by UNICEF-Bangladesh. Undoubtedly, Naripokkho strategically mobilized international actors to leverage the acid campaign onto the international discourse on gender violence, leading to the creation of ASF. However, the choices that the newly engaged actors made were often contradictory to those of the local women's groups as well as ground realities. For example, unlike Naripokkho's survivor-centered program, the UNICEF-funded ASF focused on "rehabilitating and reintegrating" victims of violence into society. Although the alliance with UNICEF broadened the scope of the campaign and opened up access to resources previously out of reach of the survivors, it led to the loss of Naripokkho's critical role in shaping a survivor-centered campaign with a vision of structural change.

Bina Goes to America

One direct consequence of internationalizing the anti-acid violence campaign was "Faces of Hope." Various Western publications such as *Ms.* (1999) and *Marie-Claire* (1998) and TV networks and programs such as CNN (1999), BBC (1999), and the *Oprah Winfrey Show* (1999) had already reported on acid violence in Bangladesh. Thus, "Faces of Hope" held the promise of generating further attention of an international community.

Connie Chung's trip preceded Bina and Jharna's departure for the United States for medical treatment, ultimately influencing the angle of her report to be spun as a "story of arrival." Chung's opening remarks were conscientious in reminding the viewers that the report in no way implied that acid throwing was a cultural practice of Bangladesh, nor was it an Islamic tradition. The escalating phenomenon was described as one of revenge committed by spurned suitors and was common among the poor. Bina was introduced as a brave young woman living a desperate life in one of the world's poorest nations, who awaited the help of American surgeons to reclaim her shattered life. Said the voice of the savior, John Morrison, a British expatriate philanthropist who was appointed by UNICEF as director of the Acid Survivors Foundation at its inception, "This is one of the most barbaric acts there can possibly be. What it does is not only disfigure a woman for life, but it also ruins her life" (Whitcraft 1999).

In 2002, the "Foreign Relations" desk of the *Daily Star* ran a press release on behalf of the British High Commission on John Morrison's anointment as Officer of the Order of the British Empire (OBE) by Queen Elizabeth II on the occasion of the "Birthday Honors" in her Golden Jubilee year. The press release reported that Morrison "was the motive power that brought together various Bangladeshi organizations to provide help and assistance for those injured and disfigured by acid violence" and that it was because of "his efforts, the Acid Survivors Foundation was established" (*Daily Star* 2002). The article affirmed ASF as having "a high domestic and international profile," where Bangladesh nationals work "ceaselessly under the direction of Dr. Morrison." True to this heroic representation, Morrison asserted in the "Faces of Hope" report the need for urgent action and was seen at work with top executives from fifteen national and international nonprofit organizations.

In the report, Chung continued to trace the events of Bina Akhter's life and arrived at the moment of providence, or the beginning of Bina's journey to Cincinnati, where laid the promise of American surgeons repairing her ravaged face. Healing the Children, an international NGO, organized for Bina Akhter and Jharna Akhter to be treated at Shriner's Hospital and to reside with a foster family in Cincinnati, Ohio. Chung's crew accompanied the two teenagers through tearful goodbyes at Dhaka International Airports on their way to "a new home, a new family, and perhaps a new face." So, the story of arrival unfolded, "Thanks to the generosity of so many Americans, Bina is about to taste a life she never imagined," said Jack Ford, Chung's co-anchor. An announcer's voice stated, "A journey to America brings new hope" (Whitcraft 1999).

From the one-room hut in Hazaribag, Dhaka, shared by seven family members, Bina arrived at her new home, likened to a palace by Chung, that raised "her hopes higher than they've ever been" (Whitcraft 1999). Viewers watched Bina accompany her host family to the sights of Cincinnati and the quintessential American experience of a Cincinnati Reds game. Bina apparently "was happier than she'd ever been" (Whitcraft 1999).

Bina even faced the news of her irrevocably damaged eye with grace and heroism. She was ready to face anything, free as she was finally from the repression of her past. "As long as I'm here for the treatment, I'll be safe," she said. "If I were still in Bangladesh, I might have been kidnapped or killed by now." Chung's voiceover said, "For the first time in a long time, she wasn't afraid." We watched "Windy," Bina's nickname among friends in Bangladesh for her athletic talents, running in slow motion on screen and her voice of hope saying, "America is a big country. If we all work together and stand as one, we can conquer the world" (Whitcraft 1999).

"Faces of Hope" imagined Bina as a grateful recipient of aid and as a good victim. It indicated an inability to understand the lived realities of her situation or to understand her as a complex subject who participated in the negotiations that brought her to Cincinnati. The program gave wide exposure to a critical campaign and reproduced colonial images of victimized third world women being rescued by benevolent first world institutions, reinscribing the historically asymmetrical relations of ruling that frame such representations. What the story failed to reflect and resonate with were the lived realities of the so-called beneficiary of first world benevolence. Bina's own role in shaping her future was obscured, as was the role of the advocacy work done by Naripokkho members.

We knew that Bina Akhter had declined an offer of going to Spain because she had not felt ready. The decision to accept Shriner's Hospital's invitation was, thus, well thought out and not a sudden stroke of sheer luck. The terms of Bina's arrival, stay, and treatment were also carefully dictated by the sponsors and the hosts and were not altogether rosy, as Chung would have the audience believe. The fiery Bina Akhter, who spoke out against women's oppression, demanded justice from the government and delivered impassioned speeches at women's rallies, was reduced to a childlike figure bedazzled by America.

Bina Spins Her Own Narratives

In 2000, Bina Akhter applied for political asylum status in the United States, defying the terms of her contract with Healing the Children, the sponsoring aid organization. Consequently, she was no longer able to maintain her previous working relationships with Healing the Children and Naripokkho. Bina and Jharna moved in with a Bangladeshi expatriate family in Cincinnati. Although Healing the Children abandoned the sponsorship of the two girls and tried to return them to Bangladesh, truncating their medical treatment, the doctors at Shriner's Hospital continued to care for them pro bono. It was understood that by staying Bina would jeopardize chances of any other acid survivor to come to America for medical treatment; be responsible for Naripokkho's loss of face in the national and international advocacy communities; and betray the trust of the international community, which had come forth with assistance. Furthermore, in Bina's absence, a trial could not be held to prosecute her attacker, Dano, in Bangladesh, which Naripokkho believed to be a serious setback in the acid campaign.[2] Because Bina's story had received media coverage nationally and internationally, this trial would have been particularly significant for the larger campaign. On her eighteenth birthday, Bina Akhter moved into her own apartment as she attended high school diploma coursework by night and a nursing assistant program by day. This new location was important for her because she no longer felt obligated to attend Bible study and other religious education courses in which her host family demanded her participation in exchange for room and board.

It was a lonely life in Cincinnati, yet Bina Akhter believed that she could contribute to the campaign against acid violence in Bangladesh from the United States. She had begun touring the country, giving presentations on violence against women in Bangladesh, her own experiences, and girls' education programs in Bangladesh. Bina Akhter had a star quality about her—the ability to draw crowds, to stir emotions, and to question people about their own assumptions and beliefs. The same characteristics that had made her the leader of the acid survivors' network in Naripokkho now brought her international fame. Nasreen Huq had said as much during an interview, "Bina gave the acid campaign its stature, she was the star. In turn, her time in Naripokkho contributed to her growth as a feminist."

Incidentally, the establishment of Acid Survivors Foundation (ASF) as a consolidated body in 1999 coincided with the dissolution of Naripokkho's direct involvement with the acid campaign. Simultaneously, several key activists who had led the anti-acid violence campaign left Naripokkho to pursue other interests. Weaving together these seemingly disparate events, the establishment of ASF, the departure of key campaign activists from Naripokkho, and Bina's decision to reside in the United States, helps us better understand the current trajectory of the anti-acid violence campaign in Bangladesh.

The ASF was set up in 1999 with joint funding from UNICEF and the Canadian International Development Agency (CIDA). This was when Bina and Jharna, among the first of a list of twenty acid survivors, made their way to Cincinnati for medical treatment. With Bina's departure, Naripokkho had lost a full-time intern to continue the nationwide networking of acid survivors. Nurun Nahar, another survivor, had taken on that position; but as a full-time student, she was not able to keep up with the volume of work. Nasreen Huq, who until the establishment of ASF had been coordinating Naripokkho's acid campaign, took on the role of board member at the newly founded ASF.

A member of Naripokkho, Khan (a pseudonym) had organized a pipeline of twenty survivors to receive medical treatment at the Shriner's Hospital in Ohio. She had been instrumental in mobilizing Bangladeshi medical professionals in the United States, who had in turn set up a sponsorship program with Healing the Children. Bina Akhter's decision to seek asylum, which jeopardized the pipeline of survivors set to come to the United States, upset her relationship with Naripokkho.

Naripokkho's virtual withdrawal from the work that it initiated is not unprecedented in regards to intraorganizational dynamics in women's advocacy groups. For instance, Honor Ford-Smith (1997), a member of the Sistren Collective, an organization in Jamaica that worked with women both culturally and politically, describes the crossroads that members of well-intentioned women's groups often encounter. Despite goals to work in the interest of social justice, women's groups can reenact historically determined power relations in new forms. Colonial narratives unwittingly regulate the production of the development worker in the image of the missionary.

Although ostensibly advancing gender justice and seemingly adapting democratic practices, Naripokkho had its own hierarchical and class structure regulating the organization. Smith argues, "A language is needed that will help to analyze and address the contradiction between the emancipatory goals of groups and their internal practice, between their interest in transforming social relations toward liberatory power relations and the tense, conflicted organizational culture of many women's groups" (216). There is need for language that can address the complexity of the lived crises and often unspoken causes behind conflicts that shape complicity and resistance in feminist spaces.

Furthermore, Ford-Smith (1997) discusses the contradictions of funding that often dictate the development of women's organizations and how those can consequently affect the group's democratic practices. The insistence on delivering products, which are measured in technical terms, and the perennial search for the grassroots women by funding agencies, contribute to a cycle of eternal dependency. For instance, to be able to expand and to function efficiently within a globalized environment, organizations need to attract members with a certain level of skill and consciousness and provide its grassroots members with the resources to acquire such formal training. However, acquiring those skills would automatically mean that they were no longer eligible for grassroots funding. Such is the catch-22 situation for many women's groups. Thus, a hierarchy inevitably surfaces between those group members with the desirable skills (e.g., connections, efficiency in English, Western-educated, etc.) and those without.

This scenario is recognizable in the dissolution of Naripokkho's involvement in acid work, which I contend occurred not simply because of the emergence of ASF but rather because of a combination of interconnected events. Bina Akhter, the so-called grassroots beneficiary and activist, had provided currency to the organization and helped bring unprecedented national and international support. When she had ceased to be grassroots, she also lost the nurturing relationships with her sponsors, Healing the Children (and by association ASF, CIDA, and UNICEF), who had found the measurable product of their work in Bina, and her mentors in Naripokkho, who had found in her the poster child of their campaign. Bina's defection only served to quicken the disintegration of Naripokkho's involvement, as internal conflicts were already under way. The acid campaign had been designed by a small group of activists who had gradually gained the support of many key institutions. Just as the Naripokkho campaign gained its legitimacy because of a few, if influential, actors, the organization's role also disintegrated because of the withdrawal of the same few. Those are the risks of campaigns that are not mass-based but rather instigated by few committed members of society.

This problem is not singular to Naripokkho. Honor Ford-Smith (1997) asserts that women's groups often act on ad hoc strategies due to external pressures. She argues that the dictates of international funding agencies exacerbate internal contradictions around structures of race and class, specifically on issues having to do with power and authority. Consequently, the organization can become constrained in terms of what it offers the community, its capacity to develop clear and effective organizational support, and its ability to satisfy members' needs.

While the acid campaign can be defined as successful because of the emergence of ASF's coordinated efforts, it lost one of its critical characteristics: the involvement of Naripokkho. This, perhaps, was inevitable once the proliferation of discourses and diversification of actors were under way. The benefits of the proliferation in discourse had led people like Khan to successfully organize a pipeline of survivors to receive medical treatment in a Western country, but it had limited the same opportunities, which backfired—a transnationalism reversed (Friedman 1999). Significant in this equation is who had the privilege to abdicate. When asked why the organization had discontinued its work against acid violence, Khan stated, "The campaign just got too big. Naripokkho works on a volunteer basis, they don't have the time or the resources for work of that scale. Naripokkho can raise awareness; it can work as an activist organization. It couldn't provide all the services that the survivors needed. We are more equipped to do the research work. Besides, ASF is doing it now. We didn't want that level of involvement." According to Bristi Chowdhury,

> I think the way we first launched the campaign could have been better orchestrated. We got ahead of ourselves. We should have done more research. Second, and this is connected to the first, we could have avoided an ASF. Instead, we should have gotten involved with other women's organizations. We tried, but in-politics both within our own organization and amongst various women's organizations kept us from it. Third, Naripokkho's Executive Committee could have been in the know from the beginning. We didn't have clear goals and we kept changing our plans and strategies. Most of the time, Nasreen and I made the decisions according to the needs of the moment. So, much of the blame also fell on us when things went wrong.

Her reflections had turned to Bina as a vital part of the equation: "I believe it was a mistake to choose Bina as the Naripokkho intern. We should have groomed someone else. We knew from the outset that she was a star. But, she was also a child. Nonetheless, Bina also did a lot of good work for Naripokkho. She brought a lot of glory to the organization. And, it's better that she tells her story than John Morrison [ASF's first director who was a British national], who goes around representing barbaric brown practices. If Bina had stayed on track, if she had come back to Bangladesh, she could have become the director of ASF one day."

But, why couldn't Bina speak from her own perspective? We hardly ever questioned the authenticity of the knowledge of middle-class feminists who wrote about the plight of their downtrodden sisters. Why was Bina held to a double standard? Bristi Chowdhury berated the donor community for hijacking the acid campaign and undermining the work of the local women's advocacy group. She believed that Naripokkho's work reflected a truly organic approach where Bangladeshi women worked with Bangladeshi women and the survivors of acid violence worked to help themselves. Simultaneously, she believed that Bina, the star of the home-grown campaign, needed to be guided and groomed by her better educated and savvier sisters. Bina was being shunned because she had acted as the ungrateful and wayward child of the campaign that had brought her into the limelight. From Naripokkho's point of view, Bina had betrayed the campaign because she had chosen to put her own needs over those of not only fellow survivors of violence but also the aspirations of the women's advocacy group.

It might be important to understand the international cultural difference here (Sharpe 2003). The international civil society crosses borders in the name of women and develops policy on development and human rights, which they profess are for the lowest strata in the developing world. The reality on the ground, however, is quite different. The international collaboration resting upon the UN mandate on helping victims of violence enabled Naripokkho members to organize a pipeline of twenty acid survivors to go for medical treatment to America. When the pipeline fell through, the euphoria and enthusiasm of the activists dissipated along with their interest to support the lowest strata—in this case, the survivors— because of a failure to understand their lived realities. It is not my intention here to pass judgment on Bina's or other Naripokkho members' actions and decisions. However, at the end of the day, it is she and the eighteen survivors who were not able to go to America for treatment who bore the most abject consequences of the international and intranational negotiations.

Concluding Remarks

Bina continues to advocate for what she had always desired: justice. Bina wanted Dano to be punished. And, she wanted to continue her engagement with the women's movement in Bangladesh, positioned as she might be, in the United States. My central purpose has been to tell a more complex story of the anti-acid violence campaign by the interweaving of multiple narratives over time. A corollary to that purpose has been to make central and visible the ongoing efforts of the women activists of Naripokkho in shaping this campaign. An organization mainly sustained by volunteers' contributions of time and funds, Naripokkho's involvement with the acid campaign was small in scale but expansive in vision. Initiated by promoting women's rights, the organizational support gained momentum with more and more staff and members offering the young girls assistance: finding places to stay for family members while survivors underwent long and arduous medical treatment in Dhaka, providing emotional support to the survivors in the hospital, assisting in bringing charges against the perpetrators, and building a network with the survivors as main actors. Naripokkho's strategy was to centralize the survivors' voices, highlight their experiences, encourage them to take over the leadership, and determine the direction of the campaign as part of the larger movement against women's oppression. Bina, for instance, during her internship at Naripokkho was moved by the organization's struggle to protect the rights of sex workers against government led rehabilitation programs. This critical feminist consciousness led her to be involved in other program areas and assume the leadership in organizing Naripokkho's International Women's Day Rally in 1998.

However, the organizational development of the acid campaign took on a different trajectory. An undoubtedly important and urgent service provider, the consolidation of ASF has had unintended consequences for the campaign. Nicoletta del Franco (1999) characterized ASF as espousing a welfarist approach, targeting the rehabilitation and reintegration of the survivors into society. To that end, ASF responded mainly to survivors' immediate need of medical and financial assistance. Over the years, however, ASF has adopted, if only in rhetoric, the vision of Naripokkho activists where the survivors themselves are at the center of the gradual process of social change. In reality, however, their programs still relegate the survivors to secondary roles and spaces that adhere to rehabilitation schemes or as workers in the service industry, thereby furthering a framework where proposed solutions for women's victimization lies at the individual intervention and salvation rather than in structural changes (Grewal and Caplan 1994).

It would be remiss not to mention that Naripokkho was in a better position than a foreign aid driven organization to put forward policies and strategies consistent with gender analyses of acid violence within the framework of women's oppression. As Nasreen Huq pointed out, it was her intention to develop an ASF within Naripokkho, but she had been obstructed by intramovement struggles among campaign leaders, members, and clients. The focus of such an ASF within Naripokkho would have been the empowerment of the survivors, so that they could become active agents in the process of transformation and social change. The lives of the survivors would not be "cases" of acid attacks, but "stories," which would be told and listened to in order to move forward, an alternative discourse to self-validating progress narratives.

In this chapter, I have aimed to broaden the understanding of the logic of local versus transnational women's activisms. Over the last decade, in particular, transnational feminist organizing has resulted in the realization of important and far-reaching accomplishments, particularly for women's groups representing the economic South. Local activists have used transnational contacts as a way to construct, reconstruct, and legitimize politically marginalized issues within the nation-state and to establish strategic bonds of solidarity with others who share in the process of such marginalization. Also, activists have organized across borders in an effort to affect public policy to enhance their local political leverage by the boomerang pattern of influence (Keck and Sikking 1998). The boomerang pattern means transnational coalitions of nongovernmental, governmental, and intergovernmental actors exerting pressures on one another as well as other influential political bodies to invoke desired policy change. Yet, the same transnational coalitions have often co-opted and eclipsed local women's issues and have rested upon uneasy alliances such as the one explicated between Naripokkho, UNICEF, ASF, Healing the Children, and survivors of violence. Furthermore, local women's issues have been represented as a monolith hiding the intramovement dynamics, which are at once ambiguous and contradictory. For instance, the internal disagreements and class-based divisions within Naripokkho unwittingly hindered the campaign from moving forward.

In this particular story of acid violence, the campaign had consistently struggled with issues of class, power, and imperialism. The campaign had been birthed by a group of middle-class, urban, socially committed women who had been moved by the injustices meted out to younger, poorer women. The implicit strategy of the campaign had entailed the transformation of the young survivors, nurturing them into becoming activists for women's empowerment. This construction of the victim-survivor-change-agent, however, did not represent the lived realities of the women in question. Although very keen on helping the survivors, the activists leading the campaign had been acutely aware of their own role as guardians and educators of the young girls. When that role was tested, for example, by Bina, who had decided to defy the terms of the agreement put in place to help her, the system of support crumbled. We must also remember that global inequalities lead to such impossible situations where victims are bound by contracts between nation-states with asymmetrical relations of power. Bina's defiance of the contract resulted in the abject loss for other victims. Yet, Bina's decision and its consequences must be understood in the context of larger global inequities.

Bina's role as the self-serving survivor had defied sociocultural imaginations of a good victim that are routinely perpetuated by the media. Powerful assumptions of womanhood and directives of appropriate female behavior governed the movement actors' understandings and expectations of how a victim should act. Naripokkho campaign leaders' shunning of Bina was also reflective of their disapproval of her disobedience as well as jeopardizing other survivors' medical treatment.

The struggles to define the acid violence campaign were not limited within Naripokkho but spanned the terrain of acid violence–related work. ASF and Naripokkho had their own clashes. The selection of John Morrison, a white British philanthropist, as the executive director of ASF reeked of colonial legacies. Even after his departure in 2001, the colonial legacies lingered. Having major donors like UNICEF and CIDA certainly made ASF resource-secure, but the guiding vision and long-term strategies, which drove the Naripokkho-led campaign, was compromised. ASF pitched itself as a service provider and remained limited to such work. Survivors received centralized medical, legal, and rehabilitative services like never before. However, when it came to systematically challenging the socially sanctioned crime of acid throwing, the organization lacked radical vision.

This analysis has implications for understanding local women's groups' relation to transnational feminist politics. Indubitably, there is a need to expand our theoretical understanding of local women's organizing and the context in which they operate. In her discussion of the campaign, Bristi Chowdhury pointed out the dependency on international aid agencies as a failure of the campaign. After all, Western funding is impermanent and a domestic funding base will ultimately be necessary if the local women's organizing efforts are to attain sustainability. Donors and NGOs have begun to supplant a weak and inefficient state in providing social services and thereby gain direct access to the public and private lives of ordinary citizens. This has been noted as an intrusive form of foreign aid and new means to govern subordinate populations (Stiles 2002). Regardless of the outcome, Naripokkho was able to use the international and national organizations to write a new chapter in transnational feminist organizing.

ACKNOWLEDGMENTS

I am grateful to the women of Naripokkho and Bina Akhter, who so generously shared their experiences with me.

NOTES

1. Research for this essay was conducted over a number of staged dialogic encounters during Bina Akhter's visit to New York from Cincinnati, November 19–21, 2002. Interviews with her and Naripokkho activists were in English and/or Bangla. The author personally conducted and translated all interviews.

2. Dano, the perpetrator, had been held in prison for two years after Bina's departure for the United States. He was subsequently released because Bina's uncle repeatedly failed to appear in court to make a statement. Naripokkho activists believed that he had been bought off by Dano's family, while Bina believed he had been threatened by Dano's supporters.

REFERENCES

Abedelkarim, M. D., and A. Riad. 2003. A surge in hate crimes followed by official U.S. targeting of Muslim, Arab men. *Washington Report on Middle East Affairs* (April 1): 51–52.

Abraham, M. 2000a. Isolation as a form of marital violence: The South Asian immigrant experience. *Journal of Social Distress and the Homeless* 9:221–236.

———. 2000b. *Speaking the unspeakable: Marital violence in South Asian immigrant communities in the United States.* New Brunswick, NJ: Rutgers University Press.

———. 1999. Sexual abuse in South Asian immigrant marriages. *Violence against Women* 5:591–618.

———. 1998. Speaking the unspeakable: Marital violence against South Asian immigrant women in the United States. *Indian Journal of Gender Studies* 5:215–241.

———. 1995. Ethnicity, gender, and marital violence: South Asian women's organizations in the United States. *Gender and Society* 9:450–468.

Acevedo, M. J. 2000. Battered immigrant Mexican women's perspectives regarding abuse and help-seeking. *Journal of Multicultural Social Work* 8:243–282.

Acker, J., K. Barry, and J. Esseveld. 1991. Objectivity and truth: Problems in doing feminist research. In *Beyond methodology: Feminist scholarship as lived research,* ed. M. M. Fonow and J. A. Cook, 133–153. Bloomington: Indiana University Press.

Agnew, V. 1998a. Tensions in providing services to South Asian victims of wife abuse in Toronto. *Violence against Women* 4:153–179.

———. 1998b. *In search of a safe place: Abused women and culturally sensitive services.* Toronto: University of Toronto Press.

Ahmad, F., S. Riaz, P. Barata, and D. E. Stewart. 2004. Patriarchal beliefs and perceptions of abuse among South Asian immigrant women. *Violence against Women* 10:262–282.

Ahmad, M. 2004. A rage shared by law: Post September 11 racial violence as crimes of passion. *California Law Review* 92:1259–1330.

Ahmed, K. 1999. Adolescent development for South Asian American girls. In *Emerging voices: South Asian American women redefine self, family, and society,* ed. S. Gupta, 37–49. Thousand Oaks, CA: Sage.

Albina, M. 2003. The effects of trauma on family life. *World Vision* (April 14). Retrieved May 1, 2005, from http://meero.worldvision.org/news_article.php?newsID=123.

Alexander, D. 2000. Addressing violence against Palestinian women. *International Development Research Centre,* June 23. Retrieved May 1, 2005, from http://www.idrc.ca/en/ev-5311–201–1-DO_TOPIC.html.

Al-Hibri, A. 2003. An Islamic perspective on domestic violence. *Fordham International Law Journal* 27:195–200.

Alliance of South Asians Taking Action. 2000a. *Fight sexual and labor exploitation.* Berkeley, CA: ASATA.

———. 2000b. *ASATA mission statement.* Oakland, CA: ASATA.

AllPsych Online. 2004. *Psychiatric disorders: Anorexia Nervosa* (May 15). Retrieved July 17, 2005, from http://allpsych.com/disorders/eating/anorexia.html.

Almeida, R. V., and K. Dolan-Delvecchio. 1999. Addressing culture in batterers intervention: The Asian Indian community as an illustrative example. *Violence against Women* 5:654–683.

Almjeld, K. 2003/2004. Clear Act threatens immigrant women victims of violence. *National NOW Times* (Winter). Retrieved September 14, 2004, from http://www.now.org/nnt/winter-2004/clear.html?printable.

Alvarez, S. 2000. Translating the global: Effects of transnational organizing on local feminist discourses and practices in Latin America. *Meridians: Feminism, Race, Transnationalism* 1:29–67.

American Civil Liberties Union (ACLU). 2004. *Sanctioned bias: Racial profiling since 9–11* (February). Retrieved February 20, 2005, from http://www.aclu.org/SafeandFree/SafeandFree.cfm?ID = 15102&c = 207.

———. 1998. *Press release: ACLU represents parents in abortion case* (July 23). Retrieved August 25, 2004, from http://www.aclumich.org/.

American Medical Association (AMA). 2005. *Diagnostic and treatment guidelines on domestic violence.* Chicago: American Medical Association.

Amnesty International. 1999. *Pakistan: Violence against women in the name of honor* (AI Index: ASA 33/17/99). New York: Amnesty International USA.

Angless, T., M. Maconachie, and M. Van Zyl. 1998. Battered women seeking solutions: A South African study. *Violence against Women* 4:637–658.

Armas, G. C. 2004. Asian population surging across America. *Detroit News Census: 2000* (May 1). Retrieved June 20, 2005, from http://www.detnews.com/2005/census/0502/10/census-139111.htm.

Artz, M. 2004. Reddy saga ends with last defendant spared jail sentence. *Berkeley Daily Planet,* June 8.

Asian Pacific Post. 2004. Where have our husbands gone? October 21. Retrieved August 5, 2005, from http://www.asianpacificpost.com/news/article/225.html.

Ashcroft, B. 2001. *Postcolonial transformation.* New York: Routledge.

Associated Press. 2004. Father accused of raping daughter, mother accused of attempted murder, May 10.

At Health. 2000. Emotional eating and binge eating disorder. Retrieved July 17, 2005, from http://www.athealth.com/Consumer/disorders/BingeInterview.html.

Awad, A. 2002. Family law. *New Jersey Law Journal* (July 2). Retrieved April 9, 2006, from http://www.law.com/jsp/article.jsp?id = 1024078931709.

Ayyub, R. 2000. Domestic violence in the South Asian Muslim immigrant population in the United States. *Journal of Social Distress and the Homeless* 9:237–248.

———. 1998. *Survey on the incidence of domestic violence in the Muslim Population.* Unpublished data. New York: Committee on Domestic Harmony, Islamic Center of Long Island.

Badlishah, N. N. N., and N. Kaprawi. 2004. *Hadith on women in marriage.* Malaysia: Sisters in Islam.

Baker, N. V., P. R. Gregware, and M. A. Cassidy. 1999. Family killing fields: Honor rationales in the murder of women. *Violence against Women* 5:164–184.

Bandler, J. 2003. Tarrytown judge's remark sparks outrage. *Journal News* (Crime/Public Safety) (May 21). Retrieved September 9, 2004, from http://www.nynews.com/newsroom/052103/a0121tarryjudge.html.

Bandyopadhyay, M. 1995. "My husband, good or bad": Closures in Bankimchandra's novels. In *Indian women: Myth and reality*, ed. J. Bagchi, 119–132. Hyderabad, India: Sangam Books (India) Limited.

Banerjee, N. 2001. Fighting back against domestic violence: Asian American women organize to break the silence. *Asian Week*, June 22–28. Retrieved July 29, 2005, from http://www.asianweek.com/2000_12_01/feature.html.

Bannerji, H. 1993. Popular images of South Asian women. In *Returning the gaze: Essays on racism, feminism, and politics*, ed. H. Bannerji, 144–152.Toronto: Sister Vision Press.

Barai, S. B. 1999. Beyond the rhetoric: Negative implications of "multiculturalism" for the anti-domestic violence work of Asian women's centers in London. Master's thesis. London: London School of Economics.

Basu, A. 2000. Globalization of the local/localization of the global: Mapping transnational women's movements. *Meridians, Feminism, Race, Transnationalism* 1:68–84.

BBC News. 2004. Sikh father guilty of death plot. December 15. Retrieved January 22, 2005, from http://newsvote.bbc.co.uk/mpapps/pagetools/print/news.bbc.co.uk/2/hi/uk_news/england/kent/4099053.stm.

———. 2002a. Television link to eating disorders. May 31. Retrieved July 17, 2005, from http://news.bbc.co.uk/2/hi/health/2018900.stm.

———. 2002b. Eating disorders rise in Zulu women. November 4. Retrieved July 17, 2005, from http://news.bbc.co.uk/2/hi/africa/2381161.stm.

Bernstein, N. 2004. From immigrants, stories of scrutiny, and struggle. *New York Times*, July 20.

Berrick, J. D., and N. Gilbert. 1991. *With the best intentions: The child sexual abuse prevention movement*. New York: Guilford Press.

Berry, D. B. 1995. *The domestic violence source book*. Los Angeles: Lowell House.

Bhattacharjee, A. 2001. *Whose safety? Women of color and the violence of law enforcement*. Philadelphia: American Friends Service Committee and Committee on Women, Population and the Environment.

———. 1997. A slippery path: Organizing resistance to violence against women. In *Dragon ladies: Asian American feminists breathe fire*, ed. S. Shah, 29–45. Boston: South End Press.

———. 1992. The habit of ex-nomination: Nation, women and the Indian immigrant bourgeoisie. *Public Culture* 5:19–43.

Bograd, M. 1988. Feminist perspectives on wife abuse: An introduction. In *Feminist perspectives on wife abuse*, ed. K. Yllö and M. Bograd, 11–26. Newbury Park, CA: Sage.

Boonzaier, F., and C. De La Rey. 2003. "He's a man, and I'm a woman": Cultural constructions of masculinity and femininity in South African women's narratives of violence. *Violence against Women* 9:1003–1029.

Bordo, S. 1993. *Unbearable weight: Feminism, western culture, and the body*. Berkeley and Los Angeles: University of California Press.

Breznikar, E. 2003. Ethnic groups question police chief on hate crimes; Arab Americans question. *(Haynard, CA) Daily Review*, April 3.

Browne, A. 1991. The victim's experience: Pathways to disclosure. *Psychotherapy* 28:150–156.

———. 1987. *When battered women kill*. New York: Macmillan/ Free Press.

Buel, S. 1999. Fifty obstacles to leaving, a.k.a., why abuse victims stay. *Colorado Law Review* 28:19–26.

Bui, H. N. 2003. Help-seeking behavior among abused immigrant women: A case of Vietnamese American women. *Violence against Women* 9:207–239.

Bui, H. N., and M. Morash, 1999. Domestic violence in the Vietnamese immigrant community: An exploratory study. *Violence against Women* 5:769–95.

Bullock, K. 1998. *Canadian Muslim women: The hijab experience*. Plainfield, IN: Islamic Horizon.

Burge, S. K. F. D. Schneider, L. Ivy, and S. Catala. 2005. Patients' advice to physicians about intervening in family conflict. *Annals of Family Medicine* 3:248–254.

Cable News Network. 2002. "Bring it down" was about a car, students' lawyer says. September 15. Retrieved May 3, 2005, from http://archives.cnn.com/2002/US/09/15/fla.terror.students.

Chandrasekhar, S., ed. 1984. *From India to America: A brief history of immigration; problems of discrimination, admission and assimilation*. La Jolla, CA: Population Review.

Chapman, D. 1962. A brief introduction to contemporary disaster research. In *Man and society in disaster*, ed. G. Baker and D. Chapman, 3–22. New York: Basic.

Childress, S. 2003. 9/11's hidden toll: Muslim-American women are quietly coping with a tragic side effect of the attacks—a surge in domestic violence. *Newsweek*, August 4, 37.

Chiu, D. C. 1994. The cultural defense: Beyond exclusion, assimilation, and guilty liberalism. *California Law Review* 82:1053–1125.

Clark, A. H., and D. W. Foy 2000. Trauma exposure and alcohol use in battered women. *Violence against Women* 6:37–48.

Cleaver, E. 1968. *Soul on ice*. New York: Dell Publishing.

Coalition to Support South Asian Survivors of Sexual and Labor Exploitation. 2000a. Press release. Berkeley and Oakland, CA: Coalition.

———. 2000b. Talking points for coalition. Berkeley and Oakland, CA: Coalition.

———. 2000c. Meeting minutes on January 25, 2000. Berkeley, CA: Coalition.

———. 2000d. Flyer from the coalition to support South Asian survivors of sexual and labor exploitation's candle light vigil. Berkeley, CA: Coalition.

———. 2000e. Handout at candle light vigil, January 29, 2000. Berkeley, CA: Coalition.

Coker, D. 2003. Enhancing autonomy for battered women: Lessons from Navajo peacemaking. In *Feminist legal theory: An anti-essentialist reader*, ed. N. E. Dowd and M. S. Jacobs, 390–403. New York: New York University Press.

———. 2001. Crime control and feminist law reform in domestic violence law: A critical review. *Buffalo Criminal Law Review* 4:801–860.

———. 2000. Shifting power for battered women: Law, material resource, and poor women of color. *U.C. Davis Law Review* 33:1009–1055.

Coleman, D. L. 1996. Individualizing justice through multiculturalism: The liberals' dilemma. *Columbia Law Review* 96:1093–1167.

Coomaraswamy, R. 1995. Some reflections on violence against women. *Canadian Woman Studies* 15:19–23.

Cornell News. 2004. Fear factor: 44 percent of Americans queried in Cornell national poll favor curtailing some liberties for Muslim Americans. December 17. Retrieved January 20, 2005 from http://www.news.cornell.edu/releases/Dec04/Muslim.Poll.bpf.html.

Council on American Islamic Relations. 1998. *Good news alert*. June 12. Washington, DC: CAIR.

Cowen, R. 1998. Slain woman was vulnerable: Deportation fear paralyzed victim. *(Bergen County, NJ) Record*, June 29.

Crenshaw, K. 1997. Mapping the margins: Intersectionality, identity politics, and violence against women of color. *Stanford Law Review* 43:1241–1299.

Cresswell, J. W. 1994. *Research design: Qualitative and quantitative approaches*. London: Sage.

Cunradi, C. B., R. Caetano, and J. Schafer. 2002. Religious affiliation, denominational homogamy, and intimate partner violence among U.S. couples. *Journal for the Scientific Study of Religion* 41:139–151.

Curtis, C. 2005 Pope calls gay marriage "evil." February 22. Retrieved on June 23, 2005, from http://gay.com/news/article.html?2005/02/22/1.

Daily Star. 2002. Queen Elizabeth honours director of Acid Survivors Foundation in Bangladesh. *Daily Star*. Retrieved June 10, 2002, from http://www.dailystarnews.com/200206/18/n2061808.htm.

Dahir, M. 2001. When label-ees become the labelers. *Bay Windows Online*. October 18. Retrieved June 28, 2005, from http://www.baywindows.com/media/paper328/news/2001/10/18/Columns/Mubarak.Dahir-128800.shtml.

Das, V. 1995. *Critical events: An anthropological perspective on contemporary India*. New Delhi: Oxford University Press.

Das, A., and S. Kemp. 1997. Between two worlds: Counseling South Asian Americans. *Journal of Multicultural Counseling and Development* 25:23–33.

Dasgupta, S. D. 2003. Sexual abuse. Children: South Asia. In *Encyclopedia of women and Islamic cultures: Family, law and politics*, vol. 2, ed. S. Joseph, 465–466. Leiden, The Netherlands: Brill.

———. 2002. A framework for understanding women's use of nonlethal violence in intimate heterosexual relationships. *Violence against Women* 8:1364–1389.

———. 2000a. Charting the course: An overview of domestic violence in the South Asian community in the United States. *Journal of Social Distress and the Homeless* 9:173–185.

———. 2000b. Broken promises: Domestic violence murders and attempted murders in the U.S. and Canadian South Asian communities. In *Breaking the silence: Domestic violence in the South Asian-American community*, ed. S. Nankani, 27–47. Xlibris Corporation, http://www2.xlibris.com.

———. 1998a. Introduction to *A patchwork shawl: Chronicles of South Asian women in America*, ed. S. D. Dasgupta, 1–17. New Brunswick, NJ: Rutgers University Press.

———. 1998b. Women's realities: Defining violence against women by immigration, race, and class. In *Issues in intimate violence*, ed. R. K. Bergen, 209–219. Thousand Oaks, CA: Sage Publications.

———. 1998c. Gender roles and cultural continuity in the Asian Indian immigrant community in the U.S. *Sex Roles* 38:953–974.

Dasgupta, S. D., and S. DasGupta. 1997. Bringing up baby: Raising a "third world" daughter in the "first world." In *Dragon ladies: Asian American feminists breathe fire*, ed. S. Shah, 182–199. Boston: South End Press.

DasGupta, S., and S. D. Dasgupta. 1998. Sex, lies, and women's lives: An intergenerational dialogue. In *A patchwork shawl: Chronicles of South Asian women in America*, ed. S. D. Dasgupta, 111–128. New Brunswick, NJ: Rutgers University Press.

DasGupta, S., and S. D. Dasgupta. 1996. Women in exile: Gender relations in the Asian Indian community in the U.S. In *Contours of the heart: South Asians map America*, ed. S. Maira and R. Srikanth, 381–400. New York: Asian American Writers' Workshop.

Dasgupta, S. D., and S. Warrier. 1996. In the footsteps of "Arundhati": Asian Indian women's experience of domestic violence in the United States. *Violence against Women* 2:238–259.

———. 1995. *In visible terms: Domestic violence in the Asian Indian context, a handbook for intervention*. Bloomfield, NJ: Manavi.

Davar, B. 1999. *Mental health of Indian women: A feminist agenda*. New Delhi: Sage.

de Lauretis, T. (Ed). 1986. *Feminist studies, critical studies*. Bloomington: Indiana University Press.

Del Franco, N. 1999. Changing gender relations and new forms of violence: Acid throwing against women in Bangladesh and the NGO response. Master's thesis, University of Sussex, Brighton, UK.

Denzin, N., and Y. Lincoln. 1994. Introduction: Entering the Field of Qualitative Research. In *Handbook of qualitative research*, ed. N. Denzin and Y. Lincoln, 1–17. Thousand Oaks, CA: Sage.

Derné, S. 1999. Making sex violent: Love as force in recent Hindi films. *Violence against Women* 5:548–575.

———. 1995. *Culture in action: Family life, emotion, and male dominance in Banaras, India*. Albany: State University of New York Press.

Desai, S. 1994. *India: Gender inequalities and demographic behaviors*. New York: Population Council.

Dion, K. K., and K. L. Dion. 1993. Individualistic and collectivistic perspectives on gender and the cultural context of love and intimacy. *Journal of Social Issues* 49:53–69.

Dobash, R. E., and R. P. Dobash. 1979. *Violence against wives: A case against patriarchy*. New York: Free Press.

Domestic Violence Research Project. 2001. *Project AWARE: Asian women advocating respect and empowerment.* Washington, DC: Asian/Pacific Islander Domestic Violence Research Project.

Dugger, C. W. 2001. Abortion in India is tipping scales sharply against girls. *New York Times,* April 22. Retrieved July 20, 2005, from http://www.nytimes.com/2001/04/22/world/22INDI.html?ex = 1122004800&en = a3c05a758259b258&ei = 5070.

Duncan, O. D. 1961. A socioeconomic index for all occupations. In *Occupations and social status,* ed. A. J. Reiss Jr., 109–138. New York: Free Press.

Durvasula, R., and G. Mylvaganam. 1994. Mental health of Asian Indians: Relevant issues and community implications. *Journal of Community Psychology* 22:97–108.

Dutton, M. A. 1992. Treating battered women in the aftermath stage. *Psychotherapy in Private Practice* 10:93–98.

Dutton, M. A., L. Orloff, and G. A. Hass. 2000. Characteristics of help-seeking behaviors, resources, and service needs of battered immigrant Latinas: Legal and policy implications. *Georgetown Journal on Poverty Law and Policy* 7:245–303.

Ebrahim, N. 2001. *Annual report 2001: Muslim women's helpline.* Retrieved April 2, 2005, from http://www.mwhl.org/fnf01.htm.

Egan, T. 2001. A nation challenged: The Muslims; tough but hopeful weeks for the Muslims of Laramie. *New York Times,* October 18.

Ellsberg, M., T. Caldera, A. Herrera, A. Winkvist, and G. Kullgren. 1999. Domestic violence and emotional distress among Nicaraguan women: Results from a population-based study. *American Psychologist* 54:30–36.

Engel, D. 1998. How does law matter in the constitution of legal consciousness? In *How does law matter?* ed. B. Garth and A. Sarat, 109–144. Chicago: Northwestern University Press.

Engelsman, J. C., ed. 2000. *Helping victims of domestic violence: A guide for religious leaders.* Madison, NJ: Clergy Partnership on Domestic Violence.

Erez, E., and S. Bach. 2003. Immigration, domestic violence and the military: The case of "military brides." *Violence against Women* 9:1093–1117.

Espenshade, T. J., J. L. Baraka, and G. A. Huber. 1997. Implications of the 1996 welfare and immigration reform acts for US immigration. *Population and Development Review* 23:769–802.

Espin, O. 1999. *Women crossing boundaries: A psychology of immigration and transformations of sexuality.* New York: Routledge.

Espiritu, Y. 1997. *Asian American women and men: Love, labor, laws.* Thousand Oaks, CA: Sage.

Evans, M. 2003. Fremont won't tolerate hate crimes; Officials vow aggressive action as locals voice fear of backlash. *(Pleasanton, CA) Tri-Valley Herald,* March 27.

Faizi, N. 2001. Domestic violence in the Muslim community. *Texas Journal of Women and the Law* 10:209–220.

Federal Bureau of Investigation (FBI). 2004. *Uniform crime reports: 2003 hate crime statistics.* Washington, DC. Retrieved May 6, 2005, from http://www.fbi.gov/ucr/03hc.pdf.

Feldman, S. 1998. (Re)presenting Islam: Manipulating gender, shifting state practices, and class frustrations in Bangladesh. In *Appropriating gender: Women's activism and politicized religion in South Asia,* ed. A. Basu and P. Jeffery, 33–52. New York: Routledge.

Fenton, S., and A. Sadiq-Sangster. 1996. Culture, relativism and the expression of mental distress: South Asian women in Britain. *Sociology of Health and Illness* 18:66–85.

Fernandez, M. 1997. Domestic violence by extended family members in India. *Journal of Interpersonal Violence* 12:433–455.

Fernea, E. W. 1998. *In search of Islamic feminism.* New York: Doubleday.

Fischbach, R., and B. Herbert. 1997. Domestic violence and mental health: Correlates and conundrums within and across cultures. *Social Science and Medicine* 45:1161–1176.

Flyvbjerg, B. 2001. *Making social science matter: Why social inquiry fails and how it can succeed again.* Cambridge, UK: Cambridge University Press.

Foa, E. B., M. Cascardi, L. A. Zoellner, and N. C. Feeny. 2000. Psychological and environmental factors associated with partner violence. *Trauma, Violence, and Abuse* 1:67–91.

Foderaro, L. W. 2004. A 9/11 lesson: Don't photograph the water. *New York Times*, June 6.

Ford-Smith, H. 1997. Ring ding in a tight corner: Sistren, collective democracy, and the organization of cultural production. In *Feminist genealogies, colonial legacies, democratic futures*, ed. J. Alexander and C. Mohanty, 213–258. New York: Routledge.

Fortune, Rev. M. M., and Rabbi C. G. Enger. 2005. Violence against women and the role of religion. *VAWnet: Applied Research Forum*. March. Retrieved September 1, 2005, from http://www.vawnet.org/DomesticViolence/Research/VAWnetDocs/AR_VAWReligion.php.

Foucault, M. 1978. *The history of sexuality: An introduction*. Vol. 1. New York: Random House.

Friedman, E. 1999. The effects of "transnationalism reversed" in Venezuela: Assessing the impact of UN global conferences on the women's movement. *International Feminist Journal of Politics* 1:357–381.

George, M. S., and L. Rahangdale. 1999. Domestic violence and South Asian women. *North Carolina Medical Journal* 60:157–159.

Gerson, D. 2003. For some, harder times after 9-11. *New York Sun*, October 1.

Gibson, P. N.d. Gay male and lesbian suicide. *Lambda GLBT Community Services*. Retrieved May 6, 2005, from http://www.lambda.org/youth_suicide.htm.

Gill, A. 2004. Voicing the silent fear: South Asian women's experiences of domestic violence. *Howard Journal* 43:465–483.

Gilman, S. 1985. *Difference and pathology, stereotypes of sexuality, race, and madness*. Ithaca, NY: Cornell University Press.

Glaser, B., and A. Strauss. 1967. *The discovery of grounded theory: Strategies for qualitative research*. Hawthorne, NY: Aldine de Gruyter.

Gleason, W. 1993. Mental disorders in battered women: An empirical study. *Violence and Victims* 8:53–67.

Gone, J. 2001. Affect and its disorders in a northern plains Indian community: Issues in cross-cultural discourse and diagnosis. Ph.D. diss., University of Illinois, Urbana-Champaign.

Gour's empowerment of women in India. 2003. Allahabad, India: Law Publishers (India).

Greaves, L., A. W. Wylie, C. Champagne, L. Karch, R. Lapp, J. Lee, and B. Osthoff. 1995. Women and violence: Feminist practice and quantitative method. In *Changing methods: Feminists transforming practice*, ed. S. Burt and L. Code, 301–326. Peterborough, ON: Broadview Press.

Grewal, I., and K. Caplan, eds. 1994. *Scattered hegemonies: Postmodernity and transnational feminist practices*. Minneapolis: University of Minnesota Press.

Guhathakurta, M. 1994. The aid discourse and the politics of gender: A perspective from Bangladesh. *Journal of Social Studies* 65:101–114.

Gupta, G. 1976. Love, arranged marriage, and the Indian social structure. *Journal of Comparative Family Studies* 7:75–85.

Gurnani, A., S. Kaushal, S. D. Dasgupta, and S. Lodhia. 2005. *Resources, strategies and barriers in assisting women abandoned in South Asia*. Presented at Aarohan 2005, September 9–11, New Brunswick, NJ.

Haddad, Y. Y. 1986. *The Muslim world today*. Washington, DC: American Institute of Islamic Affairs.

Hallak, M., and K. Quina 2004. In the shadows of the twin towers: Muslim immigrant women's voices emerge. *Sex Roles* 51:329–339.

Halttunen, K. 1999. Cultural history and the challenge of narrativity. In *Beyond the cultural turn*, ed. V. E. Bonnell and L. Hunt, 165–181. Berkeley: University of California Press.

Hammersley, M. 1992. *What's wrong with ethnography?* New York: Routledge.

Handa, A. 2003. *Of silk saris and mini-skirts: South Asian girls walk the tightrope of culture*. Toronto: Women's Press.

Hasnat, N. 1998. Being "Amreeken": Fried chicken versus chicken tikka. In *A patchwork shawl: Chronicles of South Asian women in America*, ed. S. D. Dasgupta, 33–45. New Brunswick, NJ: Rutgers University Press.

Hass, G. A., M. A. Dutton, and L. E. Orloff. 2000. Lifetime prevalence of violence against Latina immigrants: Legal and policy implications. *International Review of Victimology* 7:93–116.

Hegde, R. S. 1999. Marking bodies, reproducing violence: A feminist reading of female infanticide in south India. *Violence against Women* 5:507–524.

Heise, L. 1993. Violence against women: The hidden health burden. *World Health Statistics Quarterly* 46:78–85.

Heise, L. L., A. Raikes, C. H. Watts, and A. B. Zwi. 1994. Violence against women: A neglected public health issue in less developed countries. *Social Science Medicine* 39:1165–1179.

Hennink, M., I. Diamond, and P. Cooper. 1999. Young Asian women and relationships: Traditional or transitional. *Ethnic and Racial Studies* 22:867–891.

Herman, J. 1992. *Trauma and recovery: The aftermath of violence—from domestic abuse to political terror.* New York: Basic Books.

Herron Zamora, J. 2000a. US jury likely in Berkeley landlord sex case. *San Francisco Examiner,* January 21.

———. 2000b. Sex case landlord's shabby past. *San Francisco Examiner,* January 23.

Herron Zamora, J., and E. McCormick. 2000. Sex case landlord's shabby past. *San Francisco Examiner,* January 23.

Herron Zamora, J., and M. Yi. 2000. Lurid charge in Berkeley sex case. *San Francisco Examiner,* January 27.

Hines, P. M., N. Garcia-Preto, M. McGoldrick, R. Almeida, and S. Weltman. 1992. Intergenerational relationship across cultures. *Families in Society* 73:323–328.

Hing, B. O. 2004. Between two Americas. *ColorLines,* vol. 7. Retrieved October 2, 2004 from http://www.arc.org/C_Lines/CLArchive/story7_3_01.html.

Hirschel, D., and E. Buzawa. 2002. Understanding the context of dual arrest with directions for future research. *Violence against Women* 8:449–1473.

Holmes, K. E. 2005. Muslims strike at spouse abuse. *Philadelphia Inquirer,* June 17. Retrieved June 22, 2005, from http://www.philly.com/mld/inquirer/news/front/11914551.htm.

Huckerby, J. 2003. Women who kill their children: Case study and conclusions concerning the differences in the fall from maternal grace by Khoua Her and Andrea Yates. *Duke Journal of Gender Law and Policy* 10:149–185.

Huisman, K. A. 1996. Wife battering in Asian American communities: Identifying the service needs of an overlooked segment of the U.S. population. *Violence against Women* 2:260–283.

Human Rights Watch Women's Rights Project. 1998. *The human rights watch global report on women's human rights.* India: Oxford University Press.

Immigration and Naturalization Service Center (INS). 2002a. *Report on characteristics of specialty occupation workers (H-1B): Fiscal Year 2000.* Washington, DC: U.S. Immigration and Naturalization Service.

———. 2002b. *Report on characteristics of specialty occupation workers (H-1B): Fiscal Year 2000.* Washington, DC: U.S. Immigration and Naturalization Service.

———. 2000c. *Characteristics of specialty occupation workers (H-1B): May 1998 to July 1999.* Washington, DC: U.S. Immigration and Naturalization Service.

———. N.d. *United States immigration lottery/diversity visa Regions.* Retrieved May 10, 2004, from http://www.formdomain.com/regions.htm.

indiatimes. N.d. Ash—The darling of India. Retrieved July 17, 2005, from http://people.indiatimes.com/articleshow/699627.cms.

Indo-Asian News Service. 2002. Brother who suspected own sister of infidelity helped husband kill her. *News India-Times,* September 13.

International Eating Disorder Referral and Information Center. N.d. Binge eating disorder. Retrieved July 17, 2005, from http://www.edreferral.com/binge_eating_disorder.htm.

——. N.d. Bulimia nervosa. Retrieved July 17, 2005, from http://www.edreferral.com/bulimia_nervosa.htm.

International Gay and Lesbian Human Rights Commission. 2003. *Where having sex is a crime: Criminalization and decriminalization of homosexual acts.* Retrieved May 5, 2005, from http://www.iglhrc.org/site/iglhrc/content.php?type = 1&id = 77.

——. 1995. *The international tribunal on human rights violations against sexual minorities.* Retrieved May 5, 2005, from http://www.iglhrc.org/files/iglhrc/reports/Tribunal.pdf.

Iyer, D. 2003. A community on the front lines: Pushing back the rising tide of anti-immigrant policy since September 11th. *Subcontinental* (Autumn): 3. Retrieved June 20, 2005, from http://www.saalt.org/pdfs/dIyer1–3.pdf.

Jalal, A. 1991. The convenience of subservience: Women and the state of Pakistan. In *Women, Islam and the state*, ed. D. Kandioyoti, 77–114. Philadelphia: Temple University Press.

Janofsky, M., and D. W. Chen. 2001. Mail scrutinized across U.S. *(Quincy, MA) Patriot Ledger*, October 16.

Jayakar, K. 1985. Women of the Indian subcontinent. In *Women of color: Integrating ethnic and gender identities in psychotherapy*, ed. L. Comaz-Diaz and B. Greene, 161–180. New York: Guilford Press.

Jiwani, Y. 2005. Walking a tightrope: The many faces of violence in the lives of racialized immigrant girls and young women. *Violence against Women* 11:846–875.

Johnson, A., and Z. Nadirshaw. 1993. Good practice in transcultural counseling: An Asian perspective. *British Journal of Guidance and Counseling* 21:20–29.

Johnson, P. S., and J. A. Johnson. 2001. The oppression of women in India. *Violence against Women* 7:1051–1068.

Jones, L., M. Hughes, and U. Unterstaller. 2001. Post-traumatic stress disorder (PTSD) in victims of domestic violence. *Trauma, Violence and Abuse* 2:99–119.

Jorgensen, B. 2002. *Visa approvals take a nosedive; fewer H1Bs this year, but not because of the cap.* November 1. Retrieved May 27, 2004, from http://web.lexis-nexis.com.

Joseph, G. 2002. Pakistani faces life sentence for killing niece's husband. *India Abroad*, April 26.

Joshi, C. L. 1995. Unravelling a cover-up. *India Today*, June 30.

Joshi, M. 2004. Women activists win struggle to pray with men in mosque. *India Abroad*, June 18.

Journal of Social Distress and the Homeless. 2000. Special issue: Domestic violence in the South Asian immigrant community. Vol. 9, no. 3.

Kabeer, N. 2000. *The power to choose: Bangladeshi women and labour market decisions in London and Dhaka.* London: Verso.

Kantrowitz, B., and J. Scelfo. 2004. American masala. *Newsweek*, March 22. Retrieved April 2, 2004, from http://www.msnbc.msn.com/id/4522891.

Kanuha, V. 1987. Sexual assault in southeast Asian communities: Issues in intervention. *Response* 10:4–6.

Kasturirangan, A., S. Krishnan, and S. Riger. 2004. The impact of culture and minority status on women's experiences of domestic violence. *Trauma, Violence, and Abuse* 5:318–332.

Katz, J. 2003. Urban legend: Culture clash. *City Limits Monthly.* January. Retrieved April 2, 2005, from http://www.citylimits.org/content/articles/articleView.cfm?articlenumber = 926.

Kazarian, S. S., and L. Z. Kazarian. 1998. Cultural aspects of family violence. In *Cultural clinical psychology: Theory, research, and practice*, ed. S. Kazarian and D. Evans, 316–347. New York: Oxford University Press.

Keck, M., and K. Sikking. 1998. Transnational advocacy networks in the movement society. In *The social movement society*, ed. D. Meyer and S. Tarrow, 217–238. Lanham, MD: Rowman and Littlefield.

Kerouac, S., and J. Lescop. 1986. Dimensions of health in violent families. *Healthcare for Women International* 7:413–426.

Khaitan, T. 2004. Violence against lesbians in India. *Alternative Law Forum*. December 21. Retrieved May 5, 2005, from http://www.altlawforum.org/Resources/lexlib/document. 2004–12–21.9555696555.

Khan, E. 2004. Help is at hand for abandoned NRI wives. *India Abroad*, October 15.

Khouri, N. 2003. *Forbidden love: Love and betrayal in modern-day Jordan*. London: Doubleday.

Kim, E. A. 2003. Asian American eating disorders: A silent struggle. *Seattle Post-Intelligencer*, January 28. Retrieved July 17, from Model Minority: A Guide to Asian American Empowerment, at http://www.modelminority.com/article298.html.

Kim, M. 2002. *Innovative strategies to address domestic violence in Asian and Pacific Islander communities: Examining themes, models and interventions*. San Francisco: Asian and Pacific Islander Institute on Domestic Violence.

Kirk, G., and M. Okazawa-Rey. 2004. *Women's lives: Multicultural perspectives*. 3d ed. New York: McGraw-Hill.

Kishwar, M. 1995. When India "missed" the universe. *Manushi* (May–June): 9–19.

Kleinman, A. 1980. *Patients and healers in the context of culture: An exploration of the borderland between anthropology, medicine, and psychiatry*. Berkeley: University of California Press.

Kocot, T., and L. Goodman. 2003. The roles of coping and social support in battered women's mental health. *Violence against Women* 9: 323–346.

Koss, M. P. 1990. The women's mental health research agenda: Violence against women. *American Psychologist* 45:374–380.

Koss, M., L. Goodman, A. Browne, L. Fitzgerald, G. P. Keita, and N. Russo. 1994. *No safe haven: Male violence against women at home, at work, and in the community*. Washington, DC: American Psychological Association.

Koss, M. P., L. Heise, and N. F. Russo 1994. The global health burden of rape. *Psychology of Women Quarterly* 18:509–537.

Krause, I. 1989. Sinking heart: A Punjabi communication of distress. *Social Science and Medicine* 29:563–575.

Krishnan, S. P., M. Baig-Amin, L. Gilbert, N. El-Bassel, and A. Waters. 1998. Lifting the veil of secrecy: Domestic violence against South Asian women in the United States. In *A patchwork Shawl: Chronicles of South Asian women in America*, ed. S. D. Dasgupta, 145–159. New Brunswick, NJ: Rutgers University Press.

Kristof, N. D. 2005. When rapists walk free. *New York Times*, March 5.

———. 2004. Sentenced to be raped. *New York Times*, September 29. Retrieved September 30, 2004, from http://www.nytimes.com/2004/09/29/opinion/29kris.html?oref = login.

Kumar, R. N., A. Singh, A. Agrwaal, and J. Kaur 2003. *Reduced to ashes: The insurgency and human rights in Punjab*. Final report: Volume 1. Kathmandu, Nepal: South Asia Forum for Human Rights.

Kumar, U. 1991. Life stages in the development of the Hindu woman in India. In *Women in cross-cultural perspective*, ed. L. L. Adler, 142–158. Westport, CT: Praeger.

Lambda Legal. 2005. *Summary of states which prohibit discrimination based on sexual orientation*. Retrieved May 5, 2005, from http://www.lambdalegal.org/cgi-bin/iowa/news/resources. html?record = 185.

Lee, C. 2001. Equal right to fear. *Village Voice*, October 1, p. 44.

Lempert, L. B. 1996. Women's strategies for survival: Developing agency in abusive relationships. *Journal of Family Violence* 11:269–289.

Levi Holtz, D. 1999. Malfunctioning heater leads to tragedy in Berkeley: Carbon monoxide kills girl, hurts sister. *San Francisco Chronicle*, November 26.

Levi Holtz, D., and C. Squatriglia. 2000. Berkeley landlord depicted as overlord of India village. *San Francisco Chronicle*, January 22.

Levinson, D. 1989. *Family violence in cross-cultural perspective*. Newbury Park, CA: Sage.

Lind, A., and J. Share. 2003. Queering development: Institutionalized heterosexuality in development theory, practice and politics in Latin America. In *Feminist futures: Re-imagining women, culture and development*, ed. K. Bhavnani, J. Foran, and P. Kurian, 55–73. London: Zed Press.

Lloyd, K. 1992. Ethnicity, primary care and non-psychotic disorders. *International Review of Psychiatry* 4:257–265.

Lohr, K. 1998. Courts allow late term abortion. *Morning Edition*, July 29. Washington, DC: National Public Radio.

Loomba, A. 1998. *Colonialism/postcolonialism*. New York: Routledge.

Lopez, I. F. H. 1996. *White by law: The legal construction of race*. New York: New York University Press.

Lorde, A. 1984. *Sister, outsider: Essays and speeches*. Trumansburg, NY: Crossing Press.

Lull, J. 2000. *Media, communication, culture: A global approach*. New York: Columbia University Press.

Lykes, M. B., and A. J. Stewart. 1986. Evaluating the feminist challenge to research in personality and social psychology: 1963–1983. *Psychology of Women Quarterly* 10:393–412.

Maguigan, H. 1995. Cultural evidence and male violence: Are feminist and multiculturalist reformers on a collision course in criminal courts? *New York University Law Review* 70:36–99.

Maitri. 2000. Flyer from maitri's demonstration at Pasand restaurant in Santa Clara, January 29, 2000.

Mani, L. 1993. Gender, class and cultural conflict: Indu Krishnan's knowing her place. In *Our feet walk the sky: Women of the South Asian diaspora*, ed. The Women of South Asian Descent Collective, 32–36. South Francisco: Aunt Lute Books.

Manzione, L. L. 2001. Human rights in the kingdom of Nepal: Do they exist on paper. *Brooklyn Journal of International Law* 28:1–35.

Mankekar, P. 1999. *Screening culture, viewing politics: An ethnography of television, womanhood, and nation in postcolonial India*. Durham, NC: Duke University Press.

Marrett, P. N.d. Jainism explained. Retrieved August 23, 2005, from http://wwwedit. cs.wayne.edu:8080/~manishk/JainismDocuments/JainismExplained.pdf.

Marsella, A., M. Friedman, E. Gerrity, and R. Scurfield, eds. 1996. *Ethnocultural aspects of post-traumatic stress disorder: Issues, research, and clinical applications*. Washington, DC: American Psychological Association.

Martin, M. E. 1997. Double your trouble: Dual arrest in family violence. *Journal of Family Violence* 12:139–157.

Martin, S., B. L. Lowell, and P. Martin. 2002. U.S. immigration policy: Admission of high skilled workers. *Georgetown Immigration Law Journal* 16:1–18.

Matlock, J. 1995. *Scenes of seduction: Prostitution, hysteria, and reading difference in nineteenth century France*. New York: Columbia University Press.

Matloff, N. 2003. On the need for reform of the H-1B non-immigrant visa in computer-related occupations. *University of Michigan Journal of Law Reform* 36:1–99.

Mazumdar, R. 1998. Marital rape: Some ethical and cultural considerations. In *A patchwork shawl: Chronicles of South Asian women in America*, ed. S. D. Dasgupta, 129–144. New Brunswick, NJ: Rutgers University Press.

McElvaine, R. S. 2001. How men created God in their image. *Washington Post*, November 18.

McMahon, M., and E. Pence. 2003. Making social change: Reflections on individual and institutional advocacy with women arrested for domestic violence. *Violence against Women* 9:47–74.

Mehrotra, M. 1999. The social construction of wife abuse: Experience of Asian Indian women in the United States. *Violence against Women* 5:619–640.

Merchant, M. 2000. A comparative study of agencies assisting domestic violence victims: Does the South Asian community have special needs? *Journal of Social Distress and the Homeless* 9:249–259.

Mernissi, F. 1996. *Women's rebellion and Islamic memory*. London: Zed Books.

———. 1989. *Doing daily battle: Interviews with Moroccan women*. New Brunswick, NJ: Rutgers University Press.

———. 1987. *Beyond the veil: Male-female dynamics in modern Muslim societies*. Bloomington: Indiana University Press.

Merrill, G. 1998. Understanding domestic violence among gay and bisexual men. In *Issues in intimate violence*, ed. R. K. Bergen, 129–140. Thousand Oaks, CA: Sage.

Merry, S. E. 2001. Rights, religion, and community: Approaches to violence against women in the context of globalization. *Law and Society Review* 35:39–88.

Merx, K. 1999. Brother sentenced for rape. *Detroit News*, February 19.

Miles, A. 2000. When words abuse. *Clergy Journal* (March): 39–42.

Miller, S. L. 2001. The paradox of women arrested for domestic violence. *Violence against Women* 7:1339–1376.

Mills, L. G. 1999. Killing her softly: Intimate abuse and the violence of state intervention. *Harvard Law Review* 113:550–613.

Minter, S., and R. Rosenbloom. 1996. Sexual orientation, violence, and international human rights. *NCADV Voice: The Journal of the Battered Women's Movement* (Summer): 26–28.

Moghadam, V. M. 1992. Patriarchy and the politics of gender in modernising societies: Iran, Pakistan and Afghanistan. *International Sociology* 7:35–53.

Mohammad, A. 1967. *Quran*. Lahore, Pakistan: Kashmir Bazar Press.

Mohanty, C. T. 2003. *Feminism without borders: Decolonizing theory, practicing solidarity*. Durham, NC: Duke University Press.

Moltman-Wendel, E. 1978. *Liberty, equality, sisterhood*. Philadelphia: Fortress Press.

Molyneux, M., and S. Razavi, eds. 2002. *Gender justice, development, and rights*. Oxford: Oxford University Press.

Morrison, L. L., and J. L'Heureux. 2001. Suicide and gay/lesbian/bisexual youth: Implications for clinicians. *Journal of Adolescence* 24:39–49.

Muller, F. Max, ed. 1993. *Manu Smriti*. Trans. G. Bühler. New Delhi: Motilal Banarsidass.

Mumford, D. B., A. M. Whitehouse, and M. Platts. 1991. Sociocultural correlates of eating disorders among Asian school girls in Bradford. *British Journal of Psychiatry* 158:222–228.

Mutua, M. 2001. Savages, victims, and saviors: The metaphor of human rights. *Harvard International Law Journal* 42:201–246.

Nagpaul, A. 2005. Panel discussion at the INCITE! Color of Violence Conference III, March 12, New Orleans.

Nandu, S., and S. Nandu. 2004. "We want to live together till our death." Interview. *Savvy* (February): 16–22.

Nankani, S., ed. 2000. *Breaking the silence: Domestic violence in the South Asian-American community*. Xlibris Corporation, http://www2.xlibris.com.

Narayan, U. 1997. *Dislocating cultures: Identities, traditions, and Third World feminism*. New York: Routledge.

Narayan, U. 1995. "Male-order" brides: Immigrant women, domestic violence and immigration law. *Hypatia* 10:104–116.

Naripokkho. N.d. About Naripokkho. Retrieved September 10, 2002, from http://www.naripokkho.org.

Nason-Clark, N. 2000. Making the sacred safe: Woman abuse and communities of faith. *Sociology of Religion* 61:349–368.

Natarajan, M. 2002. Domestic violence among immigrants from India: What we need to know—and what we should do. *International Journal of Comparative and Applied Criminal Justice* 26:301–321.

National Asian American Pacific Islander Mental Health Association. 2004. Eating disorders information sheet: Asian and Pacific Islander Girls. Retrieved July 17, 2005, from http://www.naapimha.org/issues/AAGirls.pdf.

National Eating Disorders Association. 2002. Eating disorders information index. Retrieved July 17, 2005, from http://www.nationaleatingdisorders.org/p.asp?WebPage_ID = 294.

National Immigration Law Center. 2005. *Overview of immigrant eligibility for Federal programs.* March. Retrieved June 21, 2005, from http://www.nilc.org/pubs/guideupdates/tb11_ovrvw_fed_pgms_032505.pdf.

nationmaster.com. 2004. Map and graph: Mortality: Eating disorders. Retrieved July 17, 2005, from http://www.nationmaster.com/graph-T/mor_eat_dis.

Nayar, A. 2004. NRI bride mart: Case of runaway grooms. *Tribune (India)*, June 13. Retrieved August 5, 2005, from http://www.tribuneindia.com/2004/20040613/spectrum/main1.htm.

Newham Asian Women's Project. 1998. *Growing up young, Asian, and female in Britain: A report on self harm and suicide.* London: Adept.

Newton, H. P. 1972. *To die for the people.* New York: Writers and Readers Publishing.

Ngyuen, A. 1999. High tech migrant labor. *American Prospect* 11:38.

Nisperos, L., and D. Levi Holtz. 2000. Disbelief in India. *San Francisco Chronicle*, January 20.

NRIinternet.com. 2004. 12,000 cases in Gujarat of women abandoned by their NRI husbands, a figure higher than Punjab. November 23. Retrieved August 5, 2005 from http://www.nriinternet.com/Marriages/Desrted_Wife/2004/3_Gujrat.htm.

Nugent, K. 2004. Father is held in rape of child, mother accused of slashing baby. *Worcester Telegram and Gazette*, April 7.

Office of Immigration Statistics. 2004. *Characteristics of specialty occupation workers (H-1B): Fiscal year 2003.* Washington, DC: U.S. Department of Homeland Security.

———. 2003. *Characteristics of specialty occupation workers (H-1B): Fiscal Year 2002.* Washington, DC: U.S. Department of Homeland Security.

Office of Immigration Statistics, Office of Management, and Department of Homeland Security. 2002. *United States citizenship and immigration service statistical yearbook*, 2002. Retrieved May 10, 2004, from http://uscis.gov/graphics/shared/aboutus/statistics/Yearbook2002.pdf.

Office of the Inspector General. 2005. *The September 11 detainees: A review of the treatment of aliens held on immigration charges in connection with the investigation of the September 11 attacks.* June. Retrieved May 1, 2005, from http://www.usdoj.gov/oig/special/0306/full.pdf.

Okin, S. M. 1999. Is multiculturalism bad for women? In *Is multiculturalism bad for women?* ed. J. Cohen, M. Howard, and M. Nussbaum, 9–24. Princeton, NJ: Princeton University Press.

Oldenburg, V. T. 2002. *Dowry murder: The imperial origins of a cultural crime.* Oxford and New York: Oxford University Press.

O'Malley, S. 2004. *Are you there alone? The unspeakable crime of Andrea Yates.* New York: Simon and Schuster.

Orloff, L. 2001. Lifesaving welfare safety net access for battered immigrant women and children: Accomplishments and next steps. *William and Mary Journal of Women and the Law* 7:597–658.

Panchanadeswaran, S., and C. Koverola. 2005. The voices of battered women in India. *Violence against Women* 11:736–758.

Pande, M. 2003. *Stepping out: Life and sexuality in rural India.* New Delhi: Penguin.

Patel, D. R., E. L. Phillips, and H. D. Pratt. 1998. Eating disorders: A pediatric perspective. *Indian Journal of Pediatrics* 65:487–494.

Patton, C. 2004. *Anti-lesbian, gay, bisexual and transgender violence in 2003.* New York: National Coalition of Anti-Violence Programs.

———. 2003. *Anti-lesbian, gay, bisexual and transgender violence in 2002.* New York: National Coalition of Anti-Violence Programs.

——. 2002. *Anti-lesbian, gay, bisexual and transgender violence in* 2001. New York: National Coalition of Anti-Violence Programs.

PDRhealth. 2004. Battling anorexia, bulimia . . . and obesity. *Family guide to women's health and prescription drugs.* Retrieved July 17, 2005, from http://www.pdrhealth.com/content/women_health/chapters/fgwh35.shtml.

Pence, E. 2001. Advocacy on behalf of battered women. In *Sourcebook on violence against women*, ed. C. M. Renzetti, J. L. Edleson, and R. K. Bergen, 329–343. Thousand Oaks, CA: Sage.

——. 1999. Some thoughts on philosophy. In *Coordinating community responses to domestic violence: Lessons from Duluth and beyond*, ed. M. F. Shepard and E. L. Pence, 25–40. Thousand Oaks, CA: Sage.

Pence, E. L., and M. F. Shepard. 1999. An introduction: Developing a coordinated community response. In *Coordinating community responses to domestic violence: Lessons from Duluth and beyond*, ed. M. F. Shepard and E. L. Pence, 3–23. Thousand Oaks, CA: Sage.

Pendleton, G. 2003. *U visas for victims of crime.* June 24. Retrieved August 4, 2005, from http://www.ilw.com/lawyers/seminars/july2004_citation2d.pdf.

Perlez, J. 2001. After the attacks: The diplomacy. *New York Times*, September 13.

Pickett, D. 2002. Cable guys aren't meant to be U.S. spies. *Chicago Sun Times*, July 29.

Pinto, N. 2004. *Personal notes.* Berkeley, CA: Natasha Pinto.

Pluralism Project. N.d. *Statistics by Tradition: Jainism.* Retrieved September 2, 2005, from http://www.pluralism.org/resources/statistics/tradition.php#Jainism.

Poore, G. 2004. Overlaps between incestuous sexual abuse and domestic violence in South Asian communities: Advocate survey report. January 29. Retrieved February 22, 2005, from http://www.shaktiproductions.net/dv_overlaps.html.

——. 2000a. *The children we sacrifice.* Video documentary produced, directed, and written by G. Poore. Silver Spring, MD: SHaKTI Productions.

——. 2000b. *The children we sacrifice: A resource book.* Silver Spring, MD: SHaKTI Productions.

——. 1997. Re-examining definitions of domestic violence. *Options* 9:14–18.

Prasad, S. 1999. Medicolegal response to violence against women in India. *Violence against Women* 5:478–506.

Prashad, V. 2000. *The karma of brown folk.* Minneapolis: University of Minneapolis Press.

Preisser, A. B. 1999. Domestic violence in South Asian communities in America: Advocacy and intervention. *Violence against Women* 5:684–699.

Puri, J. 1999. *Woman, body, and desire in postcolonial India: Narratives of gender and sexuality.* New York: Routledge.

Puri, S. Forthcoming. Happiness in quotation marks. In *Stories of illness and healing: Women write their bodies*, ed. S. DasGupta and M. Hurst. Kent, OH: Kent State University Press.

Purkayastha, B. 2005. Skilled migration and cumulative disadvantage: The case of highly qualified Asian Indian immigrant women in the US. *GeoForum* 36:181–196.

Purkayastha, B., S. Raman, and K. Bhide. 1997. Empowering women: Multifaceted activism and SNEHA. In *Dragon ladies: Asian American feminists breathe fire*, ed. S. Shah, 100–107. Boston: South End Press.

QSR NVivo 1.3 Computer Software. 1999. Doncaster, Australia: QSR International Pty Ltd.

RAHI. 1999. *Voices from the silent zone: Women's experiences of incest and childhood sexual abuse.* New Delhi: RAHI.

Raj, A., and J. G. Silverman. 2003. Immigrant South Asian women at greater risk for injury from intimate partner violence. *American Journal of Public Health* 93:435–437.

——. 2002a. Violence against immigrant women: The roles of culture, context, and legal immigrant status on intimate partner violence. *Violence against Women* 8:367–398.

——. 2002b. Intimate partner violence against South-Asian women in greater Boston. *Journal of American Medical Women's Association* 57:111–114.

Raj, A., J. G. Silverman, J. McCleary-Sills, and R. Liu. 2004. Immigration policies increase South Asian immigrant women's vulnerability to intimate partner violence. *Journal of American Medical Women's Association* 60:26–32.

Rajan, V. G. J. 1996. Will India's ban on prenatal sex determination slow abortion of girls? *Hinduism Today*. April. Retrieved July 17, 2005, from http://www.hinduismtoday.com/archives/1996/4/1996-4-04.shtml.

Ramakrishnan, A. 2005. *South Asian committee's web survey findings by New Visions: Alliance to End Violence in Asian/Asian American Communities.* Presented at Aarohan: South Asian Women RISE UP Against Violence conference, September 9–11, New Brunswick, NJ.

Rao, S., S. Levy, and B. Bhattacharya. 2002. Women's health. In *A brown paper: The health of South Asians in the United States,* ed. South Asian Public Health Association, 24–34. Berkeley, CA: South Asian Public Health Association.

Ratan D., D. Gandhi, and R. Palmer. 1998. Eating disorders in British Asians. *International Journal of Eating Disorder* 24:101–105.

Razack, S. H. 1998. *Looking white people in the eye: Gender, race, and culture in courtrooms and classrooms.* Toronto: University of Toronto Press.

Real Sikhism. N.d. *Do not relate turban with terrorism.* Retrieved June 27, 2005, from http://www.realsikhism.com/turban.html.

Reddy, V. 2000. Wild accusations. *India Currents,* April.

Renzetti, C. M. 1998. Violence and abuse in lesbian relationships: Theoretical and empirical issues. In *Issues in intimate violence,* ed. R. K. Bergen, 117–127. Thousand Oaks, CA: Sage.

Rianon, N. J., and A. J. Shelton. 2003. Perception of spousal abuse expressed by married Bangladeshi immigrant women in Houston, Texas, U.S.A. *Journal of Immigrant Health* 5:37–44.

Richman, J. 2004. Sentencing delayed in sex-slave case. *Oakland Tribune,* March 30.

Roland, A. 1988. *In search of self in India and Japan.* Princeton, NJ: Princeton University Press.

Rosinski, J., and F. Richardson. 2004. Mom allegedly tries to kill toddler, self. *Boston Herald,* April 6.

Rozario, S. 1998. Disjunctions and continuities: Dowry and the position of single women in Bangladesh. In *Negotiation and social space: A gendered analysis of changing kin and security networks in South Asia and sub-Saharan Africa,* ed. C. Risseeuw and K. Ganesh, 259–275. London: Sage.

Rudrappa, S. 2004a. Radical caring in an ethnic shelter: South Asian American women workers at Apna Ghar, Chicago. *Gender and Society* 18:588–610.

———. 2004b. *Ethnic routes to becoming American: Indian immigrants and the cultures of citizenship.* New Brunswick, NJ: Rutgers University Press.

Runkle, S. 2004. Manufacturing beauties: India's integration into the global beauty industry. *Manushi* (July–August): 14–24.

Russell, D. E. H. 2000a. Flyer. Berkeley, CA: Diana Russell.

———. 2000b. Educational leaflet. Berkeley, CA: Diana Russell.

Ruttenberg, M. H. 1994. A feminist critique of mandatory arrest: An analysis of race and geder in domestic violence policy. *American University Journal of Gender and the Law* 2:171–199.

Sabbagh, S. 1996. *Arab women between defiance and restraint.* New York: Olive Branch Press.

Said, E. W. 1978. *Orientalism.* New York: Vintage Books.

Salcido, O., and M. Adelman. 2004. "He has me tied with the blessed and damned papers": Undocumented-immigrant battered women in Phoenix, Arizona. *Human Organization* 63:162–172.

Schechter, S. 1982. *Women and male violence: The visions and struggles of the battered women's movement.* Boston: South End Press.

Seattle Post-Intelligencer Reporter. 2003. Asian Americans and eating disorders: A Silent Struggle. January 28. Retrieved July 17, 2005, from http://www.psycport.com/stories/seattlepi_2003_01_28_eng-seattlepi_eng-seattlepi_081525_683654306331701688.xml.html.

Segal, U. A. 1991. Cultural variables in Asian Indian families. *Families in Society: The Journal of Contemporary Human Services* 72:233–241.

Seigel, J. 1999. Problematizing the self. In *Beyond the cultural turn*, ed. V. E. Bonnell and L. Hunt, 281–314. Berkeley: University of California Press.

Sen, A. 1990. More than 100 million women are missing. *New York Review of Books* 37, December 20. Retrieved June 13, 2005, from http://ucatlas.ucsc.edu/gender/Sen100M.html.

Sen, A., and S. Seth. 1995. Gender identity of the girl child in India. *Canadian Woman Studies* 15:58–63.

Sengupta, U. 1989. Rape of justice. *India Today*, May 31.

Senturia, K. D., C. M. Sullivan, S. Shiu-Thornton, M. Crandall, and S. Ciske. 2003. Domestic violence resource utilization and survivor solutions: Voices of ethnic minority and LGBT women. MS. Seattle, WA.

Sethi, R. R., and M. J. Allen. 1984. Sex-role stereotypes in Northern India and the United States. *Sex Roles* 11:615–626.

Sewell, W., Jr. 1999. The concept(s) of culture. *Beyond the cultural turn*, ed. V. E. Bonnell and L. Hunt, 35–61. Berkeley: University of California Press.

Shah, C. 1993. *Woman and nature in Jainism.* Paper presented at the 7th Biennial JAINA Convention, July 2–4, Pittsburgh.

Shah, N. 1998. *Jainism: The world of conquerors.* East Sussex, UK: Sussex Academic Press.

Shah, S. 2003. Presenting the blue goddess: Toward a national pan-Asian feminist agenda. In *Women: images and realities: A multicultural anthology* (3d ed.), ed. A. Kesselman, L. D. McNair, and N. Schniedewind, 539–542. New York: McGraw-Hill.

Sharma, A. 2001. Healing the wounds of domestic violence: Improving the effectiveness of feminist therapeutic interventions with immigrant and racially visible women who have been abused. *Violence against Women* 7:1405–1428.

Sharpe, J. 2003. A conversation with Gayatri Chakravorty Spivak: Politics and the imagination. *Signs* 28:609–627.

Sheikh, A. 2000. Gender and levels of acculturation as predictors of attitudes toward seeking professional psychological help and attitudes toward women among Indians and Pakistanis in America. Ph.D. diss., Rutgers, The State University of New Jersey, New Brunswick.

Shepard, M. F., and E. L. Pence, eds. 1999. *Coordinating community responses to domestic violence: Lessons from Duluth and beyond.* Thousand Oaks, CA: Sage.

Shirwadkar, S. 2004. Canadian domestic violence policy and Indian immigrant women. *Violence against Women* 10:860–879.

Shuriquie, N. 1999. Eating disorders: A transcultural perspective. *Eastern Mediterranean Health Journal* 5:354–360. Retrieved July 17, 2005, from http://www.emro.who.int/Publications/EMHJ/0502/20.htm.

Siddique, K. 1985. *The struggle of Muslim women.* Kingsville, MD: American Society for Education and Religion.

Sikora, D. 2001. Differing cultures, differing culpabilities? A sensible alternative: Using cultural circumstances as a mitigating factor in sentencing. *Ohio State Law Journal* 62:1695–1738.

Singh, O. 2003. The blackest day in their lives. *India Abroad*, January 10.

Singh, R. N., and N. P. Unnithan. 1999. Wife burning: Cultural cues for lethal violence against women among Asian Indians in the United States. *Violence against Women* 5:641–653.

Singh, S. 1995. *Statistical profile on women in Nepal.* Kathmandu, Nepal: Strii Shakti.

Sinha, A. 2001. Domestic violence and U.S. asylum law: Eliminating the "cultural hook" for claims involving gender-related persecution. *New York University Law Review* 76:1562–1598.

Spencer, J. 2002. Woman is found guilty of attempt to kill sons. *Austin American-Statesman,* June 27.

———. 2001. A shattered union, and a woman who feared shame; Mother, facing attempted capital murder charges, is stripped of parental rights. *Austin American-Statesman,* November 24.

SodomyLaws.org. 2005. *Sodomy laws of India.* Retrieved May 5, 2005, from http://www.sodomylaws.org/world/india/india.htm.

So-Kum Tang, C. 1997. Psychological impact of wife abuse: Experiences of Chinese women and their children. *Journal of Interpersonal Violence* 12:466–478.

Solomon, A. 2004. We are all New Yorkers. *Village Voice,* August 31, p. 32.

———. 2003. From Baghdad to Brooklyn. *Village Voice,* April 8, p. 26.

Sorenson, S. B. 1996. Violence against women: Examining ethnic differences and commonalities. *Evaluation Review* 20:123–145.

South Asian Journalists Association. 2005. *Tips for converging Nepalese in the US.* March 21. Retrieved June 13, 2005, from http://www.saja.org/tipsnepal.html.

South Asian Leaders of Tomorrow. 2001. *American backlash: Terrorists bring home the war in more ways than one.* Retrieved June 20, 2005, from http://saalt.org/pdfs/biasreport.pdf.

Stack, M. 2002. Killings put dark side of mom's life in light. *Los Angeles Times,* July 8.

Stark, E., and A. Flitcraft. 1996. *Women at risk: Domestic violence and women's health.* Thousand Oaks, CA: Sage.

Stiles, K. 2002. *Civil society by design: Donors, NGOs, and the intermestic development circle in Bangladesh.* London: Praeger.

Strauss, A., and J. Corbin. 1990. *Basics of qualitative research: Grounded theory procedures and techniques.* Newbury Park, CA: Sage.

Subedi, P. 1997. *Nepali women rising.* Kathmandu, Nepal: Sahayogi Press.

Sundaram, V. 2000. Berkeley landlord in sex scandal. *India West,* January 28.

Supriya, K. E. 1996. Confessionals, testimonials: Women's speech in/and contexts of violence. *Hypatia: A Journal of Feminist Philosophy* 11:92–106.

———. 1995. Speaking others, practicing selves: Representational practices of battered immigrant women in Apna Ghar ("our home"). *Women and Performance: A Journal of Feminist Theory* 7:241–266.

Suri, A. C., trans. 1933. Purushaartha siddhyupaaya: Scriptural view of nonviolence. Trans. A. P. Jain. *Jain Study Circular* 141:4.

Sutherland, C. A., C. M. Sullivan, and D. I. Bybee. 2001. Effects of intimate partner violence versus poverty on women's health. *Violence against Women* 7:1122–1143.

Swarns, R. L. 2003. Thousands of Arabs and Muslims could be deported: Officials say. *New York Times,* June 7.

Swarns, R. L., and C. Drew. 2003. Aftereffects: Immigrants; fearful, angry or confused, Muslim immigrants register. *New York Times,* April 25.

Tanneeru, M. 2001. *A glance at the South Asian population in the state of Georgia.* Atlanta: Raksha. http://www.raksha.org/raksha/demographics.html.

Tervalon, M., and J. Murray-Garcia. 1998. Cultural humility versus cultural competence: A critical distinction in defining physician training outcomes in multicultural education. *Journal of Health Care for the Poor and Underserved* 9:117–125.

Tewari, N., A. Inman, and D. Sandhu. 2003. South Asian Americans: Culture, concerns and therapeutic strategies. In *Culturally diverse mental health: The challenges of research and resistance,* ed. J. Mio and G. Iwamasa, 191–209. New York: Brunner-Routledge.

Thibodeau, P. 2004. H-1B backers want bigger increase in cap. *Computerworld,* November 29.

Thompson, G. 1999. Afraid of husbands, and the law; deportation risk grows for abused illegal residents. *New York Times,* April 18.

Tjaden, P., and N. Thoennes. 2000. *Extent, nature and consequences of intimate partner violence: Findings from the national violence against women survey.* Washington DC: U.S. Department of Justice.

UNICEF. 2000. *Countering acid violence and supporting survivors in Bangladesh.* Dhaka, Bangladesh: UNICEF.

United Nations Development Group. 2003. *Indicators for monitoring the millennium development goals.* Retrieved June 13, 2005, from http://www.sasurf.undp.org/mdgs/docs/MDGs_ Indicators.pdf.

UN Development Programme. 2003. *Human development reports: Nepal, gender-related development index 2002.* Retrieved May 10, 2004, from http://hdr.undp.org/statistics/data/ cty/cty_f_NPL.html.

Upadhyay, P. 1991. The social assimilation of Nepali immigrants in the United States and the role of English language training in the process. Ph.D. diss., University of Connecticut, Hartford.

U.S. Census Bureau. 2000a. *U.S. census 2000.* Retrieved November 23, 2003, from http:// www.census.gov/.

U.S. Census Bureau. 2000b. *Census 2000.* Retrieved October 2, 2004, from http:// infoplease.com/ipa/A0778584.html.

———. 1990. *U.S. census 1990.* Retrieved November 23, 2003, from http://www.census.gov/.

U.S. Department of Homeland Security 2003. *Characteristics of specialty occupation workers (H-1B): Fiscal year 2002.* Report mandated by Public Law 105–277, Division C, American Competitiveness and Workforce Improvement Act of 1998. Washington, DC: Office of Immigration Statistics.

———. 2002. *2002 yearbook of immigration statistics.* Electronic version. Washington, DC: U.S. Citizenship and Immigration Services.

U.S. Department of Justice. 2001. *Fact sheet: Worker exploitation.* March 27. Washington, DC: U.S. Department of Justice. Retrieved July 17, 2005, from http://www.usdoj.gov/ opa/pr/2001/March/126cr.htm.

Vaid, J. 1989. Seeking a voice: South Asian women's groups in North America. In *Making waves: An anthology of writings by and about Asian American women,* ed. Asian Women United of California, 395–405. Boston: Beacon.

Vandello, J. A., and D. Cohen. 2003. Male honor and female fidelity: Implicit cultural scripts that perpetuate domestic violence. *Journal of Personality and Social Psychology* 84:997–1010.

Vaughan, J. 2003. *Shortcuts to immigration: The "temporary" visa program is broken.* Washington, DC: Center for Immigration Studies.

Venugopal, A. 2005. Conservative Muslims protest as first woman leads prayer. *India Abroad,* April 1.

Vijayanthi, K. N. 2002. Women's empowerment through self-help groups: A participatory approach. *Indian Journal of Gender Studies* 9:263–274.

Violence against Women. 1999. Special issue: Violence against South Asian women, part 2. Vol. 5, No. 6.

Violence Logbook. 1996. A Naripokkho report. Dhaka, Bangladesh: Naripokkho.

Visweswaran, K. 2004. Gendered states: Rethinking culture as a site of South Asian human rights work. *Human Rights Quarterly* 26:483–511.

———. 2002. *Women's rights as human rights: Domestic violence and the problem of culture.* Keynote address. Aarohan: South Asian Women Rise Up Against Violence conference. September 13. Manavi, New Brunswick, NJ.

Volpp, L. 2003. *The excesses of culture: On Asian American citizenship and identity.* Fourth Annual Korematsu Lecture, April 24, New York University, New York.

——. 2000a. (Mis)identifying culture: Asian women and the cultural defense. Reprinted in *Asian American studies: A reader*, ed. J. Yu-Wen Shen and M. Song, 391–422. New Brunswick, NJ: Rutgers University Press.

——. 2000b. Blaming culture for bad behavior. *Yale Journal of Law and the Humanities* 12:89–116.

Walker, A. 1989. Psychology and violence against women. *American Psychologist* 44:695–702.

Walker, L. E. 1999. Psychology and domestic violence around the world. *American Psychologist* 54:21–29.

——. 1984. *Battered woman syndrome*. New York: Springer.

——. 1981. Battered women: Sex roles and clinical issues. *Professional Psychology* 12:81–91.

——. 1979. *The battered woman*. New York: Harper and Row.

Walsh, C. 2004. Girl, 2, in foster care, parents in prison. *India New England—Community Issue*, May 1. Retrieved June 28, 2004, from http://www.indianewengland.com.

Wang, A. 2001. Beyond black and white: Crime and foreignness in the news. *Asian Law Journal* 8:187–189.

Ward, O. 2005. "Runaway grooms": Documentary points to young Indian expatriates who marry for cash and then desert their wives. *Guelph Mercury*, April 22.

Warrier, S. 2000a. *(Un)Heard voices: Domestic violence in the Asian American community*. San Francisco: Family Violence Prevention Fund.

——. 2000b. Social, legal, and community challenges facing South Asian immigrant women. In *Breaking the silence: Domestic violence in South Asian-American communities*, ed. S. Nankani, 89–97. Xlibris Corporation, http://www2.xlibris.com.

Waters, A. B. 1999. Domestic dangers: Approaches to women's suicide in contemporary Maharashtra, India. *Violence against Women* 5:525–547.

Weisberg, D. K. 1996. Battered women. In *Applications of feminist legal theory to women's lives: Sex, violence, work, and reproduction*, ed. D. K. Weisberg, 277–295. Philadelphia: Temple University Press.

Wessler, S. 2002. *After 9–11: Understanding the impact on Muslim communities in Maine*. January 29. Retrieved March 13, 2005, from http://cphv.usm.maine.edu/911%20Report.pdf.

Whitcraft, T., C. Chung, and J. Ford. 1999. "Faces of hope." *ABC news 20/20*. Broadcast November 1 by American Broadcasting Company, New York.

Wing, A. K. 1997. A critical race feminist conceptualization of violence: South African and Palestinian women. *Albany Law Review* 60:943–976.

Winter, K. A., and M. Y. Young. 1998. Biopsychosocial considerations in refugee mental health. In *Cultural clinical psychology: Theory, research, and practice*, ed. S. Kazarian and D. Evans, 348–376. New York: Oxford University Press.

Withey, S. 1962. Reaction to uncertain threat. In *Man and society in disaster*, ed. G. Baker and D. Chapman, 93–123. New York: Basic.

Wu, M. W. C. 2003. Comment: Culture is no defense for infanticide. *American University Journal of Gender, Social Policy, and the Law* 11:975–1025.

Yi, M. 2000a. Landlord's record probed in sex case. *San Francisco Examiner*, January 22.

——. 2000b. Report from India: A tale of two worlds. *San Francisco Examiner*, April 5.

——. 1999. Search for better life ends in family tragedy. *San Francisco Examiner*, November 27.

Yi, M., and R. Delgado. 2000. Landlord sex charges. *San Francisco Examiner*, January 19.

Yi, M., J. Herron Zamora, and A. Wadhwani. 2000. Cops hunt victims in landlord sex case. *San Francisco Examiner*, January 20.

Yick, A. G., and P. Agbayami-Siewert. 1997. Perceptions of domestic violence in a Chinese American community. *Journal of Interpersonal Violence* 12:832–846.

Yllö, K. 1993. Through a feminist lens: Gender, power, and violence. In *Current controversies on family violence*, ed. R. C. Gelles and D. R. Loseke, 47–62. Newbury Park, CA: Sage Publications.

Yoshioka, M. R., L. Gilbert, N. El-Bassel, and M. Baig-Amin. 2003. Social support and disclosure of abuse: Comparing South Asian, African American, and Hispanic battered women. *Journal of Family Violence* 18:171–180.

Yoshioka, M. R., J. DiNoia, and K. Ullah. 2001. Attitudes toward marital violence: An examination of four Asian communities. *Violence against Women* 7:900–926.

Yuval-Davis, N. 1997. Ethnicity, gender relations, and multiculturalism. In *Debating cultural hybridity: Multi-cultural identities and the politics of anti-racism*, ed. P. Werbner and T. Madood, 193–208. London: Zed Books.

AUTHOR BIOGRAPHIES

RUKSANA AYYUB is a Pakistani American. She is a public speaker, published author on domestic violence, and a proud mother of two sons.

RUPALEEM BHUYAN is a second-generation immigrant of Assamese heritage. She is an assistant professor in social welfare at the University of Kansas.

PRAJNA PARAMITA CHOUDHURY is a Bangladeshi American woman working for the past decade to alleviate domestic violence, hate crime, sexual assault, and HIV/AIDS through education, advocacy, and counseling. She is an award-winning LGBT community activist in California and is a practitioner of traditional Chinese medicine.

ELORA HALIM CHOWDHURY is an assistant professor of women's studies at the University of Massachusetts, Boston. Her fields of interest include critical development studies, Third World/transnational feminisms, and feminist ethnography.

SHAMITA DAS DASGUPTA is a psychologist, a cofounder of Manavi, and teaches at the New York University Law School. She is an adoring mother and grandmother.

MANDEEP GREWAL has extensively researched the connections between effective policy making and the communication patterns of marginalized populations. Her other research interests include examining the mass mediated dimension of gender roles and the significance of different communication channels in the lives of immigrant Indian women in the United States.

SANDEEP HUNJAN is a clinical psychologist in Ontario. Her research interests are in the area of gender, trauma, and culture, with an emphasis on South Asian contexts.

SHASHI JAIN is a New Jersey and New York licensed psychologist and works for the Department of Human Services. She is a cofounder of Manavi and actively volunteers her services for battered women.

SUJATHA ANBUSELVI JESUDASON is a doctoral candidate and has worked as an organizer and advocate in communities of color and on women's liberation issues.

Her current work highlights the feminist, eugenic, and social justice concerns with the new reproductive and genetic technologies.

DIYA KALLIVAYALIL is a doctoral student in clinical/community psychology. Her research and clinical interests include the impact of trauma, violence, sexual harassment, and migration on women's mental health, as well as emotion and family socialization among immigrant families.

GRACE POORE is a founding member of the South Asian Collaborative to End Child Sexual Abuse (SACECSA) and has served on the Leadership Team of Generation Five, which works to prevent child sexual abuse. Community-based organizations use her award-winning documentaries widely.

SUNITA PURI, a Rhodes Scholar, is a medical student in the Joint Medical Program of the University of California, Berkeley and San Francisco. She has worked at women's shelters in both the United States and Britain and plans a career combining woman-centered clinical medicine, teaching, and research.

BANDANA PURKAYASTHA, an associate professor of sociology and Asian American studies at the University of Connecticut, is originally from Kolkata, India. Her work focuses on Asian American women with a comparative global perspective on poor women in South Asia. She is the cofounder of The South Asian Tree (TSAT), an organization that builds ties between South Asian communities.

V. G. JULIE RAJAN'S doctoral research focused on women's resistance writing in post-1947 India and Pakistan. She is on the editorial board of *Catamaran*, a South Asian Literary Journal; *SAGAR*, a South Asian academic journal; and the *Subcontinental*, a South Asian American political journal.

BIDYA RANJEET, a native of Nepal, is the director of Student Support Services at the University of Connecticut. She holds leadership positions in community building and regional educational opportunity organizations, where she specializes in issues of diversity and community. Bidya is cofounder of TSAT.

SHARMILA RUDRAPPA is assistant professor in sociology and Asian American Studies at the University of Texas at Austin. Her research interests focus on race, citizenship, and nationalism.

SHIVALI SHAH is a New York–based lawyer and a founder of Kiran, Domestic Violence and Crisis Services for South Asians in North Carolina. She teaches at Rutgers University and is advocating and lobbying for H-4 visa holders.

MAUNICA STHANKI is an attorney and activist with roots in India, Uganda, and Louisiana. She is currently the national student vice president of the National Lawyers Guild and is seeking employment in immigration law with a focus on post-9/11 issues.

SHELAGH TOWSON, a social psychologist, immigrated to Canada and has an abiding interest in the negotiation of identity in multicultural societies. She is privileged to work with graduate students whose contributions are freeing North American psychology from its cultural myopia.

ANITHA VENKATARAMANI-KOTHARI is a student of clinical psychology and researcher of domestic violence and women's rights. Through her affiliation with Asian American Federation of New York (AAFNY), Anitha has provided services to Asian American victims of 9/11 and recently conducted a needs assessment survey to recommend services for families of victims of the tsunami.

INDEX